# A CIVIL WAR

ALSO BY JOHN FEINSTEIN

A Good Walk Spoiled

Hard Courts

Forever's Team

A Season Inside

A Season on the Brink

Play Ball

Running Mates
(A Mystery)

Winter Games
(A Mystery)

# A CIVIL WAR

## ARMY VS. NAVY

*A Year Inside College Football's
Purest Rivalry*

John Feinstein

Little, Brown and Company

Boston   New York   Toronto   London

First Edition

The author is grateful for permission to include the following
previously copyrighted material:

Lyrics of "Blue and Gold." Reprinted by permission of the United States
Naval Academy Athletic Association.

Library of Congress Cataloging-in-Publication Data

Feinstein, John A.
   A civil war : Army vs. Navy / John Feinstein. — 1st ed.
      p.    cm.
   Includes index.
   ISBN 0-316-27736-3
   1. United States Military Academy — Football — History.   2. United States Naval
Academy — Football — History.   I. Title.
GV958.U5F45   1996
796.332'63 — dc20                                                      96-24675

10  9  8  7  6  5  4  3  2  1

Published simultaneously in Canada by Little, Brown & Company (Canada) Limited
Printed in the United States of America

FOR TIM MALONEY . . .

*From all the Feinsteins*

# CONTENTS

# INTRODUCTION

PEOPLE often ask me how I come up with ideas for the books I write — whether I have a system of some kind, or does my publisher make recommendations, or am I trying to write about every sport in existence until I finally get to tae kwon do.

The answer is none of the above. It is far more random than that. I can, however, tell you the exact moment when I knew I wanted to write about the Army-Navy rivalry.

It was in 1990, the year I first went to see the Army-Navy game. I'd made trips to see both Army and Navy play while growing up, and of course I'd watched many Army-Navy games on television over the years. But this was the first time I'd seen the real thing, live.

The game was everything I had expected: intense on both sides, with emotions on a ragged edge as the fourth quarter wound down. It didn't have the kind of melodramatic finish that has become, it seems, a tradition in recent years, but it was one hell of a football game.

When the game ended, I watched as the players on both teams shook hands and, in some cases, exchanged hugs. Nothing special there. But then I saw something I had never seen in all those years of watching the game on TV. Together, all the players walked to the end of the field where the Brigade of Midshipmen sat on one side, the Corps of Cadets on the other. Since Army had won the game, they walked first to the Navy side. And then they stood, together, hands

ix

on hearts, while the Navy band played "Blue and Gold." Then they all walked to the other side of the field and stood at attention while the Army band played "Alma Mater."

As I watched, a chill ran right through my body. This was the year that American troops were in the Persian Gulf preparing for what would become, six weeks later, Desert Storm. It occurred to me that the seniors on these teams might in the not too distant future be team- mates in a battle far more important than any football game. That's when I knew I wanted to write this book.

Football coaches love to equate themselves with military leaders and talk about battles in the trenches and going to war. At Army and Navy, the players understand the difference between football and war. That doesn't mean they play any less hard or care one bit less. If anything, they play with even more commitment than players at other schools. But as much as the players want to beat each other, as impor- tant as it is at both schools to win that football game, there is a bond between the players and their schools like no bond between any other rivals in sports. Army and Navy players *have* fought together in wars, have *died* together in wars, and will almost certainly do so again in the future. There is also a shared experience: only a cadet can truly appreciate what a midshipman goes through; only a midshipman has a clear understanding of life as a cadet. That's why there's no rivalry like Army-Navy.

So, at exactly 6 A.M. on the morning of October 25, 1995, nearly five years after my first Army-Navy game, I drove my car through the Washington Gate of the United States Military Academy. Over- head, stars were everywhere. It would be a cold, clear day when the sun came up, but that was still an hour away.

As I steered slowly down the dark hill to the parking lot behind the building that houses the athletic offices, it was impossible not to notice that the place was already full of life. There were cadets every- where, some of them out for a morning run, others making their way back to the barracks area for morning formation. Clearly, the day at West Point begins long before the sun shows up to make it official.

After I had parked my car, I walked over the "Beat Navy" Tunnel and past the statues of Colonel Sylvanus Thayer (the founder of West Point) and General Douglas MacArthur (known to the cadets as

"MacStatue") and then along the edge of the Parade Ground. In front of me, every room in the cadet barracks was ablaze.

My memories of the West Point Parade Ground go back to boyhood, when my parents and I would make the drive from New York City to see a game in Michie Stadium. Watching the cadets go through their military paces before the game always seemed thrilling. My assumption then was that the cadets found it just as thrilling as I did.

Of course now I knew different. Saturday mornings at West Point are regarded as a giant headache. There is Saturday morning room inspection, the most stringent inspection of the week; putting on full dress uniform for the parade; returning to the barracks to get into a different uniform; then, if your regiment has been selected that week, having to march onto the football field before kickoff. For those of us watching, it all seemed great. For those performing, it was extra work in a life already filled with work.

I sat down on the steps of the mess hall, which are a few yards from yet another statue — George Washington on a horse — to await my escort for the day, Army football team senior cocaptain Jim Cantelupe. I had told Cantelupe I would meet him at 6:15. I was ten minutes early. At 6:10, Cantelupe appeared. This wasn't surprising. Army cadets and Naval Academy midshipmen are never late. More often than not, they're early.

Cantelupe has a very unmilitary mischievous smile and he was wearing it as he approached. "Just couldn't wait to get here, could you?" he said.

"I figured I'd be in trouble if I missed formation," I answered, ducking as the doors behind me opened and plebes started pouring out of them. Plebes are expected to be lined up and already in formation by the time the upperclassmen report at 6:25. That means they start showing up at 6:15, *after* they have carried out their morning duties, which usually include making certain that every upperclassman in the company has a copy of the *New York Times* on the step when the door is opened in the morning.

"Plebes are usually up by five-thirty, sometimes earlier," Cantelupe said as we made the short walk to where his company — H-3, aka "The Hurricanes" — was forming. There are thirty-six companies at both West Point and Navy, each with about 110 to 120 members. As we walked up, one of Cantelupe's fellow first classmen was ripping a plebe for failing to deliver the newspapers on time.

"Not only do I expect the *New York Times* waiting for me when I get back from breakfast," he was yelling, "I expect you to be able to tell me everything that's in it!"

"Yes sir."

"Will this ever happen again?"

"No sir."

"For your sake, I hope not."

Cantelupe watched the scene with a bemused grin on his face. "The guy's a jerk," he said, nodding at the first classman. "Most of us, by now, we don't want to give the plebes a hard time. It's something you grow out of."

At precisely 6:25, all the company commanders made their morning announcements: haircut inspections were the highlight of the list. Cantelupe, standing at the back of the formation, wasn't really listening.

"I've been up at this hour almost every day for four years now," he said. "You'd think you would get used to it, but you don't."

Looking around at the entire Corps of Cadets, it occurred to me that Cantelupe and his teammates on the Army football team had to be the only Division I football players in America who were awake at that moment. Two hundred and fifty miles away, Navy's players would just be rolling out of bed for their 7 A.M. formation and, two time zones away, the cadets at Air Force wouldn't be up for their 7 A.M. mountain time morning formation for another few hours.

Only at the military academies do athletes routinely wake up at 6 A.M. and worry about things like haircut inspections. The difference between playing football at the military academies and at the other 103 Division I schools was probably best explained by Fred Goldsmith, a onetime Air Force assistant who is now the coach at Duke.

"At every other school in America, the hardest part of any football player's day is football practice," he said. "At the military academies, the *easiest* part of a football player's day is football practice."

It has become de rigueur in recent years to put down the Army-Navy game. After all, what used to be college football's most glamorous national rivalry hasn't involved a Top Ten team since the 1960s.

The last Heisman Trophy winner from either school was Navy's Roger Staubach, and that was in 1963. According to the critics, only tradition keeps Army and Navy on national TV every year; and the people at Air Force constantly ask why, when their football team has dominated both schools for the last dozen years, people are still fascinated by Army-Navy.

Although Army-Navy may not decide national championships anymore, it means just as much to the players as it ever has — perhaps even more now than in days of greater glory. In ninety-nine cases out of a hundred, the seniors know that the Army-Navy game — always the final game of the season for both teams, barring bowl appearances — is their last football game. Once every decade or so, someone will go on to the pros after military service, but that is the rare exception.

Everyone thinks that their rivalry is the best, the most special, the one that stands above others. But Army-Navy is unique. It is played with the fervor of people who know they are doing something that they love for a final time, that they are closing a chapter in their lives. And it is played by teams who try to crush each other for three hours, then stand at attention together when the game is over.

It is also the tradition and the uniqueness of the scene inside the stadium that makes the rivalry unique. After all, it is the only college football game played each year that is attended by the entire student body of both schools.

But it is more than that. For all their flaws, West Point and the Naval Academy still represent what this country *can* be. When we look into the faces of the cadets and the mids, we see the future. We see potential. We see, in most of them, a willingness to die so the rest of us can go on living the way we have for the past 220 years.

There is no questioning the fact that in their long histories — 194 years at Army, 151 years at Navy — there have been scandals and very serious problems. There still are. During the 1995–96 school year, the Naval Academy was beset by one controversy after another. Drug arrests in the fall were followed by a series of embarrassments in the spring that included one active mid and several ex-mids being involved in a car-theft ring; another accused of molesting a two-year-old child; another accused of sexual harassment. In August, fifteen midshipmen implicated in the fall drug investigation were expelled. Five others were court-martialed. They represented less than one-half of one percent of the brigade. And yet, everyone at the academy would agree that the episode was a huge embarrassment.

What's more, the suicide last May of Admiral Jeremy (Mike) Boorda, the Chief of Naval Operations, rocked the entire military, from President Clinton down to the lowest-ranked plebes at the Naval Academy.

Whether Boorda killed himself because of an impending controversy over his right to wear medals given only to those who have been in combat or because of reasons that went beyond that may never be known. What is known is that he was a popular leader and had given a rousing speech at the academy only two weeks before his death. In fact, he had been scheduled to present diplomas to the class of 1996 at graduation on May 24.

Instead, his death cast a shadow over what should have been a glorious day for the 916 graduates. All the speakers felt compelled to invoke Boorda's name and to imply that he somehow died a hero, but the words sounded hollow.

Just prior to Boorda's death, an academy professor wrote a scathing piece in the *Washington Post* tracing the recent problems of the entire navy back to a lack of leadership and integrity at the academy. He insisted most mids were perpetually unhappy. He was right in part — *all* mids are unhappy *at some point* in their four years at the academy. If they weren't, they wouldn't be breathing.

In contrast to the last major scandal at the academy, the electrical engineering cheating fiasco of 1992–93, football players were not involved in any of the '95–96 troubles. Even so, there are still many who believe that the lowering of academic standards at both Army and Navy in the name of winning football games is wrong and lowers the quality of the future officers the schools are producing.

There is no doubting that both academies are a long way from perfect. Many of their rules are anachronistic, and the often stifling nature of military life is bound to lead to rebellion that can be both embarrassing to the academies and threatening to their future if the leadership doesn't take them seriously.

The leadership at the Naval Academy is taking these most recent troubles seriously. The superintendent, Admiral Charles R. Larson, ordered the entire brigade to "stand down" for a week in April, meaning all four thousand midshipmen were placed on restriction. Even the first classmen were denied liberty. Larson is a four-star admiral, one of the most respected men in the entire U.S. military hierarchy. He was sent back to Annapolis in 1994 to find out exactly what had gone wrong and fix it. My guess is he will come as close as is humanly possible to doing just that.

Imperfect though the academies may be, they are still filled with outstanding young people. If the football players I had a chance to get to know at both schools are going to be this country's future leaders, the future is, in my biased opinion, in very good hands.

That's why the football game remains special: because of the people who play it.

Everyone who plays in the Army-Navy game, especially as a senior, is an extraordinary person. They have to be blessed with mental and physical toughness to survive Beast Barracks at Army or Plebe Summer at Navy. They have to be intelligent, because both schools are tough places academically, with the SAT scores of the most recent entering classes averaging slightly more than 1200. (Sit in on an engineering class at Navy if you want to understand the true meaning of the phrase "that's Greek to me.") They have to be extremely patient, because a large portion of the military training at both schools is designed to test your patience. Impatient people do not do well in battle. The academies try to see to it that none end up there.

And they have to be leaders. The best definition I heard of leadership came from Al Roberts, who played defensive tackle for Army as a junior and a senior even though he weighs only 225 pounds.

"Leadership," he said, "is convincing people they can do something they shouldn't be able to do."

There is no way that Army should be able to come within a foot of beating Notre Dame. There is no way that Navy should be able to dominate teams like SMU, Duke, and Tulane. Those schools have 1,000 advantages in recruiting — 999 of them being that no one there has to go into the military after graduating — and can consistently recruit bigger, faster, and stronger people.

Football coaches spend their lives trying to get their players to be bigger and stronger. The first thing Army and Navy do with their football players (along with every other plebe) is put them through a summer almost guaranteed to leave them weak as kittens. Then, after they have survived their plebe year, they send them off to summer camps where they again routinely lose fifteen or twenty pounds.

In the spring of 1995, Eddie Stover, one of Army's best offensive linemen, wasn't allowed to participate in spring drills. The reason? He hadn't run the obstacle course in his PE class fast enough. I wonder how many other football teams in America had *that* problem to deal with.

Army and Navy don't have the glamour they once did. In this day and age, when anyone with even a glimmer of hope to play pro football will run like the wind to get away from a military commitment, they simply can't recruit the top-of-the-line players the way they did in the old days. What they do recruit are smart, tough kids who love to play the game. Often they are kids whose only chance to play in Division I is at Army or Navy. They usually start out with about 120 plebes out for football and about 25 of them still playing as first classmen. At schools where time management is almost as important as breathing, the number of hours a commitment to football takes guarantees a high attrition rate.

Over the door leading to the Army locker room is a sign that acknowledges the difficulty of sticking it out for four years. It says: ''Those Who Stay Will Be Champions.'' The sign is accurate. Those who stayed — at both schools — regardless of how many football games they won or lost, most definitely became champions.

# A CIVIL WAR

# 1

# BROTHERHOOD

ALMOST thirty minutes after the last play of his college football career, Jim Cantelupe, still dressed in the black uniform with the gold number 22 on the back and front, walked down a dank, winding hallway in the bowels of Philadelphia's Veterans Stadium.

The scene on the field immediately after the final gun had been chaotic. In between hugs from teammates and the screams and yells of the West Point cadets who had poured onto the artificial playing surface, Cantelupe had searched unsuccessfully for Andrew Thompson.

He knew Thompson was devastated. Four years of playing football for Navy had just ended with a fourth-straight hard-to-believe loss to Army. Four games, four Army victories. Total margin: six points. This time it had been Army 14, Navy 13, the Cadets driving 99 1/2 yards to score the winning touchdown with 63 seconds to play.

It was an unforgettable drive. One that Army's players would savor forever; one that Navy's players would be haunted by for just as long.

Cantelupe, Army's defensive captain, and Thompson, his counterpart at Navy, had met twelve days earlier at the annual Army-Navy press conference. Each had understood immediately that the other was a soul mate. Neither was blessed with superior speed or size or ability. Neither had been recruited by any big-time football schools. Both simply loved the game, the competition, the camaraderie. Both had put up with the frustrations and vagaries of military academy life for four years for one reason: the chance to play big-time football.

3

"If you can't play *for* Notre Dame," Cantelupe liked to say, "the next best thing is to play *against* Notre Dame."

Cantelupe knew how badly he wanted to win his last football game. He knew Thompson had wanted to win just as much. And so, while his teammates continued to hug and pummel one another in celebration, he quietly slipped out of the locker room and walked down the hall in the direction of the Navy locker room.

"Is it OK if I go in there?" he asked a security guard.

The man looked at him quizzically, as if to say, "Why would you want to do that?" But seeing the Army uniform, he nodded his head and stepped aside. Cantelupe walked through the doorway, took three steps into the locker room, and came to a dead halt.

His stomach twisted into a knot and for a split second he thought he might get sick. The silence in the room was deathly. Players in various stages of undress stood in groups of two and three, hugging one another or talking in hushed tones. Others sat in front of their lockers staring into space.

Father William Devine, one of Navy's team chaplains, his eyes puffy and red too, stood a few feet from the doorway when Cantelupe walked in. "Father," Cantelupe said softly, apologetically, "I was hoping to see Andy Thompson."

Devine nodded and pointed his hand at a locker several feet away. Thompson was sitting there, still in uniform, his head down, staring at the floor. Cantelupe could see that he was still shaking from a crying jag. Gingerly, he stepped over a couple of towels and gently put a hand on Thompson's shoulder.

Thompson looked up, expecting to see another teammate or a coach or a member of the Navy brass. When he saw Cantelupe, he jumped to his feet, threw his arms around him, and began to sob again. Cantelupe put his arms around Thompson and said softly, "I know."

They walked into the hallway so that Thompson's teammates would not have to look at a player in black and gold.

"Dammit, I wanted to kick your ass today," Thompson said, his voice hoarse from shouting and crying. "Just once I wanted to know what it felt like to beat you guys. Now, I'll never know."

"You're a hell of a football player," Cantelupe said, meaning it, remembering the panic he had felt when Thompson had sacked his quarterback, Ronnie McAda, for a 12-yard loss on Army's final, desperate drive.

Thompson almost smiled. "That's the worst part, Jim. We're not football players anymore. It's all over now."

Cantelupe had thought about that a lot during the week prior to the game. He and his fellow first classmen had talked about it at length the night before. A few minutes earlier, one of his teammates, Eddie Stover, had gone crazy in the locker room at the thought of not being a football player anymore.

"How will I live without football?" Stover had screamed. "It's all I've ever known!"

Cantelupe wasn't very different from Stover. Or Thompson. Now, it was real. He wasn't a football player anymore. "They can't take away the memories," he said to Thompson. "They can't take away the way it felt out there today."

Thompson's eyes were still glistening. "We're brothers now," he said. "For the rest of our lives."

"Damn right," Cantelupe said.

This time, he hugged Thompson, the gold letters that spelled out Army on his chest colliding with the blue letters that said Navy on Thompson's. The closeness they felt at that moment is usually only felt by men who have gone to war together.

Of course, they had been to war. Just on opposite sides.

THE notion of football as war has been used as a metaphor for as long as the game has been played. Coaches see themselves as generals, their assistants as the officers, the players as the soldiers. The violent nature of the sport lends itself easily to the notion that every game is about killing or being killed.

It is logical, then, that the military academies, which train young men — and, for the last twenty years, women — to fight wars, would play football with great passion. And once upon a time, when there was a military draft that meant many athletes *had* to serve in the armed forces, when being a military officer paid as much as or more than a job in the National Football League paid, and when the United States was undefeated in war, truly great and gifted football players flocked to West Point to play for Army and to Annapolis to play for Navy.

The football history of the two academies dates back to 1879, when Navy played the Baltimore Athletic Club to a scoreless tie, and to 1890, when cadet Dennis Michie challenged Navy to a game at West Point. The Midshipmen won easily, 24–0, but 105 years later the Army media guide makes the point that "the Midshipmen were a far more experienced team." No one concedes anything in this rivalry without a fight.

The football history of both academies is full of glory and glamorous names, whether they are Glenn Davis, Doc Blanchard, and Pete Dawkins at Army in the forties and fifties or Joe Bellino and Roger Staubach at Navy in the sixties. All won Heisman Trophies. All played for powerful, nationally ranked teams. All went on to serve their country.

Once upon a time, Army-Navy was *the* game of any college football season. Often when they played, the national championship was at stake, especially during the forties, when Army won the championship three straight times ('44–46) and went undefeated five times in six years from '44 through '49.

The entire nation would come to a standstill for one Saturday afternoon while the Cadets and Midshipmen, America's best and brightest, dueled on the gridiron. Every major newspaper in the country covered the game, often with two or three reporters and several photographers. The outcome was the lead story in every sports section the next day. Often it was front page news.

The last vestiges of that glory were played out in the 1960s. Staubach led Navy to a 9–1 record, a berth in the Cotton Bowl and a number two national ranking in 1963, his Heisman Trophy season. Four years later, Army was 8–1 going into the Navy game and was invited to the Sugar Bowl. The Pentagon, concerned about security in the midst of the growing controversy surrounding the Vietnam War, would not allow the Cadets to accept the invitation.

The morning after the announcement was made, the Corps of Cadets marched into the mess hall for breakfast and found clumps of sugar piled up in the middle of all the tables. From the poop deck in the middle of the huge room hung a sign: "No Sugar Bowl for the football team; no sugar bowls for the corps."

The cadets cheered the sugar bowl thieves wildly. That was the last time either Army or Navy has been invited to a major bowl game.

Vietnam was a major turning point in the history of military academy football. The popularity of the military dropped considerably during those years, and with graduates from West Point and Annapolis being shipped to Vietnam almost the moment they were commissioned as officers, the notion of a four-year postgraduate military commitment wasn't nearly as romantic as it had once been.

Beginning in 1969, Army had two winning seasons (both times at 6–4) in fifteen years, including an 0–10 season in 1973. Coaches came and went. The school had five of them during that period. Navy suffered through seven straight losing seasons from 1968 through 1974 before George Welsh, a 1956 graduate of the academy, returned to resurrect the program, producing five winning seasons in seven years and three bowl appearances.

By that time, Army-Navy had lost a good deal of luster, at least in the eyes of big-time football fans across the country. The game was still on national TV and always drew a respectable rating, but it wasn't the media event it had once been. Both schools began playing easier schedules, adding games against smaller schools from Division I-AA and dropping some of the national powers that had once been traditional opponents. Many in the national media suggested they should give up big-time football altogether and play an Ivy League type of schedule. Yale and Harvard seemed like far more reasonable opponents than Notre Dame and Tennessee.

The losing and the watered-down schedules caused considerable grumbling among the old grads around the country who simply couldn't understand why beating Notre Dame and Oklahoma and Penn State was any more difficult in the eighties and nineties than it had been in the forties and fifties. When the two schools actually *lost* on occasion to schools like Delaware and Boston University and — God forbid — The Citadel, the screaming from alumni could be heard from one corner of the nation to the other.

Even worse, the steady slide at Army and Navy coincided with the rise of the upstart Air Force Academy. While the two tradition-laden schools were struggling to get to .500 even against weaker schedules, Air Force had joined the Western Athletic Conference and had built a solid program that produced winning seasons consistently and bowl trips often. Beginning in 1982, Air Force dominated both Army and Navy, winning the Commander in Chief's Trophy nine times in twelve years. The CIC, as it is called at the three academies, goes to the school with the best record in inter-academy play each season.

Air Force became so dominant in CIC play that in 1995 several of their players said publicly that winning a Western Athletic Conference title was more important to them than the CIC. The players at Army and Navy were galled and hurt by the comments. But Air Force still beat them both — again.

In spite of their preeminence on the field against their military brethren, Air Force chafed because it could not compete with Army-Navy in terms of tradition or national attention. While CBS and ABC were both bidding for the Army-Navy contract in 1994, no one was lining up for the chance to televise Air Force–Army or Air Force–Navy. And while the players at Air Force made a point of looking down their noses at Army and Navy on the football field, the other two schools did the exact same thing off the field. The cadets and midshipmen mockingly called Air Force ''The Country Club Academy'' because of the relatively plush dorms and more relaxed campus atmosphere.

Air Force won the football games; Army and Navy won just about everything else. Air Force was the little brother screaming for attention. No matter how good it got, no one seemed to take much notice.

Which is not to say that the ongoing struggles at Army and Navy did not cause a good deal of consternation at the schools. When Welsh, feeling he had gone as far as he could at his alma mater, left for Virginia in 1982, the Navy program went into a steady downward spiral. Gary Tranquill, Welsh's successor, went 6–5 in his first season. After that it was one losing season after another, including back-to-back 1–10s under George Chaump in 1991 and 1992. By the time Chaump became the third post-Welsh Navy coach to be fired in December of 1994, Navy had been through twelve straight losing seasons.

Army had experienced a Welsh-like renaissance in the 1980s when coach Jim Young, after a 2–9 rookie season in 1983, decided that the best offense for a school that couldn't recruit six-foot-five-inch quarterbacks with shotgun arms or 300-pound linemen was the wishbone. That way the quarterback had to throw only rarely, and quickness and toughness were as important on the offensive line as size and strength.

Army went 8–3–1 in 1984 and appeared in its first bowl game ever, the now-defunct Cherry Bowl. It was 9–3 a year later and played in the Peach Bowl and went to a third bowl in 1988, the Sun Bowl. In all, Young and his wishbone produced six winning seasons in seven from 1984 through 1990 before he retired, turning the job over to his defensive coordinator, Bob Sutton.

Sutton had never been a head coach before, and following in Young's large footsteps wasn't easy. During his first four seasons, he had a winning record once (6–5 in 1993), and by the end of a 4–7 1994 season Sutton was under considerable pressure, much of it from those old grads who still couldn't quite understand why Army hadn't recruited the next Blanchard or Davis yet.

Sutton, who became Army's thirty-first coach six weeks before he turned forty, might not have been retained for the final year of his five-year contract if not for his ability to steal final-second victories from Navy. After losing his first Army-Navy game as a head coach in 1991, Sutton won in 1992 on a 49-yard field goal on the game's final play; won in 1993 when Navy missed an 18-yard field goal as time expired; and won in 1994 on a 52-yard field goal. Three games, three victories. Total margin: five points.

But when Sutton assembled his 1995 team for spring practice, he knew that a victory over Navy was not going to be enough to earn him a new contract. A winning season would probably be needed, and a victory over Air Force — which had last happened in 1988 — might also be required. At Navy, the goal for 1995 was more direct: "Beat Army?" Absolutely. But for starters, beating *anyone* would be just fine.

# 2

# SQUARE ONE

WHEN the Navy football players gathered in the auditorium of Mitscher Hall on the afternoon of January 8, 1995, to meet their new head coach, they did so with a mixture of anticipation and anxiety, optimism and pessimism, joy and concern.

The last time they had been called together as a group had been on the evening of December 4, one day after their 1994 season had ended with yet another heartbreaking loss to Army. When the meeting had been called, all of them knew exactly what it was about: their coach, George Chaump, was going to be fired.

Very few of them were disappointed by this development. Some were relieved; others were delighted. Chaump had come to Navy five years earlier with a sparkling coaching résumé. He had coached under Woody Hayes at Ohio State and had been hugely successful as a head coach at Marshall, a Division I-AA power. But Chaump and Navy had never been a good match. After going 5–6 in his first year with a team built around players recruited by his predecessor, Elliot Uzelac, Chaump had gone 1–10, 1–10, 4–7, and 3–8. Even though bad luck had clearly been a factor, his record against Army was 1–4.

Worse than that, Chaump had lost the support of his players. He had trouble remembering names and he never seemed willing to take the blame when things went wrong. He fired assistant coaches constantly. And he was always telling the media that his players just weren't good enough to compete with the teams they were losing to, and that there wasn't much more he could do as coach given the lack of talent.

The players knew they weren't as talented as Notre Dame or Nebraska or Penn State. But being told by their own coach week after week that they weren't any good beat them down emotionally. They had stopped believing in Chaump, and when a football team does that it has no chance to succeed.

The relationship between the players and their coach had been crystallized during the week of the 1994 Army game when Jim Kubiak, the team's captain and quarterback, had been asked if the players wanted to win the Army game to try and save their coach's job. Instead of falsely affirming the team's devotion to Chaump, Kubiak had answered the question honestly: "We're not playing this game for Coach Chaump. We're playing it for ourselves."

Chaump responded by relegating Kubiak to the second team for two straight days of practice.

"We had gotten to the point where the only way Coach Chaump really could have helped us was to go into the other locker room before a game and give the other team's pregame pep talk," said Mark Hammond, a starting defensive tackle. "Every time he opened his mouth, it was a downer."

Hammond was one of twenty-five rising seniors on the team who had been through three years that had been filled with heartache and misery that went far beyond the twenty-five losses in thirty-three football games. The Naval Academy had been a troubled place throughout those years, a place where the football team had almost become a symbol for the frustrations of the entire brigade.

More and more, five letters had been appearing on the walls of Bancroft Hall, the giant dormitory that housed the entire four-thousand-member brigade: IHTFP — "I Hate This Fucking Place." The profane graffiti represented a mind-set that had permeated the entire academy. What's more, the relationship between the brigade and the football team could not have been worse. The football players tended to look down at the brigade, referring to them as "the nerds," and the brigade saw the football players as spoiled, arrogant failures. It was bad enough that the entire brigade was forced to go to every home football game — "mandatory fun," they called it — but then they had to stand there for three hours and watch the team get pounded.

"They hated us and we hated them," Kubiak said. "They weren't wrong in a lot of cases about the football players. A lot of the guys were arrogant and acted like jerks. But it's also true that a lot of the people in the brigade judged you harshly just because you played football and never gave you a chance to prove that you were different."

The years 1993 and 1994 had been awful for the Naval Academy. Hard on the heels of the Tailhook sexual harassment scandal in 1991, which gave the entire navy a black eye, had come "Double E," a scandal involving 134 members of the class of 1994 who had been caught cheating in an electrical engineering class that every member of the junior class is required to take. Although the cheating took place in the fall of 1992, the academy's administration, then under the direction of Admiral Thomas C. Lynch, moved very slowly in adjudicating the scandal. As with Tailhook, the media was stonewalled, which ultimately made the academy look even worse.

Eleven of the 134 midshipmen who were implicated were football players. Two of them, Javier Zuluaga and Max Lane, were stars and team leaders. When they were among twenty-four mids expelled — "separated," in academy lingo — their younger teammates were devastated.

As it turned out, Double E was only the beginning of a horrifying fall. The 1993 football season had started with hope; the Mids had jumped to a 4–2 beginning, helped by an easy schedule (Eastern Illinois, Bowling Green, and Colgate) and a shocking upset victory over Air Force, the first since Coach Welsh's departure eleven years earlier.

But that early hope had quickly turned to dust with four straight losses by an average margin of thirty points. Still, a victory over Army would have given Navy five wins for the first time since Chaump's first year and, perhaps more important, their first CIC Trophy since 1981. There was still plenty to play for.

But on the Wednesday before the Army game, the entire academy had been rocked by horrifying news: three recent academy graduates had died in a double murder/suicide at the Naval Amphibious Base in Coronado, California, just outside San Diego. Kerryn O'Neill, who had been a cross-country star at Navy, had broken off her engagement with George Smith. Apparently that had been more than Smith could handle and he had snapped. He had gone to O'Neill's room at 1:45 in the morning and found her there talking to a friend. Armed with two pistols, Smith shot O'Neill's friend four times, then shot O'Neill in the back of the head before finally turning the 9 mm Ruger pistol on himself.

When the football players heard the name of O'Neill's murdered friend, they could not believe their ears: Alton Lee Grizzard.

No one symbolized what was good about Navy football more than Alton Grizzard. He had been a four-year starter at quarterback, the team captain in 1990, and had remained someone whom everyone associated with the program pointed to as the kind of person the Naval Academy was capable of producing.

Grizzard was so tough, so inspiring to other players, so respected that when *Army* players talked about the player who best represented what the Army-Navy game was all about, they brought up Grizzard's name. When Army coach Bob Sutton, who barely knew Grizzard except as an opponent, heard the news that Grizzard was dead, he sat down and cried. "He stood for everything you want the academies to stand for," Sutton said. "He was indomitable."

No one at Navy had been surprised when Grizzard applied for SEAL training after graduation. Ask anyone in the military and they will tell you there is nothing tougher than being part of the elite special forces known as SEALs. Even Doug Pavek, who had been captain of the Army football team in 1985 and had gone on to be a Ranger, the Army's version of SEALs, conceded that SEAL training was tougher: "They do everything we do," he said, "but they have to do it under-water."

Grizzard had last been at Navy in the fall of 1992 on the day Navy played Tulane. The Midshipmen were 0–7 going into the weekend and Chaump had asked Grizzard to speak to the team before the game. By the time Grizzard was finished, he was in tears and there weren't a lot of dry eyes in the room. He talked about pride and staying to-gether and what the Naval Academy and Navy football and Navy foot-ball players meant to him. The Midshipmen beat Tulane that day. It was their only victory of the season.

And now, on a frigid, rainy afternoon, just three days before the

Army game, Chaump had to tell his players that Alton Grizzard was dead. He broke down, and so did a lot of the players. "We almost didn't believe it," Kubiak remembered. "It didn't seem possible that it was true. The whole thing was a nightmare."

They wore the name "Griz" on their gold helmets that Saturday in the New Jersey Meadowlands and, down 16–0 at the end of the three quarters, they improbably battled back, cutting the margin to 16–14 in the final minutes. When their defense held Army again and the offense got the ball back at its own 20 with more than four minutes remaining, they knew that they were going to win the game they had dedicated to their fallen leader.

They drove the ball 79 yards to the one yard line with less than a minute to play. On third down, Chaump called a running play designed to ensure that the ball would be in the center of the field if the touchdown wasn't scored. That would leave plenty of time for a chip-shot field goal that was all that was needed to win the game.

Kubiak handed the ball to halfback Brad Stramanak, who started to the left but then saw a gaping hole to the right. Instinctively, he cut back toward the hole and seemed certain to score until Army linebacker Pat Work somehow lunged sideways and made a shoestring, diving tackle. Stramanak landed no more than a foot from the goal line. Fourth down. Six seconds left.

Chaump sent in the field goal team, which was led by Ryan Bucchianeri, a baby-faced freshman who had become the team's placekicker four weeks earlier. On that afternoon, against Notre Dame, he coolly kicked two field goals on national TV in his college debut. Bucchianeri had been all-state and all-American at Ringgold High School in Monongahela, Pennsylvania. He had a strong leg and loads of confidence. He trotted onto the field believing it was his destiny to win the Army-Navy game with a last-second field goal.

What happened next is a piece of Army-Navy lore that still affects not only the people who were involved but every single person who has any connection to either academy. Kubiak, who still gets angry replaying those moments, never wanted to kick the field goal. The field was wet and slick from a steady rain, the angle wasn't very good, and even though Bucchianeri had kicked well against Notre Dame, he didn't like the idea of putting the entire game into the hands — or, more accurately, onto the foot — of a plebe.

"I wanted to go for it," he said. "I was certain we'd get in. Certain."

Players always feel that way. Clearly, the correct play was the field goal. Even on a wet field, with a tough angle, it was still only 18 yards — shorter than an extra point. Bucchianeri trotted on with holder Tony Solliday. Army called time-out.

On the sideline, Sutton couldn't help but think about the mistakes his team had made to blow what had seemed like a safe lead. "I was thinking about how this game always seems to be that way," he said. "No lead is safe. We knew that and yet we had let them come back anyway."

In the press box, Bob Beretta, then Army's assistant sports information director, was surprised to find himself almost wanting Bucchianeri to make the kick. "I wanted Army to win the game, obviously," he said. "But I couldn't help but think to myself that the consequences for a kid of missing a kick, especially such a short one, in that situation, would be absolutely unbearable. I just couldn't make myself *want* anyone to go through that kind of misery."

Army had won the game a year earlier on Patmon Malcolm's 49-yarder. Now, all the Cadets could do was hope for a miracle — a block or, even less likely, a Bucchianeri miss. The time-out ended. Bucchianeri lined up. The snap was perfect, the hold was good. Bucchianeri swung his leg through the ball and it sailed over the arms of the flailing Cadets. But as soon as it came off his foot, he knew something was wrong. The ball didn't hook as much as he had thought it would, and it sailed 18 inches to the right of the near goalpost.

*Wide right.*

Those two words would echo in Bucchianeri's ears forever. They seemed to follow him off the field, up the tunnel, through the locker room, and onto the team bus. He couldn't know it then, but those two words would become his legacy, a larger-than-life one, at Navy. At that moment, though, no one on the field understood what a life-changing moment that had been. The Army players knew they had survived, that they had won a game that had seemed lost. The Navy players were completely devastated, crushed by an awful defeat only days after the Coronado tragedy. They cried on one another's shoulders, stood bravely in the rain while the two alma maters were played, and then walked silently into their locker room.

Since Bucchianeri wore number 15 and Kubiak number 16, their lockers were right next to each other. When Navy sports information director Tom Bates quietly asked Bucchianeri if he wanted to come outside to speak to the media, Bucchianeri asked Kubiak what he thought.

"Should I go out there?" he asked.

At that moment, Kubiak was too stunned to empathize with Bucchianeri. "Booch, if I were you, I'd never walk out of here," he said.

Bucchianeri went with Bates. During a press conference that lasted less than five minutes, he unwittingly made himself into a hero. As a plebe, a midshipman is allowed three answers when addressing an upperclassman:

"Yes sir."

"No sir."

"No excuse sir."

The last is a critical part of training at the academies. If someone else splatters mud on your boots, you do not explain that to an upperclassman when he demands to know why they're muddy. You simply say — you *must* say — "No excuse sir." No one else is responsible for your failures. And so, when the media offered Bucchianeri excuses — the wet field, the angle, the pressure, perhaps even the hold or the snap — he kept shaking his head and saying — in essence — "No excuse sir."

"I missed the kick," he said repeatedly. "I did my best. I tried. I missed the kick."

In an era when athletes blame everyone and everything for their failures, Bucchianeri's simple "no excuse sir" treatise became national news. An entire country, it seemed, wanted to put its collective arms around him and say, "It's OK." Bucchianeri received hundreds of letters, from little kids to admirals to the Secretary of the Navy to congressmen and senators. Nine months later, in its college football preview issue, *Sports Illustrated* devoted seven full pages to Bucchianeri. William Nack, one of the magazine's most poetic and gifted writers, re-created what had happened during that week and on that day in a story that made Bucchianeri a national hero all over again.

Sadly, the saga had not ended, as it turned out, with the missed kick or the "no excuse sir" press conference. About fifteen hours

after Bucchianeri missed the kick, a Ford Bronco carrying four midshipmen back to Annapolis from the Meadowlands had come to the
crest of a hill about one mile from the gates to the academy. The spot
is known to the midshipmen as "Oh Shit Hill," because as you reach
it, the academy comes back into your vision and your immediate response is to say, "Oh shit."

This time, though, on a rainy, windswept morning, Brian Clark,
driving the Bronco, could barely see anything beyond his windshield.
He never saw the huge rotted willow tree that fell right across the
car's path, shearing off the Bronco's roof. Clark's three passengers,
fellow senior Lisa Winslow and sophomores Autumn Pevzner and
Robin Pegram, were killed almost instantly. Clark, the only survivor,
spent four days in the hospital.

The caravan of buses carrying most of the brigade arrived back at
the academy on that Sunday at about 2:30. Thirty minutes later, they
all filed solemnly into the academy chapel for Grizzard's memorial
service. It was during the service that Superintendent Lynch made the
announcement that three midshipmen had been killed that morning.
He didn't announce the names because the three families had not yet
heard the news.

By dinnertime, everyone knew the three names. An immense sadness settled over the Yard, as the academy campus is called. Mark
Hammond's feelings went beyond sadness. Robin Pegram had become his best friend. They were in the same Spanish class and Hammond often dropped by her room so they could study together. Other
times, he stopped in just to talk. At first he made up excuses for the
visits. After a while, he stopped bothering.

Most football players at Army and Navy give up their social lives
during the football season. There just isn't any free time, even on the
weekends, to deal with anything as serious as a girlfriend. Those that
have girlfriends explain to them that they aren't likely to see much of
them between August and early December. Sometimes the girlfriends
don't understand. Often they become ex-girlfriends.

Hammond had big plans for the end of the season. He had told his
friends that he was going to tell Pegram how he felt about her on the
Monday after the Army game. He was fairly certain she felt the same
way about him but, nonetheless, he was nervous about opening him-

self up to rejection, the way any not quite twenty-year-old would be. He had waited for the end of the season because he wanted to have time to spend with Pegram once — if — they began dating.

And then the accident happened. Hammond never got to tell Pegram how he felt. Late that night, he went out to Oh Shit Hill and just sat in the rain by the side of the road, crying. Some of his friends came and got him, brought him back. Technically, they were all in violation of academy rules, being off the Yard that late on a Sunday night. No one said a word.

Don DeVoe, Navy's basketball coach, still remembers that week at the end of 1993 vividly. Every day, it seemed, another funeral procession passed by his office. First Grizzard and O'Neill. Then Pegram, Pevzner, and Winslow. "It was as if a black cloud was sitting right on top of the academy and just wouldn't go away," he said. "Every day seemed bleaker than the last one."

Never before had the academy catchphrase "The sun always shines on the Midshipmen" seemed more empty.


INEVITABLY, the tragedies hung over the academy long after they had taken place. Although Lynch certainly wasn't held responsible for that awful first week in December, he was considered culpable in the Double E cheating scandal and for the low morale that had permeated the campus even before December. John Dalton, the Secretary of the Navy, had a number of staffing decisions to make in the spring of 1994, including finding a new Commander of Naval Operations, worldwide.

Admiral Charles R. Larson, who had been superintendent of the Naval Academy from 1983 to 1986, had been a finalist for the Joint Chiefs of Staff position in 1993 when Colin Powell stepped down. When he didn't get that job, he began making plans to retire. He would be fifty-seven in 1994, thirty-six years removed from his graduation as the brigade commander at the academy in 1958. Dalton asked him to postpone his retirement until after he had decided who he wanted to appoint as CNO.

Larson agreed, although he told Dalton at the time, "There are some very qualified younger guys who you can give the job to."

Dalton eventually gave the job to one of them: the ill-fated Admiral Mike Boorda. Then he called Larson and said, "I'd like you to consider going back to the Naval Academy."

Larson's initial response? "I thought it was someone pretending to be the Secretary, playing a joke on me," he said. "The thought of going back never crossed my mind."

Others, including Dalton, thought differently. Larson had been a very popular "Supe" with the midshipmen, someone who commanded absolute respect without being intimidating. Dalton's thinking was simple: Larson knew the academy better than anyone, having been a midshipman and the superintendent. He had never failed to do a job well, and the academy needed serious help.

Larson went back to his wife, Sally, and asked her what she thought. Both had mixed emotions: they loved the academy but were ready to get on with their lives. Another former superintendent, Admiral Ronald Marriott, called. "Chuck, the place needs you back," he said.

Larson decided to do it — on certain conditions. He would choose his own commandant (second in command) and the key people on his staff. The changes he made would be made quickly. "I didn't want to go in and start making the change of the month," he said. "I wanted to do it all the first thirty days and I wanted to tell the midshipmen *why*. I didn't want any nickel-and-dime stuff. I wanted them to understand why these things were important."

Dalton agreed. Larson returned in August of 1994, and since he didn't require the normal shakedown period that an officer normally needs in a new command, he went right to work.

"We had drifted," he said. "Not dramatically, but too much. We had become more civilian, too civilian. We had relaxed our standards and our accountability."

Once, only seniors — the first class — had been allowed to have civilian clothes and cars. By 1994, the second class and the third class (juniors and sophomores) had them. Larson took them away from the third class. He brought back mandatory breakfasts — too many mids were showing up for formation at 7 A.M., then diving back into bed. He changed the deadline for returning from weekend liberty from 11 o'clock to 6 o'clock so that everyone would be back on campus for

Sunday dinner with time to get a good night's sleep and "clear their heads for the week to come." Everyone — including first classmen — would stay on the Yard on Wednesday nights.

What's more, the academy's standards of behavior would be enforced more strenuously. During the previous two school years not a single first classman had been separated for major conduct offenses. During Larson's first year back, fourteen were separated, including three less than a month from graduation.

"The message was, the longer you're here, the more we expect out of you, not less," Larson said. "The two previous years we had just as many seniors charged with conduct offenses, but none separated. We wanted the first class to know they weren't exempt from the rules just because they had been here three years."

Given the morale at the academy, given the number of IHTFPs scrawled on the walls, it would seem unlikely that more rules and more discipline would have been greeted by the brigade with enthusiasm. But Larson didn't just announce the rules and then retreat to his office. He met with each class individually to explain what he was doing, and he began eating with a different squad each week to hear what they were thinking and feeling. He was a Supe the mids could touch, and they loved him for it.

Larson also knew he had a problem with the football team — on and off the field. Larson was in a far better position to attack the football problem than Lynch had been. Although he was a big fan of the football team, he hadn't been a player, the way Lynch had been. In fact, Lynch had captained the 1963 Cotton Bowl team. When he returned to the academy, he was immediately labeled a football Supe. No matter what he did, the brigade was convinced that his first priority was the football team.

The football team *was* important — to any superintendent. It is, without question, the most visible part of the academy, both to those out in the fleet who follow the team avidly, and to those in the civilian world who still remember Staubach and Bellino and, more recently, Napoleon McCallum and Phil McConkey, both of whom went on to NFL careers after serving their time in the navy.

McCallum had been on the team during Larson's first tenure as Supe, and even though the team didn't have a winning record in any year between '83 and '86, there were moments, including a victory over second-ranked South Carolina in 1985 when the Gamecocks arrived in Annapolis 9–0.

"We had some good wins," Larson said. "We beat North Carolina one year and Virginia and South Carolina the next. We weren't great, but people respected us."

Now, almost no one respected them, including their fellow midshipmen. Larson saw surveys that made it clear that most of the brigade saw the football players as pampered and spoiled, privileged and protected.

At his first meeting with the brigade before the start of fall semester, Larson told them that he hoped they would support one another more than they had in the past, that he believed that anyone who was involved in a "time intensive" activity, whether it was the glee club or the debate team or the football team, deserved everyone's support. He also encouraged them to stop using football games as an excuse for mischief. "Instead of sneaking out at two o'clock in the morning to hang a banner on a firehouse, why not go by the football practice field in the afternoon and let the team know you're behind it," he said.

After that, Larson met with the football team. He told the players he knew they didn't think they had the support of the brigade, but support was a two-way deal. He told them to become more involved with their companies, to show up for all their classes and try to be alert and attentive, to act like midshipmen rather than like football players who happened to wear a midshipman's uniform.

"You do that," he said, "and the brigade will come to you, regardless of what's happening on the field."

"It was like a marriage in trouble," Larson said. "The brigade and the football team were like an estranged couple. There was tension and there was resentment on both sides. We needed to clear the air."

Larson also took on some of the perception issues that had popped up in the survey. Because football players were expected to meet with their position coaches for noon meetings each day, they did not have to line up for lunch formation and march into King Hall with the rest of the mids. Larson made a change: every Thursday, there would be no position meetings and the players would march to lunch with everyone else. It was a small change — but the brigade noticed.

There was nothing, however, that Larson could do about what was happening on the field that fall. Chaump had been given a one-year extension following the 1993 loss to Army because athletic director Jack Lengyel believed that every coach deserved five years to turn a program around.

But things weren't going to turn around when the entire offensive line had graduated; when the defense was working with a third coordinator in three years; when the coach and the offensive coordinator began the season not speaking to one another.

The 1994 opener was at San Diego State, a talented Western Athletic Conference team. Garrett Smith, who was one of four new starters on the offensive line, remembers the first play of the new season vividly:

"It's your first game, you're all fired up and ready to go," he said. "First play, I come off the ball with everything I have, throw my entire body into the guy I'm blocking, and pick myself up two yards behind the line of scrimmage. I said, 'Uh oh.' I went back to the huddle and I said to Bryce [Minamyer], 'How's your guy?' He said, 'Brutal.' Then I asked Alex Domino the same thing and he just shook his head and said, 'A monster.' Right then, I knew we were in trouble."

It was worse than that. At halftime it was 42–0. San Diego State called off the monsters in the second half, and the final was 56–14. The next day, things got worse for the offense. Chaump announced to them that he had fired Greg Briner, the offensive coordinator.

"With Greg there we at least felt we had a chance because he knew what he was doing," Kubiak said. "When Coach Chaump said he was gone, there were a lot of us who figured, 'That's it, we might as well turn in our uniforms now.'"

Kubiak was so upset that he drove to Briner's house that night, breaking academy rules by leaving the Yard on a Sunday night. Briner convinced him that quitting, for him or anyone else, was the wrong thing to do. When Kubiak returned, he couldn't find a place to park. The Naval Academy is only 382 acres in size — compared to more than 1,600 acres at both West Point and the Air Force Academy — and parking on the Yard at night can often be impossible.

Knowing his car would get towed if he parked it illegally, Kubiak reported to the officer of the day to explain that he couldn't find any-place to park his car. When the OOD asked him why he was parking his car at so late an hour, Kubiak, remembering the academy's strict honor code, said, "I was driving around."

"Were you driving off the Yard?" the OOD asked.

Kubiak couldn't lie. "Yes sir," he answered.

"I thought I was a dead man," Kubiak said. "I was going to get fried big time."

"Fried" is the academy term for punishment. You can be fried for as little as a "1,000," which means you have committed a minor offense and are basically being told not to do it again, up to a "6,000," which means separation. Get fried often enough and you find yourself on restriction, usually meaning you can't leave the Yard on weekends. Continue to get fried after that and you will probably be hauled before some kind of board that will consider further punishment up to and including separation.

Kubiak had been fried periodically throughout his four years at the academy. Like a lot of players, his decision to attend Navy had little to do with the military. "They ran a passing offense and I thought I'd get a chance to play," he said.

The following day, Kubiak was called in by his company officer. Although each company has leadership from within the brigade, it also has a company officer, usually a Navy lieutenant, who runs the company on a day-to-day basis, especially when serious discipline is involved. Kubiak told him exactly what had happened: Briner had been fired on the heels of a 56–14 loss that started his last season of college football and he felt the need to talk to him. He knew he was wrong. The company officer decided not to fry him.

Kubiak escaped the noose of navy justice, but he couldn't escape the depressing reality of what was happening to the football team each week. The Mids lost to Virginia 47–10, to Bowling Green (Bowling Green!) 59–21, to Duke 47–14, and to Air Force 43–21 in a game that wasn't that close. The Falcons led 43–7 before Navy scored twice in the fourth quarter against their scrubs.

It was humiliating and disheartening. Each week, Kubiak, as the team captain, would stand up in front of the brigade, look at the Supe and say, "And this week's going to be different. We're going to go out there and bring you back a victory!"

Kubiak didn't believe it, the team didn't believe it, the brigade didn't believe it. Even the Supe didn't believe it. The players began calling it the "Lie of the Week."

They finally stopped lying in week six, squeaking out a 7–0 win over Division I-AA Colgate. The players were relieved to win a game, but hardly overjoyed. "I walked off the field in tears that day," Mark Hammond remembered. "It was an awful game."

The next week it was back to normal, a 35–14 loss to Louisville, followed by the annual Notre Dame thrashing, this time 58–21. Just when it seemed that a third 1–10 year in four was a lock, the team somehow managed to beat Tulane and Rice.

"What that told me," Larson said later, "was two things. Our guys hadn't quit on themselves, and we *did* have some talent."

Admiral Larson and Athletic Director Lengyel had been talking all season about the coaching situation. Both liked Chaump and thought he was a good man. Lengyel was especially uncomfortable with the notion of making a coaching change because the school was about to complete an $8 million overhaul of the football facilities that would include a new locker room, a huge new weight room, new meeting rooms, and expanded coaches offices. All of this was going to help recruiting considerably.

Part of Lengyel wanted Chaump to have the chance to use the new facilities. But he knew the players were unhappy. There was a sense of being rudderless inside the locker room, and there was little doubt going into the Army game that a change would be made — regardless of the outcome.

By that point, Chaump was convinced that his players — at least some of them — had turned against him. He even told several of them, Kubiak and wide receiver Matt Scornavacchi among them, that he knew they were trying to get him fired. Those whom Chaump made these comments to became known jokingly among the players as "the conspirators." It was more a badge of honor than anything else to be included in the group.

In fact, it was even worse than Chaump imagined. Garrett Smith said later that at least a dozen players had told him during the season that they wouldn't play football in 1995 if Chaump was back. Lengyel had heard all these rumblings, and he told Larson that there really wasn't any choice.

And so it was no surprise to anyone when they were told to meet in the Mitscher Auditorium a little more than twenty-four hours after the loss to Army. The game had not been as torturous as the previous year, but it had been painful nonetheless. Throughout pregame warm-ups, Bucchianeri had been serenaded by the cadets with chants of "Wide right, wide right." Then, on the opening drive of the game, Navy had reached the Army 20 and stalled. In came Bucchianeri to try a 37-yard field goal. The "wide right" cries filled the Army side of the stadium. Bucchianeri swung his leg through the ball, had plenty of distance, and missed — wide right.

The game went back and forth, until, with 6:52 left, Army's Kurt Heiss came on to try a 52-yard field goal — the longest of his career. Naturally, he made it. Navy couldn't score again and the final was 22–20.

When the players were settled in their seats on the day after the game, Chaump addressed them briefly. He told them that he understood that coaches who don't win get fired and that's what had happened to him. Then he walked out of the room. No one clapped, no one got up to shake his hand or say goodbye. Just like that, after five years and a won-lost record of 14–41, he was gone.

Lengyel then told the players there would be a search committee formed to interview candidates for the coaching job and that, for the moment, any problems should be addressed to the one coach guaranteed to return — strength and conditioning coach Phil Emery.

Thirty-six days later, the players filed back into Mitscher to meet their new coach. His name was Charlie Weatherbie, and the players knew little about him other than what they had read in the paper: he would be forty that month, and in three years as the head coach at Utah State he had a 15–19 record. During his second year, Utah State had won six straight games to finish 7–5. He had been a quarterback at Oklahoma State, had played in the Canadian Football League and then been an assistant coach at Wyoming, at Air Force for six years, and at Arkansas before getting the Utah State job.

And he slicked back his hair. Joe Speed and Andy Person, the two players who had been on the search committee had told them that. "We all thought that was kind of cool," Person said.

It didn't take long to learn more. As soon as everyone was settled,

Weatherbie dropped to a knee, reached his hand out in the direction of the players sitting in the front row, and said, "Men, let's all grab a hand and start with a prayer."

Some were delighted; some were taken aback; some were confused. All of them were surprised. The only time Chaump's teams had prayed was before the game, and then he had always asked one of the players to lead the prayer.

That would not be the case with Weatherbie. "It was a surprise," Andrew Thompson said. "But I think most of us were impressed because he had the confidence to walk into a roomful of strangers and say, 'This is who I am, this is where I'm coming from.' I think we all respected that about him right away."

The next surprise came shortly after Weatherbie had concluded the prayer and had started to address the team. Omar Nelson, a junior fullback, came in and slid quietly into a seat. He was about two minutes late.

"Son, I want to tell you something," Weatherbie said, not raising his voice. "To be early is to be on time. To be on time is to be late. To be late is to be forgotten." He looked around the room. "All of you need to remember that."

A tone had been established. In less than five minutes, Weatherbie had revealed a large chunk of his personality to his new players. They had learned that he was a man of deep religious convictions, a coach who was a great believer in punctuality and, more generally, in discipline. He smiled a lot and had cool hair, but he was deadly serious about football and about coaching football.

Tracing these traits wasn't terribly difficult. Weatherbie had grown up in a strict Baptist home in a small town in the southeastern corner of Kansas. He can't remember ever hearing either of his parents swear. They didn't drink or smoke either, and their three children — Charlie was the youngest — were brought up to understand that straying outside those boundaries was not advisable or acceptable.

Charlie was a typical younger brother, always trying to compete with Mike, who was fifteen months older than he was. Eventually, he caught him, beating him out for the quarterback job in high school. Although basketball was his first love, Charlie recognized early that it was football — specifically his right arm — that was going to take him places. He could always throw the ball harder and farther than any of his peers, and he knew he was good. In the sixth grade he announced to his father one night that he intended to play in the National Football League.

"You can do that," Bill Weatherbie answered, "but you'll have to work really hard."

Charlie did that, becoming a star quarterback in high school. He was heavily recruited by most of the Big Eight schools, although Florida State, the place he really wanted to go to, never came calling. He settled on Oklahoma State because coach Jim Stanley ran a passing offense and Weatherbie thought he would get to play early.

He got to play his freshman year as a backup and was a starter by his sophomore year. As a junior, he broke a collarbone and missed eight games. The injury proved to be a turning point in his life. Even though he had gone to church every Sunday as a boy and had accepted Christ into his life in the eighth grade, Weatherbie had never paid that much attention to religion or Christianity.

Getting hurt was about the worst thing that had ever happened to him, and, as many athletes do, he kept asking the question "Why me?" Kent Shirley, a friend and teammate who was a devout Christian, visited him often in the hospital and told him repeatedly that there was a reason for what had happened but he needed to turn to God in order to find it.

"I had been trying to get through life without His help," Weatherbie says now. "When I got hurt, Kent helped show me that I didn't have to do that, and, what's more, I couldn't do that. I needed him in my life. That was when I turned my life entirely over to Him."

That spirituality is at the very core of what Weatherbie is now. He is a big believer, not only in prayer but in reading the Bible over and over again. He starts each day with a reading, and tries to read one chapter of Proverbs every day. Since there are thirty chapters, he starts over on the first day of every month. If he quotes a verse, he can immediately tell you what chapter it is from — "Today's the fifteenth, so I was reading Chapter 15."

During the football season Weatherbie doesn't read newspapers — "I get the news from CNN at night," he says — or anything else except the Bible. In his car he has Bible tapes that he listens to driving to and from work. His new players would learn quickly how important faith was to Weatherbie: he started every gathering of the team or of his coaching staff with a prayer, and he quoted often from his readings.

One of the first quotations he brought up to them was from Jeremiah 29:11: "For I know the plans I have for you, declares the Lord; plans to prosper you, not to harm, plans to give you a hope and a future." He would use that quote over and over again when he talked to the team. Eventually, it was posted on the bulletin board in the locker room.

Weatherbie came back from his collarbone injury to have a successful senior season, leading Oklahoma State to a shocking victory over defending national champion Oklahoma and a Big Eight cochampionship, but much to his disappointment, he wasn't taken in the 1977 NFL draft. That summer he began a three-year odyssey that took him into several NFL training camps and all over Canada. He quarterbacked in Ottawa and Hamilton (twice) and had tryouts in Houston and Cleveland and San Diego. He got into one NFL exhibition game and completed one pass.

By the end of the 1980 season, Weatherbie knew it was time to put away childish things. His wife, Leann, had been very patient as he kept packing and repacking his bags. Now though, with a two-year-old son and a second on the way, it was time to move on. Weatherbie knew he wanted to coach. So he put on a suit and tie and showed up at the NCAA convention in 1981 looking for work. He found it, at the University of Wyoming, and off he went: three years at Wyoming, six at Air Force, two at Arkansas.

At Air Force, he came to know both the Army and the Navy programs well. Air Force had found prosperity running the wishbone, first under Ken Hatfield, then under Fisher DeBerry. DeBerry hired Weatherbie to coach quarterbacks and fullbacks in 1984. In 1989, having been part of a staff that had beaten Navy six straight times, he called Navy's Jack Lengyel after Lengyel had fired coach Elliot Uzelac. Lengyel was blunt: "I'm looking for someone with head-coaching experience."

Weatherbie knew that to become a head coach, he probably had to be an offensive coordinator first. So, when Jack Crowe offered the coordinator's job at Arkansas, he took it, even though he and his family loved living in Colorado Springs. "I hated to leave," he said. "But Fisher's staff is so stable, there was no way to move up, and I felt like I had to make the move if I wanted to be a head coach."

Two years later the move paid off. Utah State was looking for a coach. Fresno State athletic director Gary Cunningham, who had been the AD at Wyoming when Weatherbie was there, put in a good word for him with Utah State's Rod Tueller, and Tueller called Weatherbie and asked him to come in for an interview.

Weatherbie makes a very good first impression on most people. He is friendly and outgoing and is good at making people feel comfortable. He is full of self-confidence and, unlike a lot of coaches who are shy by nature, he loves being in the spotlight. Utah State offered him the job. He and Leann had just moved into a house they had spent a year building in Fayetteville, but there was no question about going.

Weatherbie signed a five-year contract that said he would be the head football coach. Officially, that was what he was. Unofficially, he was also the chief fund-raiser, number one alumni glad-hander, and public relations centerpiece. Once a week he would fly in a helicopter from Ogden to Salt Lake City for a press conference. Since it was tough for the media to get to him, he went to them. He flew and drove all over the state, speaking to alumni groups and potential donors.

He was a respectable 5–6 his first year, but started out 1–5 the second. Then some of the junior college players he had recruited began to jell, and suddenly the Aggies won their last five games to win the Big West Conference championship. That put them in the Las Vegas Bowl, their first bowl game in thirty-two years, and they won it, beating Ball State 42–33.

Weatherbie was now a hot young coach. He had not only proven he could win but that he was not afraid to be outrageous. During a rout of Nevada–Las Vegas that season, he had decided that the crowd was not as into the game as it should be. So, he marched behind the bench to a flagpole, shinnied up it — with some help from below — and began madly waving his arms at the crowd.

He got their attention.

Weatherbie also put the pads on for practice one day, playing scout team quarterback because he didn't feel any of his backup quarterbacks were equipped to run the opposition's offense. He came home very sore, and was informed by Leann that if he ever pulled a stunt like that again, coming home that night wouldn't be necessary.

"I didn't do bad for thirty-eight," he said, remembering the day.

Utah State lost its entire offensive line after the '93 season and, as often happens when a team rebuilds through the junior college route, got caught short in '94. The result was a 3–8 record. But the memories of '93 lingered in the coaching community, and, when Pat Jones was forced to resign as the coach at Oklahoma State, Weatherbie's name immediately came up as a possible replacement.

The notion of returning to Oklahoma State had always been on Weatherbie's mind. In fact, when he had signed his contract at Utah State, he had included a clause that allowed him to leave the school for Oklahoma State without a buyout.

"It was a dream," he said. "That's where I went to school, it's where our families live. If it had happened, it would have been a great thing."

But Weatherbie knew he wasn't a lock for the job. And so, when he heard that George Chaump had been fired at Navy, he called Lengyel again. "I've got head-coaching experience," he told him, remembering their conversation five years earlier.

"Send me your résumé," Lengyel said.

Weatherbie did, then didn't really think much about it as the Oklahoma State search neared a close. Since Oklahoma State had finished its season two weeks earlier than Navy, its search committee was much further along.

On the night of December 16, Weatherbie got a call from a friend on the Oklahoma State search committee. The school was going to announce that it had hired Bob Simmons, a Colorado assistant, to replace Jones. Weatherbie was disappointed but fell back on Jeremiah 29:11: "I have plans to prosper you, not to harm you. . . ."

The next day he called Lengyel again to find out his status in the Navy search. Lengyel wanted to meet with him. Weatherbie flew to Baltimore-Washington Airport and met with Lengyel for several hours in an airport hotel. Then he flew back to Ogden. Lengyel called the next day and asked if Weatherbie was willing to fly back to meet with the search committee. Certainly, Weatherbie said.

"Fine," Lengyel said. "You make your own plane reservations and your own hotel reservations. I don't want anyone to know you're flying in to interview. We don't want anything leaking to the media."

Weatherbie hadn't thought that the search for a new Navy football coach was that high a priority with the media in the Washington-Baltimore-Annapolis area (it wasn't), but if Lengyel wanted it that way, he would do it that way.

He flew in two days after Christmas and met with all the members of the search committee and then with Superintendent Larson, who interviewed all the coaching candidates separately from the committee. Larson also sat in on the search committee's deliberations but said nothing about any of the candidates. "I didn't want to influence anyone by voicing an opinion," he said.

Most of the Navy players expected their new coach to be Tom O'Brien, a 1971 academy graduate who had been an assistant during the Welsh era and was now his offensive coordinator at Virginia. But when search committee player representatives Joe Speed and Andy Person met O'Brien, they found him cool, almost detached. They both came away with the sense that O'Brien felt he would be doing everyone at Navy a big favor by taking over the football program. Weatherbie, on the other hand, was full of enthusiasm. He was six years younger than O'Brien and looked even younger than that with his slicked-back black hair and the wide, friendly smile he wore all the time. When Lengyel asked Speed and Person who they liked best among the candidates, their answer was emphatic: Weatherbie.

Larson had been impressed by both Weatherbie and O'Brien. Like a lot of people, Larson had thought at the start of the search that O'Brien would ultimately be the choice. But when the committee decided it was time to take a vote the result was unanimous: all twelve members chose Weatherbie.

He had brought an enthusiasm and a zeal to the interview process that O'Brien lacked. Although O'Brien's experience at Navy as a player and a coach worked in his favor, Weatherbie's six years at Air Force countered that. Like O'Brien, he had worked with military academy kids and he knew what it took to recruit at an academy. He also understood the rigors the players faced on a day-to-day basis that just didn't exist at civilian schools.

Weatherbie didn't go home after his interview because he was scheduled to work at a pre–Fiesta Bowl coaching clinic in Phoenix. On the morning of December 29, Lengyel tracked him down there.

"If we offer you the job," he asked, "will you take it?"

"Absolutely," Weatherbie answered.

"Then be here tomorrow," Lengyel said. "We'll schedule a press conference."

And so, on December 30, 1994, Charlie Weatherbie, nineteen days shy of turning forty, became Navy's thirty-fourth head coach. Most of the players were home on Christmas break that day. Andrew Thompson, who had been the team's leading tackler the previous season, was sitting in his parents' living room, feet on the couch, half-dozing and half-watching *Sportscenter* on ESPN, when he heard someone say that Navy had a new football coach. Then he heard him say the new coach's name.

"Who in the world," Thompson wondered, "is Charlie Weatherbie?"

Many people wondered not just who he was but why Weatherbie — why any coach — would want the Navy job. After all, it had been twelve years since Navy had had a winning season, and the only news the school had made in recent years had been bad news: Double E, Grizzard and O'Neill, Bucchianeri, the car accident.

Weatherbie saw the job as a chance to make a name for himself nationally. Winning at Navy certainly wouldn't be easy, but if he did — and his Air Force experience convinced him that he could — the whole country would notice. When he won at Utah State, only everyone in Utah noticed.

Of course it wasn't long before Weatherbie was asked about Army-Navy. "Oh, it's a great rivalry," he said, smiling. "It's just like Oklahoma–Oklahoma State or Alabama-Auburn, any of the big games like that."

He would coach his first Army-Navy game in 337 days. Not until then would he know how wrong his assessment was.

# 3

# LAST CHANCE

THERE had been no traumas at Army like the ones at Navy. But the nineties had been a major letdown for the football team and coaches.

In the spring of 1990, after eight years as coach, Jim Young had decided to retire at the end of the season. He had engineered a remarkable turnaround during his tenure, taking over a program that had averaged 3.3 wins a year during the previous ten seasons and, after a 2–9 record in 1983, averaging seven victories per season for the next seven years and leading Army to three bowl games.

The key factor in the turnaround was Young's decision at the end of 1983 to go to a wishbone offense. The wishbone had been *the* offense of the late sixties and early seventies in college football, first practiced by Texas, then adopted by Oklahoma, Alabama, and other national powers.

Eventually, though, the best teams figured out how to diagnose the triple-option look, assigning specific defensive players to specific offensive players, thus making some of the offensive trickery less effective. The other problem with the wishbone was that coming from behind with it was almost impossible since 95 percent of the plays were running plays and most wishbones only had one deep-threat receiver.

By the time Young decided to put it in at Army the only other Division I-A team using it was Air Force. It was not, by any means, a coincidence that two military academies would decide to employ it.

Like Air Force, Army was able to build a rushing offense around quick, intelligent quarterbacks and durable linemen who much preferred going forward to run block than stepping back to pass block. Size, something the military academies always lack, wasn't as important in the blocking schemes as quickness and technique.

The wishbone did several things for Army: it kept the offense on the field for long periods of time, grinding out long ball-control drives. That meant the defense was almost always rested and the opposition could not afford to make mistakes on offense because it wasn't going to get the ball as often as it normally did. It also made preparing to play Army more difficult because the odds were pretty good that it was the only game all year when an opponent would face the wishbone.

Young also benefited during this period from a change in scheduling philosophy. Understanding that the forties and fifties and even the sixties were long gone, the Army brass had toned down the schedule. Instead of playing Penn State every year, Army now played Colgate. Instead of traveling to Stanford, the Cadets played Montana.

Not that there weren't still tough games on the schedule. In '84, Army played Tennessee, Duke, Boston College, and Syracuse in addition to the annual games against Air Force and Navy. The next year it played Boston College, Notre Dame, and Illinois. But there were also games against Harvard and Penn, Western Michigan and Yale. That didn't make Young's job easy, because the Ivy League teams were probably recruiting a lot of the same players he recruited. But it did make it reasonable.

What's more, Army acquitted itself well against quality opponents during the Young years: it tied Tennessee in front of 95,000 fans at Neyland Stadium in Knoxville in 1984 and won there in 1986; it beat Michigan State and Illinois in bowl games; and in 1988 it lost to Alabama 29–28 in a thrilling Sun Bowl game.

Any team that could play Alabama virtually even for sixty minutes was doing just about as well as any rational West Point alum could hope. But after a disappointing 6–5 season in 1989 ended with a 19–17 loss to Navy, Young began wondering if he still had the spark he needed to keep on coaching. Friends say that Young is one of the most single-minded people alive, someone who focuses 100 percent of his time on a job until it is done. When he began to feel that drive and focus slipping, he knew it was probably time to get out.

That spring, during preparations for the 1990 season, he called in Bob Sutton, who had been his defensive coordinator at Army from the start, and told him he was seriously thinking about retiring at the end of the season. If he did retire, he told Sutton, he wanted him to be his successor.

Sutton had mixed emotions. He hated to see J.Y. leave. But if he was going to leave, he wanted the job. Sutton had known in high school that he wanted to coach. He had started his career as an undergraduate assistant at Eastern Michigan. Even though he was not yet forty, he had been coaching for almost twenty years. This, he thought, should be his time to take the step up.

Because of his record, Young had enough pull at West Point to see to it that he could all but name his successor. Thus, when he announced that summer that he would step down at the end of the season, the school announced at the same time that Sutton would be the new coach.

Army went 6–5 again that year, finishing with an emotional 30–20 victory over Navy in Young's last game. Sutton became the head coach the next day. It was not an easy adjustment. Instead of just worrying about the defense he had to worry about the entire team. He had to be more intimately involved with recruiting and with what his assistant coaches were doing. Quiet and shy by nature, he had to talk to the media on a regular basis and to alumni groups. It was not something that came naturally or easily to him.

Those are normal adjustments, though, ones that every coach makes when he becomes the boss for the first time. But it was more difficult in Sutton's case, in part because he was taking over a group of players who thought of him as an assistant coach. Football players are always closer to the assistants than they are to the head coach. In fact, to a large degree, the head coach coaches the assistants, who then coach the players. Sutton had to take a step back from the players, and he had to spend more time with the offense than he had in the past.

Finally, there was the specter of Young. Almost all new coaches take over for someone who has failed. Coaching changes are made ninety-nine times out of a hundred because the team is losing. That was certainly the case when Weatherbie took over at Navy in 1995. Almost anything he produced was going to be an improvement on the recent past.

Nothing was farther from the truth when Sutton succeeded Young. OK, it wasn't like Phil Bengston trying to succeed Vince Lombardi in Green Bay or Ray Perkins attempting to follow Bear Bryant at Alabama, but it was Sutton stepping into the breach left by a man whose record during the past seven seasons had been 49–30–1 after a ten year run of 33–72–3 prior to his arrival. Young may not have been the savior at Army, but he was a reasonable facsimile.

Sutton's first season produced a 4–7 record that included two humiliating losses: one to The Citadel, a West Point wannabe; the other by a 24–3 score to a Navy team that arrived in Philadelphia with an 0–10 record. The next two years produced marginal improvement: 5–6 in '92 (with another loss to The Citadel thrown in) and 6–5 — thanks to Bucchianeri's wide right — in '93. By the time Sutton began his fourth season in 1994, the old grads were beginning to grumble.

Some of the players even wondered about Sutton as a head coach. There was no doubting his understanding of the game, and they all liked and admired him as a person. But he wasn't the kind of leader Young had been. Despite the emphasis at West Point on leadership within the Corps of Cadets, the football coach was, by nature, a quiet, unassuming guy who would probably just as soon break down game film as charge into battle.

Needing some breaks to go his way in '94, Sutton watched helplessly as the season started out with nothing but bad ones. The first came six plays into the opener against Holy Cross when quarterback Rick Roper went down with a torn knee. He would be gone for the season. Army still won that game easily, but five days later, playing a Thursday night prime-time game on national TV against Duke, Roper's backup, Mike Makovec, also went down, with torn ligaments in his ankle.

That left Army with Steve Carpenter, who had started the season as a halfback, playing quarterback. Before the long night was over, Duke had humiliated the Cadets 43–7, continuing to throw the ball late in the fourth quarter. The last touchdown, with less than two minutes to play, came on a seven-yard pass. It was as if the Blue Devils, having already body-slammed the Cadets, wanted to rub their noses in the dirt for good measure.

"We'll remember this," Jim Cantelupe vowed later. "I guarantee you it'll be different when we play them next year."

There was still plenty of this year to worry about, however. Next came three straight losses in games Army led in the fourth quarter — to Temple, to Wake Forest, and to Rutgers. The first two losses were the direct result of late fumbles. One of the keys to running the wishbone is taking care of the football, and with fourth-string quarterback Ronnie McAda now running the team — Carpenter had been returned to his halfback slot — the offense simply wasn't in sync the way a wishbone has to be to be successful.

The losing streak finally ended the next week against Louisville. This time it was Army's turn to score late, McAda leading a 77-yard drive that produced the winning touchdown with 3:17 left in the game for a 30–29 victory. The joy of the win was muted by another injury: this one to fullback Akili King. The most talented player Sutton had ever recruited, King had been brilliant at times in his Army career and injured at other times. He had also been in almost constant trouble within the corps, including an incident in a bar in early 1994 in which he had been stabbed in the butt during a fight.

King was now a junior. When he hurt his knee against Louisville, it was apparent he wouldn't play for the rest of the season. The Cadets were now 2–4 and had lost both their quarterbacks and their best running back — arguably their best player. They had also lost their best wide receiver. But that was a different story.


THE wide receiver not catching passes for Army that fall was Leon Gantt. No one suffered more watching the Cadets struggle during that fall of 1994 than Gantt. This was supposed to have been Gantt's senior season, the year in which he and his classmates finally produced the kind of team they had all dreamed about when they first arrived at West Point in the summer of 1991.

But Gantt wasn't on the team. He wasn't even enrolled at West Point even though his grade point average for three years was 3.0.

Every week, hearing about the struggles of his former teammates, he felt sick to his stomach.

"It was no one's fault but mine," he said. "If I had listened to my mother in high school, it never would have happened."

What happened was junior English, or in cadet terminology, "Cow English," juniors at West Point being referred to as cows. (Freshmen and sophomores are called plebes and youngsters at both Army and Navy, and the seniors at both schools are called first classmen, or firsties. Only the junior classes are different. Navy simply calls its juniors second classmen).

Gantt had been a typical teenager growing up in Livingston, Texas: a star athlete who never had any trouble in school, and if he did there was usually a sympathetic teacher around to help him out. Natha Gantt constantly badgered her son about the fact that he never read anything, but he wasn't listening. "Whenever she told me I should read a book," he said, "I told her I would go see the movie when it came out."

Unlike most football players at Army, Gantt was widely recruited as a senior. He took official visits to Texas A&M, LSU, Texas, and Houston. He was generally considered the best receiver coming out of Texas in the fall of 1990. Sutton had seen him on film and had taken note of his high grades and solid — almost 1100 — SATs. Shortly after becoming head coach, he called and asked if Gantt could meet with him. Gantt figured, why not?

At the time he knew very little about West Point. Like a lot of football players, he knew about the Army-Navy game but had thought for years that it was a game between *the* army and *the* navy. He hadn't understood that there were colleges involved. Sutton convinced him to make a visit to the campus. Gantt agreed. When he got there he was impressed by one thing that most teenagers usually don't want to hear about: the discipline.

"I knew I was a good football player," he said. "But my dream was to someday go to medical school. I knew that if I went to one of the other schools and got hurt playing football, that was it, I was done. At West Point, I could play football but I also had a guaranteed job when I got out, and medical school would be there no matter what if I did well in school.

"I wasn't a wild kid or anything, but I knew if I went to a civilian school I would end up pledging a fraternity and going to a lot of parties. I really didn't want that. I wanted the challenge.''

And so, much to his parents' surprise, he said no thanks to the bigtime schools and decided to enroll at West Point.

Plebes do not report to West Point at the end of the summer. They must report at the end of June for what is known as ''Beast,'' the six-week training and orientation period that quickly weeds out anyone who isn't certain whether a military academy is the right place for him or her.

The first day, ''R-Day'' (for ''Registration''), is a complete shock to everyone. Most of the time, the about-to-be-plebes have arrived a day or two early with their families. They have toured the campus, which on a summer day overlooking the Hudson is about as pretty a place as one can imagine, and scoured the area for restaurants. Occasionally they have made the fifty-mile trip to New York City. All very pleasant and idyllic.

Then, on R-Day, they all walk into the auditorium of the Holleder Center, which sits directly across from Michie Stadium, and hear the superintendent talk about the journey they are about to embark on. After that, an announcement is made: all plebes are to report to the back of Holleder Center. Goodbyes are said quickly and the plebes stumble into the hot sun to find first classmen — almost always angry first classmen — waiting for them. Within minutes, they have been told that they are, without doubt, the worst-looking lot of plebes ever to arrive at West Point.

''It all happens so quickly,'' Gantt remembered. ''One minute, you're a kid sitting there on a summer day, the next minute you walk through a door and there are all these first classmen *screaming* at you. You think, 'Oh my God, I'm in the *army!*' ''

A few minutes later, they are in the army — officially. Before being issued uniforms they each have to recite the cadet oath:

> I, Gennie Leon Gantt, do solemnly swear that I will support the Constitution of the United States, and bear true allegiance to the National Government; that I will maintain and defend the sovereignty of the United States, paramount to any and all allegiance, sovereignty, or fealty I may owe to any state or country

whatsoever; and that I will at all times obey the legal orders of my superior officers, and the Uniform Code of Military Justice.

The rest of the first day is, for every plebe, a blur. It is a terrifying trip through the looking glass into a world none of them can possibly have imagined, no matter what they have heard or read. West Point even recommends to incoming plebes that they read *The Long Gray Line,* Rick Atkinson's superb book on the class of 1966, which spells out in great detail what Beast is like.

And, although Beast has been toned down considerably in recent years — just as Plebe Summer has been at Navy — to remove some of the emotional and physical hazing, it is still an exhausting, brutal experience. It is designed to test the will of each plebe, to find out right away if someone is not going to be able to deal with military life. No one goes through Beast or Plebe Summer without thinking about quitting at least once a day.

"It's all a mind game," Gantt said. "Once you figure that out, you can get through it. All the running and memorizing and harassing and yelling and lack of sleep and lack of eating. It's all for a reason. You just can't let it get to you."

Gantt was a fairly typical plebe. He spent three weeks absolutely convinced he wanted to go home, then decided that the *last* thing he was going to do was give up. He arrived for Beast weighing 185 pounds. By the time he reported for the first day of plebe football practice in early August he weighed 165. Most plebes lose anywhere from ten to forty pounds during Beast or Plebe Summer. That is a fact of life that academy coaches must deal with: while freshmen at other schools spend their summers working on weight programs to increase their strength, plebes at Army and Navy usually report for football practice weak and exhausted.

"We're probably the only schools in the country where the players actually look *forward* to two-a-days in the summer," Bob Sutton says. He smiles when he says it, but there's a lot of truth in the comment.

Like most plebes, Gantt spent his freshman season playing on the JV team. The coaches had decided to convert him from wide receiver to running back and he found himself relegated to the scout team during practice. At times, he wondered what the hell was going on: "Texas A&M thought I could play; Texas and Houston thought I could play. How in the world could I not be good enough for Army?'' he wondered.

He never quite mastered coming out of the wishbone stance for running backs, so the coaches moved him back to wide receiver as a sophomore. He soared to number two on the depth chart and played in every game. A year later, he was the primary target, catching twenty-one passes — a lot in a wishbone offense — for 207 yards. That should have set him up for a stellar senior year. That's when Cow English intervened.

Gantt knew he was in trouble early in the fall semester. His papers came back with all sorts of grammatical errors pointed out. The professor — at West Point they are called P's — told Gantt his vocabulary was limited, that he needed to read more. Gantt could hear his mother's voice begging him to read. He had waited for the movie. Now, it was too late.

He flunked during fall semester, the first time in his life he had ever flunked a class. He was distressed, but not panicked. He knew he had to retake the class in the spring. He also knew that West Point has strict rules about core curriculum classes: flunk it once, try again; flunk it twice, hit the road. Separation. Automatic.

Gantt worked harder than he had ever worked in a class during that spring semester. He was improving, but not fast enough. One paper came back with a three — out of a possible five. That was passing. But the next one was a two — not good enough. When the semester was over, he had two threes and three twos. He had flunked, by one point.

''It was the most devastating thing that ever happened to me,'' he said. ''I had worked so hard for so long to get where I was, and then — bang — just like that, I was separated.''

His teammates were shocked. Gantt was one of few players on the team who never seemed to have trouble academically. And now, two semesters from graduating, he was gone.

His parents suggested he come home, make up the English classes in summer school, and transfer. After all, with good grades and twenty-one catches in a wishbone offense, someone would probably take him as a transfer. He would sit out the '94 season and then play in '95. No sweat.

Gantt said no. ''I had come too far, worked too hard, made too much of a commitment to walk away,'' he said. ''I was determined to get back in school and graduate from West Point and be commissioned as an officer.''

He went to see his academic dean, Colonel Frank Giordano, to tell him he wanted to do whatever he had to do to be reaccepted to West Point the following January. Giordano was blunt with him: the odds were probably against him; separated cadets were usually not reaccepted for at least a year — if at all. But he also told him if he wanted to make the effort, he would help him in any way he could. The first thing he had to do was find a place where he could take the two English classes (he had never taken the second semester of Cow English, since he hadn't passed the first).

Gantt enrolled at Ramapo College in Mahwah, New Jersey, about a forty-five-minute drive from the academy. Following Giordano's advice, he enrolled in both the English classes and a physics class to show the admissions board how intent he was on working hard. He also took a job at a nearby McDonald's working from 5 P.M. to 2 A.M. each night to make some money to pay for his apartment and his school expenses. With his sister starting her freshman year at Southwest Louisiana University, he was determined not to have to ask his parents for any money.

''I was twenty-one,'' he said. ''I wasn't going to be a burden to them because of a mistake I had made.''

Gantt's fall schedule was brutal: the first of his three classes started at 7:30 in the morning. He would work out briefly after class, then study. If there was time, he would drive up to West Point to see the admissions people. ''I pestered them all fall,'' he said. ''I was up there at least three, sometimes four days a week. I told them my professors' names and gave them their phone numbers so they could check on my progress. I asked them if there was anything else I needed to do. Did I need any more letters of recommendation? Were there any books I should be reading? Should I have my professors write?''

Some days, after his swing through admissions, Gantt would stop at football practice. It was painful to watch his teammates going through their routines without him, but bearable. The games were not. He never could bring himself to go. ''It would have hurt too much,'' he said.

After leaving West Point, he would drive back to Mahwah to start his shift at McDonald's. As luck would have it, the Ramada Inn where the team stayed on Friday nights before home games was no more than one hundred yards away. Often, his classmates would come over on Friday evenings to cheer him up and let him know they were thinking about him.

"It made me feel great that they cared," he said. "But when they left, I would think about them going through meetings, looking at tape, getting ready to play Saturday. And I would just sit down in the back and want to cry.

"I learned a lot, though. I remember when I was in high school, people I had known would come back from college and go to work at McDonald's or some place like that and I would think, 'They must be failures, what's wrong with them?' I found out life isn't that easy or that simple. I think I grew up a lot."

He was sleeping no more than five hours a night, but after three years at West Point, he could handle that. He got A's in all his classes. In fact, his professors often used his papers as examples of how to write.

On the day that his case was to be heard by the admissions board, he finished his last class at Ramapo (the teacher in that class had allowed him to take his final early so West Point would have a grade) and raced back up the New York Thruway one more time. He had submitted a hundred-page folder that included his grades and recommendations, his renomination to West Point, and an essay on why he had been separated and why he wanted so much to return.

Giordano had made arrangements to call Gantt in Grant Hall, which is the cadet campus hang-out, as soon as he had word. The admissions board was meeting right across the street in Taylor Hall.

Gantt waited. One hour. Then two. What had gone wrong? What had he forgotten to include? He paced up and down in the lobby under the pictures of famous and not-so-famous generals who had graduated from West Point.

The phone rang. Gantt stared at it. One ring, then two. He couldn't pick it up. He sat frozen. Three rings, four. Finally, on the fifth ring, he picked it up, his hands shaking. He heard Giordano laughing on the other end. "What's the matter, Leon?" he asked. "Afraid to pick the phone up?"

Gantt's heart leaped. Giordano wouldn't have been laughing if the news wasn't good. He had been accepted. He was back. If all went well, he would graduate in December of 1995 — *after* playing one more season of football.

"I guarantee you one thing," he said, looking back. "My kids will read in high school. No movies. Books."

EVEN after the dramatic win over Louisville, things didn't get much better for Gantt's teammates. They did manage to finally beat The Citadel, escaping by a 25–24 score when Kurt Heiss kicked a field goal as time expired.

But just when it seemed that two dramatic victories might turn the season around, the opposite happened. The next three weeks produced three discouraging losses: a 30–3 rout at the hands of Boston College in front of the only Michie Stadium sellout crowd of the season; a sixth-straight loss to Air Force, this time by 10–6; and an embarrassing 21–12 loss to Division I-AA Boston University. It was true that BU was one of the top I-AA teams in the country (ranked seventh with a 9–1 record), but I-AA was I-AA.

The record for the season was 3–7 and the cries for Sutton's head grew louder each week. Lt. Gen. Howard D. Graves, the superintendent, was not in a position to turn a deaf ear. The school was trying to raise $2 million to build new athletic offices next to Michie Stadium. The money would have to come from the old grads. That meant Graves had to keep them happy. The best way to keep them happy was with a winning football team.

The most depressed of the Cadets after the Boston University game was Jim Cantelupe. The loss was bad enough, and the 3–7 record stung. Worst of all, he wasn't going to play against Navy. Late in the game, trying to make a tackle, Cantelupe felt someone fall across his right leg. The pain was sharp and immediate.

"I knew it wasn't something minor," he said later.

It wasn't. His right ankle was broken. He would have to have a rod inserted into it later in the week. After being taken to the post hospital for X rays, Cantelupe returned to the locker room on crutches just after the game had ended. He sat down on a bench directly across from Derek Klein, his best friend since Beast and his backup at free safety.

Klein wasn't surprised that Cantelupe, normally as upbeat as anyone on the team, looked depressed. The loss had been humiliating and he had been injured. "What'd they say?" he asked, almost casually, expecting Cantelupe to say something like, "It's a sprain, I'll be ready for Navy."

Instead, tears welled in Cantelupe's eyes. "It's broken, Derek. I'm done. You've got to step in and be the man."

Klein had come to Army as a quarterback and had been number two on the depth chart in the spring before his sophomore season. But he had never gotten the chance to play there and had been switched to defense as a junior. He had been fighting for playing time for three years. Now, he was going to get it — because his best friend was hurt.

"It was a weird feeling," he said. "That day, all I could think about was how awful it was for Jim. But as we got ready for the game, I couldn't help but be excited knowing I was going to be in there."

Cantelupe consoled himself by reminding himself what a great opportunity this was for his pal Klein. "If I couldn't go, I was glad that it was Derek stepping in there for me," he said. "It was comforting." And he started thinking about next year. He and Klein and all his classmates would be seniors. They would be the leaders. It would be their team.

First, there was the not so small matter of beating Navy. They did it, thanks to Kurt Heiss's miracle kick from 52 yards and because the Cadets stopped a Navy drive in the fourth quarter on a critical interception at the two yard line by an alert defensive back.

The defensive back was Derek Klein.

They celebrated with gusto when the game was over, but they all knew that the season hadn't come close to being what they wanted. And they knew they had just one chance left.

"We did not come here to be 5–6, 6–5, 4–7," Cantelupe said. "We came here to take the program beyond that. It was up to us, the seniors, to make sure what happened our junior year didn't happen again our senior year. It was our last chance. No ifs, ands, or buts. Our very last chance."

# 4

# ARMY FOOTBALL HONOR

A senior football player at Army or Navy isn't like a senior football player at other schools. For one thing, he has been through more — far more — than any of the other seniors around the country.

He has survived Beast or Plebe Summer, capped at West Point by a twelve-mile march in full combat gear under an August sun, to Lake Frederick. After three days of camping out, everyone gets to march twelve miles back to West Point.

He has lived through his plebe year, learning the answer to such vital questions as:

"Name the four Army mules."

"Name all of Navy's Heisman Trophy winners."

"What time is kickoff of this year's Army-Navy game?"

"Who is the current United States congressman from your squad leader's district?"

And the always popular "How many days till graduation?"

They had gone through summer training programs while most college kids were at the beach. They had been up at 4:30 in the morning during the summer because that was the only time to get in their off-season training before their day began at 6 A.M. They had been on guard duty and had marched for hours with a gun over their shoulder.

They had been up before the sun almost every day of their college lives and in first period classes before 8 A.M. — 7:15 at West Point, a leisurely 7:55 at Annapolis. They had been subject to punishment for everything from cutting a class to failing to turn a corner in a hallway properly to carrying a book bag over their shoulder. They had been subjected to room inspections, uniform inspections, shoe inspections, closet inspections, bed inspections, under-the-bed inspections, haircut inspections (yes, haircut inspections), and being dropped at a moment's notice for fifty or a hundred push-ups just because someone felt like dropping them for fifty or a hundred push-ups.

Most of them agreed that if they had known what life was going to be like before they signed on, they probably wouldn't have signed on. Most also agreed that they would be happy and proud in later life to tell people where they had gone to college. Almost all of them agreed on one thing: Army and Navy were great places to be from, not great places to be at.

At West Point, they were told all the time that they were getting a $250,000 education. There was no arguing with that. The saying among the cadets was, "It's a $250,000 education — shoved up your ass a quarter at a time."

Recruiting is different at the military academies than at civilian schools for the simple reason that every student at each school is on a government-funded scholarship. That means the schools do not have to concern themselves with National Collegiate Athletic Association scholarship limits.

In football, civilian schools can have no more than eighty-five players on a scholarship and can offer no more than twenty-five scholarships in a given year. Army, Navy, and Air Force can offer as many scholarships as they wish, as long as the football player meets the academic demands required to gain admission. It is virtually impossible for any of the academies to recruit blue-chip or even almost blue-chip football players, the ones who dream of playing in the NFL. Since academy graduates must make a five-year commitment to the military, almost no one who thinks he has any chance to play professionally is going to enroll at an academy.

That means the schools must take advantage of the lack of scholarship limitations and cast their nets as far and as wide as they can. Any player who shows potential and is a good student is given a hard look. A Top Ten football team will probably begin the fall with fifty to seventy-five high school seniors on its list of possible recruits. An academy may have three hundred, knowing that many will shy away, many won't qualify, and many will come to school and simply not be good enough to play.

All three academies also have prep schools. They exist primarily for students who have an interest in the academy but are not considered ready academically to enroll after their senior year of high school. The prep schools are used, most of the time, for two groups of students: minorities who need to improve their board scores and take or retake core courses, and athletes who need similar academic help. This allows the academy coaching staffs to recruit players who fall below the average SAT score for the rest of the student body, which is about 1200 at both Army and Navy.

And, while that would seem to be a terrific way to redshirt players — give them a fifth year of college the same way most civilian schools do with their football players — there are risks involved. To start with, orientation at the prep schools is a lot like Beast and Plebe Summer and often scares players away. What's more, the players who attend the prep schools are not committed to attending the academies. Often, those who show potential find themselves being recruited by civilian schools at the end of their prep seasons.

In fact, the academies sometimes have to recruit a player three different times: at the end of his senior year of high school, at the end of his prep school year, and again at the end of his sophomore year. It is then that all students at the academies have the opportunity to leave without having any obligation to the military. Once your junior year begins, you are stuck. At the academies, the decision is known as "two-for-seven" (before 1995, when the military commitment was lowered from six to five years, it was "two-for-eight"), because if you decide to stay those last two years you are committing to the military for the next seven.

Army's class of 1996 was the second one Sutton had recruited as head coach, the first that had played as high school seniors with him in command at West Point, since the class of 1995 had played their senior seasons in 1990 when Jim Young was still in charge.

About 125 of them reported for the first day of plebe practice in August. Ray Tomasits, a defensive back who had spent four years at the New Mexico Military Institute and was probably less intimidated by the burdens of Beast than anyone, remembers looking around at all the players who announced they were defensive backs and thinking, "I have no chance."

He wasn't far wrong. When the depth chart came out the next day, Tomasits was listed as eighth string — among the plebes. He would survive, though, to become a key defensive player.

Attrition happens quickly during summer ball. Some players, who see football as a way to get out of camping out at Lake Frederick, realize quickly that being at Lake Frederick is a lot easier than football two-a-days. They are back in their companies within a couple of days. Other players are told politely that they really don't belong on the football field. They too return to their companies. Others look at the varsity players when they arrive and say, "Forget this."

Life at West Point takes care of the rest. Some players leave school voluntarily; others involuntarily. Some decide after a year of JV ball that the time they're putting in isn't worth it for the return they're getting from the game. It is easier for a player at a military academy to quit football because at the academies your scholarship is unaffected. You simply go back to your company and continue working toward your degree. At a civilian school, where athletic scholarships are renewed each year at the discretion of the coaches, a player who quits the team is unlikely to have a scholarship the next year.

"The good news is that anyone who stays with the team is there because he wants to be there," Sutton says. "You don't have anyone hanging around unless they really want to be around, because there's nothing forcing them to stay. The easiest thing in the world is to take back the four or five hours a day you give up for football and put it into studying or sleeping, and no one will think any less of you for doing it."

By the time the class of '96 gathered for spring practice in March of 1995, the 125 had become 29. Relatively speaking, that was a lot. Three years earlier, Army had dressed 11 seniors for the Navy game.

Even so, almost 100 of the original 125 had left for one reason or another. Those who had stayed had become extremely close, almost like an extended family. The ones who lived nearby took the ones who lived far away home with them on weekends or holiday breaks too short to go home to places like Texas or Georgia or California or Oregon.

Eddie Stover, the right guard from Athens, Georgia, could tell you exactly how long it took to get to the home of Joel Davis, the left guard from Binghamton, New York. "It's three hours and fifteen minutes — not counting the stop at Wendy's."

All teams in all sports like to portray themselves as being families. This is especially true of football teams, where building a genuine dislike for an opponent can help a team both physically and emotionally on game day. But at Army and Navy it is perhaps more true than anyplace else.

Although morale at Army had not reached the nadir it had at Navy in recent years (the West Point cheating scandals had come earlier, back in the seventies), and the relationship between the corps and the football team had never been as bad as what had gone on between the brigade and the Navy football team, there was always a certain tension.

Some of it was for the age-old reason that affects feelings about football (and basketball) teams almost everywhere. The football players were considered privileged characters. To some degree — but far less than at civilian schools — they were. They had their own tables in the mess hall in-season, and on Saturday mornings, while the rest of the corps had to put on full dress uniforms to parade on the Plain before the public, they were resting in their hotel getting ready for a game.

At Army, football games were not mandatory for the corps. It was, however, "highly recommended" that they attend home games, and no one was allowed off the post before 6 P.M. on Saturdays when there was a game in Michie Stadium. Given the choice between studying or hanging out someplace on campus or going to the football game, most showed up at the games.

There had been one potential revolt in 1990 when members of the corps had gleefully taken off their jackets after an Army touchdown and twirled them over their heads in celebration. It was so much fun they did it again after the next score and throughout the game. That Monday, the commandant sternly announced that if the twirling act was repeated at the next week's game, the entire corps would be placed on restriction for the rest of the weekend.

The corps is used to discipline for the sake of discipline and following orders no matter how arbitrary they might seem, but this was too much. All week long the word was that the cadets were going to boycott the game en masse. They didn't. But instead of arriving ninety minutes early and instead of having one of the four regiments formally march on after the team warm-ups, they all meandered in about ten minutes before kickoff.

The jacket twirling stopped, but a point had been made: push us, but don't shove us up against a wall.

The football players at West Point, like their counterparts in Annapolis, felt underappreciated by their fellow students. They heard the grumbling about their "privileges" — some in the corps referred to football players as "get-overs" — and resented it. Their attitude was, "Fine, you come up to Michie for five hours every single day; you work out in the weight room eleven months a year; you get up ninety minutes before sunrise all summer to get your conditioning work done, and *then* come talk about how easily we're getting over." Their nickname for the anti-football whiners was "sluggos." A sluggo who went out of his way to make life difficult by doing things like turning people in who stayed up past mandatory lights-out at 11:30 or for using elevators in the barracks during the daytime was known as an "honor Nazi." And, as if to affirm that their devotion to football was separate from any connection they might have to the corps, the players substituted their own code of honor for the West Point code of honor that holds, "A cadet will not lie, cheat or steal, nor tolerate those who do." They called it "Army football honor." If you claimed to have bench-pressed three hundred pounds one day and a teammate questioned you by saying, "Army football honor?," to lie in response was considered an absolute betrayal.


ON the final day of spring practice each year, the Army football team gathers for dinner in Eisenhower Hall, a sprawling recreation facility that sits about two hundred yards from the edge of the Plain on a section of the campus that overlooks the Hudson River.

In 1995, when the spring dinner was over, the senior class stayed behind to hold the first of what would be many seniors-only meetings. Throughout off-season drills, the seniors had talked among themselves about how they could make their last season different from the first three. They had heard the seniors who had come before them talk about preseason goals and making this team different than the last one, and then they had watched as those goals turned to dust each fall.

Normally, goal-setting was done by the coaching staff. During July, most football-team members returned to West Point for ten days of Physical Individual Aptitude Development (aka PIAD), which was more a way for the coaching staff to check on what kind of shape the players had stayed in during the summer than anything else. At the end of PIAD, before the players went home for their summer break, the coaches would hold a meeting and tell the players the goals for the upcoming season.

The seniors didn't want to wait until PIAD to do that. They felt it was important to begin talking and thinking about the fall right away. And so they sat in Eisenhower Hall late into the evening to talk about what they wanted to do, what they thought was realistic, and what they thought had to be done to achieve those goals.

When they left the room that night they had established four clear goals:

- Win the Commander in Chief's Trophy. That would mean, they knew, breaking the six-game losing streak against Air Force.
- Win every home game. There were six. In 1994 the record at home had been 2–4, including the three straight losses leading up to the Navy game. That could not happen again.
- Play every game hard. A cliché, certainly, but what good did it do to play like crazy to beat Louisville and then turn around and lose to Boston University?
- Go to a bowl game. Realistically, this was the longest of long shots. Since Army's last bowl appearance in 1988, the NCAA had passed a rule requiring that a team win at least six games against Division I-A teams to qualify for a bowl. Since the Cadets played three games against I-AA opponents, they would have to go 6–2 in their I-A games. That meant going no worse than 4–2 against

superpowers Notre Dame and Washington; 1994 bowl
teams Duke, Boston College, and East Carolina; and
Air Force, which had been 8–4 in '94 and gone
uninvited.

That was a daunting task for a team that had finished 4–7 the year
before. "We came here to play the games we aren't supposed to win,"
Cantelupe told his teammates. "A lot of those teams already have us
down as a 'W.' Great. All the better for us. They'll be ripe."

The leaders of this group were Cantelupe — pronounced Cant-a-
loop, but known as Loo-pay to his teammates; and Akili King — A.K.
to everyone on the football team. They were about as different as two
players could possibly be: King a black kid from Mississippi who
had the kind of physical gifts that made him a potential NFL player;
Cantelupe, a white middle-class kid from Ohio who probably would
have gone to Pennsylvania or Bowling Green if he had not landed at
West Point.

But they were good friends and natural leaders who everyone looked
up to and respected. That was why they were the two players Assistant
Coach Mike Sullivan had sought out soon after he returned to West
Point. Sullivan had graduated from the academy in 1989. He had been
a defensive back and special-teams player on the 1988 Sun Bowl team
and had left a good deal of his soul behind when he left West Point. He
knew he wanted to coach when he got out of the military. He spent
two years as a graduate assistant at Humboldt State while finishing his
master's degree before Sutton brought him back to Army.

Sullivan told Cantelupe and King that he thought it was important
that they convince their classmates — and then Sutton — that it was
important to name team captains in the spring. Sutton had used game
captains throughout his tenure, naming the official captains before the
Navy game each year, bestowing the honor on the two players who
had emerged as the team's leaders during the season. Sullivan, whose
Army teams had elected captains each spring, thought those leaders
should be singled out sooner, rather than later.

"It gives the coaches and the players a focal point," he told Cantelupe and King. "It establishes exactly where the leadership is coming
from and who is expected to provide it. It may not seem like a big

deal, but it is. The captains grow with the responsibility and everyone else grows with them.''

Cantelupe and King put the idea to their teammates that night in Eisenhower. They agreed with Sullivan, and Cantelupe and King were named as a committee of two to take the matter up with Sutton.

Sutton is not a man who makes snap decisions about anything. He is cautious and methodical. He told Cantelupe and King he would think about their suggestion. Which he did. ''I decided that if it was important to the players, then it was the right thing to do,'' he said. ''If I've learned anything as a coach, it's how important the leadership you get from your senior class can be.''

Sutton's seniors-to-be believed that he had learned a lot more than that in his four years as head coach. They had watched him grow as a leader, becoming more confident each season. He had become more decisive as an offensive play-caller, more resolute in his decision making, more clearly the man in charge.

They knew how much he cared about them and how hard he had tried to understand what made playing — and coaching — military academy football different. Sutton had gone to class with them, gone out on recon missions, even made the march to Lake Frederick with the plebes. Unlike the Navy seniors a year earlier, who either didn't care what happened to Chaump or wanted him gone, Army's seniors not only wanted to see Sutton get a new contract, they believed part of their mission for the season was to see to it that he was still at West Point in 1996.

Joel Davis, the 305-pound offensive guard who was the team's best pure football player, told the other seniors during the Eisenhower Hall meeting: ''My goal for this season is for Coach Sutton to get a new contract. Because we all know to make sure that happens, we have to play our butts off and have a successful year.''

Davis didn't know just how accurate his comment was. Superintendent Graves had actually been under pressure at the end of the '94 season to buy Sutton out of the final year of his contract and fire him right then. If Army had not won the Navy game for a third year in a row, Graves might have been forced to make that move.

Instead, he took the position that he would decide about Sutton's future at the end of the '95 season — not a minute sooner. That didn't really make anyone happy. The old grads who wanted Sutton gone wanted him gone right away. Sutton and his supporters felt that being forced to go into the last year of a contract without even so much as a vote of confidence — much less an extension — created an air of tension around the team and severely hampered recruiting. What was Sutton supposed to tell recruits that fall when they asked — as they inevitably would — about his status? "I *hope* to be back"?

Sutton wasn't thrilled with the situation, but he understood what was going on. He had been coaching college football players since his days as a college student. He had grown up in Ypsilanti, Michigan, and stayed home to go to Eastern Michigan knowing two things: he wasn't big enough or fast enough to play college football, but he wanted to learn how to coach football.

During his sophomore year, he began making the eight-mile drive over to Ann Arbor whenever he could to watch Michigan practice. He had heard that Bo Schembechler's staff was one of the best teaching staffs in the country, and he wanted to watch Schembechler and his coaches work. Schembechler not only welcomed him but eventually made him an undergraduate assistant coach, letting him work as defensive coordinator for his freshman team during Sutton's last two years at EMU.

"I thought it was great experience, learning from the kind of people Bo had on his staff," Sutton said. "I figured I would graduate and then try to get a job coaching high school somewhere. That's what I was thinking in terms of back then, becoming a high school coach."

The year he graduated turned out to be the year that Tom Maloney, one of Schembechler's assistants, became the head coach at Syracuse. Maloney offered Sutton a job coaching the outside linebackers. Sutton took it.

That was the beginning of a coaching odyssey that was, in many ways, typical of what coaches go through. Sutton moved to Western Michigan as the defensive coordinator, then to Illinois as the defensive coordinator, and then back to Western Michigan as the offensive coordinator. He moved to North Carolina State in 1982 and there, for the first time in his career, was part of a staff that got fired.

Without a job for the first time in his life, he did what all unemployed coaches do: began calling coaches he knew to find out where there might be an opening. One of the people he called was Jim Young, who had been on Schembechler's Michigan staff when Sutton had been there. Young's answer to his question about work was cryptic: "Give me a couple of weeks," he said. "I might have something for you."

Young was as good as his word. Two weeks later, he called Sutton. He was about to be named head coach at Army. Did Sutton want to become his defensive coordinator?

Sutton wanted a job — any job. That it was a coordinator job under someone he liked and respected as much as Young was a bonus. But Army?

"I knew almost nothing about the place," he said. "I knew they hadn't had much success for a long time and I knew all the history. But I didn't really know what the school was about."

He found that out soon enough. He was Young's defensive coordinator for eight years before Young's retirement moved him up. He had known that following Young wouldn't be easy, and he also knew that winning consistently at Army was never going to be easy because of what the players go through away from the football field on a daily basis and because of the limitations that had to be dealt with in recruiting.

But he loved coaching Army players. They were tough and smart and loyal and willing to do anything to win. He was disappointed with what had happened in 1994 but honestly believed things would turn around in 1995. He knew that if they didn't, he would be looking for work in December.

That thought didn't make him happy, but he knew it came with the territory.

Leaving would be tough professionally; heartbreaking personally. But it was a possibility that had to be faced. He had known that when he first got into coaching. Coaching was all he had ever known. Debbie understood that: their honeymoon had been spring practice at Illinois in 1977. They had come to West Point when Andrew was three and Debbie was pregnant with Sarah. To the kids, this was the only home they had ever known. Sutton decided in the spring that if he was going to go down, he was going to do so coaching the team exactly the way he thought it should be coached. While the seniors were doing their ruminating, he was doing some serious thinking of his own.

The first major decision Sutton had to make concerned Akili King. Like everyone else at West Point, Sutton liked King immensely and thought he was a good person, despite his having been in and out of trouble almost from the day he first arrived as a plebe. Now he was in academic trouble and military trouble. He was a constant source of concern for the coaching staff and for his teammates, someone they could never quite figure out.

King could have gone to college almost anywhere. As a senior in Jackson, Mississippi, he was courted by most of the Southeast Conference but chose Army because that was where he had always wanted to go for as long as he could remember. His father, a minister, remembers that as a little boy Akili was always fascinated by the military. He loved G.I. Joe and watched every war movie he could find. Most kids dream about playing in the NFL; Akili King dreamed about being in the army.

He had to attend the prep school for a year because his board scores weren't high enough to get him directly into West Point, but he didn't complain. Once he did get to Army, he was a starter from day one, at halfback as a freshman, then at fullback — the primary ball-carrying position in the wishbone — as a sophomore.

When he was healthy, he was brilliant. At five eleven and 230 pounds, he was quick and powerful, almost impossible for one man to bring down. He rushed for 883 yards in seven games as a sophomore before a hamstring injury ended his season for all intents and purposes (he played very briefly against Navy), and came into his junior year as the focal point of the Army wishbone. But he pulled the hamstring again early in game three (against Temple), came back two weeks later against Louisville, and then tore his left knee up in the fourth quarter of that game, ending his season.

Throughout his time at Army, King was an enigma. Unlike most of his teammates, he could have had a full scholarship almost anyplace in the country. Yet he chose Army. He could have left after his sophomore year when he had already been in trouble within the corps (and been involved in the stabbing incident), but he chose to stay.

"It was almost like there were two A.K.s," said Cantelupe, a close friend. "The guy we saw up at Michie every day was a hard worker, a leader, someone everyone looked up to. Then, away from football, he became a different guy."

While King clearly wanted to be in the army, just as clearly he chafed at a lot of the rules and the constant badgering every cadet has to deal with. At night, when he was allowed to leave the base, he would put on his civilian clothes and slip on an earring, almost as if he were leaving Cadet King behind to go into town.

He didn't necessarily party any more than other cadets, but he did seem to have a knack for finding trouble. One of the major complaints about West Point among the cadets is its location. As beautiful as it is, with its views of the Catskills and the Hudson, it is both isolated and rural. Highland Falls, the village that sits just outside the Thayer Gate, doesn't offer very much socially for anyone, even less for college-age African-Americans. The closest place to find anything resembling a good time is twenty minutes away in Newburgh. It was there, in a black nightclub, that King was involved in the fight that led to his stabbing. The fact that he had driven there in a West Point van that he wasn't authorized to be using only made matters worse.

King hadn't been able to take part in spring drills, in part because he was still rehabbing his knee and because he had undergone minor shoulder surgery. By the time spring practice was over, Sutton knew he had a decision to make. King had a string of demerits a mile long and was constantly being placed on restriction. There was a serious question about his chances for survival at the academy into the fall semester, and even if he did make it, he would no doubt still be teetering on the brink throughout the whole season.

In short, he had gone from being a talented, likable headache to a potential time bomb. Sutton had decided that his theme for the '95 season would be "Team of Commitment." He had always believed that if everyone connected with a football team could make the total commitment to football that seniors make — knowing this is their last chance — that greatness would come from that commitment. Since he now faced a scenario not unlike that of a senior because of the contract situation, Sutton decided to do everything he could to coach as if these eleven games were the last ones of his career.

That meant eliminating all question marks and as many potential problems as possible. King was both. Before classes were over in May, Sutton called him in and told him that he had decided it would be best for everyone involved if he didn't play football in the fall.

King understood. He knew his future at the academy was very much in doubt and Sutton was already dealing with enough doubts. He needed sure things. King was anything but a sure thing. The other players were disappointed but they also understood.

"We hated to see A.K. go because he was a great player and we liked him," Cantelupe said. "But we had spent two years saying, 'Well, if we just had A.K. . . .' Now, there wouldn't be any questions about A.K. We all knew from day one that we didn't have him and we had to deal with it."

Every student at both academies spends time during the summer in some kind of military training program. The seniors had all decided to ask for summer assignments at West Point. That would allow them to work out together throughout the summer instead of just during the ten days of PIAD. Most of them found themselves assigned to Beast. It was difficult to believe that they were now the intimidating upperclassmen when just yesterday they had been frightened plebes. It reminded them all that, as difficult as their years at West Point had seemed, they were passing very fast. Too fast.

Before the underclassmen left for their summer assignments, the team gathered one more time — to elect captains. Sutton had gone along with Sullivan's idea. When the votes were counted, the choices were clear-cut: Jim Cantelupe for the defense; Joel Davis for the offense.

Cantelupe had one last thing to say before the cadets headed in separate directions for the summer. "We're all going to remember this season the rest of our lives, no matter what," he said. "Let's make sure we do everything possible to make sure the memories are happy ones."

Davis was more succinct: "When you come back in August," he said, "come back ready to kick some ass. Otherwise, don't come back."

# 5

# STARTING OVER

WORKING with new coaches was something Navy's football players had become accustomed to during the Chaump era, since Chaump changed assistants the way most people change their socks. So when Charlie Weatherbie swept into Annapolis and brought in an entirely new staff, it was neither a surprise nor a disappointment to the players.

And they still had Satan.

Satan was their nickname for Phil Emery, who had been hired after Chaump's second season as the team's strength and conditioning coach. During his three years at Navy, he had become the most stable force in the lives of the football players. There was little doubting the fact that Emery had spent a lot of his adult life around weight rooms. He was a huge man who looked perfectly capable of jumping into the middle of the line at any given moment to play nose guard and take on any three offensive linemen the opposition might offer up.

He was a master at torturing the players during their off-season conditioning drills, driving them to their absolute limits and beyond. His nickname had been born one winter morning when an ice storm had completely shut down the eastern seaboard. Since Emery lived outside of Annapolis, the players arrived for their 5:30 A.M. running and conditioning session fully convinced they would end up with a morning off. But as they walked through the darkness to Ricketts Hall, they saw a lone car sitting in the parking lot waiting for them — Emery's.

He was sitting in the front seat with the motor running to keep warm, sipping coffee. He had gotten up an hour earlier than usual to make sure he could navigate the icy roads to campus. Only the devil himself could have made it there before dawn — and taken such pleasure in being there on a totally miserable morning.

Away from the weight room, Satan was soft-spoken and friendly, with an easy smile that often fooled innocent plebes into believing he was not there to make their lives miserable. Satan's influence was a constant for four years at Navy. As Matt Scornavacchi got out of his practice uniform for the final time at the end of the 1995 season, someone asked him if it had hit him yet that he would never again go through a practice as a football player at Navy.

"No, it hasn't," Scornavacchi said. "But I've given a lot of thought to never again lifting a weight with Phil watching me."

Of course the players loved Satan. He was their rock — literally and figuratively. That became especially true during the coaching transition and throughout the winter when they were all meeting their new coaches and trying to adjust to the new system that Weatherbie was putting in on both offense and defense.

Kubiak had set numerous Navy passing records during his junior and senior seasons, in large part because Navy threw on almost every play. The Mids had absolutely no running game to speak of, gaining a grand total of 612 yards rushing (55.7 yards a game) for the entire season. Kubiak had thrown 399 passes (two less than in '93) and had completed 211 for 2,388 yards. He had also been intercepted 17 times and sacked 30 times.

Weatherbie's plan was to put in the same kind of option offense that Air Force had been running with success for years. It would feature one running back behind the quarterback, two A-backs, who would slot to either side, and two wide receivers. There would be no tight end. That came as a terrible shock to Brian Grana, who had spent three years working his way into position to be the starting tight end only to learn at the start of spring practice that his position no longer existed.

The new offensive coordinator was Paul Johnson, who had been the architect of the University of Hawaii offense that had put up scads of points during his eight seasons there. Johnson was thirty-eight, a drawling North Carolinian with a sharp-tongued sense of humor. One day in practice, when one of the offensive linemen couldn't get one of the new blocking schemes right, Johnson blew his whistle and said, "Son, if you *ever* find yourself in a game, do me a favor and call time-out."

What made Johnson OK in the eyes of the players was the fact that he could take as good as he could give. When Ken Niumatalolo, who had played and coached under Johnson at Hawaii and then come with him to Navy to coach running backs, referred to him during a meeting one day as "a heavyset hillbilly," the entire room roared. So did Johnson.

Running Johnson's option offense meant the linemen would have to learn brand-new blocking techniques and reads, as would the quarterbacks. Ben Fay, a junior, had been Kubiak's backup the previous season, but he was more of a drop-back passer than an option quarterback. When Fay missed most of spring practice with an ankle injury, the quarterback job was wide open.

The defense was more stable. Seven starters were back along with a group of experienced backups eager to show the new coaches they were ready to step in and play more than they had in the past. Dick Bumpas, the fourth defensive coordinator the seniors had worked with in four years, was also a Southerner. He had grown up in Fort Smith, Arkansas, played his college ball at the University of Arkansas, and started his coaching career there. He had been Weatherbie's coordinator at Utah State and was as quiet and intense away from the practice field as Johnson was laid back and loquacious.

Andrew Thompson and Joe Speed liked Bumpas right away. They loved listening to him talk in defensive meetings, striding up and down in the front of the room, imploring his players constantly to "make their ass want to give up the ball; hit their ass again and again; move their ass *backwards*."

Sometimes, Thompson would find himself leaning forward in his seat during those meetings, nodding his head as Bumpas spoke, wanting to jump up, run out of the room, and hit someone's ass right then and there. Speed didn't get as wound up in meetings as Thompson, but, like his best friend, he wanted nothing more than to see Navy's defense get out on the field and stuff some people.

Thompson and Speed were, without doubt, the leaders of the defense. Both were safeties, both loved to play and loved to hit. They were respected enough by their teammates that they finished first and second in the voting for defensive captain. They had been best friends since their first day at the Navy Prep School in the fall of 1991. Neither of them had been offered a Division-IA scholarship by anyone except Navy. Thompson was the youngest of three brothers; Speed the youngest of six. Both had grown up trying to impress their older brethren. They had come to Navy and, in each other, found a brother they could talk to about anything.

Thompson was a self-described farm boy, having gone to high school in Ferndale, a town of about four thousand in the northwest corner of Washington state. He spent most of his boyhood dreaming about following in the footsteps of his brother Scott, who was a linebacker at the University of Washington from 1979 to 1982, playing on four straight bowl teams, including two that went to the Rose Bowl.

"I didn't like the Huskies, I didn't love the Huskies, I *lived* for the Huskies," Thompson says, smiling at the memory. "I was seven when Scott first went there, and to me, going to the games and meeting all the big stars he played with was the absolute greatest thing in the world. All through high school, I kept a picture on my desk of the two of us when I was seven. He was in his Huskie uniform. I would look at that picture and say, 'Someday, I'll wear that uniform too.' "

There is about Thompson, even today, a kind of wide-eyed innocence that makes it easy to underestimate his toughness. He is the kid who sits in the front row of class every day, never turns in an assignment late, and called everyone sir and ma'am even before he arrived at the Naval Academy, where outsiders occasionally wonder if midshipmen receive bonuses of some kind if they can figure out how to use the word "sir" one hundred times in less than sixty seconds.

But Thompson is also a warrior and has a temper that can shock people who are used to the polite, sweet Thompson. That nature served him well as a football player, although he never did reach linebacker size the way Scott did. During the summer between his junior and senior years of high school, Thompson attended the Huskie football camp. He came home with a fistful of awards. "But they were all for things like hustle and great attitude and working hard," he said, smiling at the memory. "None of them were for being a great player. That was my first clue."

His next clue came when he never heard a word from the Washington coaching staff — or from anyone else in the Pacific-10. He wasn't shocked, but he was disappointed because he believed he could play on that level given a fair chance even if he wasn't the biggest or fastest guy around. He was recruited by a number of smaller schools, although for a while he still considered enrolling at Washington and trying to make the team as a walk-on.

But as much as he loved Huskie football, the size of the school scared him. The idea of being in classrooms with five hundred other students intimidated him. What's more, he knew his chances of succeeding as a walk-on in a program like Washington's were somewhere between slim and none. He took visits to Eastern Washington and Boise State, both of which had excellent Division I-AA programs. But Boise State wanted him to walk on and Eastern Washington offered only a half-scholarship.

Thompson was convinced he could play both places, but wasn't thrilled with their lack of enthusiasm. So he decided he would go to Western Washington, an NAIA school that played good football and had an excellent education program. His grandfather, father, and brother Steve, all of whom had gone into teaching and education, were graduates of Western Washington. The school was fifteen miles from home and his parents could come see him play every week. So it was settled.

Until the phone rang one day and a voice on the other end of the line said that he was Mike Drake and he was an assistant coach at the Naval Academy and he wanted to come to Ferndale and talk to Thompson about coming to Navy.

The call came, as far as Thompson was concerned, out of the blue. He had received application packets in the fall — like hundreds of other football players with good grades — from both Army and Navy. He had been intrigued enough by West Point to drive with his father to a "West Point Night" at a nearby community college. There, he listened to an army captain talk about the opportunities that awaited students who qualified for acceptance at the U.S. Military Academy.

When the meeting was over, Thompson introduced himself to the captain, a short, dark-haired man in a green uniform whose name Thompson can't remember, and told him he was a senior football player and was interested in the academy.

"What kind of grades do you have?" the captain asked.

"My GPA is about 3.8," Thompson said.

"How about your board scores?"

"I got 820 on the SAT," Thompson said, then added quickly, "but I'm taking it again soon."

The captain shook his head. "Forget it," he said. "You're nowhere close to being qualified to go to West Point."

He walked away, leaving Thompson feeling embarrassed and humiliated. "The guy made me feel stupid," he said. "The thing is, I'm not stupid. I always do well on papers, I work hard, and I'm good in class. But I've never tested well. I didn't test well in high school or college. It's just a struggle for me. But I do learn what I have to learn."

The meeting with the little captain left a sour taste in Thompson's mouth. Even though he had sent his applications back to both Army and Navy, he wrote them off after that incident. He assumed they wrote him off too because he didn't hear back from either of them — until the phone call from Drake.

Drake's phone call was more a fluke than anything else. That fall, Navy had been recruiting a wide receiver from nearby Bellingham High School named Ty Elmendorf. When Ferndale played Bellingham, Thompson was assigned to cover Elmendorf, who would finish the season with fifty-one catches. With no extra help, Thompson shut Elmendorf down almost the entire day. When Navy's coaches saw the film of that game, they were intrigued by the tenacious defensive back who draped himself on Elmendorf all day. They were further intrigued when they called Elmendorf's coach to find out his name and then found out that there was an Andrew Jack Thompson from Ferndale High School who had filled out an application for Navy.

The problem remained the board scores. The solution was the Naval Academy Prep School — or NAPS as everyone at Navy calls it. When Drake told Thompson he could get into NAPS because of his high grades, Thompson thought about it briefly, then accepted.

"To this day, I can't tell you why," he says, laughing. "I mean I'd never been east of Boise, Idaho, for crying out loud, and here I am agreeing to fly to Newport, Rhode Island, and enroll in a prep school I know nothing about. I had no military background in my family and I was leaving my family to go three thousand miles from home. But I still said yes. I guess I figured, what the heck, it was just one year and if I didn't like it I'd come right back home."

Even so, Thompson became more and more skeptical as the time to leave drew near. One morning he told his mother that the thought of being so far from his family terrified him. "It won't be as bad as you think," Glenda Thompson told her youngest child. "Your teammates will become your family. You'll find close friends."

Sure enough, on his first day at NAPS, Thompson found Joe Speed. They were standing in line for uniforms and started talking. Before either one of them knew it, they were laughing, each telling the other how frightening this whole deal really was.

"It was just one of those things," Speed said. "Right from the beginning, we both felt like we could tell each other anything. If Drew was struggling, he came to me. When I struggled, I went to him. And we both struggled a whole lot."

Speed had grown up in the Turner Station section of Dundalk, on the east side of Baltimore, just beyond the city limits. His father, John Speed Jr., had worked as a chauffeur as a young man before saving enough money to buy his own barbershop. He had been married once and had a twelve-year-old son named Keith when he met Courtney Lee Jackson. Even though John was fifteen years older than Courtney, they fell in love and got married. Speed's Barbershop became Speed's Barbershop and Beauty Salon and the boys came along shortly after that: John, Hartwell, Aman, Solomon, and Joe.

When Joe was four, his father died of a heart attack, leaving Courtney to run the business and raise the boys. John and Hartwell, ten and eight years older than Joe, became his protectors and father figures. It was John who signed Joe up to play for the Edgemere Falcons football team when he was six. After that, Joe played every sport he could find.

His goal was to be as good as his brothers, who always seemed to be coming home with trophies, plaques, and medals. Eventually, Joe came home with more than all of them. He was all-metro at Dundalk High School, playing both ways throughout his career. Once, he returned two kickoffs for touchdowns in a game and also threw a touchdown pass and ran for a touchdown that same day.

By his junior year, the letters were coming in from everywhere: Penn State, Nebraska, Oklahoma. Speed had good grades, and although his boards weren't great — 930 on the SATs — that wasn't considered too bad for a kid from the east side of Baltimore. It certainly would have been plenty good enough to get him into any of the football factories.

Speed also got an application form from Navy during his junior year. Since Annapolis was only thirty minutes from his house, he was more familiar with the Naval Academy than a lot of high school kids. He knew it was a pretty place, but he also knew it was extremely demanding. And the application was the longest and most complicated he had seen. By far. "I figured if I didn't have the patience to sit down and fill out the application, no way was I going to be able to make myself do all the work once I got there," he said. "I just put it on the back burner and left it there."

By late that summer, things had changed. The big-name schools hadn't followed up. As good a high school player as Speed was, he didn't have blazing speed or great size. At six one, 185, he was considered a "'tweener," not quite fast enough to be a running back or a defensive back, not quite big enough to play quarterback or linebacker. He had done some of everything in high school. That made him invaluable at Dundalk but an afterthought for Penn State, Nebraska, Oklahoma, and their ilk.

Speed was concerned. His mother was already paying tuition for his brother Solomon, who had just started at Hampton University, and he had counted on getting a full scholarship to college. The Navy packet was still sitting in a corner of his room. He called Kevin Rogers, the Navy assistant, who had contacted him the year before. Was it too late to apply? No. Speed took a deep breath and sat down to fill out the application.

He took one official visit away from home that fall, to Colgate, which had a strong I-AA team. Hamilton, New York, was the coldest place he had ever been. Speed said thanks, but no thanks. That left Navy. Speed wasn't sure if he wanted to go into the military. He had an uncle who had been in the army and had fought in Vietnam, but he knew very little about the navy. Then, when Rogers told him that his original assessment — that Speed would be able to get straight into the academy without going to NAPS — had been wrong and that he would have to spend a year there, Speed was certain he didn't want to go.

"It was eleven years they were talking about," he said. "One year at NAPS, four at the academy, and six in the navy. I would be twenty-nine, almost thirty years old before I got out. That seemed like forever to me."

But walking around Turner Station during the winter months, Speed saw a lot of young men standing on corners panhandling or drinking or doing nothing. "A lot of them were about thirty and they hadn't done a thing with their lives," he said. "I figured if I went to Navy, the one thing I would be guaranteed was that when I was thirty, I would already have done something with my life."

He told Rogers he would go to NAPS. He and Thompson were in the same platoon. Both struggled academically, but they survived. By the time they got to Plebe Summer, all the screaming and yelling had become second nature after their NAPS experience. Upperclassmen at both Army and Navy say they can spot a prep school graduate a mile away. They look older, act older, and are far less intimidated by the plebe experience. At Navy, it is known as "a Napster attitude."

The Napster attitude got Speed through Plebe Summer in good enough shape that he found himself competing for playing time with the varsity from day one. By the time the season opener against Virginia rolled around, Speed was starting at left cornerback. The game was at night and Navy–Marine Corps Stadium was full. Speed couldn't believe he was going to start in his first college football game.

"It was like a dream," he said. "The problem was, no one told Virginia that dreams are supposed to have happy endings."

On the first play of the game, Virginia went deep, testing the freshman cornerback right away. Speed saw a blur go by him, saw the ball in the air, lunged in the direction of the ball and the receiver, then watched helplessly as the receiver sprinted into the end zone. Touchdown. One play, six points. Speed wasn't the only one burned that night. Virginia won the game 53–0. Welcome to college ball, kid.

Thompson didn't play as early or as often as his pal that season.

He was having a terrible time adjusting on and off the football field. Early in the season, he broke his left hand in a junior varsity game against NAPS. That didn't stop him from playing or practicing, but it did make it a lot harder to get his schoolwork done, since he is left-handed.

By the end of the semester Thompson had worked his way up from the JVs to become a regular on special teams for the varsity and had earned a letter. That was the good news. The bad news was that he had failed both Calculus 1 and Chemistry 1. At one point in the semester he had a 0.8 grade point average.

Thompson is nothing if he is not tenacious. He retook calculus and chemistry second semester and passed them both. That still left him a semester behind his class, though, so he took Chem 2 and Calc 2 during summer school. For nine weeks his daily schedule was as follows:

5 A.M.–7 A.M. — Wake up. Breakfast. Training run with
   Satan.
7 A.M.–8 A.M. — Prepare for chemistry class.
8 A.M.–12 P.M. — Chemistry class.
12 P.M.–1 P.M. — Lunch. Get ready for calculus class.
1 P.M.–4 P.M. — Calculus.
4 P.M.–6 P.M. — Lift weights with Satan.
6:30 P.M. — Dinner.
7 P.M. until too exhausted to keep eyes open — Study chem
   and calc.

He passed both classes. Then he went to Quantico, Virginia, for three weeks of marine training. He lost fifteen pounds, virtually wiping out all the training work he had done with Satan. There were moments when Thompson wondered what the hell he had gotten himself into by not staying home and going to Western Washington. But he never felt sorry for himself.

"If you think about it," he said, "there's always someone out there who is worse off than you. A lot worse off. Was I tired? Sure. Beat up? Absolutely. But I didn't have to worry where my next meal was coming from. I didn't have to wonder if I was going to be able to feed my family. I wasn't in the middle of a war zone. And, like my mom had said, I had my teammates."

It was those feelings about his teammates that kept Thompson at Navy after his sophomore year. That was the year of the perpetual black cloud: the Grizzard-O'Neill murders, the Bucchianeri kick, and the car tragedy. It was also the year when "Double E" played itself out, with six members of the team, many of them close friends of Thompson, being separated from the academy just months before graduation.

"That was so painful for so many of us to watch," he said. "To me, guys like Javier Zuluaga and Max Lane were role models, people I wanted to be like. They were my mentors. To see them not graduate was very hard for me to take. It was heartbreaking."

Another of the team's leaders, Zuluaga's cocaptain, Jason Van Matre, was also accused in the scandal. But Van Matre turned out to be one of those who survived the investigation and, after several painful months of being under suspicion and wondering about his future, graduated. When Thompson saw Van Matre walk across the stage in May of 1994 to accept his diploma, he broke down. It was almost as if he needed some kind of catharsis after all the months of downers and tragedy. Maybe, he thought, Van Matre's graduation would turn out to be a new beginning.

That feeling, that hope, as much as anything, kept Thompson at Navy. He could have left at the end of that sophomore year, but he couldn't bring himself to do it. He couldn't leave Speed or Keith Galloway or Garrett Smith or Bryce Minamyer or any of his classmates. They had been through too much together not to stick around to go through the turnaround together. It would come, Thompson was sure of that.

"I felt I had made a commitment to a lot of people," he said. "If I had walked away from that commitment, it would have been pretty selfish. Those guys are my brothers. You don't leave your brothers in the lurch just because things get a little bit rocky."

BY the end of the '94 season Thompson was sick — literally. He caught the flu practicing in the cold the week of the Army game and spent the entire game throwing up every time he came to the sideline. When he got back to campus the next day he crawled into bed and stayed there for most of four days, leaving his room for Chaump's final meeting with the team and a couple of classes he felt he couldn't afford to miss no matter how awful he felt.

When he went home for semester break, he decided to start keeping a journal to chronicle his final year as a football player. His first entry, written on New Year's Day, mentions Navy's new football coach: "Joe [Speed] called yesterday and said our new coach, Charlie Weatherbie, is cool. I trust his judgment very much. The bowls have me thinking about our football team right now. The strong will survive in '95!"

Thompson's journal is blunt and to the point. He writes when he's angry: "Sometimes, I truly have feelings of anger and hatred towards this place," he says one night about the academy.

He is funny: "This must be noted right away: I slept 16 straight hours after taking my exams. A new record. Way to go Andrew!"

He is contemplative: "I wonder sometimes if I can grow to be the tender warrior that I believe God wants me to be. Will I be a good husband? A good father? A good person? If I can do all those things in life, I will be happy. . . ."

Always, though, his thoughts come back to football: what he can do to be a leader; how he feels about the progress being made by the new coaches; his analysis of the team and of their opponents. Most of his entries end with exhortations directed at himself: "Cut down on the cursing!" or "Work hard, 2.5 GPA this semester." Or at the football team: "The brotherhood lives"; "Don't f--- with the Navy defense"; "Think bowl game!"; or, very simply, "CIC."

Weatherbie had established three goals for the team before the start of spring practice, and he had written them down in black block letters on a white board:

"Win the Commander in Chief's Trophy."
"Winning season."
"Go to a bowl game — and win."

Initially, the last goal had been just to go to a bowl game, but Thompson had asked him to add the part about winning and he had agreed.

Those goals were extremely lofty for a team coming off a 3–8 record. Navy hadn't won a CIC Trophy since 1981. It hadn't had a winning season since 1982. It hadn't been to a bowl game since 1981 and hadn't won one since 1978. And like Army, Navy's chances of getting into a bowl were hamstrung by the schedule, since both Delaware and Villanova were Division I-AA teams, meaning that victories over them wouldn't count toward the NCAA-required six to get into a bowl. One of Weatherbie's first requests to Lengyel was a change in scheduling philosophy.

"Playing I-AA teams makes no sense," he said. "If you win, it doesn't count. If you lose, everyone counts it against you. There are plenty of I-A teams out there we can play, compete with, and beat, and have the win count in our favor."

Football teams usually schedule between five and ten years in advance. Lengyel promised Weatherbie he would work on changing the schedule as quickly as possible. In the meantime, Weatherbie was putting his team through spring practice. It was, for everyone, a learning experience. Weatherbie had put together a young staff — offensive line coach Gene McKeehan would be fifty in September, Dick Bumpas was forty-five, and everyone else was between thirty and thirty-eight — and the players liked that. He had told his coaches that if they were going to coach academy kids, they had to understand academy kids. The coaches went to class with the players; went to formation with them; ate with them in King Hall. Weatherbie insisted they all learn the words to "Blue and Gold," the school's hauntingly beautiful alma mater, so they could sing it on the field after games.

The players liked what they were seeing, but they were having trouble adjusting to the intensity the young staff brought to the practice field. At all three academies, coaches must adjust to a basic difference that is evident every day: at a civilian school, football practice is the most difficult part of most days for almost all the players, physically and, a large part of the time, mentally. At the academies the opposite is true: football practice is usually the *easiest* part of the day. It is an escape from the rigors of campus, the demands of officers and teachers.

Navy's players had grown accustomed to taking a deep breath when they walked into Ricketts Hall. They could take their ties off and not worry about snapping off a salute every five steps. The problem, at least in the minds of the coaching staff, was that they were bringing that sense of relaxation to the practice field. Even deep into the season, Weatherbie had to constantly remind them that, no matter how tired they were when they arrived, he expected their complete attention and 100 percent effort the entire time they were in a football uniform.

"Everyone else we play is coming to practice focused only on football," he said. "You guys have to be the same way if we're going to compete."

The players had no argument with what he was saying. Some days were just tougher than others. One day early in the season Weatherbie looked around the meeting room and saw a lot of heads drooping. "I don't want anyone going to sleep in here," he said angrily. "If you're tired, stand up" — that's what mids are told to do in class — "but don't fall asleep."

By the time spring practice was over, the players knew they were in the hands of a coaching staff that was completely different (except, of course, for Satan) than anything they had experienced before. But that was OK with them. All they wanted was to win. They would practice standing on their heads every afternoon if that would guarantee achieving their goals for the season.

On the day before the spring game — the intrasquad scrimmage that climaxed spring practice — they elected their captains: Andrew Thompson on defense; Garrett Smith on offense. Neither considered himself a natural leader. Both tended to be shy about speaking in public. But both saw their election as an act of faith on the part of their teammates and took that act of faith very seriously.

The spring game itself was chaotic, with Weatherbie switching players from one team to the other so often that the sports information staff, sitting in the press box, had no idea who was winning the game, the Blue or the Gold.

When it was over, there was still all sorts of confusion. The best quarterback for the new system appeared to be Chris McCoy, a quiet sophomore-to-be from a tiny town in Georgia called Randolph. McCoy had been used as a defensive back by the old coaching staff but had been scout team quarterback when Navy faced option teams. He had asked the new staff for a tryout at quarterback during the spring and had surprised everyone with his quickness and savvy. But he had never taken a college snap.

Ben Fay had missed most of spring practice, but had played well in his brief appearance in the spring game. Howard Bryant also had experience with the option, but the coaches were thinking of making him into an A-back.

The quarterback battle was confusing. But it was nothing compared to the placekicking situation. There, chaos reigned. And the spring game had only made it worse. Only one kicker had kicked the ball well all afternoon.

His name was Ryan Bucchianeri.

# 6

# THE INVISIBLE MAN

TO be fair, Ryan Joseph Bucchianeri never asked to become a national hero for missing a field goal.

To be equally fair, all Charlie Weatherbie knew about Bucchianeri when he became Navy's coach was that he had missed *two* crucial kicks. What's more, he found out quickly that those kicks were only a part of Bucchianeri's problems within the team and within the brigade.

Kickers are generally viewed with suspicion on football teams. They just aren't the same as the other players. They spend most of practice on the far side of the field, far away from the grunting and hitting and grinding that goes on for most of the afternoon. They don't need to spend as much time in the weight room during the off-season, and if they are asked to make one tackle during a season, that is a lot. Their uniforms *never* get dirty.

And the fact is, kickers *are* different. They tend to be extremely superstitious, almost obsessed with routine, and are easily thrown off their rhythm, almost like high-strung colts on race day.

That is not to say kickers can't be accepted or even liked by their teammates. Punter Brian Schrum was one of the most popular players on the team, in part because he was very good at what he did, but also because he was a good athlete and a smart, resourceful person. Schrum never complained about a high snap or a low snap or not having enough time to get off a kick. He just went about his business and was willing to do anything he could to help the team win. He had volunteered to step in as the holder on field goals, and he won the job because he had excellent hands and was athletic enough to take off with the ball if necessary and throw it or run.

Bucchianeri was different. Even as a college junior, he still looked like a ballboy who had stolen his older brother's uniform. At five eight and 155 pounds soaking wet he was the smallest player on the team. He had curly brown hair, wide brown eyes, and a round face that seemed to resonate with innocence. Around the locker room, he rarely smiled. In fact, in an environment that is usually a haven for acting childish, his serious demeanor seemed out of place.

He had never really fit in with the team, not before the infamous '93 miss and certainly not afterward. He came to Navy as one of those rare players who had lots of options but chose Navy anyway. The all-American kicker at Ringgold High School in Monongahela, Pennsylvania, had been recruited by everyone from Penn State to Notre Dame, but he had always loved the idea of military academies, the discipline, the order, the uniforms. As William Nack explained in the *Sports Illustrated* story: "Navy didn't recruit him, he recruited Navy."

After struggling early in the fall, he had become the kicker eight games into his freshman season, making the two field goals in his first start at Notre Dame. That performance was the reason he was the kicker on that fateful day against Army.

No one at Navy was prepared for what came next: the press conference at which Bucchianeri made no excuses and won the respect of the entire country. Or the hundreds of admiring letters that poured in. And then the *Sports Illustrated* story, which cemented Bucchianeri's place in the national consciousness as an example of class and guts and having the right stuff.

It also cemented Bucchianeri's place as a veritable pariah among his teammates. "I knew, when I agreed to cooperate on the story, that there was a good chance that might happen," he said a year later. "But I thought it was important that people hear what I had to say. Not because I'm important but because a lot of people go through adversity in life."

Not everyone agreed. "What he said was, 'It's OK that I missed the kick because I tried and that's all anyone can ask of me, and therefore I don't feel bad about it,'" Jim Kubiak said, his voice still rising twelve months after the story first appeared. "How can he say that? No one would get on him for missing the kick. We all make mistakes. Fine. But don't say, '*It's OK.*' It wasn't OK. A lot of hearts were broken because he missed that kick. It *should* hurt him as much as it hurt everyone else. But it didn't. That's what upset everyone so much."

Kubiak was so angry after reading the story that he fired off an E-mail message to Bucchianeri telling him what he thought. Bucchianeri was disturbed by the E-mail because he respected Kubiak and thought the quarterback had misunderstood what he was trying to say. He told Kubiak they should sit down and talk. But he never followed up.

"I just got to the point where I felt like explaining myself was pointless," he said. "No one really wanted to listen."

He was probably right in that assessment. Bucchianeri had been viewed as odd, even for a kicker, by his teammates almost from day one. Traditionally, the football team makes a point not to haze plebe football players. The less hazing they have to deal with, the more likely they are to become contributors during the season. The football tables at meals are a haven for plebes, an escape from the trivia questions and screaming that the other plebes are experiencing.

The same is true during football practice. People are judged on performance and effort by their peers, not by class rank. But Bucchianeri always seemed to keep to himself. Often, that can indicate shyness, especially when the person is a kicker. But Bucchianeri had strong opinions on subjects like weekend drinking or the bending of academy rules. He admitted that it bothered him when other mids routinely found ways around the rules. To most of his teammates, he came across more as a nerd than a football player. Rumors began to spread among the players that he was an honor Nazi on the hall and that everyone in his company was wary of him.

Bucchianeri insists none of that is true, although he has heard the accusations. "Does it bother me when I see some of the things that go on here? Yes. I'd be lying if I told you different," he says. "But have I ever once turned someone in? No. Not once. If I thought someone was really cheating, I would turn them in, but I've never seen anyone do that. But I know there are people who think that I have."

No one was going to dump on Bucchianeri for missing the kick against Army, especially in light of the tragic circumstances of that week. But by spring '94, even before the *Sports Illustrated* story, there was a sense among the players that Bucchianeri had reveled in the attention. Again, Bucchianeri insists that just wasn't the case.

"I never once asked anyone to interview me or do a story on me," he said. "Do they think I wanted to call attention to the fact that I had *missed* a kick? I tried to handle everything as low-key as possible. I got so many letters that I was swamped trying to write back to everyone." In fact, he was called in by his company officer one night because an admiral had written to him wanting to know why a lowly plebe didn't have the common courtesy to write him back when he had taken the time to share his feelings about the missed kick. "I told my company officer that I was sure the letter was in the pile, and I was getting through the pile as fast as I could but it was a big pile.

"He suggested I find the admiral's letter and move it to the top of the pile. I did."

Bucchianeri was so swamped by mail and attention that he did very poorly academically during his second semester at Navy and had to go before an academic board to explain why. He survived that trauma, only to become an even bigger star after the *Sports Illustrated* story.

His sophomore season was — for ten games — relatively quiet. Because Navy was always behind early in games, there were very few opportunities to try field goals. In fact, Bucchianeri only tried three field goals in the first seven games, making one. Then, in the victories over Tulane and Rice, he made three more (in four tries) including a 42-yarder against Rice. That meant he was four-for-seven for the season going into the Army game, and all three of his misses had been from outside 40 yards.

On the morning before the Army game, Bucchianeri woke up early, in part because he was keyed up, in part because there was a commotion in the hallway outside his room. Commotion in the halls of Bancroft during Army week is more the norm than the unusual, since Army week is traditionally a time for plebes to try and get even with the third classmen who have been making their lives miserable all semester.

When Bucchianeri opened his door there was a giant poster plastered on it. Poking his head around the poster so he could see what was on it, Bucchianeri saw, "Go Navy, Beat Army" in block lettering.

Below it was his number — 15 — and his company — 32. He smiled. This was another traditional part of Army week, the plebes making posters for football players in their companies to spur them on. But just as Bucchianeri was about to go back into his room, he noticed more writing on the bottom of the poster. This wasn't as neatly done. In fact, it looked more like graffiti. In several different colors in several different places were the same two words: "wide right."

"It threw me," he admitted. "I had heard it occasionally in the halls, even seen it written on chalkboards, but I didn't expect people in my own company to put it on my door the morning before we played Army."

Shaken, Bucchianeri joined his teammates for the bus ride to Philadelphia. The next day, during pregame warm-ups, he heard the Corps of Cadets chanting, over and over again, "Wide right, wide right." That, he said, didn't bother him. "You expect that from the other team," he said. "If anything, it psyches me up."

On the opening drive of the game, after Navy took the ball to the Army 20 and no farther, the ball was in the center of the field. There was no problem with the angle. The game wasn't on the line. The turf was dry. The attempt was 37 yards. Bucchianeri had made one from five yards farther away against Rice.

As Bucchianeri trotted on for the kick, Brent Musburger, doing the game for ABC-TV, commented that "making this kick would mean a lot, not only to Bucchianeri but to the whole Navy team. It would exorcise a lot of those ghosts lingering from last year."

Musburger didn't have time to talk about what a miss would do. Just as it had been 364 days earlier, the snap was good, the hold was good, and the kick had plenty of distance. And once again, it sailed wide right, this time by about four feet. The chants of "Wide right" engulfed the stadium again. Bucchianeri did make both his extra-point attempts later in the game, but there was no getting around another wide right; especially when the final margin was two points and the game-winner was a 52-yard field goal — by the other team's kicker.

"I saw my dream lived out," he said sadly. "A 50-yarder to win the Army-Navy game. Only I watched it instead of kicking it."

As Joe Gross, the sports editor of the *Annapolis Evening Capital,* pointed out later the next week, Bucchianeri's miss came with more than fifty minutes left to play in the football game. Navy had plenty of chances to win and made several key errors. Kubiak threw three interceptions. Three Army fumbles went uncovered. With a chance to win the game in the final minutes, the offense went nowhere. And yet, Gross noted, the general sentiment in and around Annapolis seemed to be that Bucchianeri had lost another one.

Or, as the saying now went in the brigade, he had "booched it." That month, in the on-campus humor newspaper that the mids occasionally produced, the editors put together a Letterman's Top Ten list of the reasons why their previously scheduled edition of the paper had never come out.

Reason number one: "We just booched it."

"They made me into a verb," Bucchianeri said.

If that was the worst thing they had made him into, he wouldn't have minded. This time, there was very little sympathy. It seemed to Bucchianeri that the words "wide right" followed him everywhere. He heard it in the halls, saw it written on the walls.

It was OK, though, he thought, because he knew he would come back and be a better kicker the next year. He still had two more years to make the big kick in an Army game, to dim the haunting memories of his first two years. Then, one winter afternoon, he was scrolling through E-mail messages in his computer when he came across one addressed to the entire brigade. It was from the new football coaching staff.

"Anyone interested in placekicking for the Navy football team is invited to an open tryout to be held at the football practice fields on April 6th."

Bucchianeri's heart sank. "The message was pretty clear," he said. "There weren't any E-mail messages announcing open tryouts for quarterback or wide receiver or linebacker. Just kicker. I was the kicker. They were announcing an open tryout for my job. It wasn't what I would call welcome news."

ABOUT twenty-five kickers showed up for the tryout. Todd Wright, the new kicking coach, had told Bucchianeri he didn't have to participate if he didn't want to, but Bucchianeri said he would kick like everyone else. He didn't kick all that well or that poorly — "I'd give myself a B minus for the day,'' he says — but he insists he was better than everyone else out there.

The coaches didn't seem quite as convinced. They asked nine of the kickers to participate in spring drills, not exactly a ringing endorsement for the incumbent. Then the incumbent spent a good deal of the spring watching other kickers try out for his job.

The fair-haired boy, or so it seemed, was Ryan Cox, a soccer player who had kicked field goals in high school. He had a strong leg and was getting a lot of attention from the coaches. So was Jason Covarrubias, a sophomore, who had been Bucchianeri's backup during the '94 season. According to Bucchianeri, they were given far more opportunities to kick during spring drills than he was. According to the coaches, they simply outkicked him.

The upshot was Bucchianeri being told by the coaches midway through spring practice that they had not submitted his name as one of the eighty-five players who would be asked to return to the academy in August prior to the start of classes. Under NCAA rules only eighty-five players can be on campus early, and Bucchianeri, who was now listed as the number four kicker on the depth chart — behind Cox, Covarrubias, and senior Zach Williams, who had been used for kickoffs in '94 — was not included in the eighty-five.

Bucchianeri was devastated. He was convinced he had been the best kicker in spring drills and that the coaches had not given him a fair chance. He was not going to give up, though, even if they seemed to be hinting strongly that he should. A couple of days after learning he was not a member of the anointed eighty-five, he received a copy of his fall class schedule. He had been assigned a sixth period class each day, meaning he would be late for the start of football practice. Since most special teams work is done at the start of practice, he would be missing the most vital time of the day.

Bucchianeri immediately went to try and change his schedule but was told it couldn't be done. When a varsity athlete is assigned a sixth period class, the normal procedure is to allow him to change his schedule to free that period so he can report to practice on time. But according to the academy's official records, Bucchianeri was no longer a varsity athlete and therefore not entitled to that sort of scheduling priority.

"It was as if I had disappeared from the football team completely,'' he said. "It seemed as if everyone at Navy had decided that if you try once and fail that's OK, but if you try twice and fail, then you're done trying. I wasn't done trying, though. But they wanted me gone. I had become invisible."

Panicked, Bucchianeri went looking for help. One of the deans he had become friendly with intervened on his behalf and his schedule was changed. Then he had to change his summer cruise schedule, which called for him to be in summer school early and at sea late. He wanted to reverse the schedule so he would be on campus when the football team returned.

"Even if I couldn't practice with them, I wanted to be there, working out on my own," he said. "I wasn't going to go away. No matter what, I wasn't going to quit."

And then came the spring game. One after another, Weatherbie and kicking coaches Scott Runyan and Wright trotted out field-goal kickers. No one could make much of anything. Finally, on the second kicking series of the day, Bucchianeri got his chance.

His first kick split the uprights. His second one was perfect. Same thing for the third. And the fourth. There was no doubt who had been the best kicker on the day.

"Bucchianeri kicked the best today," Weatherbie told the media afterward. "It'll be a wide-open battle for the job when we come back this summer."

Only Bucchianeri hadn't been invited to fight the battle. He left Annapolis that evening to attend his grandmother's funeral in Monongahela. When he came back two days later, he went to the locker room to pick up some equipment for off-season practice. Only there was no equipment in his locker. Nothing was in his locker. It had been completely gutted.

"The only other lockers gutted like that were the ones belonging to guys who had undergone major surgery and had no chance to play next season," he said. "It was definitely not a good sign."

He tried to find out what had happened. No one had any answers. Perhaps it had been a prank. Kevin Bull, the equipment manager, wondered if some of the student managers had done it, knowing that Bucchianeri would not win any popularity contests with that group.

Bucchianeri was still investigating locker-gate when he got a call from sports information director Tom Bates. The *Washington Post*'s Bill Gildea wanted to come up and talk to him, find out what was going on with his football career and his life.

Bucchianeri groaned. The last thing in the world he needed right then was publicity. He wouldn't feel right telling Gildea that everything was fine, because it wasn't. But he didn't want to start trouble by telling him that he felt he wasn't being given a fair chance by the new coaches. Publicity of any kind could only work against him right now.

"Please tell him that I appreciate his interest but I really don't want to do an interview right now," Bucchianeri told Bates.

Bates called back the next day. The *Post* didn't like taking no for an answer. Gildea had asked Bates to ask Bucchianeri to reconsider. Bucchianeri decided the best thing he could do was sit down and talk to Gildea, explain the delicate nature of the situation, and see if he could talk him out of writing a story. Bates set up the meeting.

The day before he was supposed to see Gildea, Bucchianeri came back from his morning classes to find a message on his door: "See Coach Weatherbie ASAP." He went into his room and checked his E-mail. Another message: "See Coach Weatherbie ASAP." As he was walking out his door to look for Weatherbie, someone was coming down the hall with another message: "See Coach Weatherbie ASAP."

Bucchianeri walked over to the temporary football offices in Mitscher Hall and found Weatherbie. They agreed to meet in his office that evening when both had free time. It would be Bucchianeri's first chance to sit and talk to Weatherbie face-to-face.

The meeting lasted almost two hours. Bucchianeri told Weatherbie he believed he had not been given a fair shot in spring ball, that he couldn't understand why he hadn't been invited in for early summer camp and why that decision had been made before the spring game — in which he had clearly been the best kicker.

Weatherbie fired right back. He had to find out about the other kickers, he said, because he knew more about Bucchianeri than the others. Right now there wasn't *any* kicker he trusted to make a big kick, and that was a major concern. Then he turned to more personal issues: why didn't he spend more time with his teammates? Why did it always seem that Ryan Bucchianeri needed special treatment?

"Special treatment? What kind of special treatment?" Bucchianeri demanded.

"Like meeting with the head coach at eight o'clock at night," Weatherbie said.

"Coach, *you* asked for the meeting," Bucchianeri said.

Weatherbie changed his tone. He told Bucchianeri the coaches had wanted to test his resolve during spring ball by making it tough on him. He promised he would get his chance in the summer even if he wasn't coming back early. Both men, player and coach, calmed down. As Bucchianeri got up to leave, Weatherbie said to him, "Now you come back this summer prepared to be the number one kicker."

Weatherbie meant the comment as encouragement. Bucchianeri took it as, if not a promise, a commitment.

They had agreed that Bucchianeri would still ask Gildea not to write the story, but if Gildea was insistent, Weatherbie said he had no problem with Bucchianeri telling him exactly how he felt. "I won't be the one hurt by it, Ryan," he said softly.

The next day, Bucchianeri convinced Gildea not to write the story. He told him there was really nothing to write, that he still planned on being the kicker next fall, and once he had done something worth writing about, he would happily talk to him. Gildea agreed.

Bucchianeri went off on summer leave and for his summer cruise, taking his footballs and his mechanical holder with him wherever he went. In Pensacola for flight training, he spent a lot of his free time driving around looking for a high school field where he could kick. He returned to the academy for summer school, his plan still being to kick on his own on an empty practice field while the anointed eighty-five went through their drills.

Even though he wasn't one of the eighty-five, Bucchianeri was told to show up for picture day. Bates had convinced the coaches that if he wasn't there, reporters would latch on to his absence as their opening day story. He had also insisted that Bucchianeri be included in the media guide even though fourth-string kickers usually didn't get a mention.

Bucchianeri went through all the motions at picture day. When it was over, Weatherbie came over to talk to him. Zach Williams was hurt and hadn't been able to come back early. Since Bucchianeri was already on campus, the coaches had decided to ask him to replace Williams.

"You're invited to camp beginning tomorrow," Weatherbie said.

"Thank you, Coach, thank you," Bucchianeri said, pumping Weatherbie's hand. He was thrilled. Weatherbie had promised him a chance. Now, finally, he was getting it.


BUCCHIANERI did get his chance — in one scrimmage. He and Cox took turns kicking field goals, since Covarrubias had a groin pull. Neither of them kicked that well, although Bucchianeri remembers making five of eight to Cox's three of eight. By now, the coaches were beginning to wonder if Cox was the answer. Brian Graham, a senior who not only wasn't in the media guide but had been assigned a number in the hundreds, was now being given a long look.

At the team's final scrimmage before the opening game with SMU, Bucchianeri didn't kick at all. Neither did Cox, who ended up quitting the team the following week. Covarrubias was now the chosen one, with Graham as his backup. Bucchianeri had started the summer at the bottom of the depth chart and hadn't moved an inch. When the travel list for the trip to Dallas came out the next week, two kickers were included: Covarrubias and Graham. Cox was gone; Zach Williams would be gone by the next week. On the depth chart that Monday, Bucchianeri was listed as Navy's sixth-string kicker.

That Friday, the travel squad gathered inside the lobby of Bancroft Hall for their pretrip inspection. Whenever a varsity team leaves Army or Navy for a trip, the athletes making the trip must appear in whatever uniform has been designated for travel and undergo inspection. It is routine stuff. Sometimes officers conduct the inspection; sometimes the team captains do it. If someone's shoes aren't shined or he's wearing the wrong uniform, he may be sent back to his room to make the appropriate changes. Very rarely is anyone written up for being less than perfect at inspection.

While the team formed up inside, the rest of the brigade was gathering outside on T-Court (named after the bronze statue of the Indian war hero Tecumseh that sits at the edge of the court area) for the team send-off. Attendance was, of course, mandatory. In addition to the send-off, a picture was to be taken of the entire brigade as part of the commemoration of the academy's 150th anniversary.

Bucchianeri stood outside on T-Court with the rest of the brigade, a book in his hands and an ache in his stomach. Now, for the first time, everyone in the brigade would see that he wasn't with the team. He knew that a lot of them would think he had quit. He hated that idea.

When the team came out the doors of Bancroft, the band struck up "Anchors Aweigh" and everyone was gathered on the steps for the birthday picture. Bucchianeri was standing just under the "HAPPY BIRTHDAY NAVAL ACADEMY" banner when he heard someone calling his name. He turned and saw a plebe named Eduardo Salazar, who was holding the "H" in "BIRTHDAY."

With his free hand, Salazar reached for Bucchianeri's hand. "Mr. Bucchianeri, I just wanted you to know how much your story inspired me," he said. "You're one of the reasons I'm here."

Bucchianeri was thrilled. And sickened. He wanted Salazar and others who remembered Wide Right I and Wide Right II to see The Make I, II, and beyond. But if they didn't give him a chance to kick, there would only be the misses to remember.

When the speeches were finished, the brigade formed a cordon along the length of T-Court for the team to walk through to the buses. Bucchianeri joined the cordon and shook hands with his teammates as they walked past him. "I wanted to jump into the middle of the cordon and get on the buses with them," he said. "But I couldn't. I had to stand there and watch them go."

When the buses pulled away, Bucchianeri remembered the book in his hands. It was *Song of the Nightingale,* a book about five Naval Academy graduates who had risen to become major influences in American life. Robert Timberg, the author, was doing a book-signing at The Mids Store that afternoon and Bucchianeri wanted to get his copy autographed.

Waiting in line, Bucchianeri was convinced that people were staring at him, wondering if he had quit the team. He wanted to jump on a chair and scream, "I didn't quit. They wouldn't let me go!" Finally, it was his turn to have his book signed.

"What's your name?" Timberg asked.

"Ryan Bucchianeri, sir."

Timberg started to write, then stopped and looked up. "You're the kicker," he said.

Bucchianeri's heart sank. When someone said, "You're the kicker," they meant "You're the kicker who missed against Army."

"Yes sir," he said.

"You showed a lot of courage," Timberg said. "You know John McCain [the former POW who had become a United States senator] told me that the adversity he went through as a POW made him a much stronger person. The same will happen for you."

"Thank you sir," Bucchianeri answered.

Timberg wished him luck for the coming season. Bucchianeri didn't have the heart to tell him the coming season would start the next night — without him.


AS soon as he heard the pregame show blasting through the hallways of Bancroft the next evening, Bucchianeri knew he had to get away. Since he had watch the next morning, he didn't have weekend liberty, so he couldn't leave the Yard. He grabbed a couple of footballs and his mechanical holder and started across campus to the football practice fields.

It was almost sunset on a gorgeous late-summer afternoon, and Annapolis Harbor, filled with boats, was a stunning backdrop to the practice fields. He spent an hour kicking all by himself on the field, the sun setting spectacularly behind him. He was tired and sweating by the time the sun was down, and he knew the game would be starting any minute.

He decided to walk over to Mitscher Hall and play the piano in the auditorium there for a while. As he walked into Mitscher, he heard the game beginning on a radio being blasted from a window. "And Jason Covarrubias will kick off for Navy. . . ."

He played for a while, then some people came in who needed to use the piano. Bucchianeri left and walked out to the far corner of campus, to the Triton Light, which sits near the corner of the seawall where the Chesapeake Bay turns to meet the Severn River. He found a bench by the light and sat and stared at the water. He closed his eyes and tried to picture the Cotton Bowl, his teammates in white, SMU in blue.

"How could this be happening?" he thought. "How can I be on the outside looking in when I waited so long to be part of a winning team here."

He sat, alone with his thoughts, until he was convinced the game was over, then started back to Bancroft. But as he walked along the road near the seawall, he heard a car radio. The game wasn't over. So he stopped at the practice field once again to kill a few more minutes. The cheers he heard coming from the direction of Bancroft told him that the game was going well for Navy.

He finally got back to his room shortly after 11 o'clock. He heard the final score walking up the steps: Navy 33, SMU 2. He didn't know how to feel. He was pleased for his teammates but felt like the kid locked out of the candy store with his face pressed against the window.

Since he had watch at 6 A.M. he tried to go to sleep. But it was no use. His stomach hurt and he felt sick. What's more, wild celebrations had broken out in the hallways. Then, just when things started to calm down at about 2:30 A.M. a fire alarm went off. Then an announcement, "There will be a spontaneous pep rally to welcome back the football team on T-Court in two hours."

Bucchianeri groaned and tried to go back to sleep. No way. The fire alarms and the announcements continued: "Pep rally in one hour" . . . "Pep rally in thirty minutes" . . . "Pep rally in twenty minutes" . . . "Pep rally in fifteen minutes" . . . "In ten minutes" . . . "In nine minutes."

The buses rolled onto T-Court just after 4:30. The welcome was jubilant and genuine. Navy football, at least for one week, was back. Bucchianeri lay back in his bed and comforted himself with one thought: "This is as low as I can go. It can only get better from here on."

He had no way of knowing that he wasn't even close to the truth.

# 7

# GETTING EVEN

THE first piece of news that Army's football players received when they returned to West Point for preseason practice was hardly a shock: Akili King had been separated from the academy.

No one thing had caused King's dismissal. He had just accumulated so many demerits and so many hours of restriction that his expulsion became inevitable. Not surprisingly, King took the news with class and dignity. He made no excuses and blamed no one but himself. In fact, when Kevin Gleason of the *Middletown Times Herald-Record* tracked him down, King told him, "I was guilty of hubris, that's why I'm not at West Point anymore."

Gleason was shocked. Never in his life had he heard an athlete use the word "hubris" before.

King enrolled at Oregon State — a school that ran the wishbone — shortly after he was officially separated. That meant he would sit out a year, then be eligible to play in 1996. He also signed up for ROTC at Oregon State. King would never graduate from West Point, but he still wanted to be in the army.

His absence left Army's fullback situation in flux — to put it mildly. The top three people on the depth chart — senior Joe Triano, senior Randy Hawkins, and junior Demetrius Perry — had never carried the ball in a varsity game. The most experienced fullback on the roster, at least in terms of varsity carries, was John Conroy. He had carried the ball once — as a sophomore — and picked up one yard.

"I got tripped by the guy blocking for me," he said. "It was at the end of the game and all the scout teamers were in. None of us knew the plays because we spent all week practicing the other team's plays."

It surprised none of Conroy's teammates to learn that he needed an entire paragraph to describe a one-yard run in the waning minutes of a 35–12 game. That is Conroy. Ask him the time, he will not only tell you how to make a watch but give you the history of watches. He is outgoing and funny, someone who has a long, detailed story to tell about almost every event in his life.

Even though he began preseason practice listed at number four on the depth chart, Conroy was convinced that his time had finally come. He was keenly aware of how close he was to the end of something that had been a huge part of his life for as long as he could remember. "When I was four, my grandfather made a video of me," he said. "In it, he asks me what I want to be when I grow up and I answer, 'I want to play quarterback for Notre Dame!' "

That answer was hardly a surprise given Conroy's upbringing. He grew up in Wrightwood, one of the Irish neighborhoods on Chicago's South Side. His father, who had been in the Air Force, was a Chicago cop for thirty-eight years, and his mother's family was heavily involved in the concessionaires union at all the ballparks and sports arenas around Chicago.

It seemed to Conroy that everyone he knew had two things in common: their father was a cop, a fireman, or worked for a union, and they all rooted for Notre Dame. "Irish-Catholic, what would you expect?" he said.

The neighborhood was divided up by parishes, the kids from each parish hanging out together and forming teams that competed with kids from other parishes. Conroy lived near St. Thomas More Parish, and he and his friends were known as "The Tommy More guys." It was, according to Conroy, a competitive neighborhood. "Sometimes the *parents* got into fights," he said. "I remember a girls' basketball game where someone's father threw a chair across the floor."

Dark haired and broad shouldered, Conroy was always one of the star athletes in the neighborhood. He played everything but loved football the most. He first remembers honing his moves as a running back playing keep-away in the schoolyard as a second-grader.

By the time he was an eighth-grader, all the local Catholic high schools were recruiting him, since recruiting is legal in the Chicago Catholic League. Conroy had high school coaches sitting in his living room explaining to him how their school was the one that would make him a star, get him a college scholarship, perhaps even get him to Notre Dame.

He chose St. Lawrence over St. Rita's, even though St. Rita's traditionally had better teams, because he and his friends decided they would all become stars faster at St. Lawrence. He did star at St. Lawrence and began hearing from colleges as a junior. A number of big-name schools expressed some interest, and a slew of Division I-AA and Division II schools were after him.

By then, Conroy had decided he didn't want to go to Notre Dame. He had gone to their football camp the previous summer and had a run in with a coach that soured him. "All I wanted to do was go someplace where I'd have a chance to kick Notre Dame's butt," he said.

That chance seemed to present itself when Northwestern offered him a scholarship. Conroy was ready to cancel all his other visits and sign with Northwestern, but at the last minute Francis Peay, then the coach, withdrew the offer. When he told the Conroy family that he had given away the scholarship because the school had recruited six offensive linemen, expecting to sign four, only to find that all six wanted to sign, Carol Conroy was furious.

John was a lot calmer. "Mom, I don't want to go someplace where they don't want me," he said.

Army did want him. So did Illinois State. Conroy visited both schools. He had a great time at Illinois State but worried that he would spend four years having a great time there and have nothing to show for it. He liked Army's discipline. Wearing a uniform to school every day didn't bother him, since he had worn one going to Catholic schools since kindergarten. A school that was 85 percent male was an improvement from all-boys St. Lawrence. It was an excellent school. "I'm going," he announced. His parents liked the idea. His friends thought he was crazy.

"They kept saying, 'Go in the army? What are you nuts?' " he said. "I figured, why not? I was pretty sure I could handle it."

The only drawback came when the admissions office told him that his 22 on the math portion of the ACT was two points shy of the 24 he needed to get straight into West Point. He would have to go to the prep school. Reluctantly, Conroy agreed.

When he arrived there he found that he was listed as the last-string fullback. "I mean, I had guys playing ahead of me who, I swear, had never played football before," he said. "I'm sitting there thinking that the coaches have to be loving me, a guy who was seriously recruited by other Division I schools, and they're acting like they've never heard of me."

Conroy made himself heard — and known — and eventually won the fullback's job. But when he got to West Point the next year, he found himself doing the last-string thing again. He had lost twenty pounds during Beast, and at six one, 185, he wasn't going to get a lot of time playing fullback. He ended up at halfback — on the scout team.

He wasn't about to give up, though, especially after the opening game, when he sat in the stands and felt miserable being there. "I couldn't stand it," he said. "I decided if I had to be on the scout team, fine, I would be the hardest-working scout team player they had. I was determined to make them notice me."

They noticed him. In fact, for eight of the final ten games that season, he was chosen as the scout team player of the week and got to travel with the team and dress for the game. That was all he got to do, though, and he hated it. When spring practice started, he had bulked back up to 205. They made him a fullback again, and by the end of spring practice he was up to second string.

Then came summer at Camp Buckner. No matter how hard Conroy tried to keep weight on, rising at 4:30 every morning to lift weights and run, he couldn't do it. He returned for preseason practice at 190. Akili King, who had somehow managed to gain weight, was switched to fullback and Conroy went to halfback again.

But at least he was on the depth chart — third string — still in a position to play. But when he got his chance in scrimmages, he wasn't doing very well. He tired easily and found himself forgetting plays because he felt weak and out of it. The doctors ran some tests: he had asthma. Medication helped, and he did get into the Lafayette game for his famous, busted one-yard run.

Again, spring practice gave him hope. He was running second string at halfback when it ended and was convinced he could beat the starter, Mike Robinson, out for the job in August. He never got the chance. The coaches moved Jeff Brizic in ahead of him. Conroy was devastated. When was he going to get to play? He talked to Cantelupe and Derek Klein, his closest friends on the team. Klein had switched from quarterback to defensive back that spring and was going to get playing time as the fifth defensive back. Maybe Conroy should think about switching to defense.

His first request, made to running backs coach Jim Simar, was rejected. Shortly thereafter, he was no longer the third-string halfback. He was back on the scout team. "This was getting completely ridiculous," he said. "I did not want to spend my entire career on the scout team. I didn't want to be one of those guys, senior year, who they said contributed to the team by working hard in practice. I respected those guys for sticking with it and working hard, but that wasn't what I wanted. I wanted to get on the field."

Cantelupe, Klein, and Joel Davis, who had been Conroy's roommate at the prep school, went to see Sutton on his behalf to ask that he be given a chance to switch to defense. Sutton called Conroy in and asked him if that was what he wanted to do. Conroy said it was.

"You know, John, I really think you have a better chance to get playing time at running back," Sutton said.

"Coach, I'm on the *scout* team at running back," Conroy said. "How much worse could my chances be at DB?"

Sutton agreed to let him move. Conroy's thinking was that he would at least get to play on special teams as a backup defensive back. It didn't happen that way. He never got off the scout team on the defensive side of the ball and never got above second string on special teams. He didn't get into a single game all season. He now had three years behind him and one rushing yard to show for it.

But he wouldn't give up. He was absolutely convinced that he would win a job on defense during spring practice. He spent the whole winter working on running backwards and trying to build his speed. Ten days into spring ball, three halfbacks had gone down with injuries. Andre Powell, the new running backs coach, wanted him back on offense. Conroy saw an opportunity: new coach, clean slate. He also could see that he was going to struggle to get playing time on defense. He agreed to move back to offense.

A few days prior to the end of spring practice, Powell told him they needed him at fullback more than at halfback, especially now that all the halfbacks were healthy. Conroy wasn't sure what to think. A few days later, he and Steve Carpenter, who was now one of the starting halfbacks, went to the football office to see Powell about summer workouts. Sitting in the office, Conroy noticed a depth chart. At fullback the list read:

A. King
J. Triano
D. Perry
L. Gibson
R. Hawkins
J. Conroy

"Sixth string!" Conroy screamed. "Steve, I'm sixth string. This is a joke! This is impossible! I'm a senior and I'm sixth string!"

He stormed out of the office, Carpenter right behind him. For the first time in his life, quitting crossed his mind. Ten seconds later, he was embarrassed for thinking it.

"You've got two choices," Carpenter told him. "You can stay bitter or get better."

Carpenter was a coach's son. Conroy knew that was a coach's saying. But it made sense.

"OK then, what do I do?" he asked.

"You gain twenty-five pounds over the summer," Carpenter said. "And you come back here next August and become the starting fullback."

Conroy decided he was right. When he went home to Chicago that summer, he told all his friends he was going to be the starting fullback in the fall. "I was sixth on the depth chart and I just went around saying, 'Yep, I'm going to be starting this year.' Since I hadn't played at all for three years, they were all amazed."

He worked feverishly in the weight room all summer and ran four miles every day to build his speed again. By the time the team reported in August, he weighed 208. At the start of the first day of practice, he was fourth on the depth chart — King was gone and Gibson had undergone knee surgery. At the end of the first day, he had moved ahead of both Perry and Hawkins. The coaches could see that he was bigger and faster.

The next day, Triano turned an ankle. On day three of summer workouts, with the season three weeks away, Conroy was just where he had told his pals in Chicago he would be: starting at fullback for Army.

ARMY'S 1995 schedule was the toughest it had been in Sutton's tenure. Notre Dame was back for the first time in ten years and a game at Washington had been added. Duke, which had gone to a bowl game the previous year, would be the second game, and after Notre Dame came a game against another bowl team, Boston College — in Boston. There were also home games against Rice and East Carolina, names that weren't likely to stir any of the old grads, but both solid teams: Rice had been 6–5 in 1994, and East Carolina had won seven games, played in the Liberty Bowl, and had eighteen starters returning.

Late in August, Sutton watched Ohio State and Boston College play in the Kickoff Classic, the first game of the college football season. During an interview at halftime, Ohio State coach John Cooper said that his team was facing the toughest nonconference schedule he had seen in thirty years of coaching with games against Boston College, Washington, and Notre Dame. Why, Sutton wondered, did those names sound familiar? Then he remembered.

The players loved the schedule. They wanted to play those teams. When Joel Davis had been told in 1991 that the coaches wanted him to go to the prep school he had balked — until they showed him the 1995 schedule. "That made it worthwhile," he said.

In the minds of the seniors, the only way truly to make a mark, to wake up the echoes of Army football, was to beat top teams. Beating Lehigh and Colgate and Bucknell wasn't going to do it. "You live to play the games people say you can't win," Cantelupe said.

The players believed, truly believed, that they could beat anyone on their schedule. Of course believing and doing were two different things. Sutton knew he had the best offensive line he had ever had, with four seniors and a junior. He had an excellent tight end in Ron Leshinski, experienced wide receivers — especially with Gantt back — and plenty of halfbacks who could run the ball. Someone needed to emerge as the fullback, and he needed a capable backup quarterback, especially after what had happened a year ago.

The defense was experienced, especially on the line and in the defensive backfield. As always, it didn't have as much size or speed as a Division I-A team would like to have, but it was full of smart, resourceful players.

By the time the team gathered on the afternoon of September 1 for their final preseason scrimmage, some of Sutton's early questions had been answered. Adam Thompson, a third baseman on the baseball team, had emerged as the number two quarterback even though he had been fifth on the depth chart at the start of summer drills. Thompson was small, five ten and 185 pounds, but he was quick and tough and learned the option reads quickly. The coaches were concerned about his lack of experience and his small hands, which sometimes gave him trouble on the exchange from center and gripping the ball.

John Conroy and Demetrius Perry were sharing time at fullback, since Triano was still slowed by his ankle injury. The kicking game would be brand-new, although J. (yes, J., not Jay, he insisted) Parker, a junior, had done good work as the new placekicker. The news wasn't as good when it came to finding a punter. None of the upperclassmen who had been given a chance had kicked with any consistency. The best punter in preseason drills had been Ian Hughes, a plebe walk-on. Sutton wasn't thrilled with the notion of throwing a plebe into the job, but it was beginning to look as if he had no choice.

The opener was against Lehigh on September 9. Traditionally, Army opened the season with a Division I-AA opponent at home. It was almost like a dress rehearsal for the real thing, which would come a week later against Duke. Even though the seniors had made "one game at a time" one of their goals, even though the coaches wouldn't dare bring up Duke until after the Lehigh game was over, that was the game that was in their thoughts more than any during preseason.

The Duke game would tell them a lot about where they were as a team. It would tell them how much they had progressed in a year since the 43–7 humiliation on national TV in Durham. It was a game they believed they could win. More than that, it was a game they wanted desperately to win in order to even the score. They all remembered the late touchdown pass.

"I don't think there's a day that's gone by in the last year that I haven't thought about that night and that feeling at least once," Jim Cantelupe said. "Now, they're coming into Michie Stadium. I promise you it will be different."

Cantelupe knew he had to be careful about promises. A year earlier he had guaranteed a victory in Durham. He wasn't about to be that brash again, but he wasn't about to back down from Duke — or anybody.

Sutton wasn't going to get as emotionally involved or as caught up in the idea of getting even as the players. But he understood the significance of the game. The four games after Duke were at Washington, Rice, against Notre Dame in the New Jersey Meadowlands, and at Boston College. Army would be a big-time underdog against Washington, Notre Dame, and Boston College; the Rice game would be a toss-up. The Duke game would set a tone, he believed, for the most difficult portion of the schedule.

First, there was the matter of dealing with Lehigh. Coaches always worry about teams that are heavy favorites looking ahead, especially with a key game the next week. Those worries faded quickly when halfback Rashad Hodge, on the first carry of his varsity career, opened the game by going 74 yards for a touchdown. Nineteen seconds into the season, Army led 7–0. Seven minutes later it was 14–0, Carpenter capping a classic wishbone drive — 66 yards in 14 plays — with a one-yard plunge. The rest of the day was a happy stroll, the offense rolling up 494 yards — 387 on the ground. Sutton even let Ronnie McAda throw the ball 10 times because he figured he would need to throw it that often (or more) in weeks to come. Cantelupe had six tackles and an interception. Conroy started at fullback and rushed for 85 yards.

Everyone went home happy. Now, they could drop the pretenses and focus completely on Duke. Sutton and offensive coordinator Greg Gregory had kept the offense simple against Lehigh, saving a number of plays that had been put in during preseason. There was no sense letting Duke see those plays on tape, especially since they weren't needed.

It was ironic that the Army players felt so much animosity toward Duke, since Duke's most famous and important figure was a West Point graduate: basketball coach Mike Krzyzewski.

Krzyzewski had graduated from the academy in 1969. He was captain of the basketball team his senior year, having survived four years under Bob Knight, who had recruited him out of Chicago's South Side. Back then, Knight was just a wild young coach — nicknamed "Bobby T" by the New York media because of his penchant for technical fouls — not the icon he would later become at Indiana University. Krzyzewski was a hard-nosed point guard who rarely scored — "Knight would never let me shoot" — but was the kind of leader West Point took great pride in producing.

After his five-year stint in the army, he went to work at Indiana under Knight for a year. When the coaching job opened at West Point, Knight recommended him for it even though Krzyzewski was only twenty-eight. Knight's influence got him the job and in five years he went 73–59, a remarkable record for Army during the seventies. That record and another Knight recommendation had gotten him the Duke job in 1980. Now, fifteen years later, he had become an icon himself, having taken Duke to seven Final Fours, winning back-to-back national titles in 1991 and 1992.

Krzyzewski still loved West Point. He talked often about the fact that the academy had taught him how to fail, a key ingredient, he believed, in his success. He also talked often about almost drowning as a plebe trying to swim across the pool in Arvin Gym carrying a brick. "That brick is probably still at the bottom of the pool someplace," he said. "Where I grew up in Chicago, they didn't teach kids how to swim."

On the night before Duke played Army, Krzyzewski came back to West Point for a dinner in his honor at the West Point Club, the on-post officers club. During the daytime, the club has a spectacular view looking down on the Hudson. When the Krzyzewski party began, there was no view of anything because the electricity had gone out.

"I think we're in trouble," Krzyzewski said. "I hear they've got Army engineers working on the problem."

When the problem was cleared up, Krzyzewski spoke emotionally about what West Point and Duke meant to him. Both, he said, were places to be admired and cherished. Earlier that year, his wife, Mickie, had taken his West Point class ring and put a Duke stone in it along with the West Point stone. "I love both schools," Krzyzewski said. "They belong together on my ring because they're together in my heart."

There would be no such love or togetherness between the two schools the next day.

WHENEVER a college football magazine starts compiling a list of the best or prettiest places to watch a college football game, Michie Stadium is invariably at or near the top of the list — especially early in the fall when the weather is still warm and the leaves are just starting to turn.

The sixteenth of September was one of those classic fall days at West Point, cool and breezy, but comfortable, with the sun poking through the clouds by the time the players took the field to warm up.

Game day for fans starts earlier at West Point than at almost anyplace else in the country because of the cadet parade on the Plain. It takes place three hours before kickoff, which means that the parking lots will start to fill with tailgaters by 9 o'clock for a 1:30 kickoff. Most fans park in the vicinity of the stadium, then take school buses to the center of campus. There, they can stroll around Trophy Point, admiring the captured weaponry from wars dating back to the American Revolution, or just gaze down at the Hudson or up at the surrounding mountains.

Saturday is one of the corps' least favorite days. SAMI — Saturday morning inspection — is the toughest and most thorough room inspection of the week. Every single thing must be in place, and one speck of dust can result in being written up if your TAC (tactical officer) is inclined to make life difficult.

Once SAMI has been dealt with, everyone must get into full dress uniforms for the parade. For the spectators, the colors and the music and the precise order of the corps as it goes through its paces is a delight. For those going through those paces it is routine, something to get through so they can retreat to their rooms to put on more comfortable clothing for the football game.

While the rest of the corps is being put through its paces, the football team is thirty miles away at the Ramada Inn in Mahwah, New Jersey. At almost the same moment that the parade begins, Sutton leads his own parade — a long lap around the hotel parking lot. The cadets wear sweats instead of dress clothes, and there is no music or pageantry anywhere in sight. Everyone walks in silence, each player and coach alone with his thoughts, trying to turn his focus to the game.

The Duke team that Army was facing was not the same team that had destroyed the Cadets a year earlier. Robert Baldwin, the tailback who had been the Atlantic Coast Conference Player of the Year, was gone, and so were some of the key offensive linemen. The Blue Devils did have Spence Fischer, their record-setting quarterback, returning, and Army's ability to control him would be critical.

Duke's coach, Fred Goldsmith, knew exactly what his team would be up against. Goldsmith had been an assistant coach at the Air Force Academy earlier in his career, so he felt he understood the mentality of an academy team. Earlier in the week, he had told his players how much Army would want to win the game. He had also told them not to expect Army to fold under pressure.

"Football's their fun," he said. "There isn't anything that's going to happen out there during the game that will be harder or tougher to take than what they go through on a daily basis just to survive in school. You'll face plenty of teams with more physical talent than this one, but you won't face any that are tougher mentally."

Goldsmith had considered asking Krzyzewski to speak to his team before the game. A year earlier, he had brought Krzyzewski in before Duke had played Navy and Krzyzewski had gotten so wound up talking about why he couldn't *stand* the thought of losing to Navy that he had launched into a profane tirade that left Goldsmith — a born-again Christian who never curses — sweating profusely. Duke won the game 47–14, and Goldsmith liked the idea of bringing Krzyzewski's fire to the locker room — with or without profanity. But he didn't feel it would be fair to ask someone who had such strong feelings for both schools to step in and speak.

"I'll save him for Navy," he said.

When the Duke buses arrived at Michie, Goldsmith walked out onto the turf for his own pregame walk. "I'd almost forgotten how pretty it is here," he said, glancing toward the trees that provide a backdrop at the far end of the stadium. He smiled. "I made a mistake last year at the end of the game. Our backup quarterback threw that last touchdown pass on an audible, but I should have told him before he went in just to run the ball into the line — no audibles. It was my fault. I know they'll use that to get ready for today."

Goldsmith didn't know how accurate his words were. All week at Army the players had reminded one another about the fourth quarter in Durham. Cantelupe's last words before he and Davis left the locker room for the coin toss were "It's time to get even, boys."

Even the head cheerleader was caught up in the notion of revenge. "It's payback time," he kept telling the corps as they settled into their seats.

It didn't start that way. After Ian Hughes's second punt of the game went only 26 yards, Fischer crisply marched Duke 40 yards down the field for the opening touchdown of the game to put the Blue Devils up 7–0.

Army's offense hadn't picked up a first down in two series. But after the Duke score, the Cadets finally began moving. They reached the Duke 24 with a fourth-and-two. McAda faked the dive to Conroy, pulled the ball out, and sprinted around left end for a five-yard pickup. Three plays later, with a second-and-goal at the four, McAda called his own number again. This time, though, he got smacked for no gain.

Worse than that, he came up woozy and wobbled to the sidelines. Adam Thompson rushed in, picked up one yard on third down, and then Parker came in to kick a 20-yard field goal. It sailed through, cutting the margin to 7–3.

There wasn't much reaction from the crowd, though, because all eyes were fixed on McAda as he sat on the bench surrounded by the Army medical staff. Bob Arciero, the team doctor, and Tim Kelly, the head trainer, tried to determine just how seriously McAda had been hurt.

"What's your name?" Arciero asked.

"Ronnie McAda."

"What day is it?"

"Saturday."

"Who are we playing?"

"Duke."

They had him stand up, extend his arms to the side, and touch his nose with one finger. No problem.

"I'm fine," McAda insisted. "Let me get back in."

"Not so fast," Arciero said. "You take it easy for a little while, then we'll check you again." Knowing that concussion symptoms don't always show up right away, he didn't want to make any snap judgments.

McAda stalked off to plead his case to Sutton, who was chewing even harder on his ever-present game gum than normal. The last thing he needed was to lose another quarterback in the first quarter of another game against Duke.

"I'm fine, Coach, ready anytime," McAda told Sutton.

"We'll see what the doctor says," Sutton said. "Go and check the play chart with Charles."

Charles Kean, Army's third-string quarterback, was in charge of signaling in plays if Sutton didn't send them in himself with one of the wide receivers. McAda walked over to him and Kean began asking him about some of the plays that had been put in that week.

"Come on, Charles, quit kidding around," McAda said. "Those aren't our plays."

Kean sensed trouble. He mentioned a couple of other plays. McAda shook his head. "Never heard of them," he said. He looked at Kean again, hoping he was joking. The look on Kean's face told him he wasn't. Kean went and found Arciero.

"He doesn't know any of our plays," he told him.

Arciero grimaced. "I think we've got a problem," he said.

They kept asking McAda about plays throughout the second quarter, and he kept shaking his head. It was all a blank. Even if he did miraculously find the plays in his brain at halftime — which Arciero thought unlikely — putting him back into the game would be high risk. Arciero is not a high-risk doctor, especially with head injuries.

Thompson, who had thrown one pass in his college career, would be the quarterback for the rest of the afternoon.

The second quarter was controlled by the defenses. Each team

moved the ball but couldn't get into the end zone. A Cantelupe interception stopped one Duke drive, and Duke settled for a field goal after
getting to the Army eight late in the quarter. Parker kicked two more
field goals, including a 47-yarder on the last play of the half. Duke
led 10–9.

Other than losing McAda — no small thing — this was the kind
of game they had expected. The defense was giving up yards but coming up with big plays whenever Duke got near the goal line. The offense was moving the ball, but the Duke defense was making similarly
important plays whenever the Cadets threatened.

Parker's kicking was encouraging, but Hughes was struggling in
the swirling wind, averaging less than 29 yards for four punts. Duke
would get the football to start the second half, and the coaches thought
a three-and-out by the defense would be critical because it would build
on the momentum gained by Parker's last-second kick and bring the
crowd into the ball game.

Instead, Fischer opened the half with a 30-yard strike down the
sideline to flanker Marc Wilson. Linebacker Ben Kotwica hit Wilson
hard in full stride and jarred the ball loose, but Wilson jumped on his
own fumble.

From there, Duke went right down the field to score. It was 17–
9, and Michie was almost silent. But Abel Young took the kickoff on
his own 18, started up the middle, broke to the outside, and was
gone — 82 yards for a touchdown. Just like that, the crowd was wild
again. Sutton went for two, wanting to tie the game, but Thompson
was tackled a yard short of the goal line. Duke 17, Army 15.

Duke responded with another field goal to make it 20–15, but on
the next series, Thompson came up with a huge play, breaking tackles
to go 56 yards on a third-and-seven option play to the Duke seven.
Two plays later, Conroy slammed into the end zone for his first touchdown as a college player. Again, the two-point conversion failed, but
with 5:08 left in the third quarter, Army finally had the lead, 21–20.

The game became a defensive struggle. A 39-yard pass play on
Duke's next series came back because of a holding call. The Blue
Devils had to punt. Army moved to the Duke 17, but Parker finally
missed — from 34 yards — and it was still 21–20.

They kept exchanging punts as the fourth-quarter clock wound down. Still, there was an uneasy feeling in the stands and on the sidelines that Duke had one last drive left in it, even though the Cadet defense had been pounding Fischer and his receivers all afternoon. When Army had possession, Sutton was loath to let Thompson throw the ball, especially going into the wind. Duke knew Army wasn't going to pass and had nine and ten defenders on the line of scrimmage.

With 6:53 left, Army forced another Duke punt. One last sustained drive could put the game away. Three plays netted nine yards. On fourth and one, Sutton gambled. Conroy followed right guard Eddie Stover and right tackle Bill Blair and picked up two yards. First down. The clock was under five minutes. Three more running plays picked up just four yards to the 35. The clock was under three minutes. Duke used a time-out.

Hughes came in to kick the ball away. Realistically, the Cadets were hoping to get 30 yards from the punt. That would mean Duke would have to drive at least 40 to get into reasonable field-goal position. Anything beyond 30 would be a huge bonus. After having to think about the situation during the time-out, Hughes shanked the punt off the side of his foot. It rolled out of bounds only 10 yards from the line of scrimmage at the Army 45.

Now, Duke had plenty of time — 2:51 with one time-out left — and only needed 20 yards to reach comfortable range for placekicker Tom Cochran. Cantelupe was screaming at his teammates in the huddle. "We need a big play! One big play and it's our ball game. Who's going to make it?"

The first big play was made by Fischer, who found a slanting Joe Opalenick over the middle at the Army 29. First down. Duke was already right on the edge of Cochran's range. The clock was under two minutes. Tailback Leymarr Marshall picked up one yard to the 28.

Ninety seconds left. Fischer dropped back to throw his 50th pass of the day. Marc Wilson slanted across the middle and caught the ball at the 20. He took one step and was slammed into by Ben Kotwica. For the second time in the half, Kotwica knocked the ball loose from Wilson. A wild scramble for the ball ensued. When they unpiled, cornerback Abdullah Muhammad was at the bottom clutching the ball.

They had made the big play! Kotwica had made the hit; Muhammad had come up with the ball. The Army bench went crazy.

There was a little more than a minute left, and Duke could only stop the clock once. All the Cadets had to do was fall on the ball three times and they would have the win they craved. Payback.

But something was wrong. The officials were huddling. Sutton sensed trouble as soon as he saw the powwow. "I thought, 'They can't possibly be thinking it was an incomplete pass . . .' "

They could. Referee Joe Soffey came out of the conference, turned on his wireless microphone, and made the announcement: "The pass was incomplete. Duke ball. Third down."

The Army players looked at one another in disbelief. Soffey couldn't be serious. Wilson had caught the ball, turned, and taken a full step before Kotwica hit him. When Sutton looked at the play later he would see Wilson take *two* steps. But the officials didn't see it that way. There is no instant replay in college football. The offense, which had started onto the field, had to come back. The defense, shell-shocked, had to line up again.

Fischer was still facing third-and-nine, but everyone on both sidelines sensed that the game's critical play had just occurred. Fischer took off on a scramble and picked up the nine yards he needed. Duke had a first down at the Army 19. Now the Blue Devils were well within Cochran's range. Sixty-four seconds were left.

Marshall picked up nine yards on the next two plays and the clock wound down to eight seconds. Duke called its final time-out and Cochran trotted onto the field. The attempt would be 28 yards. Army had survived in situations like this before. (See Bucchianeri, Ryan, circa 1993.) But Cochran wasn't a nervous freshman, he was a senior who had been Duke's kicker for four years. Army used its last two time-outs trying to get him to think about the pressure of a last-second kick. The ball knuckled slightly in the air, but easily cleared the crossbar.

Duke 23, Army 21. Final.

No one could believe it. They had done what they had to. They had rushed the ball for 305 yards and held Duke to less than 100 yards on the ground. They had pounded the Blue Devils all day. Most important, with the game on the line, they had made the big play that Cantelupe had demanded.

And the officials had taken it away from them.

Sutton didn't know what to say in the silent locker room. He was as crushed as his players. "I'm damn proud of you," he said softly. "You won that football game. As far as I'm concerned, we're 2–0 and we go from here." He felt himself choking up, so he stopped. The players saw the tears in his eyes. They couldn't remember ever seeing him as emotional after a game.

He wasn't the only one in tears. Many of the players sat in front of their lockers, too stunned to think about undressing, crying quietly. Sutton went off to talk to the media. Ever so slowly, the seniors began going from locker to locker to remind the younger players there were still nine games left to play. Suddenly, from near the doorway that led to the field, the players heard a voice say, "Excuse me, could I have everyone's attention for just one moment?"

They looked up and saw Fred Goldsmith standing there. "I don't mean to barge in here," Goldsmith said, "but I just wanted to tell all of you that I thought you deserved to win that football game. You beat us up out there. You were winners, you deserved better." He paused. The locker room was completely silent. "And I'm sorry about last year. We shouldn't have thrown that pass."

He turned and walked out. The players had mixed emotions about what they had just heard. "It was a classy thing for him to do," Cantelupe said. "But to tell the truth, right at that moment, we didn't want to hear it."

They really didn't want to hear anything right at that moment. All they knew was they had waited twelve months to get another shot at Duke. They had sold out, body and soul, for sixty minutes and gotten nothing for it.

But they had to put it behind them. Because now the tough part of the schedule lay just ahead.

# 8

# FALLEN STAR

NAVY's 1995 schedule was not exactly designed to aid a team putting in a new offense and a new defense. Three of the first four games were on the road, and the next two, although at home, were against Virginia Tech and Air Force, both teams that started the season with serious bowl aspirations.

Before the players headed off for their summer cruises and leave time, each of them had met with his position coach and with Charlie Weatherbie (although not for nearly as long as Bucchianeri). Weatherbie's message to most players was the same: give some thought every single day to our goals — CIC Trophy, winning season, bowl game victory — and ask yourself if you've done something today to help us achieve those goals.

He also gave the players a stick-on replica of the CIC Trophy to put on their watches as a reminder of their first goal. Unfortunately, the stick-ons didn't last long, especially on those watches that went to sea.

August is never an easy month in Annapolis. The weather is still blazing hot, even on the Navy practice fields, which at least catch a few breaths of wind from the nearby water. The preseason didn't become any easier when three of the team's twenty-four seniors — two of them returning starters — decided to leave the team.

The first to quit was fullback Monty Williams, who announced at the very beginning of two-a-day practices that he didn't want to play football. Williams had been the closest thing Navy had to a main man in its pathetic running game in '94, rushing for a team-leading 215 yards. He had also caught 24 passes for 138 yards and had scored eight touchdowns.

But the new offense, in which the fullback was almost always a straight-ahead runner, didn't fit him as well as it did junior Omar Nelson, and Nelson had moved ahead of Williams during spring practice. Faced with the possibility of not starting, Williams, one of the best students on the team, decided over the summer to focus on his school-work. His teammates weren't surprised. They had sensed during the spring that his desire to play was waning.

The second defection wasn't that big a surprise either. Ed Pidgeon, a backup offensive guard, had struggled academically throughout his junior year and had even been brought up on honor charges. When his case reached the commandant, Pidgeon had been terrified that he might be separated even though his crime was more one of care-lessness than anything else. Fortunately for him, the commandant saw it that way too, and although he was restricted on weekends for what seemed like forever, he was still in school.

Deeply religious, Pidgeon had prayed often during that ordeal. In his prayers, he had told God that he would give up anything, even football, if he would just get him through all this. After it was all over, Pidgeon decided that what had happened was God's way of telling him he shouldn't play football anymore.

When he explained this to Weatherbie, the coach, deeply religious himself, said he understood. But he wanted Pidgeon to be sure.

"I'm sure, Coach," Pidgeon said. "I just know God wants me to stop playing football."

"I talk to God more than you, Ed," Weatherbie said, half-joking. "And I think he wants you to keep playing."

Pidgeon wasn't swayed and Weatherbie didn't pressure him further, although he hated losing an experienced lineman, especially one who had gone through a crisis and seemed to have come out of it with some added maturity.

Losing Williams and Pidgeon was disappointing to everyone, though not shocking. But when Alex Domino walked into Weather-bie's office four days before the opener at SMU and announced he was quitting, everyone was stunned. Domino was one of the anchors of the offensive line. He and Garrett Smith and Bryce Minamyer had gone through trial by fire the previous season, and their experience was being counted on as something the team could build around, especially early in the year.

But Domino had clearly not been himself all summer. His parents were going through a bitter divorce, and it had bothered him throughout the spring and was still very much on his mind when he returned for practice in August. Since his family lived less than a hundred miles away, in Middletown, Delaware, Domino often got in his car at the end of afternoon practice and drove home, returning in time for practice the next day. A couple of times he hadn't made it back in time, which had upset the coaches. They understood he was going through a tough time, but they also felt he wasn't helping anyone — including his parents — by not getting ready for his last season as a football player.

Gene McKeehan, the offensive line coach, talked to Domino about it, and so did Weatherbie. They didn't want to seem cold or unfeeling, but there was very little Domino could do about his parents' marital problems. He was letting it affect his football. To try and get the message through to him, they dropped him to the second team for a number of practices.

They weren't getting through. Domino's play continued to be sluggish. Then, on Monday, September 4, he went to see Weatherbie. He knew he wasn't playing very well, and he didn't see how it was going to change anytime soon. He felt he had to be there whenever he could to help his mom.

"This is a big decision, Alex," Weatherbie said. "You're a senior, this is it for you. I think you ought to sleep on it overnight before you make a final decision."

Domino agreed. Weatherbie had been through this in his coaching career before. He knew when Domino left his office that day that he wasn't coming back.

His teammates weren't as convinced. A number of them went to see him in his room that night. Andrew Thompson, who had played with Domino for four years (including their year at NAPS) was completely baffled. They had been through so much and had dealt with so much frustration. Now, on the eve of their senior season, with a chance to make up for so much of that frustration, Domino was walking away.

"Alex, the hardest part is over," Thompson said. "We've put in all the work, all the hours in the weight room, in spring ball, in preseason. Now comes the fun part, the part we said we came here for."

Domino understood. But he just couldn't put his heart and soul into football at this stage of his life the way he knew he needed to; the way he knew Thompson and the other seniors would expect him to. It was better, he thought, to do it this way, make a clean break, than go out there distracted and play poorly.

Thompson was upset. The one thing that kept him going during the tough times at Navy had been the idea that the football team was a brotherhood. You didn't quit on your brothers, no matter what. You counted on them; they counted on you. He felt sorry for Domino, but he also felt betrayed and hurt.

"We'll miss you, Alex," he said. He hugged his friend and left. There were now twenty-one seniors left.

ONE senior who had trouble understanding Domino's decision was Shaun Stephenson. No one knew the importance of family more than Stephenson, and there was nothing he would not do for his mother, father, or younger brother. He was also absolutely determined to graduate from the academy and be a Marine Corps pilot. He had dreamed about that possibility for about as long as he could remember.

But there was nothing — *nothing* — that was going to deny him this last chance to play football.

Even though the season had not yet started and he had never so much as dressed out for a Navy game, Stephenson was already challenging Ryan Bucchianeri as Navy's most publicized player. Already, CNN had come in to do a feature on him, and *Sports Illustrated* was right behind. Throughout the season, anywhere Navy played, all the newspapers and magazines and TV stations — and networks — wanted to talk to one Navy player: Stephenson.

Stephenson understood. His story was full of both heroism and tragedy. His fervent hope was that, in the end, it would be a story about a good football player.

He had enlisted in the marines after high school because his father and grandfather had been marines and his older brother Dion was a marine and Shaun had always done everything Dion did. He had followed Dion to Desert Storm. There, he had been stationed on the battleship *Frederick* on the morning of January 30, 1991, when his commander called him in to give him some bad news. An Iraqi advance and attack on Khafji, Saudi Arabia, had begun the night before. One of the first American casualties in the Battle of Khafji had been Dion Stephenson.

Shaun was a week shy of his twentieth birthday. Dion was twenty-two. The marines had him escort his brother's body home. He flew with the casket to Bahrain, then to Spain, then to Delaware, and finally to Salt Lake City. After he got home, Stephenson learned that although his brother had died in combat, he had been killed by an American bomb — friendly fire. Later, he found out the details: the light armored vehicle that Dion had been in had been mistakenly marked as an enemy transport by Air Force planes flown by pilots who were members of the Air Force reserve. Two LAVs had been blown up by Maverick missiles dropped from A-10 Air Force Thunderbolts, killing fourteen Americans, Dion among them.

"What people forget is that we had a lot of inexperienced people out there," Shaun said more than four years later, able to talk almost clinically about what happened. "The training I had, that Dion had, we could identify any vehicle out there — ours, the enemies, anyone's. You had like thirty-eight different countries involved in Saudi Arabia, and they were bringing in guys who had no time to train the way we were trained. A horrible, horrible mistake was made."

The Stephenson family was first told about the possibility that Dion had been killed by friendly fire two weeks after his death. They didn't know for certain until the driver of Dion's LAV, who had been out of the vehicle when it was blown up, told them it had been friendly fire.

Understandably, many of the families involved in the disaster were bitter. Some sued the government; others were publicly critical of President George Bush and the military leadership. Not the Stephenson family. Jim Stephenson wouldn't hear a word against the U.S. government or the president. He had been a marine squad leader in Vietnam in 1965 and 1966, and he was proud of that background and of his two sons who had become marines. Over and over he was quoted as saying he knew how awful the Air Force pilots felt and that he hurt for them as well as for the families of the other thirteen dead marines.

In the story he wrote about Stephenson for *Sports Illustrated,* Rick Reilly movingly described Jim and Geri Stephenson's relationship with their three sons; how close they all were — especially Dion and Shaun — and how important the marines were to all of them.

"My dad has always believed that everyone should serve in the military at some point," Shaun said. "He thinks there's a reason why we're free the way we are and that we all owe the country something back. Dion's dying didn't change any of that."

It did, however, change the course of Shaun's life. Like Dion, he had been a superb athlete growing up, even though neither boy was very big. They had both been excellent swimmers — Dion a butter-flyer, Shaun a breaststroker. The family moved from just outside Los Angeles to Bountiful, a suburb of Salt Lake City, when Shaun was thirteen and Dion fifteen. Both boys were stars throughout their teen-age years. In high school, Dion continued to swim and played soccer. Shaun played baseball and football. His passion was football. And flying.

"All through high school, even before that, my dream was to go to the Naval Academy, play football, and then become a pilot in the marines," he said. "I remember watching the Army-Navy game with my dad when I was a kid and thinking, 'Yeah, that's it. That's what I want to do someday.'"

His memories of those games are vague — except for the gold helmets on both teams — but he remembers how much it meant to his father when Navy won.

Even though he was only five ten and barely weighed 160 pounds, Stephenson was good enough to draw some attention from Division I schools as a senior. One school that contacted him was Air Force. Stephenson didn't even write back. "I just wasn't interested," he said. "I wanted to go to Navy."

But Navy wasn't recruiting him. He applied anyway, but didn't get in even though he had a B average and 1100 on the SATs. If he had been someone the football team was recruiting, that would have been enough at least to get him invited to NAPS. But since the football staff hadn't shown any interest in him, he didn't get in.

He could have gone to junior college or gotten a Division I-AA or Division II scholarship. But Stephenson didn't want that. If he couldn't go to Navy, then he wanted to do what Dion was doing. So he enlisted in the marines. He was sent to California, to Camp Pendleton, for force reconnaissance training, the same job that Dion had been training for.

Dion was already a star in the marines. Force-recon is the top of the line in the marines, dangerous work, often done behind enemy lines. Dion craved it and said so. Shaun wanted to do whatever Dion did but wasn't as outgoing or cocky about it. Nonetheless, the brothers enjoyed being together again.

As kids, they had fought constantly about everything. Now they fought about the one thing brothers should never fight about: a woman. Neither Stephenson brother ever had trouble getting a date. They both had the kind of dark, dreamy looks that make women sigh. Dion, older and more confident, always went out with exactly who he wanted to. Shaun would never think of trying to compete with him for a woman.

It started out no different with Sandy Goss. Dion had dated her briefly and they had broken up. He introduced her to Shaun and they started dating. But then Dion changed his mind, decided he had made a mistake. He wanted to date Sandy again. Shaun liked Sandy, but he wasn't in love with her and he wasn't going to fight with Dion over her. If that was what Sandy wanted, it was fine with him.

Only it wasn't what Sandy wanted. She wanted to continue dating Shaun. When she told Dion that, he was furious. "He didn't get rejected very often," Shaun said. "He was always the top dog in everything he did, and he knew it and flaunted it. This was different. He didn't take it very well."

The brothers fought the same way they had as kids, only this time Dad wasn't there to pull out the boxing gloves and make them punch one another into a state of exhaustion. Their relationship was still a bit rocky when Saddam Hussein invaded Kuwait on August 2, 1990.

The word came down right away that Dion's unit would be one of the first shipped out as part of Desert Shield. Understanding that they were probably both going to war before this was all over, the brothers put aside their differences long enough to talk, smoke a cigar, hug, and make a pact to take care of their parents, of their little brother, Michael, and of each other if one of them should die in combat.

Four months later, Shaun was also sent to the Gulf. But he went on a ship. Dion was right at the center of the action. And so, on January 29 he was in his LAV when the worst happened.

Shaun came home to find his mother in a state of shock. She could barely speak to anyone, even her family. Dion had been her oldest and, as much as she loved Shaun and Michael, he was her special boy. Jim Stephenson was stoic in public, never turning anyone from the media away throughout the ordeal.

It was right after he had given the eulogy for Dion at the memorial service that General Alfred Gray, the Commandant of the Marine Corps, asked Shaun what he wanted to do next. Shaun knew exactly what he wanted to do: he wanted to go back to the Gulf. He wanted to pick up his fallen brother's arms and go to war. He wanted to hurt someone.

"I was hurting and I was angry," he said. "I was so angry sometimes, I couldn't even make myself cry about Dion being gone. I was just too angry."

A few days after Gray had left, he called Shaun to say he was sorry, but he wasn't going back to the Gulf. Once someone has fallen in combat, no member of his family can be sent to fight in the same theater. Gray said he would do his best to get Shaun any other assignment he wanted, but the Gulf was out of the question.

If he couldn't fight, Shaun thought, what was the point of being in the marines? The boyhood dream popped into his head. "You know, sir, I always wanted to go to the Naval Academy," he said. "Coming out of high school, my board scores weren't quite high enough to get me in."

Gray said he would see if there was anything he could do. A few days passed. Shaun was resting at home one afternoon when someone — he's not sure who because the house was still filled with friends and family — told him he had a phone call. He picked up the phone and heard a familiar-sounding voice.

"I hear," the voice said, "that you would like to go to the Naval Academy."

Stephenson found his own voice long enough to answer, "Yes, Mr. President, I would."

It was George Bush. Gray had explained Stephenson's situation to him and he had decided to get involved himself. "If that's what you want to do, young man," Bush told Stephenson, "then that's what you're going to do."

Dazed, Stephenson handed the phone to his father, who spoke to the president for several more minutes. Shortly after that, Stephenson was put in touch with Senator Orrin Hatch, who helped put together his formal application. It was Shaun, who had been out of high school for two years, who suggested the idea of prep school. "I just didn't think I would be ready for Navy academically," he said. "I needed some training."

Later, when Stephenson's story was told and retold by the media, Jim Stephenson became concerned that the public would get the idea that George Bush had stepped in and used the power of the presidency to get Shaun into Navy. That wasn't true. Stephenson's academic record was, in fact, better than many athletes who are accepted at Navy without presidential recommendations.

Before he went to NAPS, Shaun had to fulfill the final promise he had made to Dion. That last night at Pendleton, they had agreed to take care of each other if one of them should die in combat. Shaun had promised Dion — as Dion had promised Shaun — that he would take his ashes and, using the marine force-recon training that was so much a part of their lives, jump from an airplane and spread the ashes to the winds.

Before he made the jump, Shaun told his parents what Dion had wanted, to be certain they were OK with it. It was an emotional decision, but they agreed that if that was what Dion wanted, that's what Shaun should do. He flew to California, made arrangements to make the jump, and carried out his promise. He still has pictures, taken by a friend, of the moment when he let the ashes go.

SHAUN'S notion that he would have a tough time readjusting to academic life proved correct. He struggled when he got to NAPS. The military side of life there was a snap for him. But the academics, especially the math and science classes, were difficult. He finished the first semester with a 1.3 GPA.

But he had come too far to give up the dream. He stayed every day after class for EI — extra instruction — and gradually got the hang of what he was doing. His GPA second semester was 2.8, and he was voted the most improved student in the school by the professors.

Football didn't go as well. He broke two fingers early in the season, and that made it impossible for him to catch the ball. He ended up sitting out but played baseball in the spring and had a solid season. He also started dating Nikki Battaglia, another NAPster, who helped him deal with the rigors of the school and his emotions about Dion, which continued to rage inside him.

He had broken up with Sandy Goss after Dion's death, in part because he knew he wasn't madly in love with her, but more because he couldn't help but think about Dion whenever he spoke to her or thought about her.

He thought about Dion all the time, missed him terribly, and still wanted to be as much like him as possible. But he couldn't cry when he thought about him. The tears just wouldn't come. Once, when he was home on a break, he asked his father why he couldn't bring himself to cry for Dion.

"Because you know you have to be strong," his father said.

That wasn't it, Shaun knew that. His father had been strong for the whole family, but as time passed, Shaun sensed that the pain that his dad had bottled up inside was still there. Shaun felt the pain too. Sometimes, though, he felt guilty because he didn't feel more pain.

As it turned out, football provided an outlet for his pain and his anger. When he finally got to the Naval Academy in the summer of 1992, he asked George Chaump for the chance to walk-on to the football team even though the injury to his fingers had kept him from playing at NAPS. Chaump agreed and Stephenson made the team. No one practiced harder than he did. No one ran from one drill to the next the way he did. No one cared about the team more than he did. Even though he didn't get into any games that year, he became close with the other freshmen, including Thompson and Speed and Keith Galloway and Garrett Smith. He was convinced his chance to play would come the next fall.

Only it didn't. Chaump just didn't believe that a five-ten, 160-pound receiver could play Division I-A football no matter how hard he worked. Stephenson tried and tried to get the attention of the coaches, but it wasn't working. He couldn't stand the idea of another fall spent watching from the stands. Even though it killed him to leave his teammates, he decided to go out for the lightweight team, which has a 159-pound weight limit.

At both Army and Navy lightweight football is a respected nonrevenue sport. Stephenson quickly found a niche with the lightweights. He was a second team all-American as a sophomore; first team as a junior. He was the star on a team that won fifteen of the sixteen games he played. He loved playing with the lightweights, reveling in the competition and the camaraderie.

But he still missed his teammates. He cried in the stands in '93 after Bucchianeri's miss because he knew how torn up they would be. Nikki would get upset with him during games because he was so involved that he completely ignored her. "After the game, Nikki," he would tell her. She couldn't understand it.

He thought often about Dion and how he had died. Even though his father had insisted that the family would stand behind the government on the friendly fire issue, Shaun had questions. He needed to know more. He needed answers in order to deal with the anger he still felt. During the fall semester of his junior year, he asked permission to write a paper for a political science class on the topic of friendly fire in the Gulf War. The professor agreed.

The paper Shaun wrote was probably the best he had ever produced at Navy. The professor gave him a 96 for the effort, deducting a couple of points for grammatical errors. The paper was full of facts and questions and anger.

"There have been many incidents where families of friendly fire casualties were not informed of how their son or daughter had died," he wrote.

Instead, they were lied to by the government and the military and told the truth [only] by the men and women who were actually there. . . . I was told when I was less than 50 miles away from my brother in Iraq that he had been killed by Iraqi forces. My parents were told that he had been killed by Iraqi forces. A couple of weeks later, we were told about the possibility it had been friendly fire. Not until the driver of my brother's vehicle contacted us two months later were we told how he really died. By the end of March, 1991, the Marine field commanders were aware of all fourteen fatalities (at Khafji) but did not notify the families until August.

Haunting questions are raised throughout the paper:

In the Persian Gulf War, 35 of 145 killed and 72 of 467 wounded were victims of so-called friendly fire. The "fratricidal" casualty rate among U.S. forces was ten times as high as in any other battle in the 20th century. Why were there so many friendly fire incidents in the Gulf War and what have we done to prevent them? Why, being the most technologically advanced country in the world, can we not prevent the friendly fire casualty rate? These are the questions asked by countless families and countrymen who have lost loved ones and demand to hear an explanation for such tragedies.

Shaun found that some attempts to avert future tragedies were made after Khafji. In fact, a small electronics firm in New Hampshire was hired to come up with some kind of infrared beacon that might avert further accidents like the one that killed Dion. In twenty-four days the company designed, developed, tested, and produced three thousand such beacons. Two hundred of the beacons were used before the war was over.

This, Shaun wrote, raised more questions:

Why is it that a man can come up with a device that actually works in combat in a time span of 24 days and nothing was done during all the years of peacetime? Why should people who put their life in harm's way day in and day out be sacrificed for no reason? Why should families and friends suffer for the rest of their lives because a country is too ungrateful and too lazy to solve a problem that should have been solved a decade ago? These are questions that will never be answered for my family and many other families who still think of their son, daughter, brother or sister, every day that goes by.

He also noted that dealing with friendly fire has never been a high budgetary priority for the military. "The attitude taken in peacetime is that we can only afford so much, and we can fix it later. . . . We are the most advanced country in the world and all we can think of is money."

Shaun's conclusion was pragmatic, but emotional:

I have accepted the fact that in the fog of war, incidents like this will occur. Decisions must be made hastily in ground combat and, at times, innocent people will die. There is no getting around certain aspects of war; it is reality. But have we made the needed corrections for the scenarios when we have had the time? I personally feel that we have made progress, but further progress is needed. In the future, I see this progress being accomplished only by someone like myself who has personally suffered the loss of someone he truly loved and cared for.

It was all there, all the thoughts and ideas that had been bottled up inside for almost four years. Shaun showed the paper to his parents. Jim Stephenson wasn't happy with some of its antigovernment tone, but he understood what Shaun was saying and why he needed to say it. By now, Jim Stephenson was starting to show some of the pain he had bottled up in order to be strong. Shaun saw his father's pain, felt it too, and, finally, understood that the two of them had felt every single bit of the loss that his mother had felt. They had just dealt with it differently.

"It would really help me, and I think my dad too," he said, "if someday in the future I could work on helping to find ways to prevent friendly fire incidents in the future. I honestly believe I would work a lot harder at it than someone who is doing it just because it's his job."

*     *     *

TWO weeks after he had turned in his friendly fire paper, Stephenson heard that Chaump had been fired. His first thought was one of relief, for his friends, who he knew had suffered the past two seasons. His second thought was "This is my chance." He went to see Satan — Phil Emery — whom he had worked out with occasionally throughout his time at Navy. He told him he wanted a chance to play under the new coaching staff. Satan immediately made him a part of the team's off-season training program, and when spring ball rolled around Stephenson was with the team, getting his chance.

Weatherbie and his staff were amazed when they saw Stephenson. How, they wondered, could this kid have gone unused for three years? He had excellent speed — 4.5 seconds in the 40-yard dash — he was tough, he ran every pattern the way he was supposed to, and he had the best hands on the team. By the time the spring game rolled around, Stephenson had moved up to number one on the depth chart as wide receiver, ahead of players who had played and started in the past.

In the spring game, playing with a soft cast on a broken hand, he caught a 26-yard touchdown pass and was awarded the Admiral William P. Mack Award as the most improved player of the spring. His mom flew in for the game, and when it was over, Shaun got his first taste of media attention. All three papers that regularly cover Navy — the *Annapolis Evening Capital,* the *Baltimore Sun,* and the *Washington Post* — had reporters at the Blue-Gold game. All three reporters wanted to talk to one player: Shaun Stephenson.

That was fine with Stephenson. He understood his story was unique. "All I want is to have the chance to *earn* the recognition," he said later. "I've waited a long time for this season. It's my last chance. My only chance. I can't wait."

His wait was almost over as August became September and the heat began to abate. The night of September 1 was glorious in Annapolis, warm but not uncomfortable, with a breeze coming in off the Chesapeake Bay. Navy's last preseason scrimmage was almost over when Stephenson went back to return a punt. The season was eight days away. Rick Reilly had flown in for the scrimmage and to talk to Stephenson for the piece he was writing on him for *Sports Illustrated.*

Stephenson caught Brian Schrum's punt, took a couple of steps left, then tried to cut back. As he did, he was hit and he felt pain jolt through his left knee. He went down, in pain, but beyond that, frightened. "Just don't let it be anything serious," he thought.

Red Romo, who has been Navy's trainer for so long (forty years) that the new training room was named after him later that fall, and his assistant, Rob Lawton, came out to take a look. As soon as they felt the knee and saw Stephenson's pained reaction, they called for Ed McDevitt, the team doctor. They were all fairly certain the injury wasn't just a bruise. The X rays confirmed their diagnosis: Stephenson had torn the anterior cruciate ligament. The ACL has become football's most common knee injury. Once upon a time, an ACL injury meant a year off at best, a career ended at worst. But modern science has come a long way. In fact, ACL injuries don't always need surgery nowadays. McDevitt's analysis when he saw the X rays was that surgery wasn't needed. Give it a month of rest and rehab, he told Stephenson, and you should be OK.

A month! He didn't have a month or, for that matter, a week. This was his one and only chance to play football for Navy. A month would mean missing at least three games. McDevitt knew how much Stephenson wanted to play. Everyone did. But they also knew that if he forced matters, tried to come back too fast, he would only make matters worse.

Stephenson called his parents, who had made plans to fly to Dallas for the opener. He told them he wouldn't be on the trip. But he forced himself to be upbeat. "I've waited this long," he said. "I can wait a couple weeks more."

THERE would be no waiting for the rest of the team. On the morning of September 8, eight months to the day after their first meeting with Weatherbie, the sixty-five players on the travel squad for the trip to SMU gathered in the lobby of Bancroft Hall for their pretrip inspection.

Bancroft is the world's largest college dormitory, a huge building that snakes off in different directions, housing four thousand midshipmen on five floors. The public nickname for Bancroft is "Mother B." Among the midshipmen it is known as "Mother Bitch," because life there often is.

This, though, was one of the days that the football players looked forward to. The preseason work was over, it was a gorgeous day outside, and they would be leaving the academy behind for two days to play a football game. They were undefeated. Outside, the rest of the brigade gathered for the mandatory fun part of the day, the send-off.

The band struck up "Anchors Aweigh" and the players and coaches came out on the steps leading to T-Court. Most football coaches dread pep rallies; Weatherbie loved them. As soon as he was introduced, he started windmilling his arms, screaming, "Come on, let's go!" into the microphone. The mids, who had become so accustomed to the studiously low-key Chaump, loved his enthusiasm.

"Everyone's been wishing me luck around here all week," Weatherbie told the crowd. "Well, I like to say that luck is when preparation meets opportunity. We've prepared for this. Now comes our opportunity!"

The players had heard this before; it was one of Weatherbie's many sayings. That was fine, though, it seemed to stir the mids up.

Of course a Navy send-off isn't a Navy send-off unless the brass gets its chance to speak. Larson was away on a trip — he would join the team in Dallas — so the commandant and deputy commandant told the brigade how great it was that everyone at Navy was now united behind the football team.

Certainly, the brigade was a lot more behind the football team than it had been before Larson's return. Just as certainly the mids were waiting to see if things would really be different under the new regime. Still, every once in a while, the old feelings surfaced.

Weatherbie had campaigned most of the spring and summer to get his players excused from their fifth period classes on the Fridays before home games. Fifth period was the first period after lunch and got out at 2:20. If they were excused from the class, they would be able to come over to Ricketts right after lunch and rest from noon until five o'clock when they left for the hotel. Weatherbie was convinced the extra rest was vital at a school where players were often sleep-starved during the season. It was a concession Fisher DeBerry had been able to get at Air Force when Weatherbie was coaching there.

When word got out among the faculty that this was being considered, it did not go over well. The football players already missed their classes on the five Fridays that they traveled. If they missed fifth period for six more Fridays, that would mean eleven classes missed. At Navy, that's a lot. When Larson held his annual fall meeting with the brigade and faculty, one of the professors who had been told by a football player that he would be missing home game Friday fifth periods asked Larson if it was true that this was going to be allowed.

Larson said no, it was only being considered. Two days later it was no longer being considered. The answer was no. Weatherbie was upset with his players for announcing to their professors that this was going to happen before it had been cleared. Any chance of it happening had gone by the boards the minute it had been brought up in the admiral's meeting.

"Miscommunication," Weatherbie said later. "We didn't handle it well at our end. And when I thought about it later on, it probably *was* too much class for them to miss."

There was no fifth period for anyone the day before the SMU game. The team's Delta charter was in the air somewhere over the Midwest when fifth period began. It was hot and humid when the plane landed in Dallas. The team went straight to the Cotton Bowl for a brief practice.

SMU's football program had both a proud and an embarrassing history. Some of football's most glamorous names — Doak Walker, Kyle Rote, Raymond Berry, Eric Dickerson, to name a few — had come out of SMU. But the Mustangs had also been the first and only program shut down by the NCAA for multiple rules violations. In 1987 and 1988, SMU had not played any football, having received "the death penalty" from the NCAA after a second major scandal had been uncovered in a five-year period.

The sport had been revived in 1989, but on a much more low-key basis. Instead of playing home games in the 72,000 seat Cotton Bowl, SMU played on campus, in 20,000 seat Ownby Stadium. There had been some embarrassing losses since the revival (95–21 to Houston the first year), and the Mustangs had won more than two games only once in six years, going 5–6 in 1992. Now, though, the school had decided it was time to move back to the Cotton Bowl even though it was unlikely to fill the old stadium for any game, except perhaps when Texas came to town and the place would be filled with Longhorn fans.

They had gotten off to a good start the previous week, upsetting Arkansas 17–14 in the opener. But they had lost their best player, quarterback Ramon Flanigan, to a knee injury late in the game. Flanigan was a legitimate all-America candidate who had run amok on Navy two years earlier in Annapolis. With Flanigan out, the Mustangs would be just as inexperienced at quarterback as the Midshipmen were. When Weatherbie saw SMU on tape his analysis was succinct: "They're pretty good," he said. "They're also beatable."

The Cotton Bowl is located in the middle of the Texas state fairgrounds and, as the Navy buses inched through Friday afternoon traffic, Clint Bruce, who had grown up in nearby Garland, sat in the back of the bus carrying the defense and pointed out landmarks to his teammates.

In many ways, Bruce was the classic Navy football player. At six feet, 235, he was undersized for a linebacker, but he was an absolutely ferocious, driven player on the field, an emotional leader even though he was just beginning his junior year.

Earlier in the week, Bruce had gone out to a Hechinger's hardware store and purchased a twenty-five-pound, four-foot hammer that he had brought along on the trip. He had decided that each week, the defense should pass out a "hammer" award to the player who came up with the biggest hit. The winner of the hammer would have the privilege of carrying the hammer around the Yard and to and from the game the next week. For the opener, Bruce had designated himself to carry the hammer.

While there was no doubting Bruce's intensity on the football field — when the other team took the field, Bruce always stood at the far end of the sideline watching them, taking deep breaths, his fists opening and closing, saying repeatedly, almost under his breath, "Come on, come on, let's get going, let's get going" — he was as bright and entertaining as anyone you were likely to meet away from the field.

As the bus rolled past the Dallas theater district, he turned to Thompson, sitting next to him, and said, "Have you ever seen *Miss Saigon*?" When Thompson said he hadn't, Bruce told him about the Broadway musical, explaining to him the similarity in the story line between it and the famous opera *Madame Butterfly*.

Traveling with a military academy football team wasn't quite the same as traveling with other football teams. Not only did tutors routinely make the trips, but players brought books with them. They also read newspapers. At dinner that night, Garrett Smith, Bryce Minamyer, and center Brian Dreschler got into a lengthy conversation about AIDS research.

In a football season that would end with Northwestern being toasted — with good reason — for being able to win games with players who knew how to read and write, both Army and Navy routinely used players who could do those things. Those were the only kind they had.

Weatherbie, always looking for slogans, had gotten new blue-and-gold T-shirts made up for the players to wear on the road. On the front, the shirt said, "Yard Dawgs." On the back it said, "It's not the size of the dog in the fight; it's the size of the fight in the dog."

Not exactly original, but fitting.

They went through their paces in the empty Cotton Bowl, the giant state fair cowboy and the huge Texas star Ferris wheel both looming over the stadium entrance, no more than two hundred yards from the locker room doors. When the workout was over, Weatherbie gathered the team at midfield.

"I want to tell you what I see here, guys," he said. "I see a field that's one hundred yards long and fifty-three yards wide. It's no different than any field any of us have ever been on. The game's all mental now. If you play the way you can, we'll have a lot of fun out here tomorrow night."

That brought up another Weatherbie saying: "How do we spell fun?"

"W-I-N."

It had been a while since there had been very much fun at Navy.


THE coaches let them sleep until 9:30 the next morning since kickoff wasn't until 7 P.M. Football players and coaches hate night games. It means sitting around the hotel all day, killing time, getting nervous, wishing you were already out there playing. Watching afternoon games on TV just gets you more keyed up. Navy's first four games were at night. No one on the team was thrilled about that.

To break up the morning, Weatherbie brought Roger Staubach in to talk to the team after breakfast. Staubach was the most famous midshipman of them all, not only because he had won the Heisman Trophy in 1963 but because he had gone on, after his stint in the Navy, to star for the Dallas Cowboys, leading them into four Super Bowls, winning two of them.

Staubach was now a very successful businessman based in Dallas. He was fifty-two but still trim and in good enough shape to play pickup basketball several times a week. He spoke to the team quietly, without the usual rah-rah about kicking people's butts. It wasn't necessary. Staubach's record gave him authority; the way he carried himself added to it.

"I know you guys have been through a lot of ups and downs at the academy," he said. "Part of the Navy experience is learning perseverance" — he paused — "whether you want to learn it or not."

That drew a laugh. So did another story he told about an on-field fight the Cowboys had been involved in. "The first thing I did was try to find their punter," he said. Everyone hooted at that. Even Brian Schrum.

"Just remember one thing," he said in closing. "Your teammates should be the most important people in your lives outside of your families. You're individuals, yes, but you need one another to succeed tonight and the rest of the season."

They liked that. When Andrew Thompson wrote about it in his journal, his closing comment was, "Unity. That's what this is about. It was when he [Staubach] played. It is now."

Football coaches and players preaching unity is hardly a new thought. But in the case of the twenty-one remaining Navy seniors, it had meaning. They had been through so many sad times together in the last three years that staying together had been the only thing that kept them moving forward.

The day passed slowly. Most of the players turned on ESPN at noon and watched Air Force, which had opened the season a week earlier with an impressive victory over Brigham Young, crush Wyoming. More often than not, players at Navy either root for Army or don't care very much whether the Cadets win or lose. The same is true at Army when it comes to Navy. But both Army and Navy *always* root for Air Force to lose. All those years of having their faces rubbed in the dirt by the Zoomies has left scars.

The offense and the defense had their final meetings three hours before kickoff. Bumpas went over the four keys to winning the game on defense:

- No foolish penalties.
- Play with CONTROLLED fury — no mental errors.
- Eliminate big plays. Do NOT let them RUN the football into the end zone.
- Don't flinch.

His final words were direct: "Make them want to give up the football, guys. Get after their ass on every play."

IN the offensive room, Paul Johnson was far more low-key. Playing defense is much more about getting whipped into an emotional frenzy than playing offense is. Offense is almost scientific; the linemen must know their blocking techniques and remember their schemes. The so-called "skill" position players need finesse and quickness at least as much, usually more, than they need power.

"This football team has no identity right now," Johnson said. "I think that's exciting. You won't win this game on the first play. Just do what we do in practice every day. It's no different except you don't know the guys on the other side of the ball. You all have a special bond and camaraderie here. The only ones you're responsible to tonight are your teammates."

He finished with a story about an Indian medicine man who was reputed to know everything. One day a young "smart-ass" decided to test him. He scooped up a bird, clasped it in his hands, and said to the medicine man, "Is the bird dead or alive?" The medicine man looked at him and said, "Young man, the bird is in your hands."

Johnson clasped his hands together. "The game, fellas, is in your hands."

When Johnson and Bumpas were finished, it was Weatherbie's turn with both units now in the same room. He started with a lengthy prayer that included thanks to God for the day, for the game of football, and for the plan He had for this evening and for the football team. As was often the case Weatherbie was very specific in his requests: "Lord, give us the ability to focus until the clock hits zero, zero, zero." He finished, as he always did: "In your name we pray, in your name we play."

Then it was final review: first the kicking game, then the offense, then the defense. Weatherbie would go through essentially the same speech eleven times before the season was over. He is a believer in repeating things time after time so they become habit.

"We must execute the five dos of the kicking game," he said. Sometimes, he asked the players for them. On this day, he listed them:

- DO stay onside.
- DO stay off the kicker.
- DO block above the waist.
- DO block in front of the body.
- DO catch all balls.

"Offense: It's our football, men. We can't play without it. Remember, low man wins" — a reference to getting underneath the defender when blocking. "We will move the football on this team. They won't be ready for our speed.

"Defense: We will win this game in the trenches. Do your job on every play. Don't worry about anyone else's job. Wrap up on every play. Grab cloth and hold on. Knock them on their butts, help them up, and knock them on their butts again."

And finally, to everyone: "You do not have to play a perfect game to beat SMU, men. The good Lord didn't make anyone in this room perfect. Don't go out and win the game in warm-ups. Get loose and ready, but that's all. If you're tired, let us know, we'll get someone else in there for you. When the game is over, you should have nothing left — nothing.

"Let's go turn it loose — and have fun. How do we spell fun?"

"W-I-N."

The speech was not very different from the pregame speeches being delivered that day and every Saturday all over the country. But for this team, the way Weatherbie delivered it, his face full of fire and eagerness, pacing up and down like a caged animal ready to bust loose and get after someone, was important. They needed someone who came to the game as ready to play as they were. They had missed that earlier in their careers. The message didn't matter as much as the delivery. They knew what had to be done; what they needed more than anything was confidence in their ability to do it.

AS luck would have it, Navy's bus arrived at the stadium at almost the exact same moment as SMU's. The Cotton Bowl locker rooms were directly across from one another at the top of the ramp leading to the field. The players piled off the buses, each side eyeing the other, sizing it up.

The contrast was striking. The Navy players were dressed identically: summer dress whites, complete with ties and hats. The SMU players were dressed in normal hot weather college gear: shorts and T-shirts, caps turned backwards, earrings dangling. Navy's footwear was black shoes, polished to a perfect shine. SMU's ranged from flip-flops to more fashionable sandals to, in the case of the serious fashion-plates, Nikes or Reeboks.

It was a striking reminder to the players of Tommy Raye's favorite saying: "Our way of life against theirs." Raye was the linebacker coach, and if Clint Bruce was the prototype let's-kick-some-butt linebacker, Raye was the prototype let's-really-kick-some-butt linebacker coach. He was thirty-two, another of the staff's Southerners, a linebacker himself at Georgia Southern before spending two years in the army. He had then coached at Auburn and Texas Christian before signing on with Weatherbie.

Raye loved the intensity of football. He loved the violence, the anger, the idea that only one team can be left standing at the end of the game. When he arrived at Navy, he realized quickly that it was very different from the places where he had been in the past. Midshipmen didn't live and die to play football the way a lot of football players did in the South. That didn't mean they weren't devoted to the game, didn't love to compete. But it was different; it was *a different way of life*. To play at Navy, you had to believe wholly in that way of life, in what the academy — flawed though everyone knew it to be — stood for. And so it became a mantra, first for Raye, then for other coaches, then for the players: "our way of life against theirs."

It was a rallying cry that would fit at least nine weeks of the season — ten if you considered the fact that the midshipmen referred to Air Force as the country club academy.

Air Force wasn't on anyone's mind at this stage. Opening night jitters were now in full force, for everyone. When the officials came into the locker room an hour before kickoff to introduce themselves to Weatherbie and ask if there were any trick plays they needed to be aware of, they asked him what numbers the Navy captains wore. Weatherbie blanked on Thompson's 32 and Smith's 63.

Sitting inside the tiny coaches' locker room, the assistants noticed their boss's nervousness. "Hell, I'm nervous too," Johnson said. "You realize last night was the first time Chris McCoy ever stayed in a hotel room?"

"Yeah," Gene McKeehan put in, "and he's starting."

McCoy had emerged during preseason as the clear choice to start at quarterback. He was quicker than Ben Fay and had more speed. What's more, bringing Fay, the better passer, off the bench if the offense wasn't moving made more sense than bringing in the better runner.

The players were rattled too. In no sport do the athletes put in more time with less chances to test themselves than in football. Players nowadays spend eleven months a year either practicing or lifting weights or conditioning themselves to play eleven games. That means every game is a very big deal. Now, having put in eight months of work, with the hour at hand the Navy players felt the pressure building. By the time they took the field to warm up, they all looked as if they should be lying on a psychiatrist's couch.

No one could catch a pass or remember a snap count or make simple cuts that they normally made in their sleep. Weatherbie liked to end the warm-up by lining the whole team up and punting the ball to a lone returner, who would make the catch and sprint toward one end zone while everyone else raced right at him, screaming and yapping, heading in the direction of the locker room. When Schrum sailed his punt to Matt Scornavacchi, everyone charged at Scornavacchi screaming.

He dropped the ball.

"I was thinking we ought to line everybody up and scrimmage for ten minutes," Raye said. "Maybe that would shake something loose."

They walked up the tunnel to the locker room twenty minutes before kickoff, no one daring to glance to the right, where the SMU players were making the same walk.

There are few things in the world quieter than a football locker room in the final minutes before kickoff. The offense sits on one side of the room, the defense on the other. Everyone stares at the wall or at the floor or into space. Occasionally, someone will yell something, mostly because their nerves are so tight they have to let something out.

As the Mids waited, Omar Nelson, the starting fullback, looked up several times and said, "I'm sick and tired of f------ losing! I didn't come here to be a loser! No way! It's our time now, our time!"

His pal, A-back Patrick McGrew, chipped in: "Kick their butts from the start, right from the start!"

And from various corners of the room: "Our way of life against theirs!"

Mostly, though, there was silence during the fifteen-minute wait for Weatherbie to come in and say a final word. There is fear in a football locker room before kickoff, the sort that is so palpable you can almost reach out and touch it. The sport's inherently violent nature and the long, emotional buildup to each game make it that way. Unspoken is a simple fact: there is going to be pain involved in the playing of the game. Not only is the potential for serious injury always there, but each hit beats up each player's body a little bit more. Most of the time, you will jump up and run back to the huddle. But after four quarters, after eleven games, after a dozen years, the hits add up and you look in the mirror at twenty-one and say, "Boy do I feel old."

Everyone wants to get on the field and get the first hit out of the way. Everyone wants to get back to the locker room in one piece. Everyone wants all the work to have meaning.

Five minutes before kickoff, Weatherbie walked back into the room. They prayed again, Weatherbie asking both for "fanatical effort" and a game in which no one was injured. Then he acknowledged the unlikeliness that his second request would be granted. "Those that are hurt, Lord, please lay your healing hand upon them."

As soon as he said "Amen," Weatherbie jumped on a chair in the middle of the room. He had nothing new to tell them: "Have fun out there . . . turn it loose . . . How do we spell fun? . . . LET'S GO OUT THERE AND KICK THEIR TAILS!"

They were ready now. They charged down the tunnel into the Texas twilight. It was a warm evening and a crowd of 20,232 filled up less than a third of the Cotton Bowl. The 2,000 Navy fans seemed to be just as loud as the 18,000 SMU fans.

Garrett Smith called heads on the coin toss and it came up heads. Smith and Thompson, as instructed, deferred, meaning Navy would get the ball to start the second half.

Bumpas had figured that without Flanigan, SMU would try to establish a running game early. The SMU coaches had figured he would figure that, and backup quarterback Chris James came out throwing deep — on the first play. He had DeAndrea Robinson open, but Robinson, proving that jitters go both ways, dropped the ball after it hit him right on the numbers.

The season was only fourteen seconds old and already the sun had shone on the Midshipmen.

The defense held, SMU punted, and Chris McCoy promptly picked up 16 yards on his first varsity play from scrimmage. The teams exchanged punts for most of the first quarter until Johnson began to open the Navy offense up on the Mids' third possession. On first down, McCoy faked the dive handoff to Nelson and found Rashad Smith wide open for a gain of 32 yards. Three plays later, the ball was on the SMU 21. Again, McCoy faked the handoff. Patrick McGrew was wide open in the end zone. But the ball fluttered just a bit and it bounced off McGrew's hands.

A collective *aaargh!* went up on the Navy sideline. Chances like that could not be wasted. The ball should have been caught. Even as everyone was shaking their head, McCoy was taking the next snap. He sprinted right, beat the defense to the corner, and was gone. Touchdown! Covarrubias kicked the extra point and, with 57 seconds left in the first quarter of the Charlie Weatherbie era, Navy led 7–0.

SMU responded with its first sustained drive of the game, but with the Mustangs on the Navy 24, cornerback Sean Andrews made a leaping interception in the end zone to end the threat. Then, before the celebration for Andrews had ended, McCoy took off again, breaking tackles, cruising 59 yards. A penalty stopped the drive, but Covarrubias coolly kicked a 21-yard field goal and it was 10–0.

Again, SMU pieced together a march into Navy territory. This time, at the 35, Joe Speed read a screen pass perfectly and slammed receiver Kevin Thornal for a five-yard loss. Then, when James tried to throw deep for Thornal, Thompson broke the play up. SMU punted, a perfect pooch kick that was downed at the four yard line.

All Navy wanted to do was pick up at least one first down to give Schrum room to kick the ball downfield. It didn't work out that way. Nelson picked up three, then three more. McCoy ran the option for 13. First down at the 23. A sigh of relief from everyone. While they were sighing, McCoy was back at it. He started left, broke a tackle, cut back, broke another tackle, then another, and was off. This time it was 69 yards to the SMU eight. The coaches had to call time to give McCoy a chance to catch his breath. He looked as if he were about to pass out in the heat.

Of course the SMU defense wasn't feeling very well either. Knowing that, Johnson sent Nelson pounding straight up the middle. He picked up five. Nelson again — touchdown. It was 17–0, Navy. They had gone 96 yards in six plays.

SMU was shell-shocked. When the half ended, the Navy players charged up the ramp, the SMU players trudged, heads down. A year ago at halftime of their opener, the Mids had *trailed* 42–0. They had swung the score by 59 points. McCoy had already rushed for 253 yards — 35 more than Monty Williams had produced for the *season* as the team's leading rusher in '94.

Naturally, the coaches were uptight. It couldn't possibly be this easy. SMU would come out firing in the second half. Weatherbie gathered the coaches in their locker room. "We can't play much better than that," he said. "I'll tell you what, if we can score on the first possession, they might just quit."

Everyone agreed. They went out to talk to their players, each position coach taking his players into a corner. Raye's voice could be heard all over the locker room as he demanded even more from the linebackers. There wasn't much Johnson could say to McCoy except "Keep it up." One could only imagine what McCoy might have done if he had spent *two* nights in a hotel room.

As it turned out, Weatherbie's prediction was right. With SMU putting everyone in Texas on the line of scrimmage to stop McCoy, he dropped back on the third play of the half and found Cory Schemm wide open for a 41-yard pickup. On the next play, from the SMU 25, McCoy started right, and as the defense closed on him, he pitched the ball perfectly to McGrew, who was gone — untouched — into the end zone. It had taken all of 91 seconds to score again.

SMU did block Covarrubias's extra point and returned it all the way to the other end zone for a two-point blocked conversion. But that was all for the Mustangs. The Navy defense was in complete command. Fernando Harris sacked James to end one series; Mark Hammond stripped him on the next one and Clint Bruce recovered at the SMU 21. That set up a 32-yard Covarrubias field goal. Andrews got a second interception and McCoy tossed a perfect shovel pass to McGrew for another touchdown. J. D. McBryde picked up another interception.

It was 33–2 and Weatherbie was able to empty the bench. The fourth quarter was little more than a Navy celebration. By the final minutes, Secretary of the Navy Dalton had come out of the stands, grabbed a cheerleader's megaphone, and started leading cheers. "Give me an 'N'! . . ."

When the clock finally hit 0:00, the Mids poured onto the field, first to shake hands with the SMU players, then to hug one another in disbelief, relief, and joy. They had played an almost perfect game. They had dominated in every way, forcing five turnovers, giving up none. McCoy finished with 273 yards rushing and 398 yards in total offense, both Navy records. In all, the team rushed for 424 yards — 368 more than it had averaged per game the previous season and only 189 less than it had produced in all 11 games total.

When they had finished celebrating, they stood in front of their cheering section and belted out "Blue and Gold," growing louder with each line. Thompson, who had made eight tackles, kept shaking his head over and over, saying, "I can't believe it. I waited four years to feel like this."

Inside the locker room, they sang an ear-splitting version of "Anchors Aweigh" and then, when Weatherbie was finished, they pushed the commandant, the Supe, and finally Dalton onto an equipment trunk so they could each give a speech. No one minded listening now.

"You started the season in the Cotton Bowl and you're going to finish it in another bowl!" Dalton told them.

"Sec, Sec, Sec!" they screamed.

As it turned out, Weatherbie had been right all along. Fun *was* spelled W-I-N.

IT was 4:30 in the morning by the time the buses reached T-Court. No one had slept on the rollicking plane ride home. They hadn't even complained when the pilots had come on the PA to congratulate them and mention that they were Air Force graduates.

"Damn Zoomies, we'll get you later!" they all screamed.

The "spontaneous" pep rally probably would have taken place even without the fire alarms and the announcements that kept poor Ryan Bucchianeri up all night. The brigade was delirious. Thompson, normally the reticent public speaker, grabbed a microphone and yelled, "We went down to Texas and we kicked their ever-loving ass!"

Thompson heard later in the week that the brass hadn't been thrilled with his choice of words, but what the hell! It was 4:30 in the morning and they were all high on winning and, the fact was, they *had* kicked SMU's ever-loving ass.

No one wanted to go to bed. Everyone right up to the Supe had to speak. It was almost 5 o'clock by the time T-Court started to clear. Sunrise was less than two hours away. There was no question that when it rose, it would be shining very brightly on the Midshipmen.

NAVY'S victory over SMU, combined with Air Force's win over Wyoming and Army's rout of Lehigh, made that Saturday the first in eight years in which all three service academies had won on the same day.

A week later, it all turned around. Army lost the heartbreaker to Duke. Air Force was shocked, 30–6, by Northwestern, a score that became less shocking as Northwestern's remarkable season unfolded. And Navy, after a week of euphoria, lost at Rutgers, 27–17.

What was most disappointing about the Navy loss was that the game was eminently winnable. The coaches had told the players all week that Rutgers had loads of good athletes but not good football players. In other words: they would make mistakes. They had turned the ball over seven times the previous week; there was no reason why they wouldn't do it again.

Rutgers jumped to a 14–0 lead, but even on the road this Navy team didn't believe it was in trouble. One victory had given the players a kind of confidence they hadn't had in years. They came back in the second quarter to tie it at fourteen, then, after a late Rutgers field goal, they moved the ball to the Rutgers 29 in just 34 seconds and Covarrubias came on to bomb a 47-yard field goal as time ran out. It was 17–17 at the half.

Everyone in the Navy locker room was convinced they now had control of the game. Johnson again told the offense that a good opening drive would make Rutgers spit the bit. "They're wanting to give up," he said. "Just give them a reason to do it."

They almost did. They took the opening kickoff straight down the field to the Rutgers 28, but on a third-and-three, McCoy was sacked for a 10-yard loss. The Scarlet Knights began breathing again. Then the Navy coaches made a mistake. After the defense had forced a punt, Rutgers was called for illegal procedure, meaning Navy — which had the ball at its own 29 after getting zero yards on the return — could force a rekick. But Weatherbie and the assistants, talking back and forth on the headsets, got confused and sent the wrong signal into the players.

"We wanted to accept, but somehow the message sent out there was to decline," Weatherbie said later. "I was going back and forth between headsets and I never made a decision that was clear enough."

Maybe the offense was a little surprised to be on the field. Maybe everyone wasn't quite prepared. Or maybe Rutgers just made a good play. In any event, on the first play from scrimmage after turning down the penalty, McCoy was hit by defensive end Charles Woolridge and fumbled. Woolridge jumped on it and, just like that, Rutgers had the ball at the Navy 26, the somnambulent crowd came into the game, and everything had turned around.

It was Navy's first turnover of the season and it hurt. Three plays after the fumble, quarterback Ray Lucas found tight end Marco Battaglia, the Knights' best player, over the middle on a post pattern. Battaglia was a step behind Joe Speed and caught the ball in stride on the goal line. Touchdown.

Navy never threatened again. A late field goal salted the game away and Rutgers, a team that would finish the season 3–8 and see its coaching staff fired, had won a game that the Mids had been one play, perhaps two, away from controlling.

Ifs and buts.

Weatherbie's message in the tiny visitors' locker room was simple. "Remember this feeling, guys. It hurts. It should hurt. That game was there. Let's learn from this."

Thompson's analysis in his journal was more succinct: "Back to earth," he wrote.

# 9

# THE FAT MEN

AT Army, they had been on terra firma all fall. Beating Lehigh was expected and the Duke loss was crushing. But even though they had lost the game — with a little help from the officials — the Cadets had come away feeling good about themselves. Just as Navy had come a long way from the one-sided routs that had dominated most of their '94 season, the Cadets of '95 were a far cry from the team that had been destroyed by Duke and Boston College and had lost to Temple and Boston University.

They were not about to get down on themselves because of one tough-to-take loss. And if by some chance any of them did start to sulk or pout, they knew they would be in trouble. They would have to answer to the Fat Men.

The Fat Men were the heart and soul of this Army team. There was no doubting Cantelupe's leadership on the defense or the importance of McAda to the offense. The junior linebackers, Ben Kotwica and Stephen King, were becoming more of a force each week, and tight end Ron Leshinski was perhaps the best pure football player on the team.

But all of them would agree that everything about Army football was embodied (no pun intended) in the Fat Men.

The Fat Men were Fat JD, Top, Bru, and Slimsy. To the rest of the world Fat JD was Joel Davis, Top was Eddie Stover, Bru was Bill Blair, and Slimsy was Mike Wells. All four were seniors. Davis and

Stover had been starters since their sophomore seasons, Blair had become a starter as a junior, and Wells had been moved from center to
left tackle and become a starter as a senior.

Wells was the ringer in the group because he didn't actually meet
the physical requirements of the Fat Men's Club. On his heaviest day
he was six four and 262 pounds, and in truth there wasn't an ounce
of fat on him — thus the name Slimsy.

"But being fat," explained Stover, the group's philosopher, "is a
state of mind. That's why we let Slimsy in."

For Stover, Blair, and Davis, fat was much more than a state of
mind. In fact, Stover had been forced to sit out spring practice because
he couldn't complete the required obstacle course run that every cadet
must complete each spring. Blair was six two, 280 and took considerable ribbing from his teammates for the stretch marks on his stomach.
"They're alligator bites," he insisted. Stover was six three, 290 and
could easily get over 300 after a long weekend of eating. And Davis,
who had arrived at the prep school four years earlier weighing 223
pounds, was six four, 305 and still a growing boy.

The Fat Men had two passions in life: football and food. They were
bonded by those passions. Almost everything they did was devoted
to the pursuit of better football and more food. Stover had memorized
the phone number of every restaurant within twenty miles of West
Point that had delivery service. He also knew what hours they were
open and how late you could get delivery or carryout.

Davis and Stover had come up with the idea to formalize the notion
of Fat into a club the previous spring. They had been at Davis's house
in Binghamton for a long weekend of eating when the idea for hats
had come up. The next day, they had them made: a large F in the
middle with M and C on either side.

At first, it was just Davis, Stover, and Blair. When it was decided
to expand the club to include the entire offensive line, Davis, Stover,
and Blair declared themselves FMC Chiefs. Wells was a kind of sub-
chief and junior Kyle Scott, the starting center, was acknowledged,
though not made a part of the power scheme.

During preseason, every Thursday night was reserved for a Fat
Fest, usually held in one of the chiefs' rooms. In order to become part
of the club, the plebe offensive linemen were required to provide the

food, usually huge amounts of pizza, subs, sandwiches, and anything else that would fit into the room. To earn a hat, new members had to perform a "Feat of Fat," which consisted of eating a remarkable amount of food, usually very quickly. If you got sick, the Feat didn't count. Part of the mentality of fatness was the notion that the food went to your bulk.

The Fat Men also had their top ten rules:

1. FMC Salute — When greeting another member of the FMC turn the top of your trousers over with your belt facing in, since this is what usually occurs when an FM stands anyway. Bill Blair can demonstrate this salute. Note: Should not be done when in [military] uniform or in the presence of non-members.
2. NEVER eat any food labeled low-fat, diet, reduced-calorie, lite, or fat-free.
3. NEVER lie on a beach by the ocean unattended because people wearing "Save the Whales" T-shirts will keep dragging you back into the ocean.
4. NEVER go to restaurants where seats are permanently attached to the tables.
5. NEVER fill the bathtub more than half full.
6. If you are swimming and hear someone yell, "Thar She Blows," get out of the water immediately.
7. It is considered bad manners for a member to sit at the salad bar.
8. If someone tells you that you're fat, just tell them that you're not fat, that your muscles are just resting.
9. If you are a male member, be prepared to explain to girlfriends that penis size is not necessarily in proportion to body size.
10. All members must make it their #1 goal to BEAT NAVY, BEAT NAVY, BEAT NAVY . . .

Although the Fat Men took considerable ribbing from their teammates, there was no doubting the respect everyone had for them. No one worked harder in practice or in the weight room than the Fat Men.

No one cared more about winning. The fact that Davis, the spiritual leader of the group, had been elected offensive captain was a clear sign of how the rest of the team felt about the FMC.

Davis was the third member of his family to play football at West Point. His oldest brother, Ted, had graduated from the academy in 1974, when Joel was one. Ted was the oldest of seven children. He had been followed by four girls and then Dan and Joel. Dan was two years older than Joel and had also played at Army. In fact, he had been the defensive captain of the '92 team.

Joel had known for most of his boyhood that he wanted to attend West Point. He can remember the night when his mother pulled out the scrapbook from Ted's playing days and explained to him what West Point was and how special it was to go to school there. "From that point on, I was pretty much hooked," he said. "Even before football became a big factor in my life."

Football wasn't that big a factor in his life until the summer before his junior year in high school. As a freshman he was, by his own description, "skinny and weak." He played on the JV team and didn't even start. The next year he made the varsity and was a backup tight end. The starter was Dan. The football bug bit him when colleges began recruiting Dan.

"I looked at myself in the mirror that spring and I was six three, 176 pounds and I was still weak and skinny. I wanted to be recruited the way Dan had. I wanted people to come to my house and ask me to go to their school. I knew I couldn't do it unless I got bigger."

Dan had been recruited fairly heavily as a senior and had almost gone to Navy. He liked the campus when he visited and, knowing Army ran the wishbone, figured he would get the chance to catch a lot more passes as a tight end in Navy's pass-oriented offense. He gave the Navy coaches a verbal commitment, then came home and told his mother he was going to Navy.

That was fine with Elizabeth Davis. She had raised Dan and Joel on her own after she and her husband had divorced when Dan was nine and Joel was seven. If Dan wanted to go to Navy, she certainly wouldn't stand in his way. But he had committed to meeting with the Army coaches and she would not let him break that commitment.

The Army coaches came to the house and convinced Dan to visit

West Point. When the Navy coaches heard Dan was visiting Army, they were furious — and said so. Dan felt they were coming on too strong. After his visit to West Point, he decided he was more comfortable there.

If there had been any doubt about where Joel wanted to go, it was pretty much ended when Dan chose West Point. During the summer after his sophomore year, he became a weight room fanatic and put on almost thirty pounds. He became a starter at tight end as a junior, and as a senior he started at both tight end and defensive end, weighing in at 223.

Naturally, West Point wanted him to join Dan. Other schools came after him, and he took visits to Penn State, Syracuse, and James Madison. He remembers looking around Penn State's facilities and thinking, "I really wish I could come here, but I just can't. I have to go to West Point."

He didn't *have* to go, but he felt as if that was where he belonged. He did balk briefly when the coaching staff told him they wanted him to go to the prep school. His SAT score of 890, combined with a B− average, made him enough of an academic question mark that everyone thought he could use the prep school year. When Davis saw the 1995 schedule and realized that his prep school year would be like a redshirt year in terms of football, he agreed.

As it turned out, prep school was the best thing that ever happened to him. He grew bigger and stronger there, and once he had dealt with the drill sergeants at the prep school nothing that happened at Beast was likely to faze him. More important, he needed the year to adjust academically. He graduated from the prep school as "The Goat," the designation given to the lowest-ranked person in the graduating class both at West Point and at the Army prep school.

"I'm one of these guys who always does just enough to get by academically," he said. "Sometimes, I cut it a little closer than I should."

It is an academy tradition at both Army and Navy that the last person in the class — referred to as "The Anchor" at Navy — is given one dollar by each member of the graduating class. That is a graduation bonus of close to a thousand dollars. The Goat and the Anchor are guaranteed to get by far the biggest cheer during the graduation ceremony, and the "honor" (not to mention the $1,000) has become prestigious enough that those near the bottom of the class have been known to jockey down the stretch to get into the Goat or Anchor position.

Class rank is not based strictly on academic standing. Fifty-five percent of it is based on academics, 30 percent on military conduct, and 15 percent on physical aptitude. Since a GPA of 2.0 is required to graduate, those in the Goat/Anchor spot may occasionally let their military rank slip just a tad toward the end of the semester — perhaps forgetting a salute at a key moment — if they feel it might win them the coveted position.

Davis didn't do any manipulating to be the Goat at the prep school — for one thing, there's no money involved — and he hovered consistently near the bottom of his class at West Point. But whenever he had to do well on a test or had to write an important paper, he got the job done. He was taking six classes both fall and spring semester in order to graduate on time. His teammates were betting that he managed.

Football came easier to Davis than academics. Even though he dropped twenty pounds during Beast, he was one of four freshmen who lettered, playing often as a backup defensive tackle. In fact, during the second half of the Army-Navy game, Army's right defensive tackle was Dan Davis and the left defensive tackle was Joel Davis.

A year later, he started all eleven games — and kept getting bigger. By the end of his sophomore season, offensive line coach Ed Warriner was begging Sutton to move Davis to the offensive line since the only person he had there of comparable size was Stover. Sutton agreed, although Davis actually played both ways part of the time as a junior, coming in at nose guard on short-yardage situations.

He was up to 285 by then and *still* growing. By the time the '94 season ended, several pro scouts had shown up at West Point to watch him. Davis was surprised at first when he heard the pros were watching him, then excited about the prospect.

"As a freshman, if you had asked me if I wanted to play pro ball, I would have said, 'Sure, who doesn't? But I've got no chance.' As a sophomore, I would have said, 'Boy, wouldn't that be nice, but no, I'm not at that level.' As a junior, I might have said the same thing — but I would have been lying to you."

Professional football is a touchy subject at all three academies.

Ironically, Navy, the school that had the least success in recent years among the three academies, had three former players in the NFL in 1995. Max Lane, who had been separated from the academy as a senior in the Double E scandal, was playing on special teams for New England; Bob Kuberski, who had been given an early discharge from the Navy as part of the downsizing of the military, was playing in Green Bay; and Kevin Hickman, who had been part of the class of '95 but hadn't graduated, had been able to buy his way out of his military commitment — courtesy of the Detroit Lions, who drafted him in the fourth round — for about $90,000.

Air Force also had one player in the league, Chad Hennings, who was a starting defensive tackle for the Cowboys. Hennings had served four years in the Air Force before going on to play in Dallas.

Army had sent the fewest players to the NFL of any of the academies. In fact, it had been thirty years since anyone from West Point had played in the NFL. Davis didn't even want to broach the subject with the powers that be until the possibility of his playing was a real one.

"If I'm good enough, I'd like to at least have the chance," he said. "But I certainly don't want to get anyone upset or burn any bridges by asking them to let me out when there's no reason to ask for it. I *want* to play football at the next level and I think I'm good enough to do it. But until someone else actually tells me I have a chance, there's nothing for me to do."

Davis knew that getting out in two years was not that difficult because of the downsizing process. Dan, who had graduated in 1993, was already out. But losing two years — not to mention losing a lot of weight, as would be required of an Army officer — might be the difference between making it and not making it.

Superintendent Graves had heard about the pro scouts' interest in Davis. "I happen to think Joel Davis will make a very good army officer," he said, "and I would hate for us to lose him. But if he has a chance to play in the NFL and there's some way to work with him within the context of his meeting his commitment, I would think we'd try to work with him."

For the moment, Davis was focused on his last year of college ball. Stover had also received some attention from pro scouts, but he didn't think much of his chances. "I have to accept the fact that this is it for me playing football," he said. "If something does come up, well, great. But I need to face up to the end because whether I like it or not, it's coming."

Davis didn't want to hear it. "Top" — as in stove-top — "you and I are both going pro, babe," he would say. "We're going together. Believe it, baby."

Stover would nod and roll his eyes. Then they would go eat.


THE Fat Men, ably aided by Scott and Leshinski, had done their job in the Duke game — the 305 yards rushing was evidence of that. But Washington would be a much tougher test: a ranked team on the road. The offense would have to control the ball because Washington's offense was full of explosive athletes who were almost bound to make a big play sooner or later if they touched the ball enough times.

Washington was ranked seventeenth in the country and was the favorite to win the Pacific-10 title. Army was considered a breather in the Huskies' schedule, coming one week after a game at Ohio State and two weeks before Notre Dame came to Seattle.

When the Cadets arrived on the West Coast, they quickly found out what people thought of their chances. Flipping through channels in the hotel room, Leon Gantt saw an ad for *Wheel of Fortune,* which was taping shows in town that week. Vanna White was asked on the ad what she thought about the Army-Washington game. Her response was to turn around letters that spelled "blowout."

"Can you believe that?" Gantt said. "Vanna White thinks we're going to get blown out."

So did the bookies: they made Washington a 26-point favorite.

That was fine with the Cadets. So was the crowd of 76,125 — a record — that poured into Husky Stadium on a warm, windless afternoon. On a pretty day, Husky Stadium, which sits right on the edge of Puget Sound, is a breathtaking setting for a football game. Many fans arrive by boat. They dock or drop anchor outside the stadium and, instead of tailgating, they stern-gate. Then they make the short walk to the stadium and expect to leave three hours later with a victory.

When the captains went out for the coin toss, Conroy, who had been named as a game captain after his performance against Duke, was surprised to see a cadre of photographers standing around at the 50 yard line.

"I'd never been out for a coin toss before," he said. "I was thinking, 'Gee, I didn't realize the coin toss was this big a deal.' Then I looked up and I saw Vanna White standing there."

White was there to toss the coin, no doubt to get the blowout started. Conroy nudged Cantelupe. "Think I should ask her if I can buy a vowel?"

Vanna tossed, Cantelupe called heads, and it came up tails. "I knew I should have asked her about the vowel," Conroy thought.

It took Army exactly ninety seconds to let the Huskies know that it would not be easy making Vanna's prediction come true. Quarterback Damon Huard fumbled on the third play from scrimmage and Ray Tomasits, who had come a long way from eighth string on the plebe team, jumped on the ball at the Washington 33.

The Cadets stalled, though, and Parker missed a 42-yard field goal. Still, a tone had been established. The game settled into a defensive struggle. Army was able to move the ball, the Fat Men opening holes for Conroy between the tackles, but the Washington defense stiffened when it had to. Even so, the Army offense was keeping the Washington offense off the field. The only points of the first half came on a 40-yard Parker field goal late in the first quarter.

As the teams headed for the tunnel at the break with Army leading 3–0, the Cadets could hear scattered boos coming from the stands. It was music to their ears. "Their fans couldn't believe it," Stover said. "They were in shock."

So were the Huskies. Going up the tunnel, the Army players could hear the Washington players yelling at one another. "They were blaming each other for mistakes and for the game being so close," Gantt said. "I thought to myself, 'We've got them fighting with each other. This is perfect.'"

Of course a 3–0 lead was far from perfect — or safe. The coaches were convinced they needed to make sure Washington didn't come flying out of the locker room after a tongue-lashing from coach Jim Lambright and jump on them quickly. When Ed Warriner saw the Fat Men celebrating in their corner of the locker room, he jumped on them.

"Hey, it's thirty minutes and we're up 3–0," he said. "This isn't a big deal. Remember, we *expected* to come out here and win. We haven't done anything yet."

They did something on the first drive of the second half. Taking the ball at their own 19, they went 81 yards down the field, staying on the ground until McAda hit Rashad Hodge with a 15-yard pass that put the ball on the Washington one. Two plays later, Jeff Brizic scored and, amazingly, Army led 10–0.

"You could have heard a pin drop," Cantelupe said. "If we had held them on the next series, they might have given up."

There is always one series in a football game when a big underdog — especially on the road — must take control. It must not let the crowd back into the game and it must not let the reeling favorite do anything to get its confidence back.

This was that series. Washington began to move the ball, but there was no need to panic, it had moved the ball before without scoring. Army had almost completely shut down the Washington running game, so Huard was throwing on almost every down. On second-and-six from the Army 41, he sent split end Leon Coleman on a streak pattern down the sideline. Abby Muhammad bit on the fake, Coleman got a step behind him, and Muhammad brought him down at the seven.

Disaster. The crowd woke up; the Washington players stopped yelling at one another. Tailback Roger Neal went the last seven yards and it was 10–7.

But the Cadets didn't fold. Late in the quarter, Conroy ripped off a 24-yard run and they moved the ball to the Washington eight before stalling. Parker kicked another field goal to start the fourth quarter and it was 13–7. Everyone on the Army bench knew that probably wouldn't be enough.

Another critical series. Another big play for Washington. This time it was Huard finding Joe DeSaussure behind Muhammad for 49 yards and a touchdown. With 13 minutes left, Washington led for the first time, 14–13. The Huskies scored again on their next series and it was 21–13. The fans hadn't gotten their blowout, but at least they could relax now and enjoy the victory.

Only they couldn't. Taking over with 5:30 left, the Cadets moved methodically down the field. McAda picked up 12, Conroy 25. McAda hit Ron Thomas for 12. They were on the Washington six with more than two minutes to go. A touchdown and a two-point conversion and they could salvage a tie.

Unfortunately, they were driving toward the closed end of the stadium. It was band day and there were three thousand high school band members sitting in the end zone. As soon as Army closed in on the goal line, they began raising a racket. Sure enough, on third down from the six, the line couldn't hear McAda and jumped. That put the ball on the 11. McAda hit Leshinski for six yards, setting up fourth and goal at the five. Now, the crowd was really screaming. McAda and Conroy both turned to referee Jim Springer and asked him to quiet the crowd — which he had the authority to do by stopping the clock until the offensive team could hear its signals.

"I'm three and a quarter yards from Ronnie and I can't hear a thing," Conroy said. "How in the world can anyone else? I turned to the referee and I said, 'Sir, we can't hear anything.' He just looked at me and said, 'I can hear fine.' "

While McAda and Conroy were trying to hear, the 25-second play clock ran out. Delay of game. Now the ball was on the 10. Forced to pass, McAda tried to find Hodge. He got the ball off just as he was buried by the Washington line.

Incomplete. Game over. Except it wasn't. Springer, perhaps feeling guilty, called the Huskies for roughing the passer. That gave Army new life — first down at the five. McAda promptly picked up four to the one. Again, the noise became unbearable. Army had no choice but to run simple plays. Carpenter was stopped for no gain once, then twice. The clock was under 20 seconds. Army had no time-outs left.

The Washington players, tired and not wanting another play, took their time getting up. A couple of them kept Carpenter on the ground to the point where Conroy almost grabbed them and pulled them off. Again, McAda pleaded with Springer to stop the clock. Again, Springer wasn't buying. He had already made one call for Army and he wasn't going to make another. Not with 76,000 people already screaming about the roughing the passer call.

The Cadets tried to line up. Three, two, one . . . zero. They never got their last play off. The Huskies raced off the field, not so much jubilant as relieved. They had survived — barely. They didn't want to spend one more second on the field with that team.

"We underestimated them," Huard admitted. "That was a good football team."

Conroy had rushed for 166 yards. Since the Washington media had no idea who he was, they surrounded him after the game. "Where in the world," one reporter asked rhetorically, "did *you* come from?"

"My name's John Conroy, sir," Conroy answered. "I'm from Chicago, Illinois."

The Seattle papers lavished praise on the Cadets. So did the papers back East. They had done everything but win the game. There was no doubt that they were a good football team. They were also 1–2.

"We aren't in this to be close," Davis said. "We're in this to win. And I guarantee you, we *will* win."

On the Tuesday after the Washington game, Conroy took the Fat Men to dinner. Many running backs will take their offensive line to dinner after a hundred-yard rushing day. At Army, *all* the running backs take the offensive line to dinner after a hundred-yard rushing day.

They don't have a choice. It is a rule of the FMC.

"Cost me 176 bucks," Conroy said. He smiled. "I think I probably got off easy."

# 10

# ROLLER COASTER

IT was 2:30 in the morning when the football team buses arrived back at T-Court after Navy's loss to Rutgers. Seven days earlier, the brigade had been waiting there to celebrate the SMU victory. They could hardly be expected to show up after a loss, especially in a drenching downpour.

But they were there. At least some of them. Encouraged — as always — by a steady stream of announcements up and down Mother B, many of them came out in the rain to greet the team. Spontaneous or not, the players were impressed — and touched.

"In the past, there's no way anyone would have shown up after a loss," wide receiver Matt Scornavacchi said. "Unless someone threatened them or something."

No threats, just nudging.

The record was now 1–1 but two road games were behind them. Four of the next five games were at home, and given the team's improved play, the crowds in Navy–Marine Corps Stadium were likely to be large and enthusiastic. What's more, the next opponent was Wake Forest. When the Midshipmen picked up their newspapers on Monday morning they saw that they were a ten-point favorite to beat the Demon Deacons.

"Ten points?" Garrett Smith said. "I don't think we've ever been a ten-point favorite over a Division I-A team since I got here. I'm not sure we've been a ten-point favorite over a I-AA team."

If Navy was going to be a ten-point favorite over anyone, it was Wake Forest. The Deacons were already 0–3, including an embarrassing loss in the season opener to Appalachian State; they had absolutely no running game to speak of and were the overwhelming choice to finish last in the Atlantic Coast Conference.

All of which terrified the coaches. "We're used to being underdogs around here," Weatherbie said. "We can't go in there and tell them they have nothing to lose because they're the underdog. They're smart enough to know that's not true."

The mood on the Yard all week still bordered on euphoric. The hot weather had broken and, for the first time, the brigade had switched from summer dress whites to fall blues. Everyone, it seemed, was looking forward to Saturday evening, a rare night game in Annapolis against a team the Mids should be able to handle.

One person who was less than euphoric was Shaun Stephenson. He had insisted after his knee injury was diagnosed that he would play in the home opener. McDevitt and Romo and Lawton had told him to shoot for Duke, a week later, but had promised to do everything they could to get him ready to play against Wake.

"There's no chance he'll play against Wake," Lawton had said the previous week. "He just hasn't accepted that yet."

Now, Stephenson had accepted it — but he wasn't happy about it. "My mind is saying one thing, my body's saying another," he said. "This is killing me."

Chris McCoy's performance in the SMU game had given the media another story to latch on to, and Stephenson was happy about that. *Sports Illustrated* was holding Rick Reilly's piece until Stephenson was cleared to play. He knew that once that story hit the stands, he would be inundated again.

McCoy had spent most of Rutgers week answering questions about his out-of-nowhere performance in Dallas. He had handled it all calmly, with the air of someone who wasn't surprised at producing 395 yards in his first college start. It wasn't so much a matter of being cocky — McCoy was anything but — as being someone who took almost everything, good or bad, in stride.

About the only time McCoy could remember being really and truly upset about something had been in the eighth grade when he had been picked to play in an all-star football game and hadn't gotten to play because he had failed a math test. His mother, who had always told him that he could play football as long as he did well in school, told him he couldn't play football until he got his math grade up.

Chris was baffled. He had felt completely confident when he had taken the test and couldn't believe he had flunked. "A B I could understand, maybe even a C, but flunk it? No way."

But he had flunked and his mother was adamant. If you didn't pass math, you didn't pass the football. McCoy got the message: his mother meant business on this school stuff. It was only after the game had been played that he got a call from the teacher. She said she owed him an apology. Somehow, in recording her grades, she had given McCoy's B+ to another student and given McCoy that student's F.

"I was upset about missing the game, but in the long run it was probably good for me because I knew my mom wasn't messing around about doing well in school," he said. "I did tell the teacher that I thought the least she could do was give me an A after what had happened."

Although he was small, barely five nine and 165 pounds, McCoy played both ways in high school, at quarterback and defensive back. He piled up lots of yardage at Randolph Clay High School, but when it came time to pick a college, he didn't have that many options because of his size.

Because of his good grades and because his board scores — 1060 on the SAT — were high for a kid from a small town in Georgia, Navy had shown interest in him early on. But when McCoy didn't hear back from the coaching staff as the national signing date approached, he decided to sign with Division II Albany State. On the day that he was going to sign a letter of intent, McCoy got a phone call from Navy. Was he still interested in a scholarship?

He was. Was he willing to go to NAPS? Yes. And so, sight unseen, McCoy decided to go to Navy.

When he arrived in Annapolis, the coaches told him they planned to use him as a defensive back. He wasn't surprised. After all, Navy ran a drop-back offense and it had a record-breaking passer in Jim Kubiak and an experienced backup in Ben Fay. He played cornerback on the JV team as a freshman, but was used to run the scout team offense whenever Navy faced an option team. When Weatherbie told the team that he planned to switch to an option offense, McCoy saw his chance.

"I really didn't think I would miss playing quarterback because I was prepared not to play there," he said. "But whenever I ran the scout team it reminded me how much I enjoyed playing the position. As soon as I heard we were going to be running the option, I went in and asked them if they would take a look at me in spring ball."

They took a long look and liked what they saw. The only question was McCoy's experience — or lack of it. He had all the correct tools to run the option — quickness, smarts, good football sense, and a better arm than the coaches had expected. In Weatherbie's mind, the two quarterbacks best equipped to run the new offense were McCoy and junior Howard Bryant. The surprise, when the team came back for preseason practice, was Ben Fay.

Everyone had assumed that Fay would emerge as the "passing quarterback," the backup designated to go in when the team got behind and needed to throw the ball on every down. But Fay, although not as quick as McCoy, proved adept at running the option; in fact he was better than McCoy at knowing when to pitch the ball or not pitch it. Early in preseason, the coaches decided that McCoy and Fay were the quarterbacks. Bryant was moved to an A-back slot and Dennis Kane, another sophomore quarterback, was moved to defense.

For Fay, the announcement that the team was switching to an option offense was anything but good news. If the old system had remained in place, he would have been the logical choice — the only choice — to replace Kubiak at quarterback. He had spent two years in the system and had been the backup in '94.

Fay's route to Navy was, if not unique, extremely unusual. He had grown up in Fort Worth and had been recruited by everyone in the Southwest Conference: he was a bright, strong-armed kid with good grades and an air about him that made him exactly the kind of leader coaches want their quarterbacks to be. Even as the backup to McCoy, Fay was still one of the team's leaders. McCoy was the quiet one, the quarterback who stepped into the huddle, called the play, and never seemed to get rattled. That was his way of leading, staying calm under fire. Fay was more verbal, the fire-in-the-belly, take-charge guy.

In fact, early in the season when he was getting very few snaps because McCoy was playing so well, Fay had gone to the coaches and asked to play on special teams, specifically on kickoff return. Initially, the coaches thought he was talking about returning kicks, which they weren't about to let him do. But that wasn't what Fay wanted. He wanted to be up front, as a blocker. "It'll give me a chance to hit someone," he said. "Feel like I'm part of the game."

Knowing what it would mean to the rest of the team to see the backup quarterback smacking into people on kickoff returns, the coaches agreed. On his first play as a special teamer Fay threw a vicious block, leveling a defender. The entire sideline erupted.

Being a lead blocker for Navy had not seemed a likely destiny for Fay coming out of high school. Navy recruited him and he was intrigued by the school. He loved the beauty of the campus, the quality of the education, and the notion of serving his country. But the football temptations of the Southwest Conference, combined with several friends encouraging him to join them at Texas Tech, had sent him to Lubbock.

By the end of his freshman season, which had been planned initially as a redshirt year, he was the Red Raiders' backup quarterback. He was happy at school and doing very well academically. But something was gnawing at him.

"I just felt as if I had let a special opportunity slip away from me," he said. "I liked Texas Tech, but it was like a lot of schools. I knew Navy was different; I knew if I graduated from there I would have a background that I couldn't get other places. And it wasn't as if I couldn't play football there too."

He went home at the end of first semester and sat up at night turning things over in his mind again and again. There was nothing bad he could think of to say about Texas Tech. He liked the coaches and was close to his teammates. Playing time would be there. But there had to be a reason why he couldn't sleep at night.

"I finally decided I would regret it the rest of my life if I didn't at least give it a shot," he said. "I told my parents I wanted to see if it was possible to transfer to Navy."

His parents were stunned. His coaches were even more stunned when he flew to Lubbock during semester break to tell them he wasn't coming back. Telling his friends and teammates was even harder. "I shed a lot of tears," he said.

But he knew this was what he wanted. He felt better from the instant he made the decision. Navy was willing to admit him, but he would have to wait until fall semester and he would have to start from scratch, enroll as a plebe since he had not yet gone through the military training or the required freshman courses that would allow him to enter as a sophomore. What's more, even though he was coming in as a freshman, he was still considered a transfer student by the NCAA, meaning he wouldn't be able to play football for a year.

Fay knew all that. He kept saying he understood what he was giving up and what he was taking on. He still wanted to do it. Then he turned up for Plebe Summer. One week in, he was lying awake in bed at night saying, "What in the world could I have been thinking about?"

Unlike the other plebes, Fay knew firsthand what life was like at a civilian school. He knew it was far removed from the hours he was keeping, the distances he was marching, or the screaming he was enduring. He had gone from being a glamour-boy quarterback on a football-obsessed campus to a know-nothing plebe at a place where most people viewed football players with suspicion.

"For a while, I really thought I had taken leave of my senses coming here," he said, laughing at the memory. "But I think everyone goes through some of that. I knew it would get better. I mean it *had* to get better."

It did. Fay practiced with the team that fall and quickly moved up to number two on the depth chart behind Kubiak the following spring. He and Kubiak were close friends, and even though it meant more snaps for him, Fay felt for Kubiak when Chaump played games with him by putting Fay with the first team at practice.

"He actually had me with the first team right before the Army game," he said. "I remember thinking, 'He's not crazy enough to start me against Army, is he?' "

He wasn't. Kubiak played the whole game. Fay did get in to three of the routs that season during the fourth quarter and threw 11 passes — seven of them against Notre Dame. Weatherbie's arrival and McCoy's emergence changed the game plan for Fay, but he adapted. He and McCoy were roommates on the road and got along well, even though both wanted to play every snap. If anything, Fay's willingness to accept the backup role without complaint and his take-charge personality made him ideal for the role of someone who was likely to get into games when the team needed an emotional boost.

No one, including Fay or any of the coaches, dreamed that the need for such a boost might come against Wake Forest. By nature, coaches are cautious. They always assume their opponent will play its best game of the season against their team and when they look at tape all quarterbacks look like Joe Montana and all defenses look like Pittsburgh's Steel Curtain of the seventies. That is usually what they will communicate to their teams to the point where players often don't bother to listen: they know that Rutgers isn't Notre Dame and Wake Forest isn't Florida State.

The approach Weatherbie and his staff took for Wake Forest was unusual: they acknowledged to the players that the Deacons weren't very good — all the while trying to warn the players that the game could still be lost.

At the weekly Thursday pre-practice meeting, Weatherbie liked to let two assistants — one from the offense and one from the defense — talk about the game and what it would take to win.

Gene McKeehan gave the offensive speech. "Don't play down to their level," he said. "Wake is not coming in here to win the football game — unless you give it to them. Don't be average; average loses games."

Gary Patterson, the defensive backs coach, was just as blunt: "They won't play hard," he said. "Give them the chance and they'll quit." He did add a warning: "They probably look at Navy as their last best chance to win a game this season."

In other words: the only team that could beat Navy on Saturday was Navy. That was a familiar refrain at Florida State and Nebraska and Notre Dame. It was not the kind of talk heard very often on the scenic practice fields overlooking Chesapeake Bay.


AND then came Saturday.

It started badly and got worse. After that, it really got ugly.

All day, there was a growing sense that something was amiss. The weather was lousy: gray, cold, and damp. For late November, it wouldn't have been very good weather; for September, it was awful.

"Real football weather," Weatherbie told the team, trying to sound upbeat. No one wanted real football weather on the third day of fall.

The coaches could tell during pregame meal that the players weren't as sharp or as ready as they had been the first two weeks. Instead of eagerness to get going, there was almost a sense of dread in the room. Weatherbie was tight too.

"He can't let the kids see that," Gary Patterson said. "They take their cue from him."

Maybe they had already seen it. Walking into the defensive meeting, Clint Bruce shook his head and said, "I'm tired of these night games. All the waiting makes me uptight. You end up thinking about it too much."

Dick Bumpas liked to let each of his coaches talk briefly to the defense during their final meeting at the hotel. Raye, sensing the uneasiness in the room, tried to shake things loose with an "our way of life against theirs" stump speech:

"Men, let's go out there and send a message," he said. "We're a family, when we're on the field we are one person, one heartbeat. You have to *focus* on every play for sixty minutes. When people look at the film of this game, make them say, 'Dadgum, that Navy defense really flies to the ball!' "

He was at full pitch. He turned the volume down: "If you win the effort and you win the contact, what do you win?"

They all shouted the answer back: "The game!"

There was no problem with anything — effort, contact, uptightness, number of heartbeats — in the opening minutes. With the stands nearly full and the brigade wired, the defense stopped Wake cold on the first series. Andy Person set the tone on the first play, busting through the line to knock quarterback Rusty LaRue's pass down almost before it was out of his hand.

The Deacons punted and the Mids swept right down the field; just as they had planned, hoped, expected. Paul Johnson started the game with a new formation, putting three wide outs to one side. Then he ran a trick play, McCoy pitching the ball to former quarterback Howard Bryant, who then threw the ball back across the field to

McCoy. The pickup was 17. The crowd loved the razzle-dazzle. This was going to be fun.

They drove to the Wake five — first-and-goal. Omar Nelson got two yards on first down. Then McCoy got two more. Third-and-one. McCoy tried to sneak it in. No. Fourth-and-inches. There was no question about going for it. The call was the same: McCoy straight ahead. Again, the Wake line didn't give ground. Later, when Weatherbie looked at the tape he was convinced McCoy *did* cross the goal line. But the officials didn't see it that way. Navy had held the ball for 12 plays and six minutes and had nothing to show for it.

But at least Wake was pinned on its own goal line. Two running plays later, Wake was still on the one. If Navy held and forced a punt, it would have great field position. But it didn't hold. LaRue dropped deep into the end zone and found receiver Marlon Estes streaking down the sideline. The play picked up 39 yards.

Suddenly, the lively, happy crowd was quiet. What was going on here? Nothing good. Three plays after the completion to Estes, LaRue again went deep on third down, this time to Dan Ballou. Again, the pass rush was feeble and the receiver had time to get open. The pickup was 47 yards to the three. John Lewis scored on the next play.

Wake 6, Navy 0. The defense had allowed the Deacons to drive the ball 99 yards. This was just the kind of start the coaches had feared. They had given Wake hope, which is the last thing you want to give to a bad team. The Mids did come back and score early in the second quarter to lead 7–6, but it was clear they weren't in sync. A holding penalty on Dennis Kane at midfield kept a Wake drive alive and, from the Navy 43, LaRue again found Estes deep to set up another short Lewis plunge, this one for a yard. It was 14–7 Wake at halftime, and for the first time all season it was an extremely tense locker room.

"They're making it hard on themselves," Weatherbie told the coaches. "They're not playing to win; they're playing not to lose. We've got to get them out of that."

Johnson stood up. "I think," he said, "I'm going to pitch me a fit."

"Fine," Weatherbie said.

Johnson's fit was just that. He called them names, told them how foolishly they had played and how silly it was to make a big deal out of all this as if they were playing a Top Ten team. Then he calmed down and clinically explained to the offensive line where their blocking had broken down.

It was the first time any coach — other than Raye, for whom a shout was a normal decibel — had raised his voice during a game.

Neither offense did anything early in the third quarter. But then Sean Andrews jumped in front of a LaRue pass intended for Ballou and ran it back to the Wake 37. It was time for Navy to take control of the game. Everyone sensed that. Which was probably the wrong way to feel. "It was as if just winning wasn't going to be good enough," Garrett Smith said later. "We went in thinking we were going to blow these guys away just like we did SMU and it wasn't happening. Instead of thinking, 'OK, let's just calm down here and make sure we get a win,' we started to think, 'Oh God, it's a close game, how embarrassing.' "

It only got worse. After McCoy had picked up a first down at the 26, they bogged down again. Wake's defensive line suddenly looked like the 49ers', penetrating into the backfield before McCoy could get moving. The field was damp and slippery and McCoy was clearly nervous about pitching the ball. Wake's defenders knew that and they weren't even bothering to play the pitch man on most plays.

Facing fourth down at the 21, Weatherbie sent Covarrubias in to get at least three points out of the drive. But Covarrubias slipped on the wet turf and shanked the ball short and way right. The big break had produced nothing.

As it turned out, that was Navy's last real chance. On the next series, McCoy threw his first interception of the season. One series later, he fumbled. Weatherbie and Johnson decided it was time to change quarterbacks. Fay came in and promptly completed three straight passes to move the ball to the Wake 31. There were still twelve minutes left. Plenty of time. But Fay and Cory Schemm misread one another on the next play and Tom Stuetzer intercepted the ball at the 27.

That made three straight turnovers after having gone 10 quarters with just one. This time, Wake took advantage. LaRue hit another bomb to Mike Braswell to take the ball to the Mids' 21. From there, the Deacons actually produced a running game, punching the ball into the end zone in five plays, Lewis going the last nine on an option pitch — the kind of option pitch Navy hadn't been able to execute all night.

That made it 21–7 with 5:22 left. Any hope of what would now be a miracle died quickly when Bryant fumbled the next kickoff and LaRue found Estes open one more time for one more touchdown. When McCoy, who came back after the Fay interception, was intercepted on the next series it meant that the Mids had turned the ball over on five consecutive series.

The final was 30–7, and by the time it was finally over the stands were virtually empty, except for the brigade. The players were in shock. The thought of losing had never crossed their minds all week. Now, they had not only lost, they had been humiliated. During the playing of "Blue and Gold," Clint Bruce stood behind the rest of the team, tears pouring down his face. He was thinking the same thing that a lot of the experienced players were thinking. Was SMU a fluke? Are we going to go through all of this again?

Weatherbie knew that was what they were thinking. He was a bit frightened by what he had seen himself. As soon as a couple of plays had been blown, complete panic had set in. When a team has a history of losing, things can go south in a hurry.

The silence in the locker room was deafening. There weren't any uplifting words to soothe this loss. Weatherbie didn't even try. "They played a good football game," he told the players. "But the fact is, they may not win again this season. They didn't rush the ball the length of my finger and they still beat us. Give some thought to what has to be done to be prepared to play each and every week."

He was more straightforward with the coaches. "We have to stop this thing from snowballing right now. We have got to be better than this or we won't be here very long. Those kids are down right now — way, way down — and we've got to get them believing again. That's going to take a lot of work."

He paused. "No finger-pointing, guys. Let's put this one on ourselves. We didn't have them ready."

It wasn't from lack of trying. But they had not been able to find the balance between being straightforward about Wake being a bad team (Weatherbie was right, the Deacons would not win another game) while making it clear that any team is dangerous when you are

Navy because you are never going to be that much better than an opponent. The ten-point line had almost become an albatross. The players were so used to the underdog role that they didn't know how to handle being favored.

For the seniors, the loss was especially disheartening. They understood that for the coaches and the younger players this was a building process. They didn't have time to wait. When Garrett Smith got home to his room that night, he looked at the schedule on his wall. The record was now 1–2 and one of the team goals was to make a bowl game. They could now afford to lose only one more game and still make a bowl. Weatherbie had talked in postgame about learning from the loss and growing. Smith understood why he would make that comment, but he couldn't help but think the time to learn and grow was behind the seniors.

He lay awake for a good portion of the night because his neck was sore from a stinger he had gotten during the game. Football, he realized, was coming to an end for him very soon. He wouldn't miss the pain or the exhaustion, that was for sure. But he didn't want it to end with memories like the one he had in his head right now: the stands emptying in those final futile minutes, the scoreboard telling them they were getting blown out by one of the few Division I-A teams in America they would be favored to beat easily.

"This can't keep happening," he thought. "We have to get better."

Then he had another thought. "Six-week exams are coming up this week. I'm going to lose a lot of sleep studying."

No rest for the weary. Or the beaten. Or the beaten and weary with sore necks.


THE coaches knew that keeping the players focused on football the next week wouldn't be easy. Midshipmen take six-week exams twice a semester. Their grades and grade point averages are updated after each set of exams. Anyone with a GPA under 2.15 for the six weeks or cumulatively is considered "unsat." That means their privileges are cut back, especially during the week. Their only free time — if they get that — is on the weekends.

No one wants to be unsat, but many football players hover around the unsat mark. Army and Navy are no different than most schools when it comes to athletes and academics. Both schools take athletes who would not be admitted if they didn't play a sport. That means there are always going to be academic question marks.

Most of the Navy seniors were in good to reasonable shape academically. Schrum had the best GPA at the start of the semester — 3.16. Ramon Vasquez, a backup A-back, was next at 3.09. Everyone else was below 3.0 but above 2.15 — in some cases, just barely. Thompson was 2.16, Stephenson 2.17, Speed 2.18. All were on schedule to graduate, though, and absolutely determined to do so with their class. Balancing football and academics was difficult right now because the players were putting so much into football physically and emotionally that they were often too exhausted to study at night. But with six-weekers coming up they had no choice.

Weatherbie was concerned about what condition the team would be in for the trip to Duke. They were already down after the loss to Wake and they were going to be tired because of exams.

The mood of the team was summed up well on Monday — an appropriately rainy, gray miserable day — when Bruce stood up in the pre-practice team meeting to announce who had won the hammer on Saturday:

"No one won it," he said. "No one deserved it." No one argued.

Weatherbie then asked the $64,000 question: "How many of you went into the game thinking we would kill Wake? Be honest."

Almost everyone raised their hand. Weatherbie nodded. "Me too. We just can't afford to do that, no matter who we play. Every game we play is winnable. But every game we play is also losable."

He had done some searching in the Bible for something inspirational to pass on to the team. To repeat Jeremiah 29:11 right now didn't seem like the right thing to do. Instead, he gave them Galatians 6:9, which reads in part, "Let us not get tired of doing what is right."

He added something someone had sent to him in the mail: "We don't look for people who never fail — we look for people who never give up."

They were nodding as he spoke; the problem was a lot of them were nodding with sleep. "Hey, guys, don't close your eyes when you're in this room," he said, his voice not raised, but sharp. "If you're tired, stand up."

The good news for the week was they were back in the role of underdog. After beating Army to raise its record to 2–1, Duke had lost to Maryland. That wasn't considered a bad loss, though, since Maryland was 4–0 and the game was played in College Park. The coaches were surprised by both teams when they looked at the tape of that game.

"Maryland isn't any good and Duke couldn't play with them," Paul Johnson said in one meeting with the offense. "I promise you they won't finish any better than 6–5" (they didn't). "If you guys will run the offense right, unlike last week, you're going to break some very big plays against these guys."

That was the theme all week: Duke isn't as good as you probably think they are, just as Wake wasn't as bad as you thought they were.

"There probably isn't anybody outside this room other than your families who thinks we can beat Duke," Weatherbie told them on Thursday. "Well, guess what. They're all wrong."

At Duke, they had looked at the Navy–Wake Forest score and figured, "same old Navy." The Blue Devils had been surprised by how tough Army had played them, but they didn't expect the same kind of fight from Navy — especially with the game being played at Duke. The general attitude in Durham was: get this win for 3–2, then worry about the ACC schedule.

NO one was more excited about the trip to Duke than Shaun Stephenson. The doctors had finally cleared him to play. Since he had been a starter when he was injured, he would return to the lineup as a starter. The only hitch came Thursday when he felt a twinge in his knee again toward the end of practice.

"This can't be happening again," he said as Rob Lawton took a look at him.

Fortunately, it wasn't. He had just twisted it slightly, and when he ran on it for a few minutes, it loosened back up. Everyone breathed a sigh of relief.

Probably no one sighed harder than Rick Reilly. His story on

Stephenson had been put on the *Sports Illustrated* schedule as soon as the magazine got word that he would play against Duke. The piece was superbly done, full of all the pain and horror the Stephenson family had endured. It painted a clear picture of the family's closeness and everything Stephenson had gone through to get the chance to play college football. Stephenson was inundated with mail.

Some of it was from women wanting to know if he was available (he wasn't); some was from families who had lost relatives in war; some was from other young athletes who had to overcome a lot to play their sport. One was from a referee: "I'm sorry I don't have any Navy games this year," he wrote. "I'd like the chance to shake your hand."

Just as Bucchianeri had done the previous year, Stephenson stacked the mail on his desk and began answering each letter. The difference was that none of his teammates resented the attention he was getting. Several of them admitted they cried reading the story.

"I knew Shaun had been through a lot," Thompson said. "But I never realized how much. I finished reading the story and I had tears in my eyes. I thought to myself, 'Nothing I've ever been through can compare with what he's been through.'"

Stephenson appreciated the story, although he worried that his dad might think he had been portrayed as too tough on his kids. He also worried that all the attention could become a burden if he didn't contribute to the team soon.

"I don't want people to think I'm someone who made the team because the coaches felt sorry for me or something," he said. "I'm a good football player and I want people to know that. I'm not Rudy."

Rudy Reuttinger had been the walk-on at Notre Dame who had hung around the program for four years in the 1970s before finally getting in for one play at the end of an already decided game his senior year. He had managed to convince a movie studio to make his story into a movie, and the sappy film — which strayed from the facts often — had ended up being a box office success. Stephenson didn't want people confusing him with some glorified mascot.

Saturday evening didn't begin well for Navy or Stephenson. All during warm-ups, the knee felt tight, especially when he tried to make a cut or push off. The doctors had told him to expect some soreness but that it shouldn't be a problem once he was loosened up. He was worried about it stiffening, so much so that while the team waited to go back on the field after warm-ups he asked Weatherbie if he could jog up and down to keep loose.

That was fine with Weatherbie. Since the visitors' locker room at Wallace Wade Stadium is small and cramped, the entire team was sitting outside on Duke's grass practice field, where it was cool and comfortable. The practice field, which is nestled cozily among soaring oak and pine trees, sits 150 yards from the open end of the stadium, once picked by *Sports Illustrated* as "the prettiest place in America to watch bad football."

No one in a Navy uniform was admiring the aesthetics at the moment. Weatherbie worked over a wad of chewing gum as the normal pregame quiet was broken by the sound of the Duke band playing the national anthem. Even though the song was muffled by the distance between the team and the playing field, all the players and coaches stood at attention until the last note died into the trees.

Once the anthem was over, they sat or knelt again on the grass. There was almost no pump-up, tension-release chatter, each of them understanding the importance of this game. The only one talking was the Reverend Robert Lewis, one of the team chaplains. "Did you hear the radio today?" he said, speaking to no one and everyone at once. "They said we were easy pickings! Easy! You hear me? It's time to get down and get dirty, men!"

Not exactly your typical pregame chaplain talk. But Lewis was anything but typical. He was the antithesis of what you would expect a chaplain to be. He was a live wire, always up, always on, and apt to say anything. During the SMU game, as Navy drove down the field for its final touchdown, Lewis's voice could be heard clearly on the sideline screaming, "Put them in the coffin. Put them in the coffin and drive in the nails!"

When someone pointed out to him that comments like that seemed a bit out of place coming from a man of the cloth, Lewis smiled and said, "There better not be anyone in an opposing uniform coming over here looking for comfort. They're in the wrong place!"

A Navy captain who had served overseas, Lewis, who probably weighed 150 pounds at most, looked more than ready to step in at linebacker if Weatherbie needed him. "I'd get after some people," he said.

Lewis and Father William Devine — who was as quiet as Lewis was outgoing — were part of Navy's sideline entourage. They were joined by the team's three officer representatives, marine colonel Mike Glynn, navy captain Tom Butler, and navy lieutenant James K. Owens (Kent to his friends), who were assigned to the football team to work as liaisons between the players and coaches and the rest of the academy.

Some members of the brigade saw the O-reps as another example of the advantages football players had. After all, most midshipmen who were having trouble with a professor or with their schedule had to fend for themselves in straightening things out. Football players could go to the O-reps for help. It was also true, though, that football players did come up against circumstances that other mids did not.

For example, four of the seniors had been unable to take a test for marine flight school early in the semester because the team had been on the road. Glynn had been able to arrange for a makeup test the Sunday after the Air Force game. To the coaches, that wasn't the best scheduling in the world since the test was extremely important to the players and it would come just twenty-four hours after what was arguably the second most important game of the season. But it was either that or not take the test at all.

Glynn and Butler were both in their fifties, veterans of the O-rep business, and very vocal on the sidelines. Owens, who had graduated from the academy in 1988, was new to the job, having been recruited by Glynn and Butler, who felt it important that a team that was about one-third African-American have at least one African-American O-rep. Owens was quieter than his two older colleagues, especially early on. But as the season moved along and Owens became more comfortable with the players and his role, he became more and more vocal. By the time the Mids played Notre Dame, he could be heard yelling at officials just as often as Glynn and Butler.

No one on the Navy sideline was doing much yelling in the early minutes against Duke. On the Mids' first play from scrimmage — the first play of Shaun Stephenson's college career — McCoy fumbled trying to fight forward for extra yardage. Ray Farmer, Duke's all-

American safety, pounced on the ball at the Navy 36 and it looked as if they were picking up from where they had left off against Wake Forest. It was the sixth straight possession on which they had turned the ball over.

Fortunately, a spectacular play by Sean Andrews in the end zone denied Duke a touchdown, and the Blue Devils settled for a Tom Cochran field goal to make it 3–0. That gave Navy a boost. On the next series, McCoy was stopped for no gain at the Duke 47 on third-and-one. Weatherbie had a decision to make. A week earlier, failing to pick up a fourth-and-inches on the goal line had been critical. To give Duke the ball back at midfield early in the game — on the road — might be just as crucial. But he had to show some faith in his offensive line. He called time-out to talk it over on the headset with Johnson, then decided to go for it.

The line drove off the ball, McCoy followed center Brian Dreschler and Garrett Smith and picked up two yards. First down. Then, thinking that Duke would be catching its breath after a key play, Johnson called a reverse for Matt Scornavacchi, who took the ball from McCoy, dodged a couple of tacklers, got to the sideline, and then outran everybody to the end zone.

Touchdown. Duke was stunned. The Mids were overjoyed. In two plays, they had turned the momentum of the game completely around. Duke did put together a drive on its next possession, but once again had to settle for a field goal. That made it 7–6 at the start of the second quarter. Midway through the quarter, with Duke backed up in its own territory, quarterback Spence Fischer fumbled the snap and Mark Hammond jumped on the ball. On the next play, McCoy went around the right side and scored. Navy led 14–6. A Covarrubias field goal just before the half made it 17–6. The Duke players, surprised and frustrated, were starting to talk trash. To the Navy players, it sounded like sweet nothings being whispered in their ears.

The only downer of the half was Stephenson. After the second series, he took himself out of the game and found Rob Lawton. "I can't go," he said. "I just can't run on the thing. I can't stay out there when I can't run the plays."

Lawton felt the knee and could tell something was loose again. He told Ed McDevitt, who shook his head sadly. There was no choice now but to do an arthroscope and find out exactly what was going on inside the knee. When McDevitt told Stephenson what he thought, he saw tears in his eyes. "There's still time, Shaun," he said. "If we can go in there and clean the knee out you can be back in three or four weeks."

Three or four weeks probably meant he couldn't play again until the Notre Dame game. There would only be four games left at that point. First he had eleven games, then eight, now four. It wasn't fair. If anyone on the team knew about life's unfairness, it was Stephenson.

The rest of the night was far more uplifting than the news on Stephenson. Like SMU in the opener, Duke never made a move to get back into the game in the second half. Once again, Navy took the second-half kickoff and roared down the field. McCoy carried the ball four straight times and then, with the Duke defense creeping up to stop him, found Cory Schemm for 36 yards to the Duke 17.

It was McCoy's second — and last — completion of the night, but it was enough. Five more running plays put the ball in the end zone, Omar Nelson going the last two, and Navy led 23–6. Duke didn't have the stomach for any kind of rally after that, and the final was 30–9.

Once again, McCoy had starred, this time with 144 yards rushing. The defense had been superb, holding Duke to 58 yards rushing and under 300 yards in total offense while not giving up a touchdown. Navy was now 2–2 and one of the victories was over a team that had beaten the Mids by 33 points a year earlier. The next three games were at home, and the victory over Duke would certainly bring the doubters in the brigade back around. There was even talk again about bowl games.

The next two games would tell them a lot: Virginia Tech and Air Force. Both those teams would almost certainly be in bowls at the end of the season. The Mids now knew they could compete with reasonable Division I-A teams. Virginia Tech and Air Force were a step up from SMU and Duke. Navy had already taken a giant step forward in the first month of the season. The next step would no doubt be far more difficult.

# 11

# ONE FOOT TO GLORY

WHEN the Army football team got back from the trip to Washington, no one knew quite how to feel. The Cadets were all justifiably proud of the way they had played in Seattle. They had scared the hell out of a ranked team, a twenty-six-point favorite on its home turf.

They had also lost. Again.

That made them 1–2. Just like Navy after the Wake Forest loss. And, just as the Navy seniors were very conscious of time running out, the Army seniors felt the same way.

No one was more aware of the ticking clock than Jim Cantelupe. Unlike his fellow cocaptain, Joel Davis, he harbored no fantasies about playing in the NFL. He knew that his last game for Army would be his last game. And moral victories had little meaning for him.

When Jack Hecker, then an assistant coach (and now Army's director of football operations) had seen Cantelupe play in high school, he had been convinced that he was the prototype Army player. He wasn't very big or very fast, but he had what Hecker calls "the eyes."

Cantelupe's vision wasn't any better than most people's. In fact, it was a little bit worse. He wore glasses to read and had serious problems seeing at night. What Hecker meant was the look in Cantelupe's eyes when he played football or even talked about football. His brown eyes would widen to the point where they looked like chocolate M&M's turned vertical. They radiated with intensity and excitement just at the thought of playing the game. Even though he was barely six feet and weighed no more than 175 in high school, Cantelupe was a vicious hitter, someone who seemed to fly in the direction of the ball on every play.

Maybe the experience of his early years, playing with older kids in his backyard, was the reason for his competitiveness. Maybe it was playing on high school teams that had been good but, at least as far as Cantelupe was concerned, not good enough. "We made state play-offs the year before I got there," he said. "Never made it back. That still hurts."

Or maybe it was just a desire to make his mother proud. Tina Cantelupe was her oldest son's best friend. They had gone through some tough times, moving from Louisiana to California with Jim's dad, Jerry, when Jim was twelve, then moving back to Maple Heights, Ohio — where Tina grew up — when Jerry and Tina split up a year later. Jim was thirteen, his sister Carice was eleven, and his little brother, Jonah, was seven.

It wasn't an easy time. Jim had to adjust to a third school in three years; he had to help his mom with Carice and Jonah and he had to prove himself to a new set of coaches in both football and baseball. Tina went to work as a hospital administrator. That paid the bills but hardly made her wealthy. And yet when she and Jim agreed that the best thing for Jim, both academically and athletically, was to attend Trinity, a Catholic school in Garfield Heights, she never once expressed concern to him about paying tuition. She would find a way. She always did.

"One of the reasons I was absolutely determined to get a Division I scholarship was I didn't want my mom worrying about paying for me to go to college," Jim said. "She had already sent me to Trinity and she's still got Carice and Jonah to worry about."

If money hadn't been a factor, perhaps Jim would have ended up at Pennsylvania. He certainly would have qualified for some financial aid there, but since Ivy League schools don't give athletic scholarships it probably wouldn't have been a full ride. Kent State and Toledo, both Division I schools, would have given him a full ride, and he seriously considered Kent. In the end, though, he couldn't resist the challenge of West Point.

"I liked the fact that it was Division I and I liked the tough schedule," he said. "I wanted to play against the best. But I also knew I wasn't going to be an NFL player, and it just seemed like coming out of West Point would help ensure my future, no matter what I decided I wanted to do."

Cantelupe also knew he had a fallback position if he didn't like it at West Point. "All the coaches at the other schools told me if it didn't work out at Army, I could transfer," he said. "I figured I would try it and if it didn't work out, I could still go someplace else. Probably Penn."

Like every plebe, Cantelupe hated Beast, although his approach to it was a little different than most. Cantelupe takes the things that are important to him very seriously: his family, his friends, his responsibilities, and his football. Beyond that, he sees most things in life as not being worth too much concern.

One of the reasons he is a natural leader is that people feel comfortable with him from the first moment they meet him. He is hardly an intimidating figure, an average-sized person in a world of giants, with short-cropped brown hair, the intense brown eyes that Hecker noticed, and a friendly smile. Walking down the hall of his dorm one night, he encountered a plebe who was being dressed down for some horrible crime by an upperclassman. As Cantelupe passed, the plebe looked away from his tormentor briefly and said, "Hey, Jim, what's up," then returned to the tirade being directed at him.

Cantelupe laughed. "You see how much respect I get around here," he said.

Cantelupe did what he had to do when it came to corps discipline. But he always did it with enough humor to keep himself sane. On one of the first nights of Beast, the first classman in charge of his squad sat everyone down after dinner and demanded that they tell him their family's origins.

"Klein," he demanded, looking at Derek Klein. "What kind of name is that?"

"Sir, it's German sir," Klein barked back.

"O'Grady," the firstie continued. "What kind of name is that?"

"Sir, Irish sir."

It continued like that until the firstie reached Cantelupe, who was both bored and bemused by the whole exercise.

"Cantelupe," the firstie roared. "What kind of a name is that?"

"Sir," Cantelupe replied, his face as straight and serious as everyone else's, "it's *produce* sir."

The firstie stared at Cantelupe in disbelief. Everyone else stared at the floor, praying they wouldn't burst into laughter. Klein was biting his lip so hard he thought it must surely be bleeding.

"Do you think that's *funny,* Cantelupe?" the firstie screamed. He then gave Cantelupe several minutes of haranguing on what happened to wise-ass plebes who didn't take their superior officers seriously.

Naturally, the story was repeated throughout Cantelupe's company and regiment and made him into a minor legend among the other plebes. "What made Jim special was that he could always figure out a way to laugh at things, no matter how bad they got," Klein said. "He just has a knack."

Cantelupe and Klein had met the night before R-Day when their families had been seated next to one another in an Italian restaurant named Joseph's, which is about a mile from Thayer Gate, in Highland Falls. The two of them had chatted in the restaurant and each had discovered the other was a football player. When they found themselves in the same company, they immediately became friends. Four years later, they were in different companies, but still best friends.

Klein had come to West Point as a quarterback. He had played for his father at Frankfort High School in Frankfort, Michigan, and the team had gone 26–0 his junior and senior seasons, winning back-to-back state titles. Klein had thought about staying home and playing at Albion College in Michigan but, like Cantelupe, couldn't turn down the chance to play at the Division I level. As a coach's son, he was one of those kids who could remember being around football since he had learned to walk, and although he joked about playing his last football game — "I guess that's why God invented golf, to give ex–football players something to do," he said — he was as keenly aware of the void it would create in his life as Cantelupe was.

Cantelupe's career at West Point had been smoother than Klein's. Neither had played very much as a freshman, although Cantelupe had gotten into four games. Klein was the JV quarterback and appeared ready to play varsity as a sophomore when he hurt his knee in spring practice. That sent him back to the JVs while Cantelupe moved into the starting lineup at free safety.

That spring Klein asked to move to defensive back and, unlike John Conroy, who also tried the switch, found playing time there. He was a backup to Cantelupe, played in nickel (five defensive back) situations, returned punts, and was the holder on placekicks. His big chance came after Cantelupe broke his leg, and he made the most of it in the Navy game.

Klein was not the happiest of campers at the start of fall semester. He was on restriction for the first six weekends because he had been caught sleeping during morning inspection (AMI) by one of the TACs and the incident had somehow turned into an honor investigation.

It all happened because Klein was doing something almost everyone in the corps does — trying to steal an extra hour of sleep. His room was on AMI, but a friend in another company was on PMI. That meant the friend and his roommate were allowed to be in bed, with the door closed, during the morning. Since his friend had class in the morning and he did not, Klein went over to his friend's room, jumped into bed, and went to sleep.

Unfortunately, his friend's TAC came into the room to leave a message for him. When he saw Klein sleeping, he took his name from his jacket, looked him up in the computer, and contacted Klein's TAC. Most TACs at West Point understand that extra sleep is vital to the cadets. No one has explicit permission to do what Klein had done, but most TACs take the approach that if no one specifically tells them about it, then it didn't happen.

Now, though, Klein's TAC had been told. Klein pleaded guilty to the crime but mentioned to the TAC that the previous semester it had been his TAC's unstated policy that sleeping in a room that was on PMI when you were on AMI was OK. Klein's new TAC called his old TAC and asked him if that was true. The old TAC, not wanting to look as if he were lax on discipline, denied it. Now Klein was in trouble. If his old TAC didn't have an unspoken policy about extra sleep, then, technically, he had lied.

His TAC brought him up on honor charges. There is no such thing as a minor honor offense at West Point. Klein knew that as well as anybody, since he had seen fellow defensive back Jerrold Tyquiengco brought up on honor charges because he had taken his clothes to the wrong laundry.

In that case, Tyquiengco, then a sophomore, had been on his way to practice one spring afternoon when he realized he had no clean clothes. There are two cadet laundries: one for the first and second regiments, the other for three and four. At the time, Tyquiengco was in the third regiment. But he already knew that he had been assigned to the second regiment for the fall semester. Since the laundry for regiments one and two was on his way to the bus up to Michie and he was late, he took his laundry there.

He filled out the laundry form, putting his regiment-to-be down on the form. Tyquiengco was born on Guam and is half-Asian. The woman in the laundry, who deals regularly with two thousand cadets, was certain she hadn't seen him before. She looked his name up on the computer and found he was in the third regiment, not the second. She turned him in. At his trial, Tyquiengco heard a number of people testify that what he had done was not uncommon. He admitted he had done it and said he was very sorry.

He expected to receive restriction and hours marching on the area. Instead, he was turned back a year, forced to take his sophomore year all over again. Because the punishment was so serious, it had to be approved by both the commandant and the superintendent.

"A lie was told intentionally," Superintendent Graves said. "That is a serious honor code violation."

One can only wonder what would have happened to Tyquiengco if he had asked for starch.

Knowing what had happened to Tyquiengco on what had seemed like a minor charge, Klein was extremely nervous. When the honor board heard the story, they threw the honor charges out. Clearly, Klein hadn't lied. At worst, a case could be made that he had misunderstood his old TAC. More likely, although the board didn't actually say it, he had been telling the truth and his TAC had been covering his own rear end.

Even so, Klein was still given thirty hours of restriction for the original sleeping-on-AMI charge. That was an extreme punishment for a relatively minor crime. It wasn't until October that Klein was free to leave the base on weekends.

"Nice way to start your senior year, huh?" he joked.

THE best way the Cadets could put the Duke and Washington games behind them was to beat Rice. The Owls were not the pushover they had once been, having put together back-to-back winning seasons in 1993 and '94 for the first time since the fifties. Still, having played Washington to the final gun on the road, the Cadets were confident they could handle Rice at home. After all, the Owls had already lost at home to Tulane and to Louisiana State. Army had played better teams and had played them tougher.

The weekend would be a festive one. Army was bringing back players from its 1944, '45, and '46 unbeaten teams for a "Weekend of Champions" to celebrate the fiftieth anniversary of Army's football heyday. Most notably, Felix (Doc) Blanchard and Glenn Davis, the famous Mr. Inside and Mr. Outside, who had won back-to-back Heisman Trophies — Blanchard in '45, Davis in '46 — would be returning. In all, more than fifty members of those teams were coming back for a Friday night dinner, a Saturday breakfast, and a wreath-laying ceremony at the grave of the team's coach Earl (Red) Blaik.

Blaik's grave is one of the first ones a visitor encounters in the West Point cemetery. It is impossible to miss since it is shaped like a huge gray football. At the bottom underneath Blaik's dates and accomplishments are the words "Fight On Old Army Team."

Unfortunately, the old Army team, even with a sellout crowd jamming Michie, forgot to fight for most of three quarters. After taking the opening kickoff and ripping off a 65-yard drive that ended with Conroy going eight yards for a touchdown, it looked as if the Cadets were capable of dominating. Instead, they spent the next two and a half quarters being the dominated, as Rice scored three touchdowns to lead 21–7. It was a little bit like being shot with your own gun, since Rice ran the wishbone almost the entire game. Desperate, the Cadets did finally fight back. A J. Parker field goal made it 21–10 and a touchdown by Steve Carpenter and a two-point conversion by Carpenter cut it to 21–18 at the end of the third quarter.

By this point, the defense had shut down the Rice wishbone. But Rice was doing just as well against Army's option. The teams traded punts until Army took over on its own 10 yard line with 4:06 to play. The Cadets picked up two first downs, but then Rice stiffened. Ronnie McAda threw incomplete passes on third down (to Conroy) and on fourth-and-five (to Coby Short), and Rice took over on downs at the Army 39 with just 2:10 left.

Heroically, the defense dug in and knocked Rice backward two yards in three plays. But all three time-outs had to be used to keep the clock from running to zero. Army did catch a break when Rice's punter, Tony Phillips, kicked the ball into the end zone. Instead of starting near the goal line, the offense was on the 20 with some breathing room. But there was only 1:46 left and there were no time-outs.

Sutton put John Graves in the game at wide receiver because he wanted an extra pair of reliable hands for a drive in which there would be no called running plays. Graves had started the season behind both Leon Gantt and Ron Thomas but had gotten the attention of the coaches in practice with his ability to get open and his sure hands. Nonetheless, as McAda and the offense trotted onto the field, Graves had caught only two passes in his Army career — one for 16 yards in the '94 opener against Holy Cross and one for nine yards in the '95 opener against Lehigh.

This wasn't Holy Cross or Lehigh. This was put up or shut up.

Quickly, Army was in trouble, facing third-and-five from the 25. McAda dropped and threw a slant over the middle to Graves, who caught the ball on his fingertips at the 38. First down. They were still alive. On the next play, Graves went to the sideline and turned back to find McAda's pass on his hands. Eight more yards. A quick slant to Thomas put them in Rice territory at the 48. The clock was under a minute.

McAda picked up six yards to the 42 on a scramble, but two incomplete passes made it fourth-and-four with 33 seconds left. Again, McAda scrambled out of trouble and dove past the first-down marker at the 36. Twenty-seven seconds left. McAda threw a surprise screen to Thomas, who picked up nine to the 27. But because he didn't get a first down, the clock kept ticking. Army was lining up, Rice was stalling. This time, McAda managed to get the play off and spiked the ball to stop the clock with two seconds left.

They had one play left. They could try a Hail Mary pass in the end zone — a long shot at best — or they could go for a tie on a Parker 44-yard field goal. Better to tie, Sutton figured, than almost certainly lose. He sent Parker in and held his breath. Parker produced. The kick sailed through the uprights as the gun sounded. Final: Rice 21, Army 21.

The good news was they hadn't lost on the final play for a third straight week. They had come from 14 points down and salvaged a tie. The bad news was that they had dug themselves that 14-point hole and had to settle for a tie because the offense couldn't do anything for most of the fourth quarter.

When he became the head coach, Sutton had started a tradition of having the whole team sing the Army fight song, "On Brave Old Army Team," in the locker room after victories. Given the way the day had started, with the wreath-laying ceremony at Blaik's grave, it would have been the perfect way for it to end. Sutton asked the players if they felt like singing the song to celebrate the fact that they had pulled out a tie.

The answer came back emphatically and in unison: "NO!"

That was exactly the answer Sutton wanted. "They understood that a tie was better than a loss, but it wasn't what we were after," he said later. "They were disappointed because they weren't ready to play early on and got so far behind that pulling out a tie was a struggle. There were some things to feel good about in the game, but we didn't walk away from it feeling good about the way we had played overall."

The players knew that a tie with Rice didn't do anything to help Sutton's cause, especially with so many of the old grads at the game for the fiftieth-anniversary reunion. In an almost cruel way, the 1995 team struggling to catch Rice from behind for a tie reminded everyone that times had changed since the days of Blanchard and Davis. The problem was, a lot of the old grads couldn't see any reason why the Blanchards and Davises of the nineties weren't at Army.

After they had showered and dressed, Cantelupe and Klein went over to the Firstie Club, an on-campus bar and restaurant open only to first classmen and officers. More often than not, officers who live on the post prefer the West Point Club, which is the modern name for the Officers Club. But in the aftermath of the game, a number of visiting alumni were at the Firstie Club.

Cantelupe and Klein had just arrived when a couple of alums walked up to congratulate them on their comeback. "You guys really hung with it," one of them said. "It would have been easy to give up."

"Thank you sir," Cantelupe said politely.

"It's just too bad," the grad continued, "that the coaching you guys are getting doesn't measure up to the talent you've got."

Cantelupe dropped the polite veneer. "With all due respect sir," he said, "you don't know what you're talking about. Our coaches do a terrific job getting us ready to play. They can't go out there and make the plays for us."

"I was talking about leadership . . ."

"Coach Sutton's done a great job leading us this season."

Cantelupe realized that the argument was fruitless. Nothing he was going to say was going to change anyone's mind. That was the trouble. The only way to prove the point was to win games. He felt guilty that the team was now 1–2–1, and as a result, no matter how well they had played against Duke and Washington, the pressure on Sutton continued to build.

Cantelupe had been around Sutton for four of his five years as coach, and he was convinced that Sutton had gotten better at the job each year. This season he had shown more fire and emotion than ever before. It was almost as if he had decided that if the ship was going to go down, it was going to go down with him coaching exactly the way he wanted and not worrying about what happened outside the team, because he couldn't control that anyway.

As they left the club that night, Cantelupe turned to Klein. "You know, if we could beat Notre Dame, we would shut all this talk about Coach Sutton up once and for all," he said.

Klein nodded assent. Of course beating Notre Dame wasn't exactly the same thing as beating Lehigh. Unlike Navy, which played Notre Dame every year and had lost thirty-one straight games to the Irish, Army played Notre Dame only on occasion. In fact, they hadn't played since 1985. Notre Dame had won the last ten meetings between the two teams.

Army's last victory had been in 1958 — Red Blaik's final season as coach.

IT helped that they had a week off before playing Notre Dame. After four weeks of preseason camp and four games, they were a little beaten up physically and drained emotionally. Sutton gave them two days off after the Rice game and then brought them back to begin the buildup before Notre Dame.

There were three games on the schedule that Sutton knew he would have absolutely no trouble getting his team ready to play: Army, Air Force, and Notre Dame. It really didn't matter whether the Irish were coming off a national championship or off an embarrassing 6–5–1 season (which they were), they would always be the most glamorous team in college football.

They were the only team in the country that had an exclusive contract with a network — NBC — to televise all their home games. Every game they played, home or away, was on either NBC (which had been nicknamed the Notre Dame Broadcasting Company in college football circles), ABC, or, at the very least, ESPN.

Lou Holtz had been hired by Gene Corrigan, then the athletic director, to coach Notre Dame in 1986. Corrigan's charge to Holtz had been to "wake up the echoes," and Holtz had done that. The Irish had suffered through five mediocre seasons in the early eighties under Gerry Faust, an extremely successful high school coach in Cincinnati who simply couldn't adjust his style to big-time college football. Faust was about as nice a human being as anyone had ever met, which was no doubt part of his problem. Nice guys rarely succeed in the thin air of Top Ten college football. A mean streak is required. Faust simply didn't have one.

Holtz did. As the coach at North Carolina State, he had once had a professor at the school who was jogging near the practice field removed by campus security because he was convinced the man was a spy for North Carolina. He went on to coach the New York Jets and quit before his first season was over because he was convinced he couldn't control players in the pros the way he could in college, and he couldn't live with *any* lack of control. He had gone on to win lots of games at Arkansas and Minnesota, although he had left Minnesota for Notre Dame in the middle of an NCAA investigation that later landed Minnesota on probation.

Holtz of course claimed innocence or ignorance or both. He was an intense, paranoid little man who tried to hide the intensity and paranoia behind a self-deprecating sense of humor that was amusing for a while, though it soon wore thin.

But he was a great coach. He had revived the Notre Dame program, winning the national championship in 1988 and contending for it most years after that. No one was better at preparing for a big game than

Holtz. And no one was better at building up an opponent than Holtz. One year, preparing to play a winless Navy team, he had said, "This is the most talented University of the Naval Academy team we've faced. They scare me to death." The scared-to-death Irish escaped with a 38–0 victory.

Naturally, Holtz was scared to death of Army — or was that the University of the Army? Amazingly, he had legitimate reasons to be nervous. Notre Dame had played at Washington the week before it played Army and had come from behind late in the fourth quarter to win, 29–21. The Irish were 4–2, the losses coming in the opener against Northwestern and two weeks earlier at Ohio State. Holtz was claiming — of course — that this was the least talented Notre Dame team he had coached. That meant the Irish probably had no more than twenty pro prospects on their roster. Army had one, two, tops.

This was the kind of game the Army kids craved. They wanted to line up against Notre Dame and measure themselves against the best. They weren't the least bit intimidated or scared. This was the kind of chance they had waited for all their lives.

The game would be played at Giants Stadium in East Rutherford, New Jersey, about a forty-five-minute bus ride from West Point. Technically, it was Army's home game. Notre Dame doesn't play Army or Navy on their campuses because neither stadium is big enough to hold the crowd that the Irish always draw. Both Army and Navy willingly move their home games to larger stadiums because it increases their payday greatly.

The players and coaches knew what that meant: they would be playing a home game in front of 76,000 people, about 70,000 of whom would be pulling for Notre Dame. The Corps, 4,000 strong, would be there and so would their families and friends. The rest would come from the endless supply of subway alumni that helped make Notre Dame so rich and powerful.

"All that does," Cantelupe told his teammates when they met the Monday before the game, "is make winning that much more fun."

The game would be televised regionally by ABC. For the Cadets, it would be their first TV appearance of any kind in 1995. For Notre Dame it would be their first non–national TV game of the season. Of the six games they had played to date, three had been on NBC and three on ABC.

Everyone at Army knew that the offense had to control the football in order for the Cadets to have a chance to win the game. Notre Dame's offensive line was, as always, huge. If the Irish were allowed to keep their offense on the field all day, their size and strength would undoubtedly wear down the Army defense.

That meant the Fat Men would have to open holes for the backs. It also meant that Ronnie McAda would have to play one of his best games at quarterback.

McAda's presence as a West Point junior was a surprise to some people — most notably McAda. The fact that he had become one of the most important players on the team at this stage of his career was a surprise to almost everyone, McAda included.

He had grown up in Mesquite, Texas, and started playing quarterback in peewee football when he was five. His dad, Ronnie Sr., a Vietnam veteran, coached him at times as a kid and was usually his toughest critic. "He could be a pain at times," Ronnie Jr. said, smiling at the memory. "I would make a mistake and he would get on me about it. I would try to get it right and I still wouldn't get it right and he'd get on me again. Sometimes I wanted to say, 'Dad, I'm not doing it wrong on purpose.' The funny thing was, as I got older, I didn't like it when I was playing ball and he couldn't be around. I wanted to know what he thought."

Eventually, Ronnie Sr. — and a lot of others — thought that Ronnie Jr. was a pretty good quarterback. He became the starter at Mesquite High School halfway through his sophomore year and, by the end of that season, was starting to receive letters from colleges. By the end of his junior year he was six three, had a strong arm, and could run effectively when he had to. Mesquite ran a run-and-shoot offense that gave him lots of chances to showcase his ability. The letters started coming in from everywhere.

"Somewhere under my bed I've got a box that has them all," McAda said. "I think there were about 450 in all."

A number of them came from West Point. Since McAda had a 3.5 GPA and had done well on the ACT — 23 — he fit the Army profile. At that stage, though, he had absolutely no interest in a military academy. "I think I took their first letter and threw it out," he said. "I didn't even know what West Point was. I knew there was an Army-Navy game of some kind but I had never really given it any thought."

Even though he continued to receive letters from West Point, McAda didn't give the school any further thought until his senior year. By then, the flow of letters had slowed, but McAda still had visits scheduled to Missouri, Rice, Texas A&M, and a couple of Division I-AA schools in Texas. Some of the big-time schools had decided that his arm wasn't quite strong enough and his feet weren't quite quick enough for their offenses. Army, however, was still very interested, and McAda's coach, Hugh Delano, told him he thought he should at least meet with Johnny Burnett, the longtime defensive backs coach who was Army's recruiter in the Dallas area.

McAda said fine. "It was more just out of respect for my coach than anything else," McAda said. "But I liked Coach Burnett, and when he asked me if I wanted to at least visit, I figured, why not?"

He visited on a cold, dreary February weekend but fell in love with the place anyway. He liked the mountains and the Hudson and the feel of the campus. He liked the players that he met and he liked the idea that Army really *wanted* him. Texas A&M was now talking about him coming as a walk-on, and Rice had signed two other quarterbacks. "It occurred to me that if I wanted a real chance to play Division I ball, this was it," he said. "I had fun on the visit and thought the military stuff wasn't going to be all that bad. At least, it didn't seem that bad when I was there that weekend."

Before he could call West Point to tell them he wanted to come, Mitch Soltis, one of the players who had taken him around during his visit, called. He wanted to be certain McAda had not gotten a mistaken impression of what life was like at the academy. "He knew I had a really good time and he said he was happy about that," McAda said. "But he didn't want me to think that was what everyday life is like. He told me that being a plebe was no fun. He said he thought it was all worth it in the end, but I should give it some thought."

One of the unique things about recruiting at the academies is the balance that everyone, players and coaches, feels obligated to strike. It is not like a civilian school, where the goal of most recruiting trips is to see to it that the recruit has the best two days of his life and can't wait to get back there to enroll as a student. At Army and Navy, the goal is to show the recruit everything that is good about the academy but also make certain he understands what he is getting into.

"There's no point telling a guy that the place really isn't hard and he'll have nothing but fun and then have him come in here and find out that's not true,'' Sutton said. ''We think there are a lot of good things to show kids, but if we don't tell them about Beast and the demands that will be placed on them that aren't placed on them at other schools, then the chances are we'll just lose them when they get here anyway. It's better to be up front with them and find out who really wants to come right off the bat.''

McAda appreciated Soltis's phone call, but he had made his decision. In the back of his mind was the highlight film the coaches had shown him, which had culminated with the '92 Army-Navy game, the one that had ended with Patmon Malcolm kicking the 49-yard field goal to give Army the victory. McAda had never seen anything quite like that: the corps on one side, the brigade on the other; everyone standing throughout the whole game; the playing of the alma maters afterward. ''I knew I wanted to be part of that,'' he said. ''It was the most awesome thing I had ever seen.''

McAda arrived for Beast prepared for the worst. Or so he thought. From day one he was miserable, absolutely miserable. Then, about halfway through, he had to go home to Texas for several days on emergency leave when his grandfather died. It occurred to him while he was home that he could drop out of West Point right then and there and enroll someplace in the fall where he would never again have to wake up at 5:30 in the morning or shine a shoe. He told his father he wasn't going to go back.

Ronnie McAda Sr. manages a car dealership in Mesquite. He had made a living most of his adult life as a salesman. He told his son he should at least wait until Beast was over to make a decision. After all, he wouldn't want to walk away when he might just be a couple of weeks away from putting the worst of it all behind him.

Ronnie bought the pitch. ''My dad,'' he said, ''can sell anything.'' Beast ended; football started. Things got no better. He was the third-string plebe quarterback, and whenever he got a chance to run the scout team in practice he couldn't do anything right. He felt like he was seven all over again trying to please his dad. The difference was, the coaches weren't his dad and instead of going home to his mom at night he was going home to a bunch of upperclassmen demanding to know the names of Army's four mules.

He called home again. He had decided to quit. ''Well, you know, you'd have to come back and sit out fall semester at this point," Ronnie Sr. said. "Probably have to get a job. Would you rather do that or see if football doesn't get better as the year goes on? You're just getting started, aren't you?"

OK, OK. Ronnie said he would stay first semester. It didn't get much better. He wasn't dressing for varsity games, he wasn't even starting in JV games because Derek Klein, then a sophomore, was. School was harder than it had ever been before, and he missed his girlfriend, who was at A&M. He came home for semester break and announced he was enrolling at A&M. He was ready to give up football; apparently he wasn't as good as he had thought.

His dad said that was fine, if he wanted to *quit* he could *quit.* Much to Ronnie's surprise, his girlfriend, Laura Barts, who had pleaded with him not to go to Army, shared his father's feelings. He had gotten through first semester; he should at least finish the year and then they could talk about it that summer. By now, Ronnie had made some friends at West Point and had to admit he didn't hate it as much as he had before. He figured he could handle one more semester.

And then came spring football. All of a sudden, he wasn't the complete flop he had been the year before. He was completing passes, making plays. He felt more comfortable in the wishbone. Since he was getting the chance to run Army's offense instead of the scout team offense, he was actually running plays that Army ran.

Recognition Day arrived. For plebes, Recognition Day is the happiest of their entire lives. Just prior to spring break, each company forms outside the barracks and the plebes line up. The upperclassmen walk through the line of plebes, shaking hands with each one of them. The plebes call the upperclassmen by their first names for the first time.

"Jim, I'm Ronnie McAda."

"Ronnie, I'm Jim Cantelupe."

It is a simple but touching and significant ceremony. It is recognition in a literal sense — the plebes are now people worthy of addressing their fellow cadets by name — but also in a more important sense: the upperclassmen recognize that the plebes have taken all that can be dished out and they are still there. They have earned the right to be part of the Long Gray Line rather than be trampled by it. It is a day no cadet ever forgets.

By the end of the semester, having been recognized as a cadet and as a quarterback with potential, McAda felt completely different about West Point. At the end of spring drills, he had moved up to number four on the depth chart, behind seniors Rick Roper and Mike Makovec and junior Steve Carpenter, who was slated to be a starting halfback and only play quarterback in an emergency. That meant McAda would be getting snaps in practice and, more important, traveling to all the games. No more sitting in the stands on game days.

He went home and told his dad he had changed his mind, once and for all. "I'm staying," he said one day while they were playing golf.

Ronnie McAda Sr. smiled. "I knew you would" was all he said. "You aren't a quitter."

"Of course," Ronnie said later, "I *wanted* to quit. He just wouldn't let me."

With two seniors slated to split time at quarterback during the '94 season, McAda figured the year would be a learning experience for him. His chance to earn a starting job would come the next spring. It didn't turn out that way. Roper went down six plays into the opener, Makovec in the first quarter at Duke. When Carpenter came in and couldn't move the team, McAda actually got in late in that game. A week later, Carpenter started against Temple. With Army down 13–0 in the second quarter, Sutton decided it was time to see what McAda could do under pressure.

Only McAda didn't feel any pressure. "We were already down 13–0, so putting me in was more or less a nothing-to-lose kind of thing," he said. "I felt very loose. I didn't think much was expected of me. I'd been fourth string two weeks earlier. I didn't even know all the plays because I didn't get all that many snaps in practice."

After throwing an interception on his first series, McAda got rolling. He led an Army rally that culminated with the Cadets taking a 20–16 lead in the fourth quarter. Temple scored late to win the game, but there was no doubt now who the quarterback was.

McAda impoved steadily the rest of the season. The only time he did get nervous was against Navy. "It just hit me that morning that this was Army-Navy and I was the quarterback. I was the guy who was expected to lead the team to victory. That was different than coming in off the bench against Temple. I got so wound up that by game time I felt exhausted."

He handled it, though, rushing for 127 yards, and even though he only threw three passes, he completed two of them for 29 yards. He was selected by ABC as Army's outstanding player of the game.

He had come a long way from wanting to go home, quit football, and enroll at A&M. He was now, quite clearly, The Quarterback, and a lot of Army's hopes for '95 had been built around his continued improvement. That was fine with McAda. He was comfortable in the spotlight. He even looked like a quarterback, with his jet-black hair, lanky body, and quick, confident smile. He had a little Clark Kent in him, putting on wire-rimmed glasses to go to class and study, then taking them off, stepping into a nearby phone booth, and emerging as Super-Ronnie, Army QB, when it was time to play.

This was now his team, his offense. Or so he thought.

"Usually, people listen to me when I talk," he said. "Not the Fat Men. One day in preseason, we were scrimmaging and I thought it was really important we move the ball. I stepped into the huddle and said, 'OK, guys, let's really show the defense something here.' Eddie Stover looks at me and says, 'Ronnie, shut up and call the play.' I thought he was kidding, so I said, 'Hey, Eddie, in this huddle I do the talking.'

"We come out and run the play, get back to the huddle, and I say something else, like, 'Let's make sure we really come off the line now.' And Eddie says again, 'Ronnie, I told you, shut up and call the play.' I started to say something back and Bill Blair, who never says anything, says, 'Ronnie, he said shut up and call the play, just do what he tells you.' I realized right then that I was *not* going to be in charge of the offense. The Fat Men were in charge."

McAda tried very hard to keep the Fat Men happy. He even paid for food so he could attend a couple of Fat Fests. "I keep trying to convince them I'm Fat," he said. "They don't buy it."

In fact, it was McAda who had to do the buying whenever he rushed for one hundred yards under the rules of the FMC.

Underneath it all, the Fat Men respected McAda. He was tough, willing to take a hit, and if he hadn't been a mere cow (junior) they might have let him talk occasionally in the huddle. "We don't let Ronnie mess with us," Joel Davis said. "But Ronnie knows we don't let anybody mess with him either."

That was about as good as it was going to get for a quarterback when it came to the Fat Men.


GAME day in the Meadowlands was warm but overcast with some rain sprinkled in. The good news was that the kickoff was at 12:08, so there wasn't that long to wait in the morning. After not having played for two weeks, kickoff couldn't come soon enough for Army.

Lou Holtz had talked all week about how much respect he had for Army's talent. A few minutes before kickoff, Tim Kelly and Andy Smith, Army's trainers, heard a more honest assessment of how Notre Dame felt about Army's talent. The Army training room was right next to the Notre Dame locker room. The walls in Giants Stadium aren't that thick. As Kelly and Smith were getting ready to join the players in the main part of the locker room, they heard one of the Notre Dame assistants talking.

"They will come at you hard on every play," he said. "But remember one thing, there's not one player in their locker room who could play for us. Not one."

Kelly and Smith were tempted to race into their locker room and repeat what they had just heard. Then they thought better of it: "No need," Smith said later. "There wasn't anything anyone could say at that point that would get them any more fired up."

Emotion, as any coach will tell you, only takes you so far anyway. Once the game starts, emotion may carry you for a play or two or even an entire series, but that's about it. Emotion can also work against you, make you tight, take away your ability to play on instinct.

The beginning could not have been tighter for the Cadets. After the offense had gone no place, Notre Dame took the ball and rammed it right down their throat, going 58 yards in 10 plays — nine of them on the ground. It was the coaches' worst nightmare come to life, the giant offensive line pushing the smaller Cadets backward play after play.

But now, the Fat Men dug in. The offense responded with an 80-yard drive, 12 straight plays on the ground until McAda crossed up the Notre Dame defense by pulling the ball out of Conroy's chest and tossing a soft one-yard pass for the touchdown to tight end Ron Leshinski. They were screaming at one another coming off the field.

"They won't stop us!" Joel Davis told the rest of the offense. "They can't stop us!"

The larger question was whether the defense could stop Notre Dame's offense. On their second possession, the Irish needed only six plays to go 70 yards. It was 14–7, Notre Dame, after one.

They traded punts to start the second quarter, but then Notre Dame went 68 yards, the key play being a 47-yard Ron Powlus to Derrick Mayes bomb over an Army defense that was jamming up front to stop the run. The extra point made it 21–7. Notre Dame had scored on three of four possessions, driving almost the entire length of the field each time. It was beginning to look like a long, gray afternoon.

The offense drove the ball into Notre Dame territory again, but the Irish stiffened and turned them over on downs at the 34. At the half, it was 21–7. The second half started the same way the first half had — with a Notre Dame drive for a score. When Mark Edwards took a Powlus screen 46 yards for a touchdown two minutes into the third quarter it was 28–7 and it looked like another case of a game but overmatched service academy team being overwhelmed by Notre Dame's talent.

But someone forgot to tell the Cadets. Ron Thomas returned the kickoff to the Army 40, and from there he and McAda and Conroy — with considerable help from the Fat Men — engineered a drive that made it 28–14. Notre Dame drove right back down the field, but with first-and-goal at the six, Edwards got clocked running up the middle, fumbled, and defensive end Tom Burrell, who was in the game because starter Adrian Calame had broken his foot in the first quarter, jumped on the ball.

Army didn't score on that drive, but it did move the ball to the 23. From there, Ian Hughes, no longer the terrified freshman he had been in the Duke game, kicked them out of trouble with a 69-yard punt. Then the defense forced Notre Dame's second punt of the day. One could almost feel the momentum switching. The Irish didn't look un-stoppable anymore. The third quarter was ending and there was still no rout; the game was within reach for Army. It wasn't supposed to be this close. But it was.

It got even closer. Army drove to the Notre Dame 10 but stalled when McAda had to come out briefly when his back stiffened after he was hit on an option run. Forced to come into the game cold on third-and-nine, Adam Thompson had no luck. He completed a screen to Leshinski, but it went nowhere. He then threw incomplete to Thomas in the corner of the end zone on fourth down. They had held the ball for more than eight minutes, running 17 plays. But they had produced no points. And now there were less than seven minutes left.

But before anyone could start talking about Army's gallant effort, Powlus tried a pass over the middle that Ray Tomasits intercepted at the Notre Dame 33. Exactly why Lou Holtz was calling pass plays with a two-touchdown lead, the world's largest offensive line, and less than seven minutes to play, no one was certain. Maybe he was embarrassed because Army had stayed close and wanted to widen the margin.

Instead, Army needed only five plays to score. McAda hit backup halfback Coby Short for a 24-yard pickup on third down, and Conroy took it the last six yards on two carries. It was 28–21 with 4:17 left.

The crowd was stirring with disbelief. A rout was now out of the question. So was a comfortable victory. The question was: could Notre Dame hold on to the ball and run out the clock?

No. On third-and-two at the Notre Dame 39, Autry Denson plowed behind the right side of the line looking for the first down. Linebacker Stephen King was waiting. He slammed Denson down a yard short. Fourth-and-one. Logic said punt the ball deep and make Army go the length of the field. But this was Notre Dame. Holtz was running his team from the press box because he had undergone back surgery in September. He had returned to the sidelines for the Ohio State game, and, when his team lost that game, decided to go back to the press box. Later, he would claim that he was trying to call time when Powlus brought his team to the line of scrimmage.

The time-out never got called. Powlus sneaked, trying to get the yard, and might have had it. But the ball popped loose when he was hit and linebacker Brian Tucker fell on it. Whether Powlus had made it was irrelevant. Army had the ball at the Irish 42.

Watching the play, McAda was shocked. When Notre Dame had lined up, he had assumed they were going to try to draw Army offside and if that didn't work, punt. The next thing he knew, the coaches were screaming for the offense to get on the field. As he went past

Sutton, the coach grabbed his arm. "Stay calm," he said. "There's plenty of time" — 2:33 — "and we've got two time-outs."

McAda nodded. He had fantasized about this situation for two weeks: down a touchdown, final minutes, with the ball. He was certain they would score. In the huddle, he looked into the eyes of the Fat Men and felt even more certain. There was no chatter at all. They knew the situation. They had waited all their lives for this chance. McAda did what he was now trained to do: he shut up and called the play.

Conroy got one yard on first down. Then McAda ran the option to the right and pitched to Thomas, who eluded two tacklers and went 19 yards to the 22. First down. The clock stopped at 1:51 as the chains were moved. They ran the option the other way and Thomas got five more. But on second down, Conroy was stuffed for no gain. Third-and-five at the 17. Army used a time-out. There was 1:08 left.

It was all option plays now, McAda having to read the defense on each play. If he thought the hole was up the middle, he would give it to Conroy. If not, he would take it himself and head for the corner. On third down, his read said give it to Conroy. He was almost right. Conroy got four to the 13. One yard short. Fourth down. They used their last time-out. This time, McAda saw that Notre Dame was jamming the middle. He took off right and, just as he was about to get hammered, pitched to Thomas. Six yards. First down on the seven. Forty-seven seconds left.

On the sideline, the defense had gathered right at the 25 yard line, the boundary line for the teams during a game. Normally, when one unit is on the field, the other is supposed to sit on the bench and rest. Not now. They had to see this.

There was no doubt in Jim Cantelupe's mind that the offense was going to score and win the game. "I kept thinking that *this* was the reason why we had to deal with the losses to Washington and Duke," he said. "We had to come through all that so we would be strong enough to come from behind and win this game. This game was going to make up for all the hurt we had felt in the other two."

Cantelupe could barely stand up at that point. He had hurt his groin and his knee during the game and he had a splitting headache. He knew he was going to be a lot more sore on Sunday. But that was OK. It would all be worth it when they won.

They had enough time to run the ball once more if they chose to. Notre Dame knew that. They keyed on the option. Counting on that, Sutton called a fake dive and quick pass to Leon Gantt. McAda pulled the ball out of Conroy's chest, stood up, and found Gantt, wide open. Touchdown. Thirty-nine seconds to play. It was just the way McAda had dreamed it.

It was 28–27, Notre Dame. The corps was going crazy. The Notre Dame fans were in complete shock. McAda glanced over to Sutton, who held up two fingers, his index finger and his pinky. If Sutton had done anything but hold up two fingers, he might have had a mutiny on his hands, led, of course, by the Fat Men.

A lot of teams in Army's position would have kicked the extra point and taken the tie. A tie against Notre Dame would have been viewed by everyone in college football as a major victory for Army; an embarrassing defeat for Notre Dame. It would have been one of the most stunning college football results in years. No one would have criticized Army for taking the tie, especially after being down 28–7.

Less than a year earlier, after coming from 31–3 down against Florida, Florida State coach Bobby Bowden had kicked the extra point and taken a tie, saying his team had come too far to lose on a two-point conversion that failed. Later in the season, Southern California coach John Robinson, after being down 21–7 to Washington, would do the same thing. Holtz had played for a tie in the past himself and snapped at NBC's John Dockery when he had the temerity to ask why.

Sutton never even considered playing for the tie. His players had given him too much effort for too many hours on too many days to ask them to settle for a tie at what could be the finest hour of their football lives. They would win or they would lose.

As soon as McAda saw the pinky and the index finger he knew exactly what play to call. It was a play they practiced all the time for two-point conversions. It was called "October-right," a quick pass in the right flat to Leshinski, the tight end. He was supposed to fake a block as McAda play-faked. Then, as McAda pulled up, Leshinski would step out into the flat, go to the goal line, turn, and catch the ball.

The play went just as designed . . . almost. The only problem came as Leshinski bounced off the line: one of the Notre Dame linemen bumped him, throwing him off balance by a stride. He was still able to get away from the line into the flat. McAda saw him and put the ball right on target. When he saw Leshinski catch it, he thought the ball game had been won. "I was about to throw my arms into the air," he said. "Then I saw that he wasn't in the end zone."

The play calls for Leshinski to catch the ball in the end zone. But because of the bump, he was on the one yard line when he caught the ball. As he gathered it in, his back was to the goal line. He needed to turn, square his shoulders, and drive into the end zone. But cornerback Ivory Covington was closing fast with a full head of speed. Covington weighs 185; Leshinski 240. The papers would make a big thing about that weight difference the next day, but the fact was Covington had a full head of steam and Leshinski was never able to get his shoulders turned upfield. If he had, he would have scored. Instead, Covington made a superb play, never letting him get turned. He used all his strength and momentum to push the receiver sideways, driving him out of bounds a foot short of the flag.

The two-point conversion was no good. Army tried an onside kick, but Notre Dame recovered and ran out the clock. It was over. Final: Notre Dame 28, Army 27. They had come up one foot short of the victory.

None of them could believe what had happened. They had done everything they had to do. They had stopped the Notre Dame offense down the stretch when they had to have the ball. The offense had produced 365 yards on the ground; 407 total. Thomas had picked up 159, Conroy 104, McAda 87. The Fat Men had never been better. They had held the ball for more than 36 minutes, which they had known would be the key to their chances coming in.

But they still hadn't won. Notre Dame walked off the field relieved and stunned. Holtz admitted they had been outplayed and lucky to escape. That was of little solace to the Cadets. They were sick and tired of being gallant losers. Even Sutton, who always seemed to find some words in crisis, couldn't find any. He wanted to go off in a corner and cry himself. They had almost made history.

Almost. Again.

# 12

# ZOOMIE WARFARE

AS devastating as the Notre Dame loss was for the Army players, they at least had the consolation of knowing they had lived up to the old football cliché about leaving everything they had on the field. That same afternoon at Navy, they couldn't say the same thing.

The Midshipmen had been as primed to play Air Force — or so they thought — as Army had been for Notre Dame. All week, the Yard had been alive with excitement and hope in spite of the previous Saturday's loss to Virginia Tech.

In the wake of the victory over Duke and everyone surviving six-weekers, the 14–0 loss to the Hokies had been a disappointment, but if the coaches were honest with themselves, not that big a surprise. Tech, as it would go on to prove by finishing 10–2 and winning the Sugar Bowl to finish ranked tenth in the country, was a very good football team — especially on defense.

It had started the season poorly, with losses to Boston College and Cincinnati, but had bounced back to beat Miami and Pittsburgh. Miami, with a new coach and an NCAA investigation unfolding, wasn't the powerhouse it had been in the eighties and early nineties, but it still had a lot of talented athletes. When the Navy coaches saw what the Tech defense was able to do in holding the Hurricanes to seven points, they knew it would be a tough afternoon for their offense.

That didn't mean they couldn't win the game. Tech's offense was vulnerable, and quarterback Jim Druckenmiller tended to make mistakes. If they could keep the game close and wait for the Hokies to make a critical error or two, they could steal the win. But that was what they would have to do: steal the game.

The day was warm and humid, more what you would expect in early September than early October. Unfortunately for the brigade, the uniform for the day was service dress blues with jackets. Those jackets could not come off, no matter how warm it got — and it was extremely sticky.

That was the least of the coaches' worries as they gathered for their morning meeting. Unlike Bob Sutton, who didn't meet with his coaches once the team had left West Point on the day prior to a game, Weatherbie liked to gather his coaches to go over things one last time at the hotel right after the pregame meal. The coaches would have been just as happy not to meet since the meeting was almost always a repetition of what they had been talking about all week and usually served to make everyone just a little more nervous about what was to come.

They all knew the game was potentially dangerous because a flat performance could produce a blowout, and that would not be good for a team whose confidence was fragile, especially with Air Force coming up in a week. Gary Patterson pointed out that even though the crowd would be over 30,000, almost half that number — 15,000 — would be Virginia Tech fans.

Weatherbie shook his head. "Six thousand," he said. "I checked."

Details, always details.

The team was healthy, except for Shaun Stephenson, who had undergone arthroscopic surgery as planned on Tuesday. The doctors had found the knee filled with floating cartilage and all sorts of junk that had to be cleaned out. They offered him two options: undergo the major surgery right now and be off crutches by the holidays or rest the knee for four weeks and see if it could be taped up to play in the last four games. There was no chance to damage it further that way; the surgery was going to be needed regardless.

Stephenson thought briefly about doing the surgery right away for one reason: if he sat out the whole season he could apply to come back for an extra semester the following fall to play football. Given his background and the fact that he might legitimately benefit academically from an extra semester, it was very possible he might be allowed to stay and play.

In the end, though, he decided against it. From his first day on campus it had been his goal to graduate with his class in the spring of 1996. He had worked long hours to make that happen, and as much as he loved football, he wasn't going to give that up. His best friends in life were his classmates. He would graduate with them. What's more, the doctors thought he could play the last four games. He had wanted eleven games; now the best he could do was four. But if he could play in those four and end his career by playing a role in the Army-Navy game, that would be good enough. He decided to hold off on the surgery.

The game went almost the way the coaches had hoped. Virginia Tech did turn the ball over — four times in the first half — but each time its defense stopped the Mids cold. About the only time they did move the ball was when sophomore Tim Cannada came in at fullback on the game's second series and ripped off two runs totaling 43 yards to move the ball to the Tech 34. But three plays later, the ball was back on the 42 and Brian Schrum had to come in to punt.

Tech's only touchdown of the first half came after a Navy mistake. The defense had stopped the Hokies and forced a punt. Adam Crecion, a plebe who had become the team's best punt blocker, thought he had a chance to get his hands on John Thomas's kick. Instead, he just missed the ball and piled into Thomas. Roughing the kicker — 15 yards. As often happens after that kind of error, the team given a second chance began to move the ball. The first quarter ended with the Hokies on the Navy 16 right in front of the brigade.

During the break between quarters, Weatherbie turned to the brigade, imploring them to make a lot of noise. They responded lustily, but on the first play of the second quarter, Druckenmiller lofted a perfect pass over Robert Green's grasp to receiver Jermaine Holmes for a touchdown.

That was Tech's only sustained drive of the first half. Navy's best chance to score came after David Viger recovered a fumble by tailback Duane Thomas at the Tech 30. The offense moved the ball exactly one yard and Covarrubias came on to try a 46-yard field goal. It flew wide right and the score was 7–0 at the break.

The mood in the Navy locker room was restless. The defense had given the offense four chances and the offense had come up empty. If anyone on the defense was going to point fingers at the offense, though, they would have to answer to Clint Bruce.

"Everyone in here better remember that we're *one* team, not two separate units," he screamed as soon as the door closed. "We know the offense will get points back, so let's just remember that. Anybody thinks different, they're going out to the woodshed. Understand?"

They understood. The coaches knew all the understanding in the world wasn't going to make it easy to score. "Their offense is doing everything it can to give us a chance," Weatherbie said. "But we're having trouble doing anything with that defense."

Paul Johnson knew that was true. But there wasn't much he could do when Tech's defensive line seemed to be in the backfield the moment McCoy took the snap. They had tried Fay at the end of the first half, and he had moved the ball briefly before throwing an interception with the clock running out. They would stick with McCoy in the hope that his speed would eventually create something.

The chance came right away. Cory Schemm, who had been weak as a puppy for two days because an abscessed tooth made it impossible for him to eat, took a McCoy pitch and picked up 13 yards for only the fourth Navy first down of the game. Then, on fourth-and-inches at their own 43, they went for it and McCoy made it with a foot to spare. Another pitch to Schemm picked up 16 more yards and they were in Tech territory at the 42. But that was when the Hokies decided they had seen enough. On fourth-and-three at the 35, McCoy took two steps to try and run an option and was plowed under before he could even think about pitching the ball.

End of drive. The defense hung tough, keeping them in the game. On one play, Andrew Thompson plowed through two blockers, tackled Thomas for a two-yard loss, and took a knee to the head. He came up dizzy. Not quite sure where he was, Thompson came off the field after Tech's punt and sat down with the linebackers.

"Are you OK?" Tommy Raye asked him.

"I'm fine, Coach, fine," Thompson said. He got up and walked over to the defensive backs. Patterson wanted to make sure he wasn't in never-never land.

"What day is it?" he asked.

"It's Saturday, Coach, and if you try to take me out of this game I'll kill you," Thompson answered. Patterson nodded and didn't say another word.

Thompson didn't even remember the conversation with Patterson or Raye after the game, but he did stay in. Tech didn't put together another sustained drive until the clock was under 10 minutes. Then, after Schrum had punted them into a hole at their own five, they finally moved the ball, going 95 yards, chewing up eight minutes of clock in the process. When Thomas finally scored on a pitch with 1:55 left to make it 14–0, it was over.

Navy had played about as well as it could have — especially on defense. Tech had simply been better. It hadn't been like Rutgers, where they had let a chance to win slip away; or Wake Forest, where they had played horribly and embarrassed themselves. They had given everything they had and it hadn't been quite enough.

Two days later when they walked into the locker room, two large handwritten signs were posted on the bulletin board. The first one read: "Jeremiah 29:11 — 'For I know the plans I have for you, declares the Lord; plans to prosper you, not to harm, plans to give you a hope and a future.' "

And right next to it: "Galatians 6:9 — 'And let us not get tired of doing what is right; for after a while we will reap a harvest of blessing if we don't get discouraged and give up.' "

That was Weatherbie's message for the week: the Lord has a plan for this team, and if we keep working and doing what is right, we will reap a harvest — that harvest being a win over Air Force.

In his journal Thompson was more direct: "Boy, do I want to beat those bastards," he wrote. "I can't forget one of those punk running backs laughing in my face after the game last year. I also won't forget the pain and embarrassment of last year's game either."

ALMOST no one at Navy had forgotten the pain and embarrassment inflicted by Air Force in recent years. Although the Navy seniors did have a win over Air Force — 28–24 their sophomore year — that victory had ended an eleven-game losing streak to the Zoomies. It was Navy's first and only win over Air Force since George Welsh's departure at the end of the 1981 season.

Since that time, Air Force had dominated CIC Trophy play. Prior to 1982, it had never won the CIC Trophy. Since then, it had won it ten times in thirteen years. Army had broken the spell in 1984, '86, and '88 but hadn't beaten the Falcons since '88. Air Force had held the trophy for the past six years. During those thirteen years, the Falcons were 12–1 against Navy and 10–3 against Army — 22–4 overall.

Some of the games had been close, notably the 1992 game in Colorado Springs, when Navy had recovered a late Air Force fumble with a 16–15 lead only to have an official incorrectly rule that the ball-carrier was already down. As in the Army-Duke game in 1995, Air Force went on to kick the winning field goal in the final seconds after the missed call. The fact that the officials publicly admitted the next week that the call had been blown did little to salve Navy's feelings.

The 1994 game wasn't nearly as close. It had been tied 7–7 in the first quarter before Air Force scored 36 straight points. The final was 43–21 only because Air Force coach Fisher DeBerry emptied his bench in the fourth quarter.

DeBerry, of course, had been one of Weatherbie's mentors. Weatherbie had worked at the academy during DeBerry's first six years as Air Force coach, and that experience was one of the reasons Weatherbie had been hired at Navy. The hope was that some of the lessons Weatherbie had learned from DeBerry about how to win at an academy would lead to success at Navy.

But all academies are not alike. In fact, each has its own distinct personality. Generally speaking, Navy is considered the most difficult academically because more engineering courses are required and because so many of the classes are extremely technical in their orientation. Army is considered to be the most difficult militarily: it has the most rules and less tolerance for breakdowns in military discipline. At Army they wake up the earliest — formation at 6:25 A.M.; first class at 7:15 — and morning formation is always outside, regardless of the weather. At Navy, they move inside when the weather turns cold, and formation isn't until 7 A.M., first class at 7:55.

Air Force's upperclassmen have carpeting in their rooms and some of them have TV sets. At Army, no one is allowed to watch television anywhere on the base until they are cows (juniors). Air Force's rooms are the most spacious, although Navy's — which are the smallest of the three — do have small showers. The West Point cadets consider this an extraordinary luxury.

Navy lives to beat Army and Army lives to beat Navy. But there is no hatred or even serious dislike between the two schools. It is an intense rivalry with a good-natured edge. There is no such amiability between Army and Air Force or Navy and Air Force. There is, if truth be told, bitterness in both rivalries.

The Air Force people can't stand the fact that nothing they can do will win them the attention that Army and Navy receive. "No one east of the Mississippi even knows we're alive or cares," one Air Force assistant said on the day Army played Air Force. "And we've kicked Army's and Navy's asses ever since we got here."

In general, Air Force players and coaches don't have a lot of respect for Army's and Navy's players and coaches. They think they're better because they have consistently *been* better. But because they don't think they receive proper credit for that dominance, they tend to pile it on at times — laughing in an Army or Navy player's face at the end of a game, for example. Thompson was not the kind of person who held grudges against people just for beating his team. Rubbing it in his face, however, was a different story.

The bitterness even carried over to the officers at Navy. During Air Force week, the players heard speeches from Secretary of the Navy John Dalton, from the Supe, from the commandant, and from the deputy commandant. Even Jack Lengyel, who normally let the officers give the speeches, got into the act at practice one day.

That was on Tuesday, after the players had sat through a two-and-a-half-hour ceremony commemorating the 150th anniversary of the academy. Practice started late as a result. About an hour in, everyone looked up and saw Dalton, Larson, Bogle, and Lengyel approaching. The last thing in the world Weatherbie wanted to do was stop practice for speeches. But he had no choice.

Dalton told the players they reminded him of Navy's 1954 "Team of Desire," which had been led by a quarterback named George Welsh and had bounced back from a disappointing 6–0 loss to Notre Dame to beat Army and then shut out Mississippi in the Sugar Bowl. Lengyel then reminded them that when they played Air Force Saturday, they weren't just playing for themselves, they were playing for the entire United States Navy and the entire Marine Corps.

The players knew this. Their locker room at the stadium had various sayings all over the walls. One was John Paul Jones, "I have not yet begun to fight." Another was Larson's credo of "excellence without arrogance," which was right over the door. And yet another was Lengyel's, "We play football for the United States Navy."

It wasn't that the players didn't respect Dalton or Larson or Lengyel or any of the officers. But they really didn't need to be told what was at stake when they played Air Force. They — not the officers or suits — had *played* in the game. They knew how awful it felt to be behind 43–7. And the last thing they needed to do was stand around on the practice field while their hamstrings tightened on them halfway through practice being told one more time how important the damn game was. But that was part of playing for Navy. Everyone liked to give speeches.

In the locker room, after wins, they were fun. They weren't even so bad at pep rallies. But not on the practice field; not on Tuesday afternoon when the workouts were long enough and tough enough to begin with.

Air Force week wasn't anything like Army week when it came to hijinks in Bancroft. Wednesday was wacky tie day and Thursday was ball cap day. And of course there was a mandatory-fun pep rally (actually it was called a Falcon Roast) on Thursday evening. Weatherbie, Thompson, and Garrett Smith were driven into the pep rally in a light armored vehicle and there were more rousing speeches.

"I am really tired of losing to Air Force," Larson said. "And I know we aren't going to lose to them on Saturday!"

They cheered wildly when he was finished. And with good reason. It was 7:55. "Thank goodness," said Marty Fisher, Thompson's roommate, glancing at his watch. "We were all worried this thing was going to make us all miss *Friends*."

If there were two things that all Army and Navy football players agreed on in life they were (A) *Friends* was not to be missed, and (B) anyone who thought Courteney Cox was half as hot as Jennifer Aniston needed to have his eyes examined.

\*    \*    \*

ANDREW Thompson was having a tough week, and it wasn't just because he wanted to beat the bastards from Air Force.

He knew it was going to be a hectic week, even without Air Force to worry about. His parents were coming to town Friday to spend a week, and even though he was excited about seeing them, their presence would make life more complicated. To begin with, his dad had a tendency to bring up the "transition" he was going to have to make, once football was over, to move on with his life in the marines and out of the game. He knew his father was right, but he also knew he didn't want to think about life after football until he had to. For the moment, everything else came second; football first.

Which brought up another problem. He had met Tracy Marini on summer cruise and they had hit it off right away. She was in ROTC at the University of Virginia and they had spent some time together during the summer and on weekends earlier in the fall. She would be coming up for the Air Force game and she and her parents were also coming to Annapolis the following week for the Villanova game. A Thompson-Marini family dinner was planned for that weekend.

Thompson wasn't comfortable with any of that. He liked Tracy, but he wasn't head over heels in love, and the truth was he was thinking of breaking up with her for the simple reason that he didn't have the energy to deal with football and school and a relationship. Right now, the relationship had to come third, and he was having trouble keeping his head above water in number one and number two.

Then there was school. Thompson was taking fifteen hours — five classes — and, as always, had to work extremely hard to stay ahead of the curve. Some classes were fun, like his first period Russian history class on Monday, Wednesday, and Friday. The professor was Arthur Rackwald, who was both brilliant and funny. He called football "an opiate for the masses" but clearly had a soft spot for the football players in his class. When Mark Hammond, who was taking two classes with Rackwald, couldn't answer a question one morning, the professor shook his head and said, "We must have discussed that on one of those Fridays you were off with the football team, eh Comrade Hammond?"

He referred to all his students as "comrade" and brooked no inattention. "You don't study physics on my time," he barked one morning at a mid trying to catch up for the next class. And when he noticed Thompson biting his nails, he lectured him on the evils of nail biting.

Rackwald was fun, even at 7:55 in the morning. The thermodynamics class that came next was one of those where Thompson and almost everyone in the class only occasionally knew what the professor was talking about. Thompson also had a naval law class, a class on Nazism, and another engineering class. He would have to take and pass eighteen hours during second semester in order to graduate. In doing that, he still didn't have it as bad as the engineering majors, some of whom had to take as many as twenty-three hours a semester, including labs.

The hours that the midshipmen spent going to class were the closest they came to feeling like normal college students. More than 75 percent of the professors at Navy are civilian — quite a few are ex-military — and although most classes begin with everyone standing to be ''presented'' formally to the professor, the classroom atmosphere is similar to what one might expect at a civilian school.

Of course, at most civilian schools class attendance is voluntary. If you don't want to show up on a given day — or on given days — you don't, and you risk missing information that may be needed on a test or, in some cases, being graded down if a professor counts class participation as part of your grade.

At the academies, class attendance is mandatory. Occasionally, if you should happen to know the student charged with handing in attendance lists, you might be able to get away with cutting, but that is extremely risky because the classes are small enough that most professors will notice an absence and because if you are caught, both you and the attendance taker are subject to an honor code charge. No one wants to mess with that. Class cuts are not unheard of, but they are rare. Additionally, if you do cut a class, the work is hard enough that it will undoubtedly hurt your grade.

Thompson had never cut a class in four years. He couldn't afford to. In each of his classes he sat in the front row to let the professor know that he was there and eager to participate. He often stayed after class when he could to ask questions, and he took all the EI — extra instruction — that he could. His attitude as much as his actual work had kept him afloat for four years, and he wasn't going to let down now with graduation in sight. Like a lot of midshipmen, he carried putty in his briefcase, and when he started to feel tired in class, he took the putty out and began squeezing it in order to stay awake. Others simply stood up when they got tired. That was allowed. Falling asleep was not.

After four years at a military academy, one gets used to the quirks of academy life, like having to salute whenever an officer walks by; having to formally ask permission to enter a room if a class is under way, or having to march into lunch every day while spectators gawk at you. But every once in a while, the quirks start to make you crazy.

As he walked into King Hall for lunch after his naval law class on the Wednesday before the Air Force game, Thompson had slung his book bag over his shoulder. His class schedule that morning had taken him from one end of the Yard to the other and back again. After his third class of the morning, he was just tired enough to leave his bag on his shoulder as he walked inside. He wasn't ten feet inside the door when he was stopped by one of the company chiefs.

"You need to get that book bag off your shoulder," the chief barked.

"Sorry sir," Thompson said.

The chief noticed Thompson's three stripes — as a senior and a football team captain he had two extra stripes. "Three-striper like you should know better than that. What kind of an example are you providing? You look completely unprofessional."

"Yes sir," Thompson answered. "You're right sir."

The chief nodded, his point made, and walked on. Thompson rolled his eyes in disgust. "That's the kind of thing around here that drives you nuts," he said. "Sometimes it seems like there's just no letup."

Actually, Thompson had gotten off easy. A few weeks later, Mark Hammond would commit the same offense and be put on restriction by his company officer, meaning he had no weekend liberty at the end of that week. Life for the first classmen was a lot easier than it was for plebes, but it was *never* easy.

Thompson's last concern that week — though not his least concern — was the marine flight test he, Shaun Stephenson, Joe Speed, and Brian Grana had to take on Sunday. It was a four-hour test and, knowing he would have trouble sleeping Friday night in anticipation of the game, and would no doubt be sore after the game Saturday night, Thompson was concerned about getting through the test. But he knew he had to do it. He wanted to fly helicopters in the marines and the only way to do that was to pass this test.

But everything — his parents, Tracy, schoolwork, the flight test — had to be pushed to his brain's back burner this week. Air Force was coming to town, and Thompson, like everyone else on the team, wanted to exorcise last year's bitter memories. There was only one way to do that.

SATURDAY dawned wet and gray. They hadn't really had a pleasant day for a home game yet. Pregame meal began with another speech. This one came from Tom Butler, the normally mild-mannered O-rep, who never seemed to get upset with anyone or anything.

Except Air Force.

"I was stationed at an air force/naval base the last couple of years and I can't begin to tell you how tired I got of the lack of respect the air force people had for our football program," he said. "That's what this is about out here today — respect.

"There's only going to be one team on that field that believes in 'excellence without arrogance,' because the other team has a lot of arrogance and they love to rub our noses in it when they beat us. You seniors know that these coaches are going to turn this program around. The question is, do you want to be part of that turnaround or do you want to read about it in the papers next year!

"This is combat. You all know you can't pick your conditions in war so we'll have to deal with the rain. Make no mistake about it, men, this is war. So enjoy your prewar meal."

The players were surprised by Butler's intensity. So was Weatherbie, who said, "A*men!*" out loud when Butler was finished. But it wasn't really anything new: Air Force was arrogant and cocky and losing to them would be no fun. They all knew that already.

By now, Weatherbie was concerned that the game might be getting *too* big in everybody's mind. When the coaches gathered for their pregame meeting, he told them he thought it was important that the players be reminded to approach this like any other game.

"That's going to be kind of hard, Coach," Gary Patterson said. "All week long, they've been told this game is bigger than the others. They've been told that by the Secretary of the Navy, by the Supe, by the 'Dant, by everyone on the Yard, and just now by Captain Butler."

Weatherbie nodded. "You're right. But I couldn't very well tell those people they couldn't talk to the team."

It was another one of those quirks about academy football. At other schools, the president of the university wasn't likely to show up on the practice field for too many pep talks. Nor were cabinet members seen giving rah-rah speeches very often. But at Navy — and Army — they were often a part of game preparation.

The bottom line was that the CIC games and Notre Dame were always going to be the biggest ones on the schedule. Weatherbie liked to say that your next game is your biggest game no matter who the opponent is, but he knew that wasn't true. He admitted as much as the meeting wrapped up.

"Well, guys," he said, "this is one of the games we were hired to win."

Dick Bumpas, who almost never said a word in these meetings, couldn't resist the opening. "I sure wish," he said, "you'd told us that before those other games. We'd have been a lot more relaxed."

The coaches did try to turn the emphasis back to football rather than bad blood or respect or lack of respect when they met with the players. In the defensive meeting, Patterson said, "I know a lot of you want to get even for last year. *Forget last year!* This is this year. Win this game. Period."

Bumpas pointed out to them that the wet weather would make it tougher for the Falcons to run their option (it would also be tougher for Navy to run its option, but that was Paul Johnson's problem). He quoted a Roman general who once said, "The god of war hates he who hesitates."

They had to be decisive against the option. Defensing the option takes great discipline because you have to stick to your assignment no matter what you think you see or where you think the ball may be going. As soon as you react to a fake and go away from your assignment, the potential for a big play exists.

Navy's job was summed up best by Rob Lawton, the assistant

trainer, who liked to put a different saying on his bulletin board in the training room each week. That week he had written: "The difference between winning and losing is not doing something right, but doing it exactly right."

"FELLAS, it's time to take it to another level. I promise you, losing to them will *not* be fun. I'll be a good Christian after we get through beating the hell out of them and wish them the best then."

It was ten minutes before kickoff. Weatherbie was still in with the coaches. The speaker was Colonel Mike Glynn, the marine O-rep. One more time the players were reminded of how awful it would be to lose to Air Force.

Maybe that was why they went out and played their worst first half of the season. Or maybe Air Force was just better than they were. In any event, with the rain having cleared off, the Mids found themselves down 17–0 before the second quarter was half over.

Things were going so badly for Navy that Ed McDevitt, the team doctor, was approached by a young midshipman early in the second quarter.

"Sir, there's a problem," the mid said. "The goat is sick."

"What do you mean the goat is sick?" McDevitt asked. "You mean the kid in the goat outfit or the real goat?"

"Both."

It was true. Apparently the midshipman in the goat's outfit had hyperventilated from all the excitement and needed to be assisted into the training room. At almost the same time the real goat, Bill XXVI — who was due to be retired the next week — also began to feel ill.

By halftime, both goats were feeling better, but the football team wasn't. The score was 17–3, Air Force, and all the coaches' worries had come into play. The offense had looked tight from the start, and the defense simply didn't have any answers for quarterback Beau Morgan, a talented, elusive runner who threw the ball effectively when he had to. The Navy offense had picked up a grand total of 95 yards — four of them through the air.

Weatherbie's message at halftime was direct: "This is the only chance you're going to get to play Air Force this year, and so far you aren't playing the way you can. They aren't beating you, you're beating you. That isn't a great team out there; it's a good team, one that will take advantage of mistakes. But it isn't unbeatable.''

They tried. Joe Speed intercepted a Morgan pass on the fourth play of the half and returned it to the Air Force 21. The crowd and the brigade stirred for perhaps the first time since the opening kickoff. But just as in the Virginia Tech game, the offense couldn't cash in. Three plays netted five yards and they had to settle for another Covarrubias field goal. It was 17–6 and the momentum that a touchdown would have given them was gone.

When Air Force scored again five minutes later to make it 23–6, Weatherbie decided it was time to change quarterbacks. McCoy still had only one completion, and down by 17 points, they had no choice but to throw the ball. Fay's first series got the ball into Air Force territory, but they bogged down again at the 27, and this time Covarrubias missed the field goal. One series later, though, Fay got them into the end zone, finding Astor Heaven from 19 yards out.

Hallelujah. It was their first touchdown since the Duke game, and the lead was down to 23–13. There were still almost 17 minutes left in the game. A comeback wasn't out of the question. Air Force picked up three yards on two plays to end the quarter. They faced third-and-seven at their own 23. Now, the crowd was really into it. On the first play of the fourth quarter, Morgan faked the option, rolled right, and found Craig Hancock open deep. Hancock gathered the ball in and would have scored if he hadn't tripped at the Navy four.

The play picked up 73 yards. The only sounds in the stadium were coming from the small cadre of Air Force cadets that sat opposite the brigade. The defense had gambled, going for a big play on Morgan, and had lost. Two plays later, Nakia Addison scored and it was 30–13.

The Mids didn't quit. They scored again on a Tim Cannada sprint up the middle with 4:17 left to cut the margin to ten. That touchdown set up Ryan Bucchianeri's first appearance on the field all season. Bucchianeri had moved up to second string on the kicking depth chart and was considered the best onside kicker the team had. Desperately needing the ball back, Weatherbie called for an onside kick and sent Bucchianeri into the game.

Most people didn't even notice. In fact, the public address announcer said, "Covarrubias to kick off for Navy," and on the official play-by-play of the game Covarrubias was listed as having kicked off.

"I finally get into a game," Bucchianeri said later. "And no one even knows that it's me."

His assignment was an unusual onside kick. Instead of kicking the ball hard into the ground and hoping for a high hop that would give a Navy player the chance to grab it out of the air, Bucchianeri was instructed to "bunt" kick. That meant kicking the ball softly along the ground, running next to it until it had gone the required 10 yards, and then diving on it.

It was a difficult, delicate play. If you kicked it too softly, a player from the other team could run up and grab it before it went the 10 yards it had to go before the kicking team was allowed to touch it. If you kicked it too hard, there was no chance to catch up to it. But they had worked on it in practice that week and Bucchianeri had actually pulled it off once.

Not this time. He came close, diving onto the pile along with a couple of Air Force players. He even got a hand on the ball briefly. But when they unpiled, Rory Rosenbach, a six-four, 240-pound defensive tackle, was lying on top of it.

Realistically, that was the ball game, although Navy did get the ball back one last time with less than two minutes to play and a chance to pull off a miracle. If they could score, onside kick successfully, and score again . . .

They couldn't. On fourth-and-four at the Air Force 43, Omar Nelson went up the middle, hoping to fool the defense. He didn't, coming up two yards short. It was over.

Navy plays two games all year when the players on both teams stay on the field for both alma maters after the final gun: Army and Air Force. Traditionally, the loser's song is played first. And so the Navy players stood at attention, the Air Force players behind them, while "Blue and Gold" was played. Then, they followed the Falcons, who were led by DeBerry, and stood silently while the Air Force alma mater was played.

Perhaps DeBerry had said something to his players about not kicking sand in the faces of the Mids. Maybe, because Navy was now

**The captains**
Joel Davis, Andrew
Thompson, Jim
Cantelupe, Garrett
Smith

**The coaches**
Bob Sutton, Charlie
Weatherbie. "The more
desperate team wins."

**Glenn Davis and Doc
Blanchard**
Their legacy is a
constant at West
Point — for better or
worse.

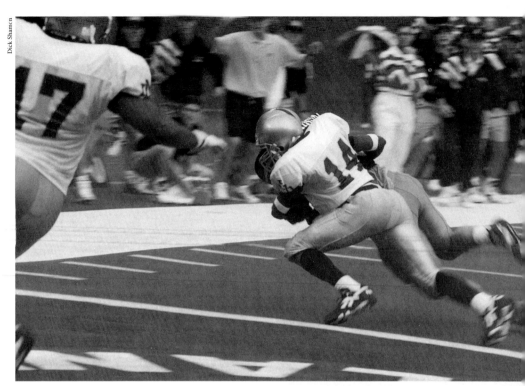

**Inches from glory**
Notre Dame's Ivory
Covington is able to
ride an off-balance
Ron Leshinski out-of-
bounds to avert one of
the greatest upsets in
football history.

**Matt Scornavacchi**
An iconoclast surviving in a
world that demands
conformity.

**Ronnie McAda (#7)**
"The day you get recognized is the best
day of your entire life."

**Marine Corps Col. Mike Glynn**
One of Navy's O-reps prepares for battle.

**Ben Fay**
He repeated his freshman year for the chance to go to Navy. "What was I thinking?"

The Corps of Cadets goes through its paces while the
Brigade of Midshipmen looks on.

Captains Thompson and Smith lead the Mids through the pregame cordon.

© Phil Hoffmann Photography

Captains Thompson and Cantelupe hug before the toss of the coin.

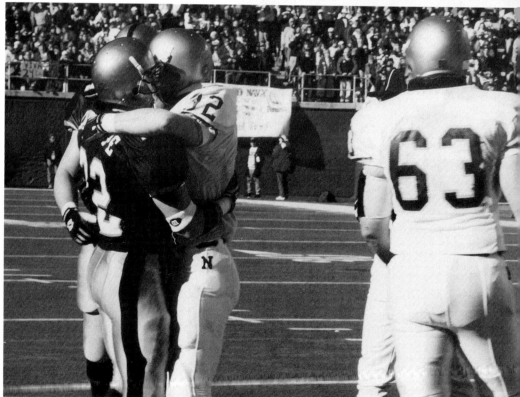

Dick Shamon

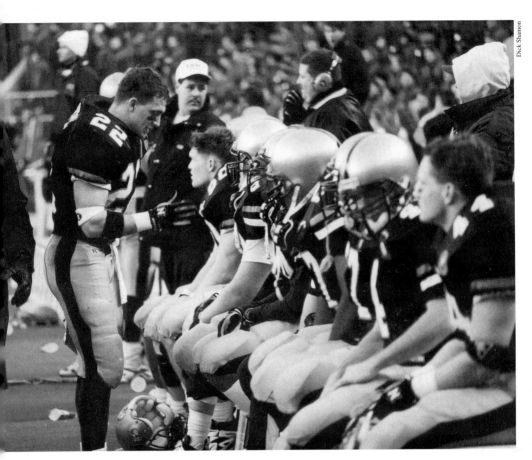

Cantelupe lectures the defense
after Navy's opening
touchdown.

Chris McCoy closes on the goal line as Cantelupe moves in to make a game-saving tackle.

**Al Roberts**
"Leadership is getting people to do something they shouldn't be able to do."

**2:49 P.M.**
The drive begins with McAda taking
the snap from the end zone and John
Conroy four yards deep preparing to
take the first handoff.

John Graves (#88) hauls in the pass a
step ahead of Kevin Lewis (#43).

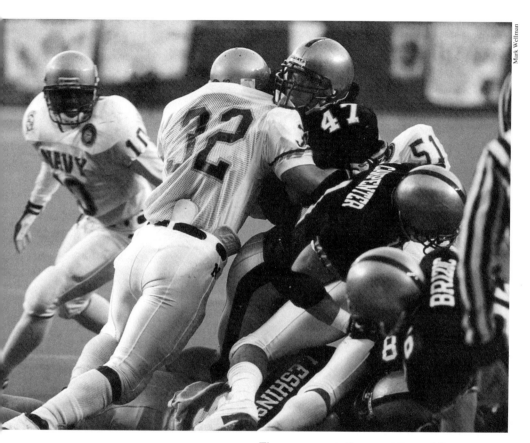

Thompson meets Conroy at the goal line:
"No, no, no!"

Mike Wells (#56 in black), Kyle
Scott (#55), and Joel Davis
(under Scott) wedge open the
hole for Conroy as McAda (#7)
gives him the ball one last time.

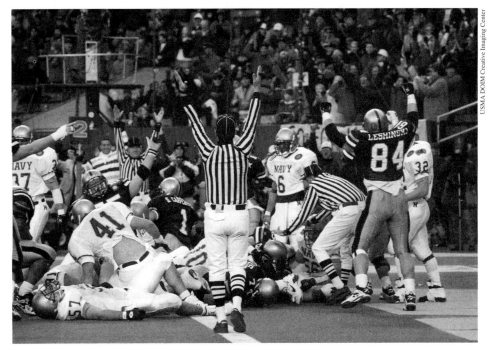

**The nineteenth play**
Touchdown. Conroy lies on top of Davis (#74) and Wells in the end zone.

**Navy's last gasp**
Donnie Augustus (#34) cradles the ball in the end zone while Jerrold Tyquiengco (#16) celebrates and Cory Schemm (#20) and Pat McGrew (#34) look on helplessly.

**The Brotherhood Weeps**
Andrew Thompson and Joe Speed

Mark Hammond breaks down during the singing of "Blue and Gold."

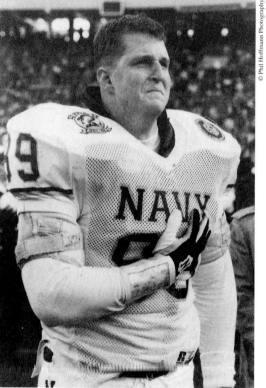

The playing of "Alma Mater." Note the two team
doctors, Bob Arciero of Army and Ed McDevitt of
Navy (hand on heart for the opponent's song),
standing together behind Abel Young (#25).

Superintendent Graves congratulates Bob Sutton but tells him there is still indecision on his job status.

The Army players get to sing "The Song" one last time.

coached by a former assistant of his, he had asked his team to show respect for them no matter what the outcome. Whatever it was, there wasn't any trash talking or sneering. The handshakes were, for the most part, silent. No one from either side lingered. By now, the rain was falling steadily. Air Force wanted to get home. Navy wanted to get as far away as possible.

DEBERRY is one of those good old Southern coaches who sounds as if butter wouldn't melt in his mouth when he talks about the opposition after a game. Navy had really battled, he said, given them one heckuva fight. There was no doubt in his mind that "Cholly" would do a fine, fine job building the program and Navy would win a lot of football games in the future. He was proud of his team for coming through on the road with a hard-fought victory over a tough Navy team.

"Cholly" wasn't feeling terribly sanguine about his team's toughness or the battle it had put up. He was disheartened because he knew his players hadn't played nearly as well as they could have. After the prayer, with Larson and Bogle standing silently by the door, he talked at length about learning how to beat good teams.

"That game could have been won, guys," he said softly. "We just made too many mistakes, hurt ourselves too many times. We didn't give ourselves a chance to win. We have got to learn how to compete against teams like this."

He paused, searching for answers that weren't there. "Someone's going to pay for the pain we feel right now," he said. "We'll come in Monday, look at this video, and kick Villanova's ass next week. We can still have a winning season and we can still share the Commander in Chief's Trophy if we beat Army and Army beats Air Force. There's a lot to look forward to and to work for."

He was groping. "We'll get better. We'll learn." He paused. "I love you guys, remember that." He stopped. The words were starting to choke in his throat. He collected himself and gave them the speech he gave them every Saturday:

"Tomorrow is the Lord's day. Get yourself to a church of your choice, and if you aren't with your loved ones, call them. There's someone out there who is responsible for getting you where you are today. Make sure you call them and thank them for that. OK, let's everyone get a hug.''

And so they all made their way gingerly around the locker room, exchanging hugs and a few words. For the first time all season, there were tears in some eyes. There had been so much buildup to this game, and it had gotten away so fast.

As he did after every game, Thompson made a point of circling the locker room to have a word with almost everyone on the team. As he started to pull his uniform off, he shook his head. ''I know I should be looking forward to dinner with everyone tonight,'' he said. ''But right now, it's hard to feel much like socializing with anyone, even my family.''

Even families have trouble understanding how much football players put into the game for those eleven chances a year to play for real. They hear about life at the academies, but they don't live it. Thompson walked out of the locker room and greeted his parents and Tracy.

''Disappointed?'' his dad asked sympathetically.

Thompson looked at him as if he had just landed from Mars. ''Disappointed? Gee, Dad . . .''

He stopped and shook his head sadly. He knew his father was on his side and didn't want him to be *too* disappointed. But how could he not be? He had played football for as long as he could remember, and now there were only five games left in his career. There would be no bowl game. There were no next years left. Five more games and the uniform would come off forever.

# 13

# FINALLY

WHEN he finally got back to his room on the night of the Notre Dame game, Jim Cantelupe's biggest problem was deciding what hurt the most.

Cantelupe had been knocked silly on the first play of the game, missed two plays, and then come back. Later, making a tackle, he had felt a sharp pain in his groin area. It was extremely discolored by the end of the game. As it turned out he had suffered a slight concussion on the first play but had fooled the doctors by answering all their questions correctly.

"I always know it's Saturday, and they would have had to knock me cold for me to forget who we were playing," he said. None of the injuries would have mattered if they had won the game. But the ache from the loss reminded him of how much his body ached.

College football players regularly take a pounding. They go through the season with cuts and bruises and nagging injuries that don't keep them from playing but can make the act of walking from one class to another painful. Cantelupe had gone a step beyond that in the Notre Dame game. He spent most of the day Sunday in bed — when he wasn't in the training room — but couldn't sleep that night because he was in so much pain from his groin and various and assorted other nicks. He also had a pounding headache.

He managed to make it to formation on Monday morning, but as soon as breakfast was over he was back in bed, since he had no first period class and he couldn't keep his eyes open because he was so exhausted.

The rules said that Cantelupe couldn't be in bed because it was morning inspection time until 9:30. No one in Cantelupe's company was going to turn him in, especially knowing his condition. But as luck would have it, Cantelupe's tactical officer, John Thomson, came into his room that morning looking for him.

Thomson had played football at Army. He had been a defensive back on the bowl teams in 1984 and '85. When Cantelupe had learned that Thomson was going to be his TAC he had been delighted. He didn't expect any special favors from him, but he had figured having a former football player running the company would make life a little easier for him. "You would expect the guy to understand what your life is like," he said. "I thought he would be somebody I could go and talk to, confide in, DB to DB."

It hadn't turned out that way. Thomson was concerned that if he showed any favoritism toward Cantelupe it would be viewed within the company as the ex-footballer taking care of the current footballer. So, he bent over backwards to be tough on Cantelupe and his roommate, Kevin Norman, who had been a punter during his first two years at the academy.

Cantelupe's relationship with Thomson was perhaps best summed up by Thomson's room inspection on the twenty-sixth of September. Most room inspections are done by first classmen. Occasionally they are done by a noncommissioned officer, and every so often by the TAC. Cantelupe and Norman had received consistently good reports throughout the semester. The worst thing anyone had written during the first four weeks of the semester was "fix up closet and tighten bed." Most of their reports had concluded with comments like "good room" or "good AMI." On September 13, the officer doing the afternoon inspection had written two words on the correction card: "GREAT PMI!"

Then Thomson showed up. His report on Cantelupe and Norman's room for the Tuesday morning after the Washington game read as follows:

Unsecured footlockers, wet sink/stopper up, dirty mirror, too many civilian clothes on display (Cantelupe), house shoes not aligned (Norman), boodle boxes improperly displayed, bed improperly made (Cantelupe), window sill cluttered and covered with food, windows open from the bottom, books not properly stored in book cases, vitamins not locked away, civilian articles hidden in green girls [the West Point nickname for the green blankets used on the beds], dusty shoes under bed, unshined and disreputable shoes under bed (Norman), dusty work areas, floor not swept under desks, too many civilian hats displayed, too many civilian shoes in coat closet, hangers not spaced properly in coat closet, short overcoats not sent out for re-striping.

A civilian walking into Cantelupe and Norman's room that morning probably would have found it neat. Thomson saw havoc. Everything Thomson mentioned was in the 464-page book of barracks regs that each cadet is issued. There are limits on everything from hats to family pictures to shoelaces. Technically, every one of Thomson's comments was accurate. But almost no one followed the barracks regs to the absolute letter of the law.

Ten days later, Thomson was back. He didn't find as many things wrong this time, but there were still "too many knick-knacks displayed; Regs and other manuals located on the wrong part of the bookshelf," and Cantelupe once again had the dreaded "loose bed."

Cantelupe didn't like the tension he felt existed between he and Thomson. He had almost always gotten along well with his TACs, which was not surprising since he was, generally speaking, a cadet who did his work, got things done on time, and stayed out of trouble. Now, as a senior, with an ex–football player as his TAC, he was having trouble for the first time in his life.

The tension simmered until the Monday morning after the Notre Dame game, when Thomson walked into Cantelupe's room and found Cantelupe asleep in bed during AMI. "He went ballistic," Cantelupe said later. "Screaming and yelling, telling me I was an embarrassment to the company and the academy. I tried to explain to him that I had been up all night in pain, but he didn't want to hear it."

Two days later, having spent most of Monday and Tuesday receiving treatment, Cantelupe walked into Thomson's room and requested a "closed door" session. At West Point, closed door is more than just a literal term. It means that a cadet has asked an officer for permission to speak his mind, without fear of reprisal if he says something that might, under normal circumstances, be considered disrespectful. A request for a "closed door" is considered serious business. If the officer does not think there is good reason for a "closed door," he may deny the request.

Thomson waved Cantelupe in and closed the door.

Cantelupe told Thomson that he had never expected special treatment from him but that he thought he was getting it — especially bad treatment. He asked Thomson if he honestly believed he would have just gone to sleep during AMI without a legitimate reason for doing so.

"The Army way is by the book," Thomson answered. "You know that."

"No, I don't know that," Cantelupe said. "A good officer uses common sense in dealing with people; he uses the book when he needs to and ignores it if and when the situation calls for it to be ignored."

They went back and forth for ninety minutes. Cantelupe felt better when they were finished because he had gotten a lot off his chest and because, even though Thomson wouldn't admit it, he knew he had made some good points. Thomson was certainly never going to be a confidant, but maybe they could have a better working relationship for the rest of the semester.

Having dealt with Thomson, he now had to focus on a larger concern: whether he would be able to play on Saturday at Boston College. The doctors had told him that practicing during the week was pretty much out of the question. Most of the time, Sutton had a no practice/ no play policy. If he was going to make an exception for anyone, it would probably be Cantelupe.

That rule would only become relevant if Cantelupe was ready to play on Saturday. On Wednesday night, after his session with Thomson, walking back down the hall to his room wasn't easy. The thought of playing football at that moment was out of the question. Still, when people asked him if he would be ready for Saturday, Cantelupe's answer was direct: "Absolutely."

Exactly what kind of shape the Cadets would be in wasn't as clear. They had now been through four straight disappointing weeks, the Notre Dame loss being the most heartbreaking of them all, not only because they were so close but because of who the opponent was and what a victory would have meant to the program — and to Sutton.

After all, unless the team completely collapsed in the second half of the season, it would be difficult to fire the first Army coach since Red Blaik to beat Notre Dame. That issue was raised during the week when Mike Vaccaro, the columnist at the *Middletown Times Herald-Record,* blasted General Graves for letting Sutton continue to blow in the wind.

Vaccaro's point was that no reasonable observer watching this Army team play could conclude that Sutton was getting anything less than the very best from it. A new contract should have been on Sutton's desk, Vaccaro wrote, after the Washington game and, if not then, certainly now. If coming within a foot of beating Notre Dame wasn't proof enough that Sutton deserved an extension, what was?

Graves had been told by the Army brass that the decision on Sutton's future was his to make. Al Vanderbush, the athletic director, very much wanted Sutton retained. Graves wasn't prepared to make that commitment. At least not yet. Since he was retiring at the end of the school year, this was one of the last major decisions he would make. He wasn't going to be rushed into it and he wasn't going to make it based on emotion. He had told Sutton and Vanderbush that he would make a decision when the season was over. He wasn't going to be swayed from that position.

Graves was certainly aware of the fact that teams that come close to winning big games and don't win them often come up flat the next week or the week after. The Cadets were 1–3–1. They had to play at Boston College, where they would be a decided underdog and, after that, had games left with Colgate, East Carolina, Air Force, Bucknell, and Navy. Only the two Division I-AA games — Colgate and Bucknell — could be considered almost lock victories. What if the team lost the other four? How would Graves look extending Sutton's contract after back-to-back seven-loss seasons?

Cantelupe was aware of what was going on. He also knew that the team needed to be as emotionally ready to play Boston College as it had been for Notre Dame. On Wednesday, after he hadn't been able to practice for a third straight day, he sent an E-mail message to his teammates:

When you win you get a feeling of exhilaration.
When you lose, you get a feeling of resolution.
You resolve never to lose again.

— Vince Lombardi

7–3–1. Boston College is in our way, let's kick their
f------ ass for four quarters!!!! This is our season! Nobody
said we have to keep the score close anymore.

Lupe.

That was the approach they needed to take going to Boston. They
assumed that they wouldn't be able to sneak up on the Eagles after
the Notre Dame game. They paid little attention when BC was listed
as a thirteen-point favorite. That was fine, they thought, but we know
better. The surprise came when they arrived in Boston Friday and
some of them picked up the *Boston Globe*. Mike Hasselbeck, who
would be starting at quarterback for the Eagles, was quoted as saying
that his team didn't expect an easy game against Army. "We expect
them to come in here and put up a good fight," Hasselbeck said.

Sutton read that quote just before he left his room to join the team
for dinner on Friday night. It brought a smile to his face. He would
certainly make his players aware of the quote before kickoff. More
important, though, it revealed something about BC's mind-set: they
were viewing this game as a good warm-up for their showdown with
Notre Dame the next week. That was just fine with Sutton.

After five years as the head coach, Sutton had become a creature
of habit on road trips. He always ate the same dinner on Friday
night — carrots, mashed potatoes, and coffee. He always sat with the
quarterbacks and the kickers, and he always asked each game captain
to say a prayer prior to a meal — one of them on Friday night before
dinner, the other on Saturday morning before pregame meal.

Those were the only times that Army prayed as a team, although the
team chaplains always conducted a Fellowship of Christian Athletes
"huddle" on game mornings. Normally about a third of the travel
squad attended. Sutton was always at the FCA huddles, in part because
he wanted to be there to share that time with his players and in part

because he often didn't make it to church on Sundays during the season.

"Two things I'm bad about during the season," he said. "Getting to church and getting my exercise. As soon as the season's over, I do a lot better job at both of them."

The contrast on the subject of religion between Sutton and Charlie Weatherbie was striking. Sutton was a religious man, but he considered religion to be a private matter. He never told his players to go to church, and since it was the players who led the prayers, it was up to them as individuals to say whatever they felt like saying. More often than not the prayers were simple blessings of the food.

At Navy, the team prayed often and almost all the prayers were led by Weatherbie, who spoke very directly to God at times — "Lord, let us play with focus and fanatical effort," "Lord, allow us to do a good job analyzing this video we're going to watch" — and always ended by making a direct reference to Christ dying on the cross.

The Navy players, much like any group of college-aged people, could probably be divided into three groups on the topic of constant prayer: some loved it, some were neutral about it, some thought it too much. They all respected the clearly genuine nature of Weatherbie's faith. Some of them had thought that Chaump didn't pray enough. But there were some who wondered if football was important enough to pray about so often. Weatherbie never asked God directly for victory, but he did often request all the elements that would lead to it.

Matt Scornavacchi, the team's resident agnostic, had wondered early on how Brian Grana, the team's only Jewish player, felt about the prayers and their very Christian nature. One day before practice he asked Grana.

"I like it," Grana said. "I don't have to go along with every word that Coach is saying in the prayer, but I think praying together the way we do bonds us and this is a team that needed bonding. I'm fine with it."

Scornavacchi was fascinated by that answer and decided if Grana didn't mind praying, then there was no reason for him to mind praying. "Tell you the truth, I can take it or leave it," he said. "Most of the time, I'd just as soon leave it. But if it helps us win games, then I'm all for it. I'll do anything that will help us win games."

No doubt the Army players would have willingly prayed four or five times a day if they thought it would help them win games. But unlike the Navy players, who had been through so much trauma in recent years and had dealt with so many events that had been divisive, they didn't need anything extra to bond them. They were already a close-knit group, with or without prayer.

Another difference between Weatherbie and Sutton was repetition: while there are certain basics that every football coach talks about each week, some coaches believe in repeating things week in and week out to make them habit. By the sixth week of the season — if not sooner — almost any Navy player could have gotten up and given a Weatherbie pregame talk almost word-for-word. He might vary it slightly depending on the quality of the opponent, but not much.

Every game was an opportunity. The kicking game would be critical and the five "dos" had to be executed. They had the best punter in the country. The offense had to protect the ball — "We can't play without it, men" — the defense had to "wrap up and grab cloth on every play." They needed focus and fanatical effort. Every player had to concentrate only on doing his job and have faith that his teammates would do theirs. They didn't have to play a perfect game. They were playing for the navy and the Marine Corps worldwide. Jeremiah 29: 11 and Galatians 6:9 would be quoted in whole or part. It was time to turn it loose and have fun. And how do we spell fun?

Sutton knew that anything a coach said was essentially the same message from week to week. But he believed it had to be said differently or the players might stop listening. That was why he always came up with a different "theme" for each game. Usually, it was a short phrase that was written on the players' travel itineraries. For Boston College, the theme was "take the hill."

Since Boston College is located in the Chestnut Hill section of Boston, that was simple and made sense. But there was more to it than that. Taking a hill is something the army is often asked to do in war. Every Friday night, the team watched a film that focused on that week's theme.

The films were put together at West Point's Center for Enhanced Performance, which worked with Army athletes in a number of areas of sports psychology and also was a reading and learning center for the entire corps. Mike Sullivan, who spent his afternoons and evenings helping to coach the linebackers, spent the early part of his days teaching at the CEP. Each week, after talking to Sutton and some of the players, he would put together the Friday night movie.

Sullivan's BC flick started with clips from the movie *Hamburger Hill,* which was based on the true story of a battle in Vietnam in which American soldiers had assaulted a hill eleven times in ten days before finally capturing it. For the players, the highlight came when an American TV reporter walked up to one of the GIs, microphone in hand, and said, "There are people who say you have no chance to take this hill."

The GI looked into the camera and said, "You listen up, newsman. We're going to take this fucking hill."

From Hamburger Hill to Chestnut Hill. As soon as the clips of Vietnam had faded, they were replaced on screen by clips of the 1994 BC rout of Army. Those were quickly replaced by shots from Army's last victory over BC, a 45–14 romp in 1985. The message was clear: people say you can't take this hill; but you know you can take this fucking hill.

"See you in the morning," Sutton said as soon as the lights came up. He didn't see any reason to add another word.


WHILE Sutton went to his room, there was one last ritual left for the players and assistant coaches: the snack.

By the time the Friday night movie was over, it had been almost three hours since the Fat Men had eaten. They had ordered pizza after arriving at the hotel and had eaten a huge dinner at 6:30. But now it was 9:30. It was time to eat again. And so they did. Huge sandwiches and desserts. Just to make certain he didn't starve overnight, each took an extra sandwich or two with him to his room.

"It's ten hours until breakfast," Eddie Stover said, walking out with a huge sandwich cradled in his arms. "We can't possibly go that long without eating."

Joel Davis nodded sagely. "It would be a very un-Fat thing to do," he said.

The coaches didn't partake of the sandwiches, but as soon as the players had cleared the room, they had ice-cream sundaes. The ORs (at Navy they are called O-reps; at Army ORs) and trainers usually joined in, and everyone sat around swapping stories until they were too tired to worry about the game anymore.

The good news about a noon kickoff is that no one spends the morning lying in bed trying to go back to sleep. The players were up at 6:30 and ate breakfast an hour later. Then they met in the parking lot for their pregame walk.

The weather report for the day called for heavy rain and high winds. The morning was gray and overcast as Sutton led his team around the hotel parking lot. Everyone walked, even Adrian Calame, who was on crutches and had been told that his football career was over. He was still part of the team, though, and that meant that he took part in the team walk, crutches or no crutches.

The rain started while the buses were winding their way to the stadium, and by the time the kicking specialists took the field for pre-game warm-ups, it was pouring.

"Perfect weather for us," Cantelupe said to Derek Klein as they walked onto the field. "It will be hard for them to throw the ball with all this wind and rain."

Cantelupe had gotten into Thursday's practice for a few plays but still hadn't been certain on Friday if he was going to be able to play. But the Indocin (an anti-inflammatory) and the painkillers he had been taking had finally kicked in, and he woke up Saturday morning feeling much better. He was ready to play.

He wasn't alone. Sutton reminded them about Hasselbeck's *Boston Globe* comment just before they left the locker room. "Let's let them know right away that we aren't here for a good fight," he said. "We're here to take the damn hill!"

At Army, everything is ritual — even leaving the locker room. A lot of teams post inspirational sayings over the door to their locker room and the players slap the sign before walking through the door. At Navy, the sign changed depending on who the coach was. Weatherbie's was: "Fun is spelled W-I-N." The sign hadn't changed at Army for so long that no one could remember exactly when it had first been put over the door. It read: "I lay me down to bleed awhile and I will rise again to fight."

As soon as Sutton was finished talking, equipment manager Dick Hall, who had grown up in the shadow of West Point, served in the army, and then returned to West Point and become the equipment manager in 1975, took up his position next to the door. As each player passed, Hall gave him a pat on the back or a tap on the helmet and said softly, "Touch the sign, Jimmy/Johnny/Ronnie. That's it, let's go." He did that for each player, then waited until the room was clear. He was always the last man out the door.

The game did not begin auspiciously. On the opening kickoff, Ron Thomas, who had played so well against Notre Dame, limped off with a sprained ankle. Tim Kelly's quick assessment wasn't very positive: high sprain. Not likely to play again today. Then, on Army's second possession, McAda limped off, his back bothering him again. Everyone groaned. When would their luck change?

Soon. Adam Thompson came in and the Cadets went right down the field and scored. Brad Miller picked up 35 yards on a pitch to the three yard line and Rashad Hodge went in on the next play. Midway through the first quarter, it was 7–0. The teams traded punts, Ian Hughes pinning BC on the four yard line with a 47-yarder. On the Eagles' second play, Hasselbeck fumbled and linebacker Matt Coldsnow jumped on the ball at the BC 10. It took three plays from there to get Conroy into the end zone. It was 14–0 after one.

By now, the rain had become monsoonlike. Alumni Stadium, which would have been sold out in decent weather, was perhaps two-thirds full, and the very wet natives were getting restless. They were even less happy when BC wide receiver Adrian King fumbled on the next series and McAda, back in and feeling fine, went 14 yards to end a 37-yard drive. Ninety seconds into the second quarter, it was 21–0.

"No let up now. Pour it on them," Davis yelled as the Fat Men came off the field. This was FMC weather. Keep the ball on the ground and let the Fat Men do their thing.

Boston College finally pieced a drive together and Hasselbeck found King in the end zone for a five-yard touchdown pass with 10:40 left. But there was a flag. Holding — Boston College. Touchdown waved off. On the next play, Hasselbeck dodged the rush and threw the ball down the middle into the end zone — and the waiting arms of Ray Tomasits. He returned the ball to the 13 yard line. By now, the BC players were starting to yell at one another in frustration.

It only got worse for them. On Army's first play after the Tomasits interception, McAda faked the dive to Conroy, pulled the ball out of his stomach, and sprinted around the right side for 34 yards. In two plays, they had gone from a BC touchdown to no touchdown and an Army first down near midfield. Effortlessly, they kept moving the ball. On second-and-seven at the 25, McAda ran the exact same option play and, untouched, raced 25 yards for a touchdown.

With 7:10 still left in the first half, it was 28–0.

"This is impossible," one BC fan screamed. "We can't be losing 28–0 to *Army!*"

They weren't for very long. Two minutes later, with the Eagles again pinned deep, Hasselbeck forced another pass over the middle and Brian Tucker intercepted it and returned it to the BC 24. By now, Hasselbeck was probably convinced that Army was going to give his team a pretty good fight. Two plays later, McAda faked the dive again and this time dropped back to pass. John Graves was so wide open in the end zone he could have sung the words to the fight song and the alma mater before anyone from BC showed up. McAda put the ball right on his numbers.

When J. Parker booted the extra point over the screen into the stands, it was 35–0. The BC fans were so upset that they refused to return the ball. Instead, they began tossing it from one section to another as security guards chased helplessly after the wayward ball. The guards had about as much luck as the home team was having catching anyone from Army. Perhaps the fans thought if they kept the ball, the game would have to be stopped.

The good news for BC was that there was only 1:14 left in the half. The bad news was that they were so messed up they couldn't even run out the clock. Starting from their 20, the Eagles moved back 10 yards on a hold, five more on a delay of game. Two running plays got them to the 14. By now, sensing another chance to score, Army was using time-outs to stop the clock. BC helped out even more: Hasselbeck tried to pass on third down. Incomplete. The clock stopped with 46 seconds still left.

BC's punt — into the wind — went out-of-bounds on their 41.

Forty seconds left. Loads of time. McAda picked up five and stepped out of bounds. Hodge got 21 up the middle. McAda hit Ron Leshinski over the middle to the one. Hodge took it in from there. They had made it with eight seconds to spare.

When time finally ran out, the scoreboard said it was 42-0. The fans, wet, cold, and angry, booed loudly. "Sweetest music I ever heard," Joel Davis said as they headed for the warm, dry locker room. If they were soaked, they hardly noticed.

Sutton tried to act as if the game wasn't over. "We're only halfway up the hill," he insisted. They knew better, but they listened anyway. "When we've been behind in games, we've said in here, 'Let's win the second half.' Same thing when we're ahead. Let's win the second half."

Around the country, as the halftime score was posted, people were looking at one another and saying, "That can't be right." The press box at Navy, where the Mids were struggling to beat Villanova, called the press box at BC to double-check the score. "We didn't think Army would be behind 42–0," sports information director Tom Bates said. "But it certainly never occurred to us that they'd be *ahead* 42–0."

It hadn't occurred to anyone. The Eagles had plenty of talent — they would be within a touchdown of Notre Dame late in the fourth quarter the following week — but not very much heart. As soon as Army knocked them backwards, they folded.

The second half was little more than a glorified scrimmage. BC finally scored on its opening drive of the third quarter, but it ran almost seven minutes off the clock. Coach Dan Henning had thrown in the towel. He wasn't even going to try to get close. All he wanted to do was keep the score as respectable as possible.

Sutton played everyone in the second half. Joe Triano, who had been the number one fullback going into preseason, only to be set back first by an ankle sprain, then by a broken wrist, got into a game at fullback for the first time all season. He ripped off a 36-yard run — only to have it called back due to a hold.

Nothing else went wrong. The four hundred cadets who had made the trip spent most of the second half chanting "Fix bayonets," meaning they were locked in on their target and ready for the kill. The kill had already taken place.

Cantelupe played and played well, although Sutton got him out as soon as there was no shutout to defend. There was no reason for him to take any more hits on this day. Cantelupe took his helmet off, hugged Klein, and shook his head.

"It's almost as if all the frustration that's been building came out today," he said. "BC was in the wrong place at the wrong time and, coming in here, they didn't even know it or understand it. We've been building to this for a month, we just didn't know it ourselves."

The final was 49–7 and, if Sutton had wanted it to be, it could have been much worse. The fourth quarter was little more than one long hug-fest along the Army sideline. By that time, the crowd had dwindled to almost nothing. The only noise in the stands was coming from the corner on the Army side where the cadets and the Army band were located.

When it was over, the BC players sprinted for the locker room, humiliated and embarrassed. The Army players, soaked to the bone, lingered to look at the scoreboard and listen to the alma mater. As they piled into the locker room, Ray Tomasits kept saying over and over, "We get to sing the song. We get to sing the song. It's been so long since we sang the song I'm not sure I remember the words."

They all remembered the words. Sutton was so happy, he was jumping into people's arms in celebration. About the only somber moment came when General Graves came up to congratulate him.

"Great win, Bob."

"Thank you sir."

Down the hall, in the interview room, several players were politely telling the Boston media that it was just their day, that things had gone their way and they had little doubt that BC would have better days because they still had a good football team.

Brian Tucker wasn't willing to go that route. Tucker had grown up in Odessa, Texas, and had played at Permian High School, which had come to the attention of the entire country in H. D. Bissinger's brilliant book *Friday Night Lights*. The book was about the hold that high school football has on much of America, and he picked Odessa and Permian as his case study. Football was an obsession at Permian, not only for everyone at the school but everyone associated with the school in any way.

Tucker had no problem with that perception. He was proud of his Permian roots and the two Texas state champions he had played on. If there was one thing he had learned at Permian and had reinforced during four years at West Point, it was that football was a tough, mean game and you never gave up no matter what the conditions or the score were. Tucker had torn up his knee in spring practice and had been expected to be out until midseason. He was back for the Duke game. As thrilled as he was with the outcome of this game, he was disgusted by the way BC had reacted to adversity.

"They quit, gave up," he told a newspaperman from Boston. "They had no heart. They disgust me."

Bob Beretta, Army's sports information director, heard what Tucker was saying and shook his head. He knew Sutton wouldn't be thrilled to hear a comment like that, no matter how true it might be. A camera crew came up to Tucker. Could they have a minute? Beretta thought for a second about grabbing Tucker and suggesting he soften his comments just a little bit. But he stopped, in part because he didn't like telling players what to say or what not to say, but also because he was certain Tucker wouldn't repeat those comments with a TV light shining in his face.

The camera went on. Tucker was asked about the game. "BC quit, gave up," Tucker said to the camera. "They had no heart." He paused. By now Beretta knew what was coming next. "They disgust me."

Beretta couldn't help himself. He started to laugh.

A few feet away, Jim Cantelupe was talking to Mike Vaccaro, who now had even more reason to write that Sutton's contract should be renewed. Graves had left the locker room and was looking for Cantelupe, who he knew had played hurt. He walked up and shook Cantelupe's hand. "Great leadership, Jim," he said. "Great win."

"Thank you sir."

Graves turned to go and saw Vaccaro standing there. They stared at one another for a moment. Graves straightened up, looked past Vaccaro, and headed for the door. Vaccaro decided this wasn't the right moment to ask about the contract.

It was the best win any of them could remember. They hadn't just beaten BC, they had completely humiliated them. They had finished the game with 555 yards in total offense. Cantelupe stared at the final stat sheet and shook his head.

"What a great feeling to have all the work finally pay off," he said. He smiled. "This may sound cocky, but we deserved this."

Every bit of it.


ABOUT the only person who had a complaint in the aftermath of the Boston College game was Ronnie McAda: he had rushed for 116 yards. That meant a night out with the Fat Men. "They're gonna kill me," he said. "I'll be in debt until I graduate."

Since the team had moved the ball almost at will on the ground (482 yards rushing) McAda had only completed two passes in the game. One had gone to tight end Ron Leshinski, who was one of those rare players who was so talented that he had started every game his plebe year. As a junior, Leshinski was perhaps as good a football player as the team had, someone who the coaches wished they could get the ball to more often.

The other completion went to John Graves. It was the *fifth* catch of his four-year Army career. One had come as a junior. The second had come in the Lehigh game. The next two had come during the desperate final drive against Rice. The catch against BC had not only been the longest of Graves's career — 26 yards — it had been for a touchdown, his first ever.

"I always figured I'd get one sooner or later," he said. "I may not be very talented, but I am very stubborn."

Make that *very* stubborn. If not, Graves wouldn't have been at West Point, wouldn't even have been playing football. He was the type of person people always underestimated. He had an aw-shucks, Arkansas drawl that made him sound more like some hick who had just wandered in from milking the cows than the highest-ranking senior on the football team academically.

"I had a 2.4 first semester my plebe year," he said. "My parents couldn't figure out what was goin' on because I had like a 3.6 in high school. I told 'em, 'This is a whole different ball game.' I kind of struggled with all the English and history they made us take. I'm a lot more comfortable in science and math."

Having found his comfort level as an economics major, he hiked his GPA to 3.5 as a junior, and with an average of just over 3.2 for three years he had the highest class rank among the seniors. Joe Triano, Mike Wells, and Jim Cantelupe were next, and the four of them were, according to unofficial calculations, the only football seniors in the top half of the class.

It was unusual for the football team not to have someone ranked very high in the class. Graves was 205th. A year earlier, the football team had produced Eric Oliver, who had finished second in the senior class and been selected for a Rhodes Scholarship (which he turned down), and Hans Pung, who had been First Captain of the Corps of Cadets — the highest rank a cadet can achieve.

But neither Oliver nor Pung was a leader on the football team. Pung was strictly a special teams player who made one tackle the entire season and lettered only as a senior. Oliver, a linebacker, was a very good player who was fifth on the team in tackles. But he was quiet, more of a scholar than an athlete, someone who was respected by his teammates but never looked to in the way Cantelupe and Davis were.

This was a senior class of grinders, hard workers for whom few things came easily but who never seemed to mind. Graves was a perfect example. As a kid, he had gone to seven different schools in seven years from kindergarten through the sixth grade. His mother, Judy, divorced his father, David Callis, when John was two. She took John and his two older brothers to live with her parents in Warren, Texas. Their house burned down — one of John's earliest and most vivid memories — and they ended up in Shreveport, Louisiana.

It was there that Judy met William Graves, who had retired from the air force to work for the Federal Aviation Administration. They got married when John was seven and moved briefly to Texas, then to Oklahoma City, to Fort Smith, Arkansas, and then eventually to Benton, a suburb of Little Rock. Even then they weren't finished moving, because after a year the family moved from one side of Benton to the other and John switched schools one more time.

When he was eight, John learned that his father had died after falling and hitting his head in the bathroom. David Callis was a recovering alcoholic who had spent a good deal of time in and out of VA hospitals (he had also been in the air force) and, according to the story John was told, he slipped in the bathroom one day, hit his head, fell, and by the time anyone found him hours later it was too late.

He was thirty-nine. "Strangest thing about it is he always told my mom he knew he wouldn't live to be forty," Graves said. "I never really knew him, since I was two when they split." He thinks of William Graves, who adopted all three of Judy's sons, as his father.

With all the moving around, the one certainty in John's early years was football. He started playing when he was six and, even though he was small, had a knack for the game from the start. Coaches always played him all over the field, on offense and defense, keeping him in the game as much as they could.

By the age of twelve, John had played so much football he was burned out. He quit in eighth grade to join the school band. He was good enough to play first trombone, but he missed football. So, at the end of his freshman year, he told the band director that he was quitting the band to take up football again, since he figured it was unlikely he could play on the football team, then join the band during halftime shows.

"Woulda been nice if I could," he said. "But I don't think the coaches would have gone for it." The band director wasn't pleased. "Worst mistake you'll ever make," he told Graves.

By the end of his sophomore year, Graves thought he might be right. He got in for a total of three plays as a halfback and was wondering if there were still any openings in the band by the time the regular season came to a close. The week before the state playoffs began, he was out on a practice field by himself, kicking field goals, just for fun. One of the assistant coaches walked by and noticed.

"You ever think about being a kicker?" he asked Graves.

Graves hadn't thought about it for a single second. The coach told him the team needed a backup kicker for the playoffs and he should be prepared to kick in case something happened to their first-string kicker. As it turned out, the first-string kicker got hurt while Benton was scoring its first touchdown of the game. Just like in the movies, Graves was sent in to kick the extra point. He made it and two others that night. He also kicked a field goal. When his junior season started, he was the field goal kicker.

He was moved to wide receiver that year, although he didn't play much, catching three passes — one for a touchdown. But he did kick a 48-yard field goal and at the start of his senior year was picked in preseason as the all-state kicker. He even became a starting wide receiver.

All of that did not have recruiters knocking his door down. He did get calls from a number of smaller schools in Arkansas, but his dream to play at the University of Arkansas clearly wasn't going to come true.

"If they had called me once, I'd have been there," he said. His older brother, James, had graduated from Arkansas. "I was a Razorback fan from the first minute I started paying attention to football."

Two Division I schools contacted him: Air Force and Army. Both schools were recruiting him and his teammate Judd Fite. "Everyone thought we would go together," he said. "Judd ended up going to Air Force and I ended up going to Army."

Graves ended up at West Point for three reasons: he didn't want his parents paying for college — "I remembered how hard it was for them every time the tuition bill for James would show up," he said; he wanted a shot at Division I football; and he visited Army before Air Force.

"I got to Army and I thought, 'I can't go wrong here,'" he said. "It's a good school, they play Division I ball, it's a pretty place. I assumed Air Force would be pretty much the same and I just wanted to make a decision and get it behind me, so I told them right then and there I would come. Never did visit Air Force."

He didn't even mind the idea of being a wide receiver in a run-oriented wishbone offense because his high school team had played the wishbone. During his senior year, Graves led the team in receiving with 22 catches. When he arrived at Army, he met wide receivers who told him they had caught 95 passes as seniors. Ninety-five passes, Graves thought, we never *attempted* 95 passes in a season.

He went through all the plebe ordeals everyone else goes through but never once told his parents how miserable he was. When a plebe first arrives at West Point, his parents are given a manual that explains to them what their son or daughter will experience. The manual warns parents to expect phone calls from their plebes, especially during Beast, saying they want to come home, that they hate Army life and don't want to stay another minute.

One evening during Graves's junior year, when he was home visiting his family, his mother asked him why she had never received that phone call. "There wasn't anything you could do about it," Graves answered. "And anyway, you know I wasn't going to quit."

He didn't quit football either, although the thought did cross his mind. There were times when he almost hoped his name would show up on a cut list. "That way I could honestly say I hadn't quit, but I wouldn't have to put up with it anymore."

He was strictly a JV player as a freshman. As a sophomore, he was about to get playing time as a punt returner when he broke his collarbone in practice. Although he did return to dress for the Navy game eight weeks later, he didn't get in for a single play. He finally got into three games as a junior, but when spring ball ended he was listed as the third-string wide receiver behind Leon Gantt and Ron Thomas.

"I just decided I was going to force them to play me, one way or the other," he said. "I was going to stay healthy and I was going to make plays. I had to. There were no more next years left."

Graves also believed that he benefitted from a change of receiver coaches. Jack Hecker, who had been on the staff for twenty years during two stints at Army, had been promoted to the newly created job of director of football operations. Hecker had been the receivers' coach and, according to Graves, had put up with a lot of silly mistakes Graves had made during his early years at West Point.

In fact, Graves had developed a whole routine explaining to people why Army ran the wishbone offense. "My first day of practice as a plebe, I ran a couple of patterns and Coach Hecker came over and told me I was the worst wide receiver Army had ever recruited. Being a plebe, I believed everything I was told. I thought, 'My God, the worst receiver ever. That's saying a lot.'

"The next day in practice, another plebe ran a few routes and Coach Hecker went over and told him *he* was the worst receiver West Point had ever recruited. I felt better, because now I was only the second worst but I thought it was amazing that the two worst receivers ever would be in the same recruiting class.

"Then the varsity came back. First day of practice, Leon Gantt ran a couple of routes and, sure enough, Coach Hecker told him that *he* was the worst receiver ever. Now, I understood. With so many horrible receivers, they had no choice but to run the wishbone."

Hecker had almost surely told every receiver he had ever coached that he was the worst ever at some point. He was still one of the most popular coaches on staff (no doubt for putting up with such a bunch of no-talents for so many years), and his decision to give up coaching was a disappointment to the receivers.

But for Graves, who had struggled at times, a new coach meant a clean slate. "When Coach [Mike] Dietzel looked at me, he saw only what I was doing that day," he said. "When Coach Hecker looked at me he probably couldn't help but think about the screwup I had been at times my first couple of years."

As luck would have it, both Gantt and Thomas came up with nagging injuries during preseason and Graves began getting more snaps in practice. The coaches couldn't help but notice that he had a way of making things happen. If he was supposed to run a route 20 yards deep and saw a defender waiting, he would run the route two yards short and get open. If a ball was anywhere near him, he not only got to it, he held on to it. When the games started, he was in the receiver rotation and, as time went on, more and more of the passing plays — not that there were many of them — were called for him.

Even Jack Hecker had joined the Graves bandwagon by midseason. "The kid knows how to make plays," he said one evening during practice. "All they have to do is put the ball near him and he'll do the rest."

Which wasn't bad for the worst receiver ever to put on a uniform at West Point.


SUTTON was concerned that the players might spend so much time basking in the glow of the Boston College victory that they would forget to show up to play Colgate the following Saturday. The truth was, there was almost no way to lose the game. Colgate was 0–7 against Division I-AA competition, and if Army played horribly it would probably win the game by a couple of touchdowns.

Sutton didn't want a letdown. He wanted to see improvement every week. His theme for Colgate week was "between the lines," meaning the game wouldn't be won because they had played well at BC or because Colgate had played poorly all season. It could only be won "between the lines" on Saturday afternoon.

The players understood Sutton's fears, and they weren't about to let down and play a sloppy game. But they also knew that the two games that followed Colgate, East Carolina at home and Air Force on the road, would both be difficult and critical. They couldn't help but look ahead to those games just a little even while the coaches were demanding that they focus their attention on Colgate.

The Boston College game had added spice to the ongoing melodrama of Sutton's contract. By now, even some of the old grads were starting to notice that this team was playing quality opponents and playing them extremely well. But General Graves wasn't going to be budged.

"The way the team has played has been wonderful," he said that week. "But the fact is, we still haven't played our two most important games. Let's see what happens in those games."

That was West Point tradition. There were three levels of importance to football games: beating teams like Duke, Boston College, even Notre Dame was OK; beating Air Force was very, very important; beating Navy was life-and-death. Playing some of those OK schools close and pounding on another one of them was nice, even very nice to Graves. But he would probably be just as inclined to rehire a coach who was 2–0 against Air Force and Navy and 0–9 against the rest as he would be to rehire a coach who was 0–2 against Air Force and Navy and 9–0 the rest of the season.

"I think football is important to the academy, because it's so visible," Graves said. "But I think there are other things about West Point that matter more than football, far more."

While the Navy players loved Admiral Larson, the Army players were more ambivalent about Graves. Unlike Larson, who was always enthusiastic and loved to jump on chairs after games and give fiery pep talks, Graves was extremely reserved. He rarely showed up on the practice field, and even when he did he had little to say to the players. He was a polished public speaker, tall and ramrod straight at sixty-three, but even in casual conversation he tended to sound as if he were delivering a speech. Larson loved to wander around practice in a windbreaker with "Supe" stitched on the chest. Graves looked like someone who woke up in the morning wearing a perfectly starched uniform.

The seniors were keenly aware of Sutton's contract situation, and that made them feel even less comfortable around Graves. They knew it wasn't their place to voice their opinions to him, but they were dying to.

"In the end, the only way to let him know how we feel is to go out on the field and kick people's butts," Cantelupe said. "That says a lot more than anything else we could say."

Graves had not been the superintendent when Sutton became the coach. But he believed that the decision had been made too quickly, that Jim Young had, for all intents and purposes, been allowed to handpick his successor without any input from other factions at West Point. That didn't mean Sutton was the wrong choice; it just meant Graves didn't think the process had been handled correctly.

Clearly, if the team were to beat Air Force and Navy, Sutton would be rehired. But if it lost to Air Force, there was some feeling that even a victory over Navy might not save Sutton. If beating Navy was the only criterion for rehiring, he would already have been rehired since he was 3–1 against the Midshipmen. Being 0–4 against Air Force didn't hurt him as much as being 0–4 against Navy would have (he would have already been fired in that case), but it was a strong second.

Sutton wasn't thinking about Air Force and Navy just yet. His worst fears about Colgate were realized in the first quarter when Abel Young fumbled the opening kickoff and Colgate promptly scored to go ahead, 7–0.

Michie Stadium was almost full on a day that had started out looking awful, with wind and rain much like what they had seen in Boston, but had cleared into a gorgeous fall afternoon. With the leaves on the trees in full color, it was the kind of Saturday when West Point was a very romantic place to be.

The Cadets weren't feeling very romantic after their start. They did drive the length of the field to score on their next drive, but only after John Conroy broke two tackles to pick up a fourth-and-two by a yard. It was still just 7–7 after one.

Everything changed in the second quarter. The defense dominated; the offense moved at will. By halftime it was 28–7 and Sutton felt relaxed enough to start the second-string offense in the third quarter. Unfortunately, before the offense could get on the field, the defense fell asleep at the switch and Colgate drove 68 yards to score. Back came the first team. It scored again to make it 35–14 and Sutton was able to get everyone into the game in the fourth quarter.

The only person hurt by the extra series given to the first team offense was McAda, who went over 100 yards rushing on that last drive. More food for the Fat Men. "This time," he said, "I'm taking up a collection."

The final was 56–14. There was one glitch in the fourth quarter: the cannon that the cadets traditionally shoot off to celebrate a touchdown ran out of gunpowder at 49–14. Several cadets scrambled to find more. They made it back to the stadium just in time for the final touchdown.

Sutton was pleased. They had gotten their act together and played well after the sloppy start. They were 3–3–1, finally back at .500. They had put themselves into position to have the kind of season they had set out to have the previous April when the seniors had gathered after the spring dinner.

The finish line was in sight. But still a long way off.

# 14

# TROUBLED TIMES

THE week after the Air Force game was easily the most difficult anyone at Navy had been through all season.

The loss itself was devastating. Even the always upbeat Weatherbie
had trouble dealing with it. He wondered where he had gone wrong
in preparing his team. He had felt completely helpless on the sidelines
wondering why his team seemed so flat and lifeless at the start of a
game in which the players should have been ready to explode on the
opening kickoff.

Some of the coaches thought they had been too ready; that all the
rah-rah and pep talks had sapped them emotionally before they got
on the field. Weatherbie wasn't buying that. ''They hear that stuff all
the time,'' he said. ''And if we think it was bad this week, wait until
we get ready to play Army.''

Weatherbie told the players that he thought they had all let a golden
opportunity slip away. ''That was not a great Air Force team,'' he
told them. ''We played awful and the final score was 30–20. Imagine
what it might have been if we had played well.''

Two of their goals were now gone: they could not take back the
Commander in Chief's Trophy since even a tie (if the Falcons lost to
Army and Navy beat the Cadets) would mean the trophy stayed at
Air Force; and they weren't going to a bowl game. The best they could
finish now was 7–4, 5–4 in Division I-A games. That would not be
good enough.

They could still have a winning season, though, and they still had Notre Dame and Army to look forward to. Weatherbie was concerned about Division I-AA Villanova because the Mids had struggled against teams like the Wildcats in recent years. In fact, Chaump's record against I-AA teams had been 5–5. Since those games were scheduled to pad the win total, that was less than excellent. Weatherbie knew how down he felt, and he was worried that the players would also have trouble bouncing back.

Their feelings were best summed up by Andrew Thompson's journal entry that week: "We've come too far and worked too hard for our last five games as football players to be a drag," he wrote. "I feel about as bad today as I have in a long time."

If their 2–4 record and the loss to Air Force weren't enough to depress the players, there was plenty going on around Bancroft Hall to make them feel rotten. When they reported back to the Yard on Sunday evening, they were all told that no one would be allowed to leave Mother Bitch until they had completed a drug test. Larson had ordered the entire brigade drug-tested immediately.

The reason was a sting operation conducted by Naval Criminal Investigative Services on the night of the Air Force game in a Holiday Inn in Glen Burnie, about thirty minutes from the academy. Two midshipmen had been arrested after attempting to buy LSD from NCIS undercover agents posing as drug dealers.

Larson had been called early Sunday morning about the arrests. They didn't come as a shock to him, since he had been told earlier that it appeared likely that there were midshipmen dealing drugs, and about the NCIS sting, but they were disappointing. A year earlier, Larson had done two random drug tests on the brigade, testing half of them one week and the other half several weeks later. Only one positive test had come back, and that was for marijuana.

"Both tests were done right after they had come back from some kind of extended leave," he said. "You would think if you were going to get back positive tests, it would be a time like that. I was very encouraged by those results."

This was discouraging. What's more, the word in the halls was that the two arrested mids had named names to the investigators of other midshipmen involved in their operations and there might be as many as forty people involved. If that was the case, Navy could be facing another Double E situation. Anyone found guilty of drug charges would face virtually automatic separation, since the Navy had a zero-tolerance drug policy. Larson was determined to do everything possible to avoid another public relations fiasco.

One way to do that was to act swiftly and publicly in reaction to the arrests. That's why the entire brigade was locked up until everyone had been drug-tested. It was also why the academy announced the arrests and the drug testing and said that the results of the drug tests would be made public.

Naturally, nerves all around the Yard were frayed. They were also frayed around Ricketts Hall. Double E had been perceived by many as a football scandal, since six of the 24 expelled mids had been football players and because investigators had reported that 11 of 14 suspects who had refused to cooperate with them were football players.

Any involvement in the LSD arrests would be disastrous, especially at a time when the program was trying to improve its image, not only on the Yard but locally and nationally. One rumor had it that an ex–football player who was no longer at the academy was involved, but that appeared to be as far as it went — at least as far as anyone knew.

The whole thing made everyone a little jumpy. Combined with the Air Force disappointment, it made for a tense week of practice. Weatherbie had hoped that his team would be so angry about what had happened against Air Force that it would make Villanova pay for that disappointment.

Instead, the day started off about as badly as was possible. It was another miserable Saturday with the same storm that was engulfing Army and Boston College also sweeping through Annapolis. Rain was coming down sideways an hour before the game, although once again it did let up just before kickoff.

It was still an awful football day, and when Villanova jumped in front 7–0, some of the seniors began to wonder if they were going to go winless at home in their final season. The offense was sputtering. Chris McCoy had struggled against both Virginia Tech and Air Force, and there had been rumblings from the brigade for Ben Fay. Weatherbie and Paul Johnson didn't want to make the switch unless they had no choice, but with the offense going nowhere in the second quarter, they were out of choices.

The decision was a correct one. With Fay providing more of a passing threat, the offense began to move. On Fay's second series, they marched 60 yards, Fay taking it in from the one on the ninth play of the drive. But Covarrubias missed the extra point — wide *left* — and it was 7–6. Villanova put together a drive of its own, but for once Navy got a break from the other team's kicking game when the 'Cats' field goal kicker, Jack Kiefer, missed a 36-yarder as time expired.

They still trailed by a point, but the Fay-led drive had given them a boost emotionally. They could move the ball and they could score. It was simply a matter of getting back some of the confidence on offense that had been lost the last two weeks. They had only produced 86 yards in total offense, but 60 of it had come on the touchdown drive.

"Killer instinct, men," Weatherbie told them. "We've got to get that back."

It took a Villanova mistake, a fumble at the 15 yard line, to finally help them find it. Backup linebacker Travis Cooley came up with the loose ball at the Wildcat 12 yard line and the offense managed to punch it in from there, Fay again scoring from the one. Then Fay ran a quarterback draw on a two-point conversion attempt and made it, giving the Mids a 14–7 lead.

But Villanova wouldn't go away. The offense went right down the field and had a first-and-goal at the Navy four as the third quarter ended. Here, Navy came up with the kind of goal-line stand that defensive coordinator Dick Bumpas always insisted would turn a game around. Tom Poulter stopped running back Anthony Cowsette for a loss of one to the five. Quarterback Clint Park, under a rush, threw the ball away on second down. Then, on third down, Sean Andrews came up with an interception — his sixth of the season — in the end zone.

Bumpas's theory about turning the game around on the goal line proved accurate. The offense promptly put together its best drive since the Duke game, going 80 yards, capped by a bruising seven-yard run by Tim Cannada for the touchdown with 10:14 left. Even though Covarrubias's extra point was blocked and Villanova did score again late, the Mids had just enough to get to the finish line ahead. The final was 20–14.

They were a lot more relieved than exuberant when they reached the locker room. A six-point win over a Division I-AA team that had turned the ball over four times was hardly a confidence builder. Weatherbie tried anyway. "Hey, men, there's no such thing as an ugly win," he said. "Any win is a pretty win. You did what you had to do, made the plays you had to make against a pretty good football team out there. Feel good about yourselves. Enjoy this."

They needed to enjoy it. They now had a week off to salve their wounds, physical and emotional. They would need the rest. The next opponent would be slightly more talented than Villanova: Notre Dame.


THE Villanova game had been a miserable one for Jason Covarrubias. He had missed one extra point by a country mile and had another one blocked. And after Navy's second touchdown, his kickoff had gone out-of-bounds, giving Villanova the ball on the 35 yard line.

The coaches were disturbed enough by Covarrubias's troubles that they let Ryan Bucchianeri kick off after the final touchdown. Bucchianeri sailed a textbook kick to the one yard line, near the corner. It was the kind of kick that is a returner's worst nightmare because if he lets it go and it doesn't go out-of-bounds, it may end up as a free ball bouncing around in the end zone. Kick returner Josh Dolbin had no choice but to field the ball, but when he started upfield, he put his foot out-of-bounds on the one. It was the perfect kickoff.

For Bucchianeri, getting into the game and executing that way was a huge thrill. It was his second play of the season — the "bunt" kick against Air Force had been his first — and the first time in close to a year that he had been involved in a play that had a happy ending for Navy.

The following week, when the team went through the kicking tape as it always did on Monday afternoons, the kickoff replay came up. As Dolbin stepped out-of-bounds with the ball, a number of voices could be heard in the darkened room.

"Great kick, Booch."

"Way to get the job done, Booch."

"Clutch play, Booch."

The words of encouragement sent chills through Bucchianeri.

Finally, he felt, he was turning the corner. He was back in uniform and back on the field. He wasn't kicking field goals again — not yet.

"It's a little bit like my freshman year," he said that week. "It seems as if I may finally get a chance against Notre Dame. The difference is, that year, I didn't deserve to kick before that. This year, I did. And I hadn't gone through everything I've gone through this year either."

Bucchianeri had thought — or at least hoped — that he had hit rock bottom the night of the SMU game, sitting by himself out by the Triton Light, staring at Chesapeake Bay while his teammates were playing 1,300 miles away in Dallas.

Amazingly, things had gotten even worse before they started to get better. The week of the Rutgers game wasn't that bad. He enjoyed seeing how much the brigade was enjoying the SMU victory, although he still had that left-out feeling, since he hadn't been part of it. "The way the Yard felt that week was what I had waited for since I first got here," he said. "I wanted it to be that way and yet I felt like I was on the outside looking in."

He read in the local paper that Weatherbie had taken Covarrubias to the weekly quarterback club luncheon and introduced him to the audience as "the man to do all of Navy's placekicking." That stung, but it was understandable and Bucchianeri knew it. Not only had Covarrubias kicked well in Dallas, but it was only natural that Weatherbie would do everything possible to build his confidence.

In fact, he made a point every week of mentioning in the team's pregame meeting that he *knew* if a kick was needed to win the game, Covarrubias would come through and make the kick. "After SMU, he was The Man in practice," Bucchianeri said. "It was almost as if the other kickers didn't exist."

The irony in Covarrubias being the kicker standing in Bucchianeri's way was that he was probably Bucchianeri's best friend — perhaps his only friend — on the team. Covarrubias was popular with the rest of the players. He was a good athlete who had played soccer growing up in Southern California. He was easygoing and funny. He also wore his black hair slicked back, à la Weatherbie.

He was cool; Bucchianeri wasn't — and had no desire to be. But the two were friends. Covarrubias respected Bucchianeri's work ethic and felt he had learned watching Bucchianeri in practice the previous year. He knew Bucchianeri wasn't likely to be elected team captain at any point in the future, but he liked him anyway.

"Ryan's different, but so what?" Covarrubias said. "I spend more time with him than the other guys so I know him better. He does have a sense of humor, they just don't see it. He's a good kicker and a hard worker. He's working as hard this year as he did last year when he was the starter. I expect him to be pushing me the rest of the time he's here. I want him to."

Even though the team lost at Rutgers, Covarrubias kicked well again, hitting a 47-yard field goal to tie the game as time expired at the end of the half. That kick turned out to be the high-water mark for the Mids that night. Bucchianeri heard about the kick after the game. This time, he had liberty and had been as far away from the Yard and the broadcast of the game as he could.

He almost felt guilty about avoiding the games, but it was just too hard to sit in Mother B and listen with everyone else. He was convinced that everyone was staring at him in the halls, anyway, that people were whispering that he had quit. He wanted to wear a sign saying, "I haven't quit, they just won't let me kick."

The Rutgers loss brought everyone back to earth a little, but the Yard was still abuzz the week of the Wake Forest game. Bucchianeri hoped against hope that he would be on the dress list, that since it was a home game the coaches would dress him, if for no other reason than out of respect for his status as the starting kicker the previous two years.

When the list came out Wednesday, his heart sank. Two kickers would travel to the Holiday Inn on Friday night: Covarrubias and Graham. There was a separate list of players who wouldn't go to the hotel but would be in uniform Saturday. That list usually consisted of seniors who were on the scout team or plebes who the coaches wanted to get a taste of the sidelines on game day. Bucchianeri didn't qualify in either category.

"Now my worst fears had been realized," he said. "They couldn't even let me put on a uniform and stand on the sidelines with my teammates. It was an awful feeling."

The worst part of it was that he couldn't hide this time. He couldn't go off and kick by himself during the game or escape the Yard. The entire brigade is required to take part in the march-on at home games (at Army only one of the four regiments actually marches on), and since Bucchianeri wasn't dressing for the game, he had to participate in the march-on. Even in those early games as a plebe he had been in uniform for home games. He had never marched on for a game and had never watched a Navy game from the stands.

Now, he had to do both.

When the brigade marches on at home games, it forms up by the seawall near the practice fields and marches the two miles from the academy to Navy–Marine Corps Stadium. It is unfortunate that the stadium is located where it is, if only because the academy itself is so pretty and the stadium, located out near Route 50, takes advantage of none of that beauty. From the very top of the stadium on a clear day, one can see a sliver of water and some of the historic buildings of downtown Annapolis. If the stadium sat where the practice fields are, it would be the most scenic in the country. It would also be virtually impossible for 30,000 people to get to it.

The brigade marches out the main gate and down Main Street to Maryland Street. There it turns left and marches over to the bottom of Rowe Boulevard. There, in the shadow of the State House and the Governor's Mansion, it turns right and marches about one mile up to the stadium. Traffic is cut off in the area during the march and crowds often gather to watch the mids as they go by.

Bucchianeri joined up with the rest of the 32nd company out by the seawall and took his place in the formation. He was trying hard to keep his eyes front and his mind blank as they turned onto Rowe Boulevard. A couple of hundred yards up, he heard one of the plebes in the company, marching a row behind him, say, "Come on, let's do it, let's do the cadence on Booch."

"Are you sure?" someone else answered.

"Yes. Call it out."

And they did.

Cadences are, of course, a regular part of military marching. Anyone who has ever seen *An Officer and a Gentleman,* or any other movie involving military trainees, has seen soldiers marching while a drill sergeant calls out cadences in a singsong voice. At Navy, the march-on cadences were a little different. They were called "slam cadences" because they slammed someone. They were written by the plebes and were generally considered a good-natured chance for the plebes to get back at some of the upperclassmen for what they were being put through.

The victims were usually people who had done something embarrassing: gotten sloppy drunk one night or showed up with an ugly date or completely botched a test. The cadences were supposed to be cleared in each company by the company's leadership since they were going to be called out on a public street. Nothing obscene was supposed to be allowed or anything that might in some way embarrass the academy. Most of them were such in-jokes that no one on the outside would know what was being talked about anyway.

Now, as they were crossing the long bridge on Rowe Boulevard that puts the marchers in sight of the stadium, Bucchianeri listened as the plebes began calling out the Booch-cadence.

> *On the field for the biggest game,*
> *Had a chance to make a name.*
>
> *All he had to do, was kick it through,*
> *Easy enough for any of you.*
>
> *Stepped to the ball, destination in sight,*
> *I hooked it up — kicked it to the right.*
>
> *Had my chance, to win it all,*
> *Coach shouldn't have let me touch the ball.*
>
> *From two years of startin' and havin' it all,*
> *Maybe there's a spot in company ball.*

There was a pause and then there was more:

> *First march over to the stands,*
> *How's it feel to be a fan.*
>
> *He can't kick and he can't punt,*
> *Should've had the laces front.*

*Since his kicks were so lame,*
*Navy lost the big game.*

*That first time he did try,*
*Even though he made us cry.*

*Second time was just sad,*
*Now we know he's really bad.*

*Since his kicks were so lame,*
*Navy lost the big game.*

*There is no one he can blame,*
*He should hang his head in shame.*

*It's been said he had bad luck,*
*We all know that he just sucks.*

*Since his kicks were so lame,*
*Navy lost the big game.*

Bucchianeri couldn't believe his ears. How could they be this cruel? These weren't just members of the brigade doing this to him, these were the people he lived with and worked with every day. "My family," he said. "If I had one consolation having to go through the march-on it was that I was with my company. I felt protected somehow. And then they did that to me."

Bucchianeri marched along, refusing to show any emotion or say anything. But he was crushed. "That was my death march," he said. "My worst nightmare come to life. I didn't think we would ever get to the stadium."

When they finally got there, Bucchianeri found a place in the stands close to the field — the brigade stands throughout the game — and watched the game unfold. That was the night when nothing went right for the Mids and Wake Forest embarrassed them, 30–7.

Covarrubias got to try one field goal, when the game was still close — 14–7 — in the third quarter. As he trotted on, the two mids on either side of Bucchianeri, who were not members of his company, began swaying from side to side, chanting, "Wide right, wide right." Others around them picked it up. It occurred to Bucchianeri that many in the brigade probably thought he was still the kicker. He considered telling them who he was, but decided against it. Instead, he stood there and watched the Covarrubias kick not only sail wide right but come up considerably short.

When the game finally ended, Bucchianeri made his way down to the field and stood watching the stands empty. He had never felt lower. He had asked one of the plebes in his company if the slam cadence was written down anywhere. The plebe produced some notepaper on which it had been written. Bucchianeri asked if he could have it. The plebe shrugged and handed it to him.

Long ago, Bucchianeri had figured out that the academy wasn't the idyllic, slice-of-Americana place he had imagined it to be. It could be a hard place, an unfair place. Now he had learned it could also be a cruel place.

"It had to be one of the worst days of my life," he said later. "I said to myself, 'Where's the justice? Where's the honesty? This is supposed to be a place where people band together and work together and take care of each other in tough times. How could this have happened to me?' What had I done to deserve this kind of treatment?"

There is no simple answer. A lot of it, no doubt, had to do with the group mentality. Individually, almost every member of Bucchianeri's company probably would have admitted to feeling embarrassed by what they had done to him. Within a group of 120, though, they were hidden, meaning the only one embarrassed was the one singled out: Bucchianeri.

But it was more than that. Bucchianeri had committed the cardinal sin in a college atmosphere not only of being different but of being different in a way that left a lot of people with the impression that he thought he was better than they were. His teammates felt that; that somehow he thought that not smoking, not drinking, adhering strictly to academy rules that others regularly bent made him superior. Bucchianeri categorically denied feeling this way, but in conversation, he would often make reference to people who "don't have the discipline to not drink or do drugs." Or those who "don't have enough respect for the rules to follow them."

Bucchianeri was completely sincere in his beliefs. And, to be fair, he wasn't some zealot who went around telling people that his way was the only way or lecturing others. He kept to himself most of the time, and that too made people suspicious of him. It was a vicious circle.

The saddest part of it all was this: if he had made the two field goals against Army, his eccentricities would undoubtedly have been seen in a far more sympathetic light. "Oh yeah, Ryan's different, but when the game is on the line, he comes through for you."

Unfortunately, he hadn't come through. He had made other kicks in his career, some of them important ones. But twice, against Army, with, as Weatherbie always pointed out, "the entire navy and Marine Corps watching," he had missed. If he had been one of the guys, he might have been forgiven. But being out there by himself to begin with *and* missing the kicks was a devastating combination.

Instead of being a sympathetic figure to the rest of the brigade, someone who had given his all even though he hadn't made the kicks, he was viewed as an oddball who was a failure. To them, he didn't deserve sympathy. As Bucchianeri said, "You can try once and fail and they'll give you another chance. But if you try twice and fail, as far as everyone around here is concerned, you're through trying."

Amazingly, after the nightmare on Rowe Boulevard, Bucchianeri still wasn't through trying. He was at practice on Monday, ready to go, still trying to prove he deserved another chance. He knew that no one would blink an eye if he walked in and quit. Which was exactly why he vowed that he never would.


WEATHERBIE would never admit it, but his life would have been a lot simpler if Bucchianeri *had* quit. It was almost as if all the bad memories of the past few years hung over his head whenever he walked on the practice field. What Weatherbie would admit was that he and everyone else in the program had to give Bucchianeri his due for not walking away.

The week after the Wake Forest game, for the first time all season, Bucchianeri climbed to number two on the depth chart. Todd Wright even told him he might make the Duke trip to kick off. But when the travel list came out Wednesday, he wasn't on it. By this time, he wasn't surprised or disappointed.

He went home that weekend to see his grandmother, who was very sick. It was a tough couple of days. He hated seeing his grandmother so weak, and he also hated all the questions from his friends and family: "Why aren't you playing?" He tried to sound optimistic, saying he thought his chance would come later in the season.

And slowly but surely, his chances did start to come. He got to dress for the Virginia Tech game as the backup kicker, then got in the games to kick off against Air Force and Villanova. With Covarrubias struggling, he thought he had an excellent chance not only to make the Notre Dame trip but to be a part of the game.

Notre Dame brought back special memories for Bucchianeri: as a freshman he had kicked the first two field goals of his career against the Irish, including one in the first half that had given Navy the lead. It had also marked the beginning of Bucchianeri's run as the number one kicker.

The days after the Villanova game brought back more fond memories. Walking the halls, Bucchianeri heard words of encouragement for the first time in what seemed like forever. People had noticed the kickoff to the corner and a number of them commented on it. "It wasn't like I kicked a game-winning field goal or anything," he said. "But it was a start. At least now, people knew I was still with the team, that I hadn't quit, that I was still a football player."

Things stayed upbeat early in the week. He was getting chances to kick off with the first team. On Tuesday evening, Todd Wright told him he might kick off on Saturday. The travel squad would be posted on Wednesday.

His parents were planning to make the trip to South Bend, as were a number of his friends from back home. But there wouldn't be much point in going if Ryan wasn't going to be there. He had not traveled to a road game all season. Logic said he would travel this week, but after what had gone on during the last several months he was taking nothing for granted.

Wednesday he arrived for practice and went straight to the locker room bulletin board, where the travel squad was posted. There were two names listed under placekicker: Covarrubias, Bucchianeri.

He was going! A wave of relief swept over him. Now, he wouldn't have to tell his family and friends to cancel their plans. He wouldn't have to go through another round of explanations about his demotion. He might even get to play.

It was windy and rainy throughout practice that evening. Both he and Covarrubias struggled with their kickoffs. The coaches wanted a middle-left/deep kickoff; meaning they were supposed to aim for the yard-line numbers on the left side of the field. Neither kicker could drive the ball as deep as the coaches wanted and both were sailing the ball a little too close to the out-of-bounds mark. Kicking out-of-bounds had been Covarrubias's problem the previous week. Still, Bucchianeri thought, the coaches would understand that it wasn't an easy day to kick, although the screaming and yelling he was hearing didn't necessarily indicate that sort of understanding.

The next day he walked into the locker room and paused by the bulletin board to check announcements and to see if an itinerary for the trip had been posted yet. While he was standing there, he glanced at the travel list. Instinctively, he looked again to see his name.

It wasn't there.

Actually, it was there, but it had been crossed off in pen and Graham's name had been written in underneath the place where Bucchianeri's name had been typed. His first thought was that it was another joke; his teammates, knowing how much it meant to him to make this trip, having some fun at his expense.

He walked into the training room to check the list posted in there. Same thing: Bucchianeri crossed off; Graham written in. Now, he was starting to get scared. If this was a joke, it wasn't terribly funny. He went and found a third list. It was no different than the other two.

"In three years at Navy, I had never seen a name crossed off a travel list," he said. "I thought this couldn't possibly be happening just the way I had thought the last few months couldn't be happening. Only it was happening."

He went upstairs and found Wright. Please, he pleaded, tell me what I saw on the travel list downstairs was a joke. Wright shook his head. It wasn't a joke. The coaches had met after practice Wednesday and had decided that he had kicked off very poorly. They had decided to take Graham, who had been kicking well in practice the last couple of weeks, and leave him home.

Bucchianeri launched into a list of "Do you mean to tell me's," as in, "Do you mean to tell me I have one bad practice and I get taken off the travel squad?'' and ''Do you mean to tell me the other kickers can be awful and no one says anything to them, just to me?'' and ''Do you mean to tell me you don't think there's a double standard at work here?''

He rattled on and on. Wright listened patiently. There was nothing he could do, he said, the decision had been made.

''So you're telling me I'm not going?'' Bucchianeri finally asked.

''Right now, I would say it's unlikely,'' Wright said, trying to soften the blow.

''So there's still a chance they might change their minds after practice today?''

Wright couldn't mislead him. ''No, Ryan, I don't think there is,'' he said.

''I'm not going, am I?''

''No. You're not.''

Bucchianeri thought he might start to cry right there in Wright's office. In a way, this was the worst blow of all because it had sneaked up on him. Everything else — except for the slam cadence — he had seen coming. But this was worse than the slam cadence because this time he had to involve his parents. He couldn't keep this secret from them. He would have to tell them he wasn't going.

He went to a phone and called his father's office. His secretary answered. ''Ryan,'' she said, ''congratulations! Your dad told me you're going to Notre Dame! That's great. I guarantee I'll be right in front of my TV on Saturday looking for you. Let me get your dad.''

Bucchianeri knew the only way he was going to be able to tell his father was just to come right out with it. If his dad started gushing like his secretary, he would lose it completely. And so, as soon as he heard his father's cheerful ''Hello, Ryan,'' he just told him: ''Dad, I'm not making the trip to Notre Dame.''

He heard his father's voice drop so low he almost couldn't hear him. He was asking questions, but Ryan wasn't hearing them. All he could hear was the way his father's voice sounded. ''Totally deflated,'' he said. ''He sounded like a child who had been crushed emotionally. I couldn't take it. It was one thing to hurt me, but not my family. I just said to myself, 'No. Not this time.' I told my dad, 'Listen, this isn't final yet. I'll call you back in a few minutes.' ''

Bucchianeri hung up with his dad and went to find Bert Pangrazio, the team's administrative assistant. Pangrazio was a marine captain who had arrived at Navy as an unrecruited walk-on and been the 1988 team's cocaptain. He was the team's troubleshooter, taking care of any logistical problems that might crop up on the road and making certain all the various details leading up to a trip — like which entrance buses should show up at after a game — were taken care of.

As an ex-player of recent vintage, Pangrazio was someone the players liked and trusted. Often they would take their troubles to him, putting him in the unofficial role of a liaison between the assistant coaches and the players. Now, Bucchianeri went to Pangrazio and laid his story out for him. This was unfair, he told him, completely unfair, and someone had to tell Coach Weatherbie that this was happening. He had told his family he was traveling because he was on the Wednesday list. Since when had that become a tentative list and not a definite one?

He was close to being out of control. Pangrazio could see that. Like everyone else connected with the team, he saw Bucchianeri as an odd duck, someone who had never quite fit in and never showed that much interest in fitting in. But what he saw now was a troubled midshipman who had what sounded to him like a legitimate complaint. Travel lists *didn't* change unless someone got hurt or got into trouble at school. He wasn't sure why the coaches had changed the list, but he thought Bucchianeri's complaint had merit.

"I want you to do two things," he told Bucchianeri. "I want you to get ahold of yourself. Then I want you to go downstairs and get dressed for practice. I'll see what I can do."

Bucchianeri started to say something else. Pangrazio held up a hand. "Ryan, let it go. Let me see if I can do anything. OK?"

Bucchianeri nodded and went downstairs. Pangrazio went down the hallway and found Weatherbie, who was about to leave his office for practice. He told Weatherbie what was going on, adding that he thought, at least this once, Bucchianeri had a point.

Since each position coach draws up the list of his players he wants to travel, Weatherbie hadn't been aware of the fact that Bucchianeri had been on and then off the list. The only time an assistant would consult him before submitting his list was if he was planning to make a major change — like not traveling someone like Chris McCoy or Andrew Thompson for some reason — and the second-string place-kicking position didn't fall into that category.

"His name was on the list and then they crossed it off?" Weatherbie asked, wanting to be sure he had his facts straight.

Pangrazio nodded.

Weatherbie shook his head. "Well, we can't very well cross Graham off now," he said. "That's just as unfair. What do we do?"

"We could get a cot put in one of the rooms," Pangrazio said, "and take all three of them."

Most football teams travel with one placekicker and have a position player who has kicked in the past available in case of an emergency. Navy had traveled with two all year because there had been so much uncertainty surrounding the position. Now they were going to travel with three? Weatherbie knew there wasn't any choice.

"Bring 'em all," he said, vowing to tell the coaches not to post any travel lists in the future until they were sure that those were the players they wanted on the trip. Pangrazio went downstairs to let Bucchianeri know he was back on the trip and to make the necessary arrangements, which included telling equipment manager Kevin Bull, who was leaving right after practice to make the eleven-hour drive to South Bend with the equipment truck, to take a uniform for Bucchianeri.

Pangrazio couldn't help but smile thinking about the look on Bull's face when he told him he would have to pack for three kickers. Bull hated kickers. He thought they were all whiny, spoiled prima donnas who blamed every kick they missed on their shoes. Bull was tough on all the players, sometimes telling them they didn't deserve the equipment they were asking him for. But he was toughest on the kickers, who kept demanding new pairs of $150 shoes every time they missed a kick and complained constantly that something was wrong with their spikes: too long, too short, too soft, too hard, too muddy, too dry. Always something.

Earlier that year, Frank Schenk, who had kicked a 32-yard field goal to become the hero of the 1989 Army-Navy game, had come back to Annapolis for a visit. He had been on the practice field one afternoon while the kickers were warming up and he had bet Bull a pair of shoes that he could make a 50-yard field goal in his street shoes.

"You're on," Bull told him.

When Schenk drilled the kick, the other kickers had gone wild. "Schenk beat Bull out of a pair of shoes," they had yelled gleefully.

"I couldn't be happier," Bull told them.

"What? Why?"

"Because he just proved that if you're a *good* kicker it doesn't matter what kind of shoes you're wearing or what kind of spikes you have. You just make the damn kick!"

Naturally, Bucchianeri was high on Bull's list of kicking prima donnas. Having to add his equipment to the truck at the last minute so that three kickers could be in uniform would probably ensure that Bull would still be grumbling when he hit Ohio on the drive west.

Bucchianeri thanked Pangrazio for his help and called his father quickly to tell him all was well and he would be making the trip. His dad wanted details, but there was no time. He had to get on the practice field.

By the time he got there, the word was already spreading that Bucchianeri was making the trip. Three kickers? they all asked. Well, the answer came back, Booch went to the coaches crying and they backed down. Once again, the legend of Bucchianeri grew a little bit more. And once again, he had one question: exactly what did I do wrong?

The answer, in this case, was nothing.

# 15

# THE SNOWS OF SOUTH BEND

EVEN without the Bucchianeri soap opera, Notre Dame week around the Yard would have been tense. Every year when Navy played Notre Dame the same question came up: why was this game still played?

There was no questioning the tradition surrounding the rivalry. The two schools had played every year since 1927, making theirs the oldest annual intersectional rivalry in college football. The only problem was that what had once been a great rivalry had become so one-sided in recent years that many considered it an embarrassment.

Navy hadn't beaten Notre Dame since 1963. That was 31 straight losses — and counting. What's more, the margin was usually huge: 37, 31, and 37 points the last three years. The last time it had been under 20 had been in 1988, a 22–7 Irish victory. Navy's last real chance to win had come in 1984, when Notre Dame had escaped with an 18–17 victory.

The game was still played for two reasons: first, it made money for Navy and, since the Naval Academy Athletic Association was a privately funded, nongovernment operation, making money was important. Although the NAAA was nonprofit, it counted on football revenue to keep it around the break-even mark each year. Giving up the money from playing Notre Dame would be a considerable hit.

But the more important reason for continuing the game was that the Navy players wanted to keep playing it. Even though it made no sense to outsiders, they craved the idea of playing the Irish every year.

Most Navy football players (like Army football players) had been told at some point in their lives that they weren't really Division I caliber. That was one of the reasons they were at Navy: for the chance to prove that wasn't true. To wade in against Notre Dame on national TV was one way to show people that they had been underestimated.

Of course the problem with that was the talent gap. Notre Dame coach Lou Holtz had, for all intents and purposes, the pick of the football litter each and every year. It was remarkable that enough mistakes had been made by Holtz and his staff that the Irish had been an embarrassing 6–5–1 in 1994, including a humiliating 41–24 loss to Colorado in the Fiesta Bowl in a game that wasn't even that close. Most years, Notre Dame had between ten and twenty players on the roster who had an excellent chance to play in the NFL. Most years Navy had somewhere between zero and one. This year was no different: the Irish were loaded with future pros. Navy had one player who might have a chance if everything broke right for him: punter Brian Schrum.

But the players still wanted to play the game. They still believed that if they played as well as they were capable of playing, they could shock America. After all, they pointed out, they had led 24–17 two years earlier at halftime. True, but the final score had been 58–27. There was one source of encouragement this year: Army's near miss. The Midshipmen knew the Cadets were essentially the same as they were — undermanned but unwilling to give up on themselves. That attitude had almost stolen the game.

For the coaches, this was an exciting week and a scary one. Like the players, they loved the idea of testing themselves against the best. Unlike the players, they worried that if things didn't go right, another rout was always possible.

In recent years, it had also become a part of Navy–Notre Dame tradition for Holtz to do his best to make Navy sound like the Dallas Cowboys in the pregame buildup. Every year, it seemed, Navy had the quickest, best prepared, strongest, most experienced team he had ever seen come out of Annapolis. Notre Dame was always beat up, undermanned, not quite playing up to par, and, no doubt, scared to death of the "University of the Naval Academy."

This had been a strange year at Notre Dame. The schedule was the easiest the Irish had played in years. Michigan was gone and so was Florida State. Penn State was no longer on the schedule either. Ohio State had been added but so had games with Vanderbilt and Army. In fact, Notre Dame was playing Army, Navy, and Air Force. Rumor had it that Holtz was hoping to add Coast Guard and the Merchant Marine Academy in 1996. In the meantime, the joke was that the Irish had to be considered the favorites to win the Commander in Chief's Trophy.

Of course that joke had almost blown up in Notre Dame's face in the Meadowlands against the Cadets. The entire year had been a struggle for the Irish. They had lost the opener to Northwestern, which had been considered a huge upset at the time since no one knew just how good Northwestern would end up being. They had been routed by Ohio State and had needed a good deal of luck to get by Washington and Army. On the other hand, they had destroyed Southern California when the Trojans were undefeated and ranked number five in the country and had pounded a Texas team that would finish 10–2–1.

In short, Notre Dame was very, very good. But also very inconsistent. Perhaps the back surgery that had caused Holtz to miss two games and spend more than a month in a neck brace had something to do with it. Perhaps the fact that quarterback Ron Powlus, who had arrived at Notre Dame with more advance publicity than anyone or anything since Halley's comet but hadn't yet become anything more than an average quarterback, was also part of it.

Or maybe Holtz had lost some of his drive. He was fifty-eight and had won his two hundredth game earlier in the season. Once again there were rumors flying that he was getting ready to quit, in spite of a long-term contract extension. In any event, this was a Notre Dame team that no one could figure out.

Of course Holtz claimed it was lack of talent. "Least talented team we've had in a long time," he insisted. No one really listened. Holtz had coached 118 games at Notre Dame and no doubt considered himself the underdog in every one of them.

That was why it was so surprising when Notre Dame's weekly press release, which was only slightly thicker than most Bibles, arrived by fax at Navy on Monday afternoon. Amid all the usual Holtzisms about the Navy juggernaut was a strange, very un-Holtzlike quote. Talking about Navy's spread offense, Holtz said, "I said years ago if you didn't care what you did, I'd run the same offense Navy is running."

*If you didn't care what you did?* What did Holtz mean by that? It sounded as if he was taking some kind of shot at Weatherbie's offense. But that wouldn't be like Holtz. Unless he was still simmering from the bad feelings that had erupted at the end of the 1994 game when Chaump had called a late time-out even though the game was out of hand and Holtz had responded by faking a punt and punching one last knife-in-the-back touchdown into the end zone. Chaump and Holtz had exchanged angry words afterward and there had clearly been hard feelings.

But that had been Chaump; this was Weatherbie. Surely, when Holtz talked by phone to the Navy beat writers on Wednesday, he would clear the whole thing up.

"What I meant," Holtz said when the quote was mentioned, "is that if you were coaching high school or something that would be a great offense to run."

*Coaching high school?*

Weatherbie, standing in the back of the room waiting to talk to the media when Holtz was finished, did a double take. Unless he had heard wrong, Holtz had just said Navy ran a high school offense. Weatherbie wasn't the only one who thought he'd said that.

"Lou, are you saying Navy runs a high school offense?" one of the writers asked.

Holtz began spluttering angrily. "I *never* said that!" he yelled. "It boggles my mind that anyone could think I said that. What I'm saying is that if we want to recruit quarterbacks here who want to go on to the NFL, we can't run an option-style offense."

That was clearer. Of course, Holtz had just recruited an option-style quarterback, because Powlus had clearly struggled in Holtz's half-pro, half-college–style offense. From there, Holtz became himself, apologizing profusely for the fake punt incident of a year ago. "It was one of the most foolish, embarrassing, humiliating things I've ever done in coaching," he said, laying it on as thick as possible.

It was too late. The high school quote was going to make the headlines. When Weatherbie sat down to take questions, someone jokingly asked him if Navy was planning to show up in Irish green uniforms on Saturday.

"Maybe," he said, half-smiling, "we'll show up in high school uniforms."


WEATHERBIE never mentioned the high school crack to his team. For one thing, he knew they would see it and hear about it. For another, getting them fired up wasn't going to be the problem this week. The problem was going to be convincing them they could win.

Thursday was unseasonably warm for the first week of November in Annapolis. The temperature was close to seventy when the team arrived at Ricketts for practice. Since the heat was on, it felt like it was about a hundred degrees inside the building, so Weatherbie took them outside for their pre-practice meeting. Everyone sat on the bleachers overlooking the Astroturf field while Weatherbie talked. Behind him, boats chugged back and forth, going in and out of Annapolis harbor.

"Timing is everything in life," Weatherbie told the players. "If my timing hadn't been right, I wouldn't be married to my wife. Our timing to play Notre Dame is right. I think they're ripe to be beaten. There are a whole lot of people who would love to be in your shoes right now: playing on national TV Saturday with a chance to pull an upset that will have everyone in the country talking about you."

He went through the usual litany of dos and don'ts. But in the midst of it he tossed in an interesting prediction: "They punt the ball on average three times a game," he said. "If we make them punt it at least six times, we'll win the football game. Their punter isn't very good. We want to get him on the field as much as possible. Remember that. Make them punt it six times and we'll win."

He didn't say anything about high school offenses or about the streak. In fact, on Wednesday, when a reporter had asked him about the losing streak, he had answered with a straight face, "What losing streak?"

He was completely aware of the streak, but he didn't want to make it into anything more than it was. He knew the players were fully aware of it too. "These players haven't lost thirty-one in a row," he said somewhat defensively. "All they know is that they want to win Saturday."

Weatherbie was also playing some mind games with the media — and Notre Dame. When he was asked in his press conference who the starting quarterback would be he had answered Chris McCoy. In reality, he and Paul Johnson had already decided to start Ben Fay. But Weatherbie saw no reason to help Holtz in his preparation by announcing that publicly.

McCoy understood the switch. Fay had come off the bench against both Air Force and Villanova and moved the team when it had been sputtering. Weatherbie hadn't made the change after the Air Force game because "Ben moved the ball but he didn't pull the game out for us." Against Villanova, he had pulled the game out. Ideally, the coaches still preferred the idea of bringing the fiery Fay off the bench.

But he had earned the chance to start. After practice on Tuesday afternoon, Johnson had kept both quarterbacks on the field a few extra minutes to tell them that Fay would start. Neither of them was surprised. The coaches didn't think Notre Dame would be surprised either, but they figured any little edge might help.

The weather was still gorgeous when they boarded the plane on Friday morning to fly to South Bend. The weather report in Indiana wasn't nearly as encouraging: snow and temperature in the low twenties, with more expected on Saturday. South Bend is one of those places that has two seasons: winter and the Fourth of July. Snow the first week in November wasn't the least bit unusual.

They were late arriving, not because of the weather, but because the plane was late leaving Baltimore. That wiped out the planned trip to the new College Football Hall of Fame. Instead, they went directly to Notre Dame Stadium for practice.

It was a classic South Bend day: bitterly cold, wind sweeping in off Lake Michigan, making twenty degrees feel like zero, snow falling intermittently. The NBC announcing crew, Charlie Jones and Randy Cross, was waiting in the tunnel, trying to keep warm, when the team arrived. Jones and Cross wanted to talk to Weatherbie, to the quarterbacks and to the captains, and, of course, to Shaun Stephenson, who would be making his re-debut the next day. The knee had progressed exactly the way the doctors had predicted. Stephenson didn't feel 100 percent, he knew he wasn't as quick or as fast as he had been before the injury, but it felt good enough to try and play.

Friday practices aren't terribly serious. On the road, it is a chance for the players to acquaint themselves with the stadium, to learn where the play clocks are, to gauge how much sideline room there is, and to get a feel for the footing. This was especially important at Notre Dame, where the sidelines were extremely tight and the swirling winds could make any kick into an adventure. It was also good for the younger players, who had never been in the place before, to walk around and get a look at the hallowed grounds of college football's most famous stadium.

This would be the last game played in the stadium before a renovation project that would expand the capacity from 59,075 to 80,000. To its credit, Notre Dame had stubbornly refused to expand the stadium for many years even though it could probably have doubled the capacity and still sold out every home game. Now, though, the time had come to cash in, and so one of the sport's most intimate and traditional venues would be added on to.

Exactly why Notre Dame needed extra money no one could quite figure out. After all, with its network contract for the broadcast of home games, and with huge TV and bowl revenues each year that it split with no one — since it didn't belong to a conference — the Irish were raking in enough money to purchase Dublin. Or so it would seem.

None of that was of any concern to the Midshipmen. They just wanted to perform well in the stadium, regardless of its past or its future. To keep everyone loose, the defensive coaches came out for practice in shorts, in spite of the frigid weather. The defensive linemen held a pass-catching contest and several of the receivers lined up to try field goals. Matt Scornavacchi nailed a 45-yarder and declared himself ready if needed. Everyone laughed — sort of. The kicking issue was still a sensitive one.

As soon as practice was over, everyone rushed for the warmth of the locker room — except for the players Jones and Cross had requested mini-interviews with. They lined up in the tunnel and waited patiently while the men from NBC asked their questions.

Inside, Bert Pangrazio was handing out a newspaper clipping that he had kept since September. It was a picture of several Notre Dame players watching the final seconds of their loss to Northwestern tick away. The caption said: "Don't worry, Irish, Navy's still on the schedule."

Pangrazio had wanted to hand the clip out twenty minutes before kickoff, but Weatherbie vetoed that. The compromise was Friday afternoon before the long bus ride back to the hotel.

They would have to ride the bus forty-five minutes into Michigan to reach their hotel since South Bend hotels refuse to take reservations for less than two nights from anyone — even the visiting team — on football weekends. Since teams always try to leave right after a game, opponents of Notre Dame always found themselves stuck somewhere out in the middle of nowhere, chugging a minimum of forty-five minutes to and from the stadium.

The motel where the team was staying was a Quality Inn that was straight out of the 1950s. It had a huge, dark lobby complete with shuffleboard court, Ping-Pong tables, a swimming pool, and a pool table. The players didn't mind. They weren't here to see the sights anyway.


WHEN they woke up Saturday morning, it was sunny and frigid outside. By the time the bus left for the stadium, it was snowing. "No big deal," one of the bus drivers said. "This is just lake-effect stuff."

As if that meant it wasn't really snow.

It wasn't snowing when the game kicked off; in fact the sun was out. All day, the weather seemed to change by the minute: from sunny to cloudy to snowy and back again. The only constant was the cold. The wind chill at game time was nine degrees. As the sun moved west, the wind chill moved south.

That was fine with the Mids. On their opening drive, they moved the ball almost at will, in spite of two penalties — one a clip after a 30-yard option run by Fay — and went 54 yards in six plays to score, Will Smith going the last 15 yards after a perfectly timed pitch from Fay. They were up, 7–0.

Of course a year ago they had gone ahead 7–0 and the final score had been 58–21. Still, it was an encouraging start, especially with Fay running the option with so much confidence. Naturally, Notre Dame came right back and scored, aided by a personal foul call for roughing Ron Powlus as he was being run out-of-bounds.

It was only the first quarter, but the Navy sideline was getting a little paranoid. The game was less than eight minutes old and Navy had already been called for 35 yards in penalties — Notre Dame none. Everyone who came into Notre Dame Stadium knew that Holtz liked to use officials from the Mid-American Conference. Why? The MAC being a smaller, less glamorous league than others, getting to officiate at Notre Dame was a big deal. The officials wouldn't want to do anything to annoy Coach Holtz and not be invited back.

Did that actually happen? Probably not very often. But in a tight situation . . .

Playing Navy wasn't supposed to be a tight situation. But when the flags started flying early, everyone on the Navy sideline began to wonder. "Hey, what's the rule around here?" Kent Owens yelled at one official. "Notre Dame has to win or you guys don't get to come back? Is that in the NBC contract or something?"

It wasn't just the officials that made everyone a little bit crazy. One of the reasons the stadium was being renovated (besides the money the expansion would bring in) was that the facility was completely outdated. The locker rooms were tiny and room for the teams on the sidelines, especially on the visitors side, was cramped. It didn't help that Notre Dame put extra bleachers in front of the first row of stands to squeeze in a few extra paying customers.

In order to make certain that the visiting team would be able to go about its business without being hassled, Notre Dame stuck about five hundred ushers and security people on the sideline. At least it felt like that many. Their job was supposed to be to keep any wanderers — spectators, photographers, roving band members — clear of the bench area.

Only they really weren't needed. So instead they took up space on the sideline and screamed and hollered for the Irish just like the rest of the fans. The difference was that they were within earshot of the visiting players — and wore guns. You told them to shut up at your own risk.

With all this going on, the Mids continued to play superbly. Late in the first quarter, still tied at 7–7, Keith Galloway and Andrew Thompson combined to down a Schrum punt on the Notre Dame one. The defense held, and just as the coaches had predicted, punter Hunter Smith launched a wounded duck that traveled a total of 18 yards. That put the Mids in business at the Notre Dame 28. They marched to a first down at the nine but stalled at the three as the first quarter ended.

They then had to wait through one of NBC's interminable time-outs. The time-outs were supposed to be three minutes — which was long to start with — but always seemed to last an extra minute so NBC could throw in an extra replay or a promo for the Saturday night lineup. It was no coincidence that NBC-televised games at Notre Dame lasted longer than any other college football games, usually between three and a half and four hours.

Covarrubias trotted on to start the second quarter with a 20-yard chip-shot field goal. Somehow, he missed it, pulling it wide left. A golden opportunity gone. It was still 7–7.

Midway through the quarter, after another short Smith punt set them up at their own 49, the Mids put together another drive. Mixing passes in with the option game, Fay moved the team briskly into the end zone, scoring himself on an option-right after the Notre Dame defense bought the initial fake to fullback Tim Cannada. With 4:03 left in the half, Navy led again, 14–7. The extra point was kicked not by Covarrubias but by Brian Graham. Weatherbie had decided after the 20-yard miss that it was time to change kickers. Bucchianeri stood and watched as Graham, who had never before been in a game, knuckled the kick through.

Bucchianeri thought he might be asked to kick off, but that job still belonged to Covarrubias. His kick was fielded by Allen Rossum at the 11 and returned to the 49. From there, the Irish quickly tied the score again, the key play being a sliding catch by all-American receiver Derrick Mayes that picked up 20 yards on a third-and-12. It was the kind of play that great players make. Mayes, a certain early-round draft pick, simply had skills that no one in a Navy uniform had.

Powlus went the last yard with 1:10 left and it seemed likely that the teams would be tied at halftime. There was nothing wrong with being even with Notre Dame at halftime. But Paul Johnson thought his offense could move the ball and, instead of running out the clock, took a shot at scoring once more.

Starting at their own 28, the Mids rolled down the field: Fay hit Cory Schemm, moving the ball to the 42. But an incompletion and a failed dive play that only picked up a yard set up third-and-nine at the 43 with 26 seconds left. Then Holtz stepped in and did Navy a favor by calling time-out. Apparently he thought his team might have a chance to block a punt. Instead, having saved a time-out of their own, the Mids picked up the first down when Fay found Astor Heaven over the middle at the Notre Dame 31. Fay spiked the ball to stop the clock, then found Heaven again, this time at the Notre Dame four. Nine seconds were left. They had one chance to throw the ball into the end zone. Fay looked for LeBron Butts, but threw the ball outside while Butts cut inside.

A mixup caused by lack of time. Two seconds left. They had to get something out of the drive. Graham came on for a 21-yard field goal. From almost the same spot where Covarrubias had missed to start the quarter, Graham hit to end it. Halftime: Navy 17, Notre Dame 14.

The crowd could be heard murmuring as the players headed for the tunnel. Things often get congested in that tunnel with both teams trying to get to their locker rooms. Once, players from Notre Dame and Southern California had fought in the tunnel before a game. Now, the only sound was the clattering of cleats. No trash talking from either side. The Notre Dame players were dazed. In a sense, so were the Navy players. They had believed they could compete with Notre Dame. But they hadn't just competed in the first half; they had dominated.

Later, Weatherbie would look back at the tape and say, "We should have been ahead at least 28–14, maybe more, maybe as much as 31–7."

The statistics bore him out: Navy had 301 yards in total offense, Notre Dame 132. Notre Dame had already punted four times — one more than they averaged per game — and two-thirds of the way to Weatherbie's goal of six. Navy had held on to the ball for almost 18 of the 30 minutes. Penalties had hurt: four for 39 yards as opposed to one for 15 yards for Notre Dame

They had the lead, but knew it could have been more. That didn't matter now. What mattered was that the game was winnable. They had spent the whole week hoping that would be the case. Now they knew it was.

Weatherbie's first job at halftime was to calm his coaches down. Even Johnson, usually so laconic and low-key, was wound up. "We have to get the ball in the end zone when we have the chance," he said. "Dammit, I should have called something different down there on the goal line."

"Hey, Coach, it was a great drive," Weatherbie told him.

"Yeah, but we could have had seven, instead of three, and we didn't get anything after the short punt —"

"Easy," Weatherbie said. "We're doing great."

"I know," Johnson said. "But I just want to win the damn game."

"We're winning it right now," Weatherbie said. "All we've got to do is keep the kids doing what they're doing. We can't ask any more of them than what they're giving us."

"Greatest group of kids I've ever seen," Tommy Raye said, speaking to no one and everyone. "They don't have any idea how hard it is to do what they're doing."

"And we have to keep it that way," Weatherbie said. "Remember, this is what we *expected*."

That was the theme throughout the break. OK, we have the lead, let's extend it. We told you that you would move the ball — you've moved it. We told you they could be stopped — you've stopped them. Just keep doing it.

They did. On Notre Dame's first series, Powlus rolled right from his own 17 and never saw Fernando Harris, who had blitzed from his linebacker spot and left the Notre Dame linemen clutching at air. Harris grabbed Powlus from behind with one hand and pulled him down hard at the eight yard line. Powlus landed on his arm and didn't get up. As it turned out, he had broken the arm. His season was over. Once the savior of the program, Powlus left in an ambulance while some Notre Dame fans nodded knowingly and said the team would be better off with backup Tom Krug at quarterback.

No one on the Navy sideline was happy to see Powlus hurt. To begin with, you never wanted to see a player hurt, even if Powlus had been trash talking throughout the game. "Like on every play," Andrew Thompson said later.

What's more, they had Powlus under control. They had shaken his confidence. Now, Krug was coming in fresh. When a star quarterback goes out, the rest of an offense tends to turn up its intensity a notch, knowing it must in order to survive. The Irish were in a semi-coma, unable to deal with the notion of a Navy team that was coming right at them, not overwhelmed physically or by the Notre Dame mystique.

"We [the seniors] had all been in the stadium before," Thompson said. "We knew they were good, but we also knew they weren't gods. Powlus *wasn't* that good. He wasn't hurting us. We were happy to see him in the game."

Krug almost got sacked on the goal line on his first play, but managed to dump the ball off at the last minute. Hunter Smith had to come in and punt with the ball on the Notre Dame seven. He got off a 37-yarder, but Mark Mill, a plebe who had gotten the coaches' attention with his aggressiveness, grabbed the line drive and returned it 13 yards to the Notre Dame 31.

They were in business. But not for long. Fay was hit trying to pitch to Omar Nelson and Notre Dame recovered. No problem. Two plays later, Thompson slammed into fullback Mark Edwards and jarred the ball free. Andy Person jumped on it and the Mids had the ball back at the Notre Dame 41.

This time, they moved the ball — and held on to it. On fourth-and-one at the 31, Fay picked up the first down, running behind Garrett Smith to pick up two yards. Patrick McGrew picked up four more to the 25. By now, Notre Dame was pinching closer and closer to the line to cut off the run. Fay faked the dive play, took a three-step drop, and found Will Smith wide open at the 10 yard line. There wasn't a defender in the same county as Smith and he walked into the end zone untouched.

The silence in the stadium — except for the small band of mids behind the Navy bench — was deafening. But a couple of yards from where Fay had thrown the ball, a yellow flag was lying on the ground, tossed there by referee Pat Holleran. His eagle eyes had spotted center Brian Dreschler holding. The Navy coaches went crazy. How could he have spotted a hold on a three-step drop? The timing of the call was remarkable.

And so, instead of being up 24–14 midway through the third quarter, the Mids were moved back to the Notre Dame 39 with second down and 20. Fay actually picked up 17 of it on a third down pass to Butts, but he came up three yards short of the first down at the 22.

What to do? Try to pick up three yards and risk getting nothing again? Or, give Graham a shot at a 39-yard field goal? Todd Wright had commented in the pregame coaches' meeting that Graham had been better on long field goals that week than anytime all season.

What Weatherbie didn't know was that Graham had gotten his foot stepped on in the crowded tunnel at halftime and had twisted his ankle badly. He hadn't told anyone because after waiting four years to get into a game and kick, he wasn't going to beg off because of a fluke injury. And so, Graham was sent on to try the field goal. It was woefully short and way wide. If Graham had known how serious his injury was, he wouldn't have tried to kick. But he didn't want to come off as a wimp the first time he had a chance to kick. By trying to suck it up and be tough, he had hurt the team.

Even after that disappointment, the defense held again and forced a punt. This time, Smith got off a respectable kick and Mill moved up to catch it at the Navy 37. But he was too eager. The ball bounced off him and into a huge pile of players. When the officials finally pulled them all apart, Ivory Covington, the man who had made the fateful tackle on Ron Leshinski on the two-point conversion attempt in the Army game, was on top of it.

The Navy sideline was like a balloon that has just had a needle stuck in it. Holtz, who would later spend most of the buildup to the Orange Bowl trying to convince the media that Tom Krug couldn't throw a football into the ocean from a rowboat, went right for the jugular. Mayes went deep down the left sideline, Krug threw the ball up, and Mayes outjumped Robert Green, who was with him all the way, for the ball. He may have pushed off to clear a little space, but there was no way *that* flag was going to be thrown. Mayes caught the ball at the two and dove into the end zone.

Two minutes earlier, it had appeared that Navy would lead, 24–14. Instead, Notre Dame now led 21–17. It went downhill quickly from there. On the first play of the next series, Fay tried to hit Tim Cannada over the middle, but linebacker Lyron Cobbins batted the ball up in the air and intercepted it at the Navy 36. Notre Dame quickly moved the ball to the six. But then Andy Person got into the backfield and jarred the ball loose from Krug as he was trying to hand off. Person chased the ball down at the 13 and fell on it.

Navy ball! They still had a chance. But no. There was another flag on the field. Navy had 12 men on the field. There had been a mixup in coverages; an extra lineman had come in, but no defensive back had come out. It was a clear-cut call; a huge mistake by the Mids. On the next play Krug floated the ball into the end zone, and again Mayes outjumped the defender for the ball. This time the defender was Sean Andrews, who hadn't been outjumped by anyone all season. But he hadn't been up against a talent like Mayes before. Touchdown, Notre Dame. It was 28–17.

The Irish tacked on another touchdown early in the fourth quarter and the last 10 minutes was little more than a scrum, Navy trying to get on the board one more time, the Irish just trying to get the game over with so they could go into the locker room and breathe a deep sigh of relief.

On Notre Dame's last meaningless drive, the officials made two holding calls against the Irish. Then, on Navy's last drive, they called a roughing the passer penalty when Fay was buried.

"Don't think I don't know what you're doing," Weatherbie yelled at the officials. "You're calling a bunch of penalties now so that the statistics will look even. I know better."

It finally ended in near darkness, three and a half frigid hours after it had started. While Notre Dame sprinted for the locker room, the Navy players stood in front of their band for "Blue and Gold." They were exhausted and sad. They had put everything they had into the game and thought they deserved better — a lot better — than an 18-point final margin. Knowing they had outplayed the Irish for much of the day was small consolation.

When the last notes drifted into the wind, they turned to leave the field and found their path to the locker room blocked. The Notre Dame band was on the field. It simply couldn't wait an extra minute to let the Navy players sing their alma mater.

"You'll have to go around," one of the ever-helpful security people told the players, pointing to the far sideline. Polite to a fault, the players turned and trotted to the far side of the field, then made their way off the field from there, the strains of the Notre Dame victory march ringing in their ears.

Holtz hadn't called any fake punts this year. But Notre Dame had piled on anyway.

Weatherbie wasn't going to let them think the officials had decided the game. He knew that wouldn't have been healthy. And as it turned out, when he looked at the tape the next day, some of the calls he had thought had been wrong hadn't been. Dreschler *had* been holding on the key touchdown pass.

"It was a hold," Weatherbie said. "But there were a lot of plays on both sides that were also holds they *didn't* call."

The bottom line, though, was simple: the officials hadn't beaten them. To a lesser extent, Notre Dame hadn't beaten them either. *They* had beaten them.

In the cramped locker room, with the players still kneeling after the prayer, Weatherbie told them that. "To beat teams like this," he said softly, "to be the team we want to be, to be a bowl team, we can't turn the ball over when the game's on the line. We can't commit silly penalties. A bad team will let you get away with that; a good team won't. We lost to a good team today. But we didn't lose to a team we couldn't beat.

"Remember that. Remember how this feels right now. And think about how good it will feel to come back next year and whip their tails.

"Keep your heads up. You've got nothing to be ashamed of."

Knowing that didn't make the loss hurt any less. As they had gotten into the habit of doing after every game, Thompson and Smith — the two captains — circled the locker room, shaking hands with their teammates, thanking them for the effort, reminding them that there was still a lot to play for.

When he reached Bucchianeri, Thompson paused after shaking hands. "You know something, Ryan, I want to tell you how much I admire the way you've hung in this season," he said. "I know it's been tough for you, but you've come out to practice every day and given everything you have."

"People like you are the reason I keep coming back," Bucchianeri said.

He meant what he said. So did Thompson. They would never be friends; they were too different. But each had earned the other's respect.

Thompson completed his circle of the locker room. His message to his teammates was simple and direct: "Winning season," he kept saying. "We can still have a winning season."

They had three games left. They would have to win all three to finish 6–5. Not a man among them didn't think it was possible.

# 16

## TRIP FROM HELL

WHILE Navy was playing three good quarters and one bad one at Notre Dame, Army was playing three bad quarters and one good one at home against East Carolina.

The emotional letdown that Sutton had feared going into the Colgate game had come a week later. Unfortunately, it had come against a team that was equipped to take full advantage of a poor Army performance. East Carolina was one of those teams that almost no one knew anything about but was loaded with talent. The Pirates, who would go on to finish with a 9–3 record that would include a victory over Stanford in the Liberty Bowl, were fast and tough and had that little extra bit of meanness that teams trying to prove themselves always have.

The Cadets knew going into the game that ECU was a good team, better than Duke and probably in the same class as Washington, but they just couldn't get themselves to the kind of emotional pitch they had reached against those teams. They fell way behind, battled back, and still had a chance to win, trailing 31–25 with the ball and three minutes left. But the third of Ronnie McAda's three interceptions doomed them. That was the final: 31–25. They were back under .500 at 3–4–1.

Jim Cantelupe summed the day up best: "We just couldn't get out of our own way," he said. "It was the worst we had played since the first half of the Rice game."

As disappointing as the loss was, it changed little in terms of the players' overall goals for the season. They could still have a winning record and, just as important, they could still win the Commander in Chief's Trophy. To do that, they would have to do something that Army hadn't done since 1977: go to Colorado Springs and beat Air Force.

Sutton called the CIC "our championship." Since Army didn't play in a league and since a bowl game had been ruled out, that was the way this team would have to make its mark, by winning the CIC. Since Air Force had already beaten Navy, a victory over Army would clinch the trophy for the Falcons for another year. Army hadn't beaten Air Force — home or away — since 1988. It had two wins total in Falcon Stadium, the one in '77 and one in '67.

"We can't go out of here without having beaten those bastards," Joel Davis told his teammates early in the week. "We've been a committed team all year. This week we have to be more committed than we've ever been."

Before the players could turn their complete attention to the job of beating Air Force, there were a couple of minor distractions. Over the weekend, eleven first classmen had rented a van and sneaked down to the Naval Academy Dairy Farm in Gambrills, Maryland, and stolen the three Navy goats. Two days later, in a separate gambit, the CIC Trophy had been stolen from the trophy case where it was housed at Air Force.

These kinds of hijinks had become fairly standard fare over the years. Everyone usually got a good laugh out of the whole thing, the stolen mascots — whether they be Navy goats or Army mules — or trophies were returned a few days later, and everyone went on with their lives.

Not this time. When word got out about the stolen goats and the stolen trophy, General Graves went ballistic. Part of it was his personality: Graves simply wasn't a hijinks kind of guy. But beyond that was the 1992 nonaggression pact that had been signed by Army and Navy, which read, "In the future, there will be no kidnapping of cadets, midshipmen, or mascots."

The pact had come about after a group of midshipmen had kidnapped the Army first captain. The Navy first captain that year was a woman. During a leadership conference at West Point, she invited the Army first captain to meet her for dinner at Joseph's, the same Italian restaurant in Highland Falls where Cantelupe and Klein had met one another for the first time. When he arrived for dinner, the Army first captain was ambushed by a group of midshipmen, thrown into the backseat of a car, and driven to Annapolis.

He was released several hours later after the Corps of Cadets had threatened to storm the Yard to get him back. In the wake of the incident the leadership at both schools decided the whole kidnapping notion had gone too far, and the nonaggression pact was signed. It had been renewed in the fall of 1995 with the two commandants and first captains meeting in Annapolis to formally reseal the agreement. A few weeks later, eleven of Graves's cadets had blatantly violated the pact. He was not the least bit happy.

He was even less happy with the stealing of the CIC Trophy because a note had been left in the empty trophy case: "Our football team is coming out here to get this on the weekend," it read. "We just thought we would remove it a little bit earlier." The note was written on Graves's personal stationery.

Graves was out of town when the kidnappings occurred, but he held a staff meeting on a conference call and gave very specific orders to the new commandant, General Robert St. Onge: get the goats and the trophy back and find out who is responsible. Right away.

St. Onge called a meeting of the entire first class for Wednesday night in Eisenhower Hall. Word spread quickly through the barracks that St. Onge's message was going to be direct: either the parties responsible come forward and admit their guilt or the entire corps would be kept on the post without liberty for the coming weekend.

Since there were no classes on Friday in celebration of Veterans Day, which fell on Saturday, that would mean a three-day weekend would be destroyed. An hour before the meeting, the eleven firsties who had pulled the goat heist came forward. The goats were returned safely and the kidnappers were given ninety hours of restriction. Of course it wasn't all bad news for them: that night at the Firstie Club all their drinks were free, courtesy of their classmates.

The next day, the CIC Trophy was also returned. Air Force quarterback Beau Morgan couldn't resist a swipe at the West Pointers in response: "Stealing the trophy is about the only way that Army's ever going to get it," he said.

Fighting words. Which was exactly the way the Cadets wanted it. They felt exactly the same way about Air Force that the Navy players did: the only thing they hated more than Air Force was losing to Air Force. Early in the week, Mike Sullivan, who had played on the last Army team to beat Air Force, asked Cantelupe how he thought the team would feel about putting camouflage on their faces just prior to the game.

"We did it in '88," Sullivan said. "It was a way of saying to one another that we had to sell out completely to win the game; that we were going to war together to win."

Cantelupe ran the idea past Davis, who liked it, and they took it to Sutton, who also approved. So it was decided: they would hand out the camo just before kickoff. The other seniors were told. None of the underclassmen knew. If they did, it would dampen the emotional effect.

Since there were no classes on Friday, and since the corps had not been locked up, the post was virtually empty by the time practice was over on Thursday night. During Jim Young's tenure as coach, he had taken the team to the nearby Bear Mountain Inn on the Thursday before Air Force trips for a team dinner and a night of player/coach skits. It was a way to relax and bring the team together in a light way before what would be a tension-filled weekend.

With everyone gone, Sutton decided it might be fun to revive skit night. Rather than take the team to Bear Mountain, he arranged for the dinner to be held in the Cadet Restaurant in the basement of Eisenhower Hall. Everyone gorged on chicken and pasta and corn and cookies. The pizza came later. The Fat Men were in heaven.

The skits were wickedly funny. Jim Zopolis, the senior defensive back who was best known for his ability to mimic anyone, did a Doug Pavek imitation that had people falling off their chairs. Pavek had been a superb defensive back on the 1984 and '85 bowl teams and had come back to West Point as a liaison between the football team and the athletic department. He was now an army captain and he often talked to the players about commitment and dedication, and he was quite proud of the fact that, at thirty-one, he could still hold his own in the weight room. He also occasionally brought up the fact that he had played in two bowl games. As soon as Zopolis said, "You know, fellas, I played in *two* bowl games," everyone knew he was doing Pavek.

Pavek, sitting in the back of the room, kept shaking his head and saying, "It's not fair, I'm telling you, the guy's just not being fair."

This was not a night for fairness. John Graves even got up and did an imitation of Sutton sending in a play in which he changed his mind three times. Graves couldn't help but notice that one person wasn't laughing: Sutton. "I thought I might never play again," he said later.

Bill Doutt, the inside linebacker, who was due to become a father on the day before the Navy game, did a dead-on imitation of linebacker coach Bill Sheridan throughout the evening. No matter what anyone said or did, Doutt/Sheridan told them they better *shut up* right now.

But it was the coaches who got in the last word with a hysterical re-creation of an offensive line meeting. Eddie Stover and Joel Davis, as played by running backs coach Andre Cooper and assistant strength coach Scott Swanson, kept interrupting Ed Warriner (playing himself) to ask why the food at the hotel couldn't be a little bit better and a lot more plentiful. When Davis was caught not paying attention to what Warriner was talking about, he would just shake his head and say, "Yeah, I know, Coach, but I *am* the sexiest man in the corps."

It was full-blown jock stuff, the kind that bonds and binds a team together. They had all been through long, tough days in practice; they had all gotten on one another and been angry at one another. But it had all been for one reason: to create a team that would leave a mark. When the skits were over and the coaches had left, Davis stood up and told the team, "This is the best team I've ever played on. But we haven't met any of our goals yet. This is our chance. Wherever I am next year, I want to know that when you underclassmen come to practice every day, you're walking past that CIC Trophy. That's what this trip is all about."

IT was snowing when they landed in Colorado Springs the next day, but that didn't surprise anybody. It was November and they were in the Rockies. Snow was part of the deal. Of course an hour later the snow stopped and the sun came out. That was part of the deal too.

The local newspapers were full of bulletin board material: several Air Force players were quoted as saying that sure, the CIC was important, but winning the Western Athletic Conference would mean much more because it was so much harder to do. One Air Force player noted that Army and Navy knew in their hearts that "we're just a tougher bunch than they are." There was also a story with the headline: "Army coach's job may be on the line Saturday."

That was the last thing Sutton wanted the players thinking about. His theme for the week had been built around numbers:

'95 team; 60 minutes; 4 ever.

This team had to give everything it had for 60 minutes in order to achieve a victory they would all remember forever. "The feeling you are going to have on Saturday walking off that field," he told them, "is like nothing you've ever felt before in your lives."

The theme of the CEP/Sullivan–produced film that night was champions and what it felt like to be one. There were shots of the U.S. hockey team in Lake Placid, of Joe Montana and the 49ers, and, finally, a clip from Joe Namath talking about winning Super Bowl III: "There was a feeling right after the game," Namath said, "that was so wonderful, so special. It was just like, *we did it, we won, we're the champions.* I'll never ever forget that feeling or that moment. It was like nothing else I've ever felt in my life."

When the film was over, Sutton and the coaches left the players alone. Cantelupe read some of the Air Force quotes and pointed out the headline about Sutton's job. "That's something we can control, guys," he said. "We can take care of that."

Davis talked again about the total commitment needed to win the game. Then, the underclassmen left and the twenty-three first classmen remained behind. They discussed handing out the camouflage the next day just before kickoff and about what it would mean to beat Air Force. Several players got up and spoke. Bill Blair, who rarely spoke in team meetings, said he had waited four years to have a chance to play on a team this good in a game this important. Landis Maddox, the only player in the room, other than Davis, who had lettered as a freshman, said they had to consider it their responsibility to win the game, that it was up to all of them to lead everyone else.

Finally Davis got up one more time. Usually when he spoke to his teammates, Davis would work his way into a frenzy, peppering his talk with what would politely be described as salty language. This time though, his voice was soft and it kept getting softer.

"Before this season started, we made a pledge to each other," he said. "We pledged not to let each other down, to not let ourselves be mediocre again.

"I got an E-mail the other day from Anthony Noto. He graduated in '91 and he was one of my coaches at the prep school. He talked about playing Air Force and he talked about not playing football anymore."

Davis held up a battered piece of printout paper that he had been carrying all week. "This is what he said to me: 'Joel, getting up in the morning to face the battle isn't what's hard; it's getting up in the morning knowing that there's no battle left to fight.'

"We've got three battles left. That's all. Three more times we go out there together."

He paused. The room was completely silent. "I don't want this season to end," he said. "I don't want it to end because I don't want to leave you guys. I love you guys."

His voice cracked as he finished. They all stood up and formed a huddle. It was Jason Moura, a scout team player for most of his career who had made himself into a contributor on special teams through sheer effort and hard work, who spoke for all of them: "There were 120 of us four years ago," he said. "Look around. This is what we've got left. Three more weeks and we'll never play football again for the rest of our lives."

Emotional rhetoric is a big part of football. The reason for that is simple: going out to play a football game — even going out to practice — isn't like other sports. To play well, you almost certainly must endure pain. You are going to be hit and you must hit back — harder. You are going to feel tired, probably exhausted, but you have to keep going. You are going to endure aches and pains throughout the season, the kind that won't go away — if they ever do — until after you stop playing the game.

That makes it important to emphasize and reemphasize the commitment individuals have to a team. If you are determined not to let your friends, your buddies, your comrades down, you will push forward even when your body is telling your mind it has had enough. If Army's seniors had done one thing in 1995 with all their meetings and all their rhetoric it was remind each other — and the underclassmen — that they were all in this together.

They had battled through the tough losses and the letdowns by constantly reminding one another that the only way for all their effort to be rewarded in the end was to keep on pushing forward. Now, with the end clearly in sight, the seniors kept telling one another that there were a lot of years of *not* playing football ahead of them. This was a time to savor, but also a time to give up their bodies one more time for the cause.

The cause was Army football. It was one that they all had come to believe in deeply. It didn't matter to them if outsiders didn't understand that or if others in the corps saw them as a bunch of get-overs. They knew better. They looked into one another's eyes, and each saw someone who he had been to hell and back with and would be friends with for life, long after the football uniforms were put away for the last time.

When they promised they would do anything for one another, it was more than rhetoric. They meant it. On their Army football honor, they 100 percent meant it.


WHAT bothered the Army players most about the losing streak to Air Force was that they couldn't figure out a reason for it. If they had lost six straight times to Notre Dame they wouldn't like it, but they would understand it. But being dominated by Air Force made no sense because the schools were similar, even if the dorms at Air Force were a little plusher and there were more television sets and a few less restrictions. There were also fewer restrictions at Navy — though not more TVs — and the gap between Army and Navy each year was usually about the width of a thumbnail.

The losing streak had fallen into a distressing pattern: at home, the Cadets would keep the game close — losing 15–3, 7–3, and 10–6.

On the road, they would get blown out: 29–3, 25–0, 25–6. In fact, Army hadn't scored a touchdown at Air Force since 1987. That was a long time to go between extra-point attempts.

When Jim Young had been coach, he had tried everything possible to find a way to play better at Air Force. One of the problems visiting teams faced was the altitude: the academy was almost a mile above sea level, and the thin air took some adapting to. Young tried arriving three days early to get used to the altitude; he tried arriving at the last minute so the team wouldn't have time to notice the difference. Once, he had the players wear oxygen masks during practice to simulate the kind of air they would be breathing. Another time, he had oxygen on the sideline for every game, home or away, so that the players would get accustomed to using it.

Nothing worked. One year Young went so far as to assign Sutton to find out the best way to deal with the thin air. Sutton called several places that dealt with oxygen debt and was told that the best way to handle it was to be in the thin air for thirty days. At that point, he was told, you wouldn't even notice the difference.

"Great idea," Sutton said, "only we couldn't exactly arrive a month early to play the game."

The thin air wasn't the reason they were getting blown out, and everyone knew it. If a game was lost in the fourth quarter on a late Air Force rally, perhaps then you could point to the thin air as a factor. In recent years the games had usually been decided long before anyone had time to feel oxygen debt.

Charlie Weatherbie pointed to the stability of the Air Force coaching staff — DeBerry had been there twelve years and had very little turnover on his staff — as a reason for Air Force's domination of the CIC. But Army, while not as stable, had been coached by Young and then by Sutton, his top assistant, for thirteen seasons. It had been using virtually the same offensive system since 1984. Yes, it had broken the pure wishbone to go to a one-back-behind-the-quarterback set, with the other two halfbacks on the wings, but Air Force had also done that. In fact, with Weatherbie's arrival at Navy, all three service academies were running virtually identical offenses.

A large part of it was recruiting. For geographic reasons, Air Force had an advantage in recruiting anyone west of the Mississippi, and it had a large edge in California, which was one of the most football-rich states in the country. While the coaches knew they weren't going to get any of the really big-time California players, who would choose between Southern California, UCLA, and Notre Dame, they would have a good chance to recruit at the level right below that. After all, they played in a solid football conference — the Western Athletic — California recruits wouldn't be that far from home, and the campus, if it wasn't buried under snowdrifts, was stunning.

More often than not, Army and Navy tended to battle over academy-type students and players from the East while Air Force had the West to itself. There were, of course, exceptions to this, but that was the general rule. Air Force could also point to its recent success: the Falcons had been in seven bowl games during DeBerry's eleven years as coach. Navy hadn't been to a bowl game since 1981; Army had last gone in 1988.

There was also the question of *who* Air Force played. There were no I-AA teams on the Falcons' schedule. They had joined the WAC in 1980 and traditionally played a very representative national schedule. Their four nonconference games in '95 were against Army, Navy, Northwestern, and Notre Dame.

Finally, there was image. Army and Navy certainly had the edge in tradition, and no game Air Force was going to play in was going to equal Army-Navy in national appeal or attention. But that was one game. Air Force sold, to put it bluntly, the Wild Blue Yonder. Tom Cruise in *Top Gun* was the best recruiter Air Force had. Come to Air Force, fly superfast jets for a living, and hang out with Kelly McGillis when you're on the ground. Even General Graves admitted that the more glamorous image of the Air Force worked in its favor.

"There is such a thing as Army Aviation," he said. "But let's face it, when you think of Air Force, you think of flying, blue skies, sunglasses and all. When you think of Army, you tend to think about activities that usually are associated with mud."

Ouch. The Army coaches would no doubt wince at that description, but there was little doubt that just as Navy pitched the romance of the sea, Air Force talked often about the glamour of the sky. Army had to sell tradition and leadership. Sometimes that worked. In recent years it had not been enough to beat Air Force.

They were convinced they had what it took this year. Air Force came into the game with a 6–3 record, and a story in Saturday morning's newspaper said that a victory would clinch a spot in the Copper Bowl for the Falcons. They were also tied for the lead in the WAC.

It was a typical DeBerry team. Beau Morgan was a talented, clever, tough little option quarterback. They had a number of solid backs and a defense that wasn't overwhelmingly big but played with the same kind of heart that Army prided itself on.

Were they as arrogant as the Army and Navy players insisted that they were? Probably not — in most cases. But having dominated the other two service academies and — in their mind — not gotten the credit they deserved for that domination, everyone at Air Force could be just a tad frosty when talking about Army and Navy. No doubt that feeling carried over to the players and was reflected in their approach to the players from the other two academies.

Everyone connected with Army had come to believe as the season had evolved that this was the year that they were going to walk into Air Force and walk out with both the CIC and a measure of restored pride. When he met with the team early Saturday morning, Sutton talked about how he felt about the way they had approached the season.

Normally, Sutton is a low-key speaker except in the moments just before and just after games. When he gets really emotional, his voice drops so low that you have to lean forward and listen intently to hear him. When he walked into the 7:30 pre-breakfast meeting, he went through his normal routine: reading the schedule for the morning and reminding the players to check out of the hotel before their walk. He paused for a moment. When he started speaking again, his voice was barely louder than a whisper.

"We talked back in August about the power of one," he said. "About not letting the guy next to you down; about how we would need that power at some point in the season. This is that moment. This is what all the work has been for. We will go onto that football field today as *one*," he said. "You've done that all season. But even though we are *one* on the field, each of us as individuals has to have something that inspires us when we walk onto the field.

"It can be matching up against a great player; it can be memories of the past, thoughts about the future. Well, I want to tell you guys what inspires me as an individual."

He stopped and looked around the room. If a pin had dropped it would have sounded like a nuclear bomb going off. "It's *you*. All of you. You inspire me because you are the best damn team I've ever coached."

The rest of the morning was a steady building of emotion. The day was perfect: cool and breezy, but almost cloudless. Kickoff was at noon, so the game would be over long before the sun began to set and the temperatures began to drop again.

The day did not, however, begin ideally. Johnny Burnett, the long-time defensive backs coach, woke up in the middle of the night with a painful kidney stone. This had happened to Burnett before, but that didn't make it any less painful. When the team went for its walk, Burnett was clearly hurting. He wasn't about to beg off, though — not from this game.

They arrived at Falcon Stadium at 9:30. There was still frost on the field, so the players who liked to walk onto the field and look around before they got into uniform had to settle for walking around the perimeter. One banner had already been hung at the far end of the stadium. It read: "Punt the Grunts." Just before kickoff, Air Force officials had it taken down. By then, of course, everyone had seen it.

Although the scenery surrounding Falcon Stadium is stunning, since it is set smack in the middle of the Rampart Range of the Rockies, the stadium itself is very ordinary. It has 52,000 bench seats and they are all set well back from the field. Clearly, the loudest noise anyone would hear all day would come from the pregame Air Force flyovers that are a part of every pregame at Air Force.

"Forget the damn flyovers," Joel Davis had told the team. "That has nothing to do with us."

The flyovers were loud. And the loudest of them all came over just as Army hit the tunnel to return to the locker room. The tunnel seemed to shake as the planes went over.

Twenty minutes before kickoff, the first classmen broke out the camouflage. The reaction was exactly what they had hoped for. "This isn't Hollywood, pretty boy stuff," Cantelupe said as he tossed it to people. "This is to show what the game means to us and to show our commitment to one another."

They greased it on one another until they were all black and green from forehead to chin. It had been seven years since an Army team had put on camo before a game. It had been that same seven years since an Army team had beaten Air Force.

Sutton talked one more time about what it would mean to them to walk off the field as champions. By now, he didn't need to say another word and he knew it. They flew out of the locker room as prepared as a football team could be to play a football game.

And for one quarter, they played about as well as a team could hope to play. Air Force went nowhere on the opening drive of the game. Army took over for its first series and sliced right through the Falcons. The coaches wanted to give Air Force something to think about right away, and that meant stepping out of character and throwing the ball.

"We have to be free-flowing and daring," Sutton had said.

They were both. On the third play from scrimmage, McAda found an open Ron Leshinski for 12 yards and a first down to the Army 45. It was the earliest the Cadets had thrown a pass all season. Three plays later, McAda tried another pass. This time it was intended for Jeff Brizic and fell incomplete. No problem. On the next play, McAda started right and pitched the ball to Ron Thomas, who beat the Air Force defense to the corner and was gone — 43 yards — for a touchdown. Less than five minutes into the game, Army led 7–0.

Air Force picked up three first downs on the next series but stalled at the Army 36 and opted to punt. Steve Carr's kick pinned Army back at the 14. Time to grind it out. McAda picked up one to the 15. Air Force moved everyone up close, determined to keep Army from picking up a first down. McAda put the ball in Conroy's stomach on the next play, then pulled it out and dropped back to pass.

No one in Colorado not wearing a white uniform had been thinking pass, not in this situation, not from Army. John Graves was behind everyone. McAda's pass floated into his waiting arms and he was long gone, 85 yards. Touchdown! After going eight years without a touchdown in this stadium, Army had scored two in less than nine minutes. It was 14–0. The flyovers were long forgotten. The Army bench was joyful. They were doing exactly what they had promised one another they would do. They were playing free-flowing and daring. Air Force was on its heels.

A fragile team might have folded right there. But years of winning keeps a team from getting down when things don't go well at the start of a game. The Falcons went right down the field themselves, Morgan finding Jake Campbell for a 25-yard touchdown pass and, after one quarter, the two teams who had combined to score 16 points against one another a year earlier had scored 20: Army 14, Air Force 6.

The wind had become a factor by kickoff. It swirled quite a bit but was clearly blowing from the far end of the field — the south — toward the north, where the locker rooms were. Army had won the toss and deferred receiving the kickoff until the second half, meaning it had the wind in the first quarter. Now, Air Force had it in the second.

The offense began to sputter. After moving to the Air Force 29 on their third possession, the Cadets stalled there, and with the wind against them, Sutton opted not to try a field goal on fourth-and-eight. McAda tried to hit Leon Gantt deep, but he was well covered and for the first time in the game Air Force had held.

The rest of the quarter was mostly spent in Army territory. Air Force kept moving the ball and Army kept making big plays when it had to. The defense stopped one drive at the 36; another at the 27 when placekicker Randy Roberts, who had missed the extra point after the Air Force touchdown, missed a 44-yard field goal with the wind dead behind him.

That might have been Air Force's last possession of the half if not for a rather strange mark by the officials after Conroy had appeared either to pick up a first down at his own 46 or come up just short of it on a second-down run. Instead, the officials ruled that he had dragged his knee on the ground at the 44. That brought up third-and-three instead of third-and-inches and McAda, trying to run wide, was stuffed for a loss of two.

That forced a punt and Air Force did get the ball back, with 2:33 left. This time, their offense didn't stall in Army territory. Instead, Morgan capped a nine-play drive with five seconds left on the clock by hitting Dustin Tyner, who had beaten Garland Gay by a step, in the corner of the end zone. The Falcons went for two and Morgan was sacked trying to scramble. So the Cadets still led, 14–12, at the break.

But the last Air Force drive had hurt. Several times, it appeared the Cadets had them stopped, especially on fourth-and-two at the 20, when Todd Eilers had looked to be hemmed in when he took Morgan's pitch but managed to slide free for eight yards. Even then, there had only been ten seconds left to go the last 12 yards. Air Force had picked it up in five seconds — and one play.

The locker room was almost muted, especially compared with the intensity before the game. "Hey," Ed Warriner shouted at one point, "we're *winning* the game, fellas. Check the scoreboard."

Clearly, the players didn't feel that way. Air Force had controlled the game on both sides of the ball after the 14–0 start, and the late touchdown had been deflating, especially since it brought back memories of Air Force's ability to make the big plays year in and year out in these games.

The coaches knew that a quick start in the third quarter would be important. They would have the ball and Air Force, they assumed, would take the wind, wanting to jump on them and keep the momentum at the start.

"We have to make some things happen right away," Sutton told the coaches when they met. "We need a jump start."

They needed a confidence boost too. Even though they were winning, it was clear they didn't feel in control. Maybe after the fast start they had expected Air Force to roll over and die the way Boston College had. But this wasn't Boston College. This was another service academy team. It was also a team that didn't believe for a second that it could lose to Army, especially not on this field.

The first mistake of the second half was made by DeBerry, who miscommunicated with his captains. They thought he wanted the wind in the fourth quarter, not the third, and so they told the officials that they would kick off into the wind. That meant Army *really* needed a quick start to try and build a margin for the fourth quarter.

Kurt Kremser boomed the kickoff all the way to the six yard line, a tremendous kick into the wind. As the ball wobbled down, having gone a lot farther than kick returners Abel Young and Jeff Brizic had thought it would go, they glanced at one another to see who should catch the ball.

Neither of them did. The ball hit Young's foot and squirted straight to the right, rolling out-of-bounds on the six. Awful field position, not to mention a deflating way to begin the half. But they had the wind and they had dug out of a similar position earlier in the game.

Not this time. Conroy got three and Thomas three more. On third-and-four, McAda tried to throw to Leshinski, but cornerback LeRon Hudgins had him dead stone covered. They had to punt. Even with the wind behind him, Ian Hughes got off a poor kick and the ball rolled out-of-bounds on the Army 47.

They had wanted a quick start. Instead, they had again pinned themselves in their own territory. It took Air Force seven plays to make matters worse. On third-and-eight from the 10, Morgan ran a textbook quarterback draw, taking two steps backward, then running straight up the middle untouched into the end zone. Now, Air Force had the momentum and the lead.

The Falcons went for two once more and again Army stopped them. That meant it was only 18–14. There was still plenty of time to get turned back around. Instead, the offense went in the wrong direction, starting at the 27 and punting, three plays and two sacks later, from the 12. Sensing the kill, the Air Force defense was swarming now, beating their men off the line consistently, getting into the backfield before McAda had time to get anything started. This time, Hughes boomed his punt and the ball rode the wind and the roll all the way into the end zone — an 88-yard kick. It hardly seemed to bother the Falcons. On the second play of the drive, Morgan got outside and took off for 55 yards. Two plays after that, he pitched to Campbell, who went the remaining 19 yards. Eighty yards, four plays. They still couldn't make an extra point — Roberts missed another kick — but that was beginning to matter less and less.

On the Army sideline, everyone could feel it slipping away and there was nothing they could do about it. It had never occurred to anyone that this game would be anything less than a dogfight that probably wouldn't be decided until the very end, just like Duke and Washington and Rice and Notre Dame. The notion that they had wanted it *too* much didn't fit because they had come out so clearly ready to play. They needed to take a deep breath, calm down, and get ahold of themselves.

But it doesn't work that way in football. Emotion can't carry you for sixty minutes, but it can get you rolling in one direction or the other, and when that happens it can be very hard to stop if you are the one getting rolled.

By now, McAda was trying too hard, feeling as if nothing he was doing was right. He ran an option left and fumbled at the 23. Air Force's Steve Fernandez jumped on the ball and, once again, the Air Force offense breezed into the end zone, Morgan running another quarterback draw for the touchdown. They even converted the extra point. It was 31–14 and there were still more than five minutes left in the third quarter.

Less than ninety seconds later it was 38–14. Air Force's Michael Dalton intercepted McAda's first-down pass at the Army 42 and returned it all the way to the 11. Morgan got nine yards and then Campbell got the last two. In 10 minutes and 31 seconds, Air Force had scored four touchdowns going into the wind. Army had been caught in an avalanche, and by the time the last rock had fallen, the Cadets were completely buried. As it turned out, DeBerry's mistake hadn't mattered even a little bit.

The Army sideline was in a state of total shock. Air Force had scored 38 straight points. When the third quarter ended, the Army players put four fingers up — as they did every game — indicating, "the fourth quarter is ours." It was a sad, futile gesture. At that stage it really wouldn't have mattered if the fourth quarter had been theirs. They weren't going to score 24 points. They weren't going to come back in this game. They had put heart and soul into preparing to win, to finally take the CIC back, and they were going to come up empty.

Adam Thompson came in at quarterback and took the team to a consolation touchdown that made the final score 38–20. What hurt the most was that there hadn't been any bad luck or any bad calls. They hadn't come agonizingly close before losing. Air Force had thrashed them. Morgan had produced 152 yards rushing and 155 passing. After the 85-yard bomb to Graves, McAda had completed one more pass the entire day.

When the gun finally sounded, they had to make the long walk across the field to congratulate the Air Force players, to see the looks on their faces that seemed to say, "We knew it all along." They had to stand at attention for the Air Force alma mater and then, as a final insult, hear the celebrating Air Force cadets in the stands doing a mock Army cheer: "Gooooo Army, Beeeeeeat Navy!" It was their way of saying, "Go and have your little game with the Mids; we whipped you both — again."

Three hours after they had poured out the locker room doors, racing onto the field for the confrontation they had waited twelve months for, they trudged back through those doors with their heads bowed. The black and green camo on most of their faces was smudged by mud and by tears. Silently, they gathered around Sutton, who stood on the same chair he had stood on earlier, to give the postmortem.

For a coach, a moment like this is as tough as any in the business. There really is nothing to say. Effort doesn't matter when you've been blown out. There's nothing to grasp. As Sutton climbed onto the chair he was aware of the fact that General Graves was standing a few feet behind him, his back against the door, surrounded by members of his staff.

Even though he didn't want to think about it, Sutton couldn't help but wonder if he and his staff hadn't just lost their jobs. His entire family, Debbie and the two kids, fifteen-year-old Andrew and twelve-year-old Sarah, had made the trip. They all knew what was going on. That was something he would have to deal with later. Now, he had to find something to say to his players, knowing how much they were hurting.

"That was disappointing for all of us," he said, starting out with the stridency he always had in his voice after games. "I know how much everyone in here wanted this game and I know how all you guys sold out to try and go out there and win it. It hurts. It hurts all of us. I know that most of all it hurts" — he paused to compose himself — "the seniors." He paused again. "I know, we all know, how much all of you have given to try and get this done."

His voice caught. He put his head down. Everyone waited. "Today was a bitter day. Bitter. But that's the risk you take when you put so much into something. We all have to understand that. There are no guarantees in this game or in life. We didn't get what we wanted." His head was up now, his voice measured and composed. "But we have to go on from here. We've got a good, solid team coming to our place next week and we have to come in on Monday and start dealing with how we'll bounce back and get that game. It's our last home game. We need to win it.''

They gathered for the traditional cheer for next week — ''Beat Bucknell!'' — but it was about as forced as a cheer will ever be.


SUTTON had to go outside and meet the press. There is a tiny interview room at Air Force, but it was reserved for DeBerry — even though DeBerry wouldn't show up until twenty minutes later. ''We were celebrating winning the CIC again with the Secretary of the Air Force,'' he explained.

Sutton stood in the tunnel between the locker rooms and started to talk, only to be interrupted by an equipment truck backing down the tunnel that almost ran everybody over. ''What is the deal here!'' Sutton screamed. ''Doesn't anyone know what's going on?''

It was as close as he would come to showing his frustration publicly. He finally moved down to the field, out of the way of all the equipment trucks, to hold his press conference. While he talked, the players dressed slowly, knowing they still had a long trip home. It would take forty-five minutes to get to the airport, then the flight would take another three hours. With the two-hour time change, it would be close to midnight before they got back to West Point.

Traffic is always slow getting out of Air Force because there is only one main road leading out of the stadium. Unlike other schools, Air Force refuses to clear a path for the visiting team's bus to get them through the traffic. And so, even though the Army buses had a police escort, it didn't do any good since all the police car did was sit in traffic like everyone else.

''It was like water torture,'' Sutton said later.

It was just getting dark when the buses cleared the traffic. Everyone put their head back to sleep during what was left of the trip to the airport. Suddenly, the buses veered off the highway at the exit for the hotel where the team had stayed. Gene Uchacz, the assistant athletic director who coordinated the team's travel, had called from the airport: there was a mechanical problem with the plane. It would be at least an hour before they could even consider leaving — probably longer. And so the buses pulled back into the hotel and everyone was dumped back into the same ballroom where they had eaten breakfast ten hours and a lifetime ago.

There was no food, nothing to do, nowhere to go. Everyone just sat, some on chairs, some on the floor, and stared into space or talked in hushed tones. Sutton walked around talking quietly to a number of players. He paused for a long time to talk to Jason Moura, who was sitting on the floor, crying. He gave Moura a long hug and moved on. The scene felt exactly the way a funeral feels: people milling around with pained, shocked looks on their faces.

Finally came an announcement from Ben Russell, another of the assistant ADs: there were pizzas on the way. Even the Fat Men were too tired and too discouraged to cheer that news, although everyone was starving. They had eaten almost nothing since breakfast because traditionally a huge dinner was served on the airplane.

Everyone was quietly munching on pizza when Athletic Director Al Vanderbush, who had gone out to the airport to consult with Uchacz and the people from World Airways, came in and started quietly telling people the plane couldn't be fixed that night. They would have to recheck into the hotel and spend the night.

"Don't go anywhere, though," Russell said. "Because if something does happen, we might call you during the night and tell you that we're leaving."

Cantelupe looked at Klein. "They wouldn't do that, would they?" he said. "I mean if we're stuck, we're stuck. Let's at least get a decent night's sleep."

Klein shrugged. "At this point, I'd believe anything."

They were handing out room keys when one of the tutors who traveled with the team stood up to announce that anyone who wanted to do a little studying with the tutors should remain downstairs because the tutors would be available. They all looked at him as if he had just landed from Mars.

It was shortly after eight o'clock when they began heading for their rooms. Some went to the hotel restaurant to get something other than pizza to eat. Others went to their rooms and turned on the Florida–South Carolina game, a one-sided Florida rout. Others just went to sleep, drained and exhausted by the events of the day.

It was about 11 o'clock when the phones started ringing in their rooms, shaking most of them from sleep. "We're leaving for the airport at 1 A.M. Be in the lobby at 12:45." Four players assumed it was just a joke and didn't bother to get up.

It was no joke. Uchacz and Russell had found another plane. The weather reports on both ends of the flight for the next day were not good. The East Coast had been buffeted all night by high winds and torrential rains. But now things had apparently calmed down. This was their best chance to get out of town.

And so, they all gathered in the lobby, most of them with their eyes half-closed. The four who hadn't believed the initial call had to be called again while everyone sat on the buses and waited. Doug Pavek spoke for everyone: "What have we done to deserve all *this?*" he said.

When they arrived at the airport, the new plane was waiting. "Rich International," it said. No one had ever heard of it, unless it was a coffee. This was a 747. Everyone boarded and tried to go back to sleep. The captain came on the PA to welcome everyone. "We just came over the mountains, folks, and it might be a tad bumpy going out of here," he said. "After that we should have a fairly smooth ride."

Everyone looked at one another. The dreaded "a tad bumpy." How bumpy could it be on a 747?

Extremely. Almost as soon as the plane took off, the roof panels began to shake and squeak. Mike Sullivan pointed at them and said, "What's wrong with this picture?" Then the tad of bumpiness showed up and the plane began rocking and rolling all over the sky. Most athletes never notice turbulence on an airplane. Young people almost never are bothered by it. Most Army cadets have studied engineering and done some flying. They understand how planes work and aren't bothered by a few bounces.

On this trip, as the plane climbed over the mountains, shaking and rolling and squeaking, everyone sat straight up, staring at the ceiling panels and at one another. "I hate this," Joel Davis said. "I just hate it."

The plane finally reached a cruising altitude and the squeaking and rolling stopped. Everyone went to sleep. Three hours later, they were awakened when the squeaking and rolling started again. The plane was now descending and the East Coast winds were at least as high as the winds in the Rockies had been. Slowly, the plane came down, rocking and squeaking.

Finally, land was spotted below. A mock cheer went up. Just as quickly, the plane began ascending again. Something had gone wrong on the approach. The pilot had to climb back through the clouds again and start all over. By now, those who had eaten the steak dinner at 5 A.M. eastern time were regretting it. Uchacz crossed himself over and over again. Rocking and squeaking, the plane began to descend again. This time, except for a few more sizable bounces, everything went fine. The plane landed and a loud cheer — a serious one — went up.

It was snowing in Newburgh. Everyone deplaned gingerly. Davis looked at his watch. It was seven o'clock in the morning. "Eleven hours," he said, "until formation."

After the last twenty-four, even formation didn't sound like such a bad thing.

# 17

# WINNING SEASON?

WHILE the week leading up to the Air Force game had been one of emotional buildup and anticipation at Army, that same week had been one of jangling nerves at Navy.

Weatherbie probably would have preferred another game against Notre Dame rather than the game he had to prepare for: Delaware. This was another of those games with a I-AA opponent that was a nothing to gain/everything to lose proposition for his team. What's more, the Blue Hens weren't just a I-AA team, they were a I-AA power. They would come into the game with a record of 9–0 and a I-AA ranking of number two in the country in one poll, number four in the other.

Delaware had been a small school powerhouse for years, led by their longtime coach Tubby Raymond, who was in his thirtieth season. Raymond had won 248 games, which made him the tenth-winningest college football coach of all time. The last two times Navy and Delaware had met had been disastrous for the Mids: a close 29–25 loss in 1991, followed by a 37–21 defeat the next year in a game Delaware had led 23–0 before coasting home.

Weatherbie was concerned that he could talk until he was blue in the face about how good the Blue Hens were and his team wouldn't take him seriously. Navy had outplayed Notre Dame in every statistic except the one that mattered (score), so how tough could a bunch of Blue Hens be?

The Monday afternoon meeting was about as tense as any all season. Weatherbie again reviewed the Notre Dame statistics to drive home the point that they had beaten themselves. He told the players that the tape had shown that many of the calls they had all thought were wrong, weren't wrong. He told them they had to deal with adversity better. "When something bad happens, don't let it lead to another bad thing happening," he said. "Never let one mistake become two. We're doing too much of that."

He was pacing up and down in front of the team as he spoke. He stopped and his voice turned sharp. "Some of you guys look half-asleep in here," he said. "Am I boring you to death?"

That got their attention. They weren't used to hearing razors in Weatherbie's voice. "There's only one question for this team this week," he said. "How bad do you want it? If you want it, we'll win the game. We can handle Delaware physically. But is a winning season really important to you? If it is, we'll get the job done. I'll tell you one thing I know for certain about Delaware: they will come in here believing in themselves. If we don't do the same thing, it will be a long afternoon."

He was still concerned about their attitude when the meeting broke. When practice was over, he called an informal meeting of the players committee, which consisted of three seniors, two juniors, and two sophomores, to talk again about the team's attitude that week. The players committee had been set up so that the team could feel as if it had spokesmen in all three of the upper classes who could talk to the coaches. Their conversations could be about things ranging from play calling to the movies being shown on Friday night to the pregame meal menu.

Now, Weatherbie wanted the committee members — seniors Andrew Thompson, Joe Speed, and Andy Person, juniors Omar Nelson and Ben Fay, and sophomores Gervy Alota and Greg Summa — to make it clear to their teammates that this was going to be a difficult week of practice. The weather was starting to turn cold, they were all a little tired and a little beat up, and they weren't playing an opponent whose presence in Annapolis would have the Yard abuzz. But they had to ignore all that and make sure they were ready to play their best game of the season on Saturday. Anything less would be a disaster.

The players were impressed by Weatherbie's concern. Although none of them had wavered in their feeling that the new coaching staff was headed in the right direction, there had been a sense that there was a sameness to the message every week. Always it seemed the game was a great opportunity; always it seemed that doing their job would ensure that God's plans not to harm them but to prosper them would eventually be revealed to them.

Now, Weatherbie was abandoning the set speech. He seemed to understand that the opportunity this week was for disaster if they didn't show up on Saturday ready to play. There could be no more flat starts at home. That had been a distressing pattern all season: in all four home games, the opposition had scored first and the Mids had spent the rest of the day trying to come from behind. They had succeeded only once, against Villanova.

Most of the problems had centered around the offense, which had been brilliant at times, mediocre at others, and on some occasions downright lousy. It was a credit to the defense, which had played excellent football almost the whole season, that there hadn't been any finger-pointing. Once upon a time that wouldn't have been true with a Navy team. The defensive players would have been walking around saying, "Well, we did our job."

This defense was too mature to let that happen. Thompson, as the captain, was the leader, but he received ample help from Speed, from the two linebackers, Fernando Harris and Clint Bruce, and from Mark Hammond and Andy Person.

Hammond and Person had both had superb seasons. Hammond, coming from the inside at his tackle position, and Person, coming from the outside at defensive end, had made big plays in almost every game. Both were intensely competitive on the field, quiet and gentle off it.

Person was one of those rare players who had been good enough to see playing time as a plebe. In fact, he, Speed, and Brian Schrum were the only three-time lettermen on the team. Person had grown up in Philadelphia and had played both ways — at tight end and at linebacker at Episcopal Academy. He had been moved to the defensive line as a freshman because at six four, 230 pounds he was big for a linebacker even though he was relatively small for a lineman. He made up for that lack of size with speed and smarts. He had a nose for the football and a knack for big plays.

It hadn't come as easily for Hammond, who had grown up forty-five minutes from the academy in Great Falls, Virginia. Hammond played JV ball as a freshman, then sat out his sophomore year after knee surgery. It wasn't until the third game of his junior year that he cracked the starting lineup. From that point on, he got better and better, and by now he had become one of the team's best defensive players.

Harris, who had started for three years, had come to the academy by an unusual route: after graduating from high school in Crockett, Texas, he had enlisted in the navy. A year later, he had been offered a spot in an officer ascension program and had enrolled at Norwich University in an ROTC program. After a year there, he had transferred to the Naval Academy. Having turned twenty-four in September he was the second oldest player on the team — behind Shaun Stephenson — and he played with quiet fury. His reaction to the play which had resulted in Ron Powlus breaking his arm had been typical: after making a great play to sack Powlus from behind, Harris didn't even celebrate the sack. He didn't regret the play — the tackle was clean and Powlus getting hurt had been a fluke — but he saw no reason to celebrate.

Often, he and Bruce would stand together on the sideline and when the offense sputtered they would say to each other: "Another chance to do our job. Ready?"

"Ready."

Then they would go out and do it.

None of the three attracted very much media attention even though each had a story to tell. Hammond was a good student and had an offbeat sense of humor. He still carried a sense of loss over the death of Robin Pegram but rarely betrayed that feeling unless the subject came up. "It doesn't hurt as much as it used to," he said. "It's just an ache that I still feel."

Person was always in the middle of locker-room hijinks and took great pleasure in making life miserable for his younger brother Chris, who was a sophomore scout team player. He was the subject of stories in the Philadelphia papers every year before the Army-Navy game, since he was the hometown boy coming home for the big game.

Harris was the quietest of the three, content most of the time to let his play do the talking for him. He did open up occasionally when the team's black players would gather after practice to swap stories and sing the occasional off-key song.

This was not a team divided by race by any stretch of the imagination. No two players were closer than Thompson and Speed, and McCoy and Fay had become close through their competition at quarterback. Room assignments on the road were done by position and class; race was never taken into consideration.

But as is the case at most colleges where African-American athletes make up a large chunk of the varsity athletes but a small chunk of the student body, there were times when the black players enjoyed spending time among themselves. Just as the black players at Army often liked to go out and seek black female companionship at the few places in the area where they could find it, the same was true of the black players at Navy.

It was not at all uncommon at both schools for black players to be among the team's leaders. Akili King would almost certainly have been a captain at Army had he stayed in school. At Navy, Chris Hart had been a cocaptain in 1994, and Speed and Nelson were not only members of the players committee, they were two of the players everyone on the team looked up to.

This was a week when all the various elements on the team needed to pull together. Notre Dame week was easy for everyone because of who the opponent was and because the game was on national TV. Everyone was talking about the game around the Yard and wishing the players luck and telling them they could do it. Delaware was entirely different. The players could almost sense a feeling in the brigade that football wouldn't really matter again until the week of the Army game. Games against Delaware and Tulane just weren't that big a deal.

They were a big deal, though, especially to the seniors. They knew that all three of their remaining games were winnable — and losable. Three wins would represent a remarkable turnaround, a winning season after the disaster that had been 1994 and an end to the Army losing streak that haunted all of them. Three losses would put them in the same boat with the seniors who had come before them: a 3–8 record was a 3–8 record, no matter how much closer the games had been or how much harder the team had played.

Andrew Thompson put it best in his journal that week: "In the end we can only be judged by what we do on Saturday afternoons. The rest just doesn't matter.''

Somewhere between Monday afternoon and Saturday at 1:30, Weatherbie's message got through. Right from the beginning, the Mids were all over Delaware. There was no slow start, no deficit to overcome. They scored first, they scored second. Ben Fay went 74 yards for a touchdown on an option run to make it 21–0. Paul Johnson would joke later that Fay took 32 seconds to run the 74 yards. It didn't matter. What mattered was that he didn't stop until he was in the end zone.

Clearly, Delaware was stunned. This wasn't what the Blue Hens had expected from Navy. The defense was flying to the ball so hard and so fast that even Dick Bumpas was caught smiling. Most amazing of all, the day was sunny and comfortable. The final was 31–7. It probably could have been worse except that the coaches got everyone into the game in the fourth quarter after the last touchdown had put Delaware away.

The victory was a huge relief to everyone. The last thing anyone wanted was a loss to a Division I-AA team to blot their record. Weatherbie was already campaigning with Lengyel to eliminate I-AA games from the schedule in the future. To make that argument more convincing, the team had to prove that it was head and shoulders above I-AA competition, something it had been unable to do in the past. Blowing out an undefeated team that was ranked in the top five in the I-AA rankings was a big step in the right direction.

The victory made them 4–5. Since the string of losing seasons had started in 1983, only one Navy team had won more than four games: Chaump's first team, which had gone 5–6 only to follow that with back-to-back 1–10 records. Beating Delaware didn't send the Yard into a state of euphoria, but if anyone had been looking closely they would have noticed that this was a team that had turned back around in the right direction. They had hit their nadir in the Air Force game, started back up the ladder against Villanova, played well for almost three quarters against Notre Dame, and then put together their best all-round performance since the Duke game against Delaware.

There was little doubt that Ben Fay's work at quarterback had something to do with this trend. Fay's skills didn't lend themselves to the wishbone the way McCoy's did, but he was a better runner (Johnson's jokes about his speed aside) than the coaches had thought. What's more, he and Clint Bruce were, without question, the two non-senior leaders on the team, and everyone on the offense — including McCoy — looked up to him.

Best of all, McCoy had handled the switch without whining or complaining. Instead, he continued to work hard in practice and was supportive of Fay just as Fay had been supportive of him when he had been starting. And contrary to what the coaches had thought, he was comfortable coming off the bench. It almost seemed as if he felt less pressure not starting. After all, as mature as McCoy seemed to be, he was still a twenty-year-old who had spent his first night in a hotel two months ago.

The coaches were thankful that McCoy had handled the switch as well as he had. In college football — even at a place like Navy where the players are used to taking orders — starters rarely handled going to the bench graciously.

All season long, the coaches had shuffled players in and out of the starting lineup, looking for the best combinations and trying to give younger players a chance if older players didn't appear to be getting the job done.

Tim Cannada had supplanted Omar Nelson at fullback, and Nelson was less than thrilled with the switch. When Kevin Lewis didn't get a lot of snaps during the second half of the Navy game in the defensive backfield, DB coach Gary Patterson, who made the decisions on who played and who didn't, found himself confronted by an angry father after the game. Monty Williams had quite the team in preseason after Nelson had outplayed him during spring practice. Zach Williams, who had kicked off for most of '94, had quit after one game when it became apparent he wasn't going to kick off anymore in '95.

Others dealt with adversity differently. When Brian Grana's position (tight end) had been eliminated in the spring, he had, by his own admission, sulked about it for a while. Then he had decided to become the best tackle he could possibly become. When Bryce Minamyer saw his name listed with the second team early in the season, he took it as a hint that he needed to play a little harder and worked his way back into the starting lineup, where he stayed for the rest of the season.

And then there was Matt Scornavacchi. For four years, Scornavacchi had been the team's iconoclast. He was not, by any stretch,
an outcast the way Bucchianeri was. His teammates liked him. They
enjoyed his wise-guy, off-the-wall humor and respected him for raising issues that others might not raise — like whether Grana, as the
team's only Jewish player, would be bothered by Weatherbie's prayers — even if they might disagree with him more than they agreed
with him.

Scornavacchi had been the team's best big-play receiver in both
his sophomore and junior seasons. He had caught 18 passes for an
average of 18 yards a catch as a sophomore and 22 passes for an
average of 20 yards a catch as a junior. And yet, within the brigade
he was known as PIF — Pass Intended For — because it often seemed
that he *almost* made big plays.

That was probably unfair. Scornavacchi was not the same kind of
possession receiver that Damon Dixon, who had graduated a year earlier, had been. Dixon had caught 51 passes as a senior for a total of
556 yards — only 116 more than Scornavacchi had picked up with
his 22 catches. In fact, Kevin Hickman, the tight end who had gone
on to the NFL, had caught 41 balls in '94 for a total of 24 yards *less*
than Scornavacchi had totaled.

Still, Scornavacchi had the PIF label. It was probably as much because of his pragmatic attitude as any dropped balls. Scorno just
wasn't a rah-rah guy. It wasn't in his nature. He laughed when people talked about the importance of the brigade as Navy's so-called
twelfth man.

"Give me a break," he said. "When we win, we win, just like
when we lose, we lose. The brigade has nothing to do with it. Most
of the time I've been here, the brigade didn't like the football team
anyway."

Growing up in Reading, Pennsylvania, Scornavacchi had excelled
at all sports and been a very good student too, with a 3.3 GPA and
1170 on his SATs. He could have gone to an Ivy League school either
as a football player or as a miler in track, but he opted for Navy because he wanted to play Division I football; he figured the education
was comparable to the Ivy League; and he didn't want his parents
paying for college.

Mike and Lyn Scornavacchi had divorced when Matt was thirteen. Matt still remembers driving with his mother and his sister Gina up to Penn State, where his brother Mike was a sophomore, to tell him about the split. "They all cried," Matt said. "I didn't really understand it completely, but it didn't seem to change things that much. Dad was never home much anyway."

Lyn Scornavacchi went back to college after the divorce and got her degree in psychology. Mike moved to Lancaster and remarried. The relationship between father and youngest son was tense, strained. "I stopped worrying about it a long time ago," Matt said, unconvincingly.

Although he got to play briefly as a freshman and extensively from the start of his sophomore year, Scornavacchi hadn't had the easiest ride during his four years at the academy. He had been in the 32nd company — "the cursed 32nd," as he called it — that Bucchianeri belonged to. He had known Robin Pegram and Autumn Pevzner and had been in the same squad as Lisa Winslow. Gil Green, the linebacker who hanged himself in January of 1993, had also been in his squad. He had seen one roommate transfer and another close friend, Tom Pritchard, thrown out of school for using a fake ID to get into a bar.

"They didn't have to throw him out for that," Scornavacchi said. "But they were looking to nail him."

As a junior, he was labeled as one of the "conspirators" by Chaump, a label he joked about without making any bones about his dislike for Chaump. "I wouldn't have played another year for him," he said. "When he was fired, I wasn't going to go around and say, 'Oh, isn't that too bad,' because I didn't think it was. I was glad he was fired. Anyone would have been an improvement."

Weatherbie hardly seemed like an ideal replacement from Scornavacchi's point of view. He was planning a ground-oriented option offense, which meant less chances for the wide receivers. He was deeply religious and Scornavacchi was an agnostic. He was a stickler for little things — like taping your ankles — and Scornavacchi didn't like to tape his ankles.

"I don't care if I don't catch a single pass all season," he said. "All I want to do is win games. I'll play tackle to win games. Coach Weatherbie has a great, upbeat attitude. I don't have to buy into everything he says to believe in what he's doing as a coach."

But he still didn't tape his ankles. Instead, he had the trainers put just enough tape above his socks to make it look like they were taped.

During the season, Scornavacchi's playing time had dwindled as younger players had improved. Mark Mill had become the punt returner and Neal Plaskanos the main kickoff returner. Even with Shaun Stephenson hurt, Scornavacchi was sharing time at the wide-out spots with Astor Heaven and LeBron Butts and Plaskanos.

But he never complained or stopped giving 100 percent every day in practice. He took almost everything in stride, with the possible exception of the food in King Hall. "I hate it," he said and backed that up by buying his own food and cooking for himself most nights in his company's wardroom.

Unlike the rest of the seniors, Scornavacchi didn't dread the end of his days as a football player. "I've been beaten up playing the game," he said. "I've talked to guys who have played in the pros and seen what it does to their bodies. Not for me. I'm ready to move on, get on with my life. I'm lucky, because I've got a job guaranteed next year. I have a lot of friends back home who have college degrees who are working for lawn care services or as chauffeurs."

Now, though, as he and the other seniors faced the last home game of their careers, they all had to admit that it was difficult to believe it was all ending so quickly. There would be twenty-one seniors in uniform for the Tulane game. Although they all felt in some ways as if they had been plebes only five minutes ago, each of them had to admit it had been a long, difficult road since those first days of Plebe Summer.

It was not a cliché to say they had arrived as boys and would leave as men. They had seen death and dealt with failure and firings and dissension. They had seen more than one hundred other players who had started with them not make it to the finish line. They had been embarrassed at times, infuriated at others. None of them would say they wanted to do it all over again. All of them would agree they had learned a lot — more, really, than they had bargained for — about the realities of life.

The night before the game, when the defense met, Bumpas asked the seniors to talk about how they felt about wearing their blue uniforms for the last time. Each of them got up and talked about what it had meant to them to be Navy football players. Thompson talked about "the brotherhood" that had kept them all together. Speed said he never would have made it through four years without his teammates.

Each of them thanked the coaches for helping them to become a good defense. A year ago, they had given up 399 points for the season. Through nine games this season, they had given up 168. "I've probably made half as many tackles as I made last year," Thompson said. "I don't care. I'm playing on a defense that makes me proud. I'm grateful for that."

It was an emotional session, the seniors imploring the underclassmen to build on what had been started. "This is just the beginning," Person said. "I expect to be cheering you guys in a bowl game next year."

There would be no bowl game for these seniors. But they could still go out the way they most wanted to go out — as winners. Each of them would be introduced before kickoff along with their parents or someone close to them if their family couldn't make it to the game.

Shaun Stephenson's parents were flying in from Utah. Shaun had played in both the Notre Dame and Delaware games but hadn't had a pass thrown in his direction. Now, he would play his last home game one week after playing his first. Joe Speed's mom came over from Dundalk. Andrew Thompson's parents didn't make the long trip from Seattle, but a close friend of the family, Bill Huntington, came down from Delaware. Thompson threw his arms around him and cried when he trotted onto the field to join the other seniors. Andy Person's mom and dad were there and so were Mark Hammond's.

Lyn Scornavacchi was there too. Mike Scornavacchi wasn't. Matt had called him earlier in the week to see if he was going to come. "Sorry, son," Mike Scornavacchi had said. "I'm going hunting this weekend."

In the locker room before the game, Scornavacchi shook his head recounting the conversation. The tough, I-can-take-anything look was long gone. His blue eyes looked just a little bit misty. "Can you believe the guy," he said. "Hunting. I hope he has a good time."

Even without Mike Scornavacchi, the day turned out to be a good time for his son and his son's team. It didn't start all that well. The weather was cold and miserable, a steady, misty rain coming down when the game began. The team didn't even get its signals straight on leaving the locker room. When the seniors went out to be introduced, the underclassmen followed them out.

Weatherbie hadn't wanted that. He had wanted the seniors to have their moment and then have the rest of the team take the field. But no one had told the underclassmen. Weatherbie walked back into the coaches' locker room for a moment after the seniors had left and came back to find an empty locker room.

He was not pleased.

He felt better — at least a little better — once the game started.

The good news was that the Mids completely dominated the first half. The bad news was that they only led 7–0 at the break. They outgained Tulane 181 yards to 34 but once again found a variety of ways to keep themselves off the scoreboard.

The kicking game continued to be a problem. Looking for something — anything — the coaches had put in a fake field goal, having Brian Schrum flip a quick shovel pass to the fullback. They tried it on the first series, bringing Covarrubias in, ostensibly to try a 41-yarder, then having Schrum toss the ball to Tim Cannada. The play came up short of the first down and was quickly put back into mothballs.

Two possessions later, they drove the ball to the Tulane seven. But on third down, Fay was sacked for a four-yard loss and Covarrubias came on for what should have been a routine 28-yard attempt. Only nothing was routine in the Navy kicking game at this point. He hooked it left.

In the stands, Ryan Bucchianeri winced. After the Notre Dame, on-the-list/off-the-list debacle, he hadn't made the dress list for either the Delaware game or this one. An hour earlier, he had marched onto the field with his company — there were no more slam cadences — and had walked almost directly underneath the goalpost Covarrubias had just hooked the ball to the left of.

Navy finally got into the end zone with McCoy at quarterback, driving 74 yards late in the second quarter. Even then, it took a fourth down conversion and a gutsy call by Johnson: a fake dive play followed by McCoy rolling right and finding LeBron Butts in the end zone for a 17-yard touchdown pass.

The kicker on the extra point was Graham, bad ankle and all. The coaches had lost all confidence in Covarrubias, and with Bucchianeri consigned to the stands, the third dressed kicker was Tom Vanderhorst, a plebe who had started the year at number eleven on the depth chart and had kicked with the JV team all season. Graham's kick cleared the goalpost by about a foot, but it was good. He hobbled off into a celebration that might have made you think he had just kicked the winning field goal against Army. Even extra points had become an adventure.

That was all the first-half scoring. The defense had dominated Tulane's offense from the start. Person, Hammond, Harris, Speed, and Thompson were determined to make their last memories of this stadium happy ones. All they needed was some help from the offense.

"Hey, guys, there's no reason for this to be close," Johnson told his offense during the break. "Don't let them hang around. You let a team hang around, it's dangerous, something will happen. There's no reason why we can't score on every possession of this half if you'll just stay calm and make the plays. We're moving the ball every damn time. Why not score?"

Weatherbie was nervous as a cat. Even though his team was ahead, the game brought back memories of Wake Forest, a team they had dominated in the first half only to fall apart in the second after failing to take control of the game. His message all week had been that they had to get to five (wins) before they could get to six. He reiterated it one more time before they went back on the field.

"Everything we've worked on for the last ten months is on the line right now," he said. "Number five is out there for us, but we've got to go and take it. They aren't going to hand it to us."

They didn't have to. With Fay back at quarterback, they went right down the field after taking the kickoff. Fifty-nine yards, six plays, with Cannada breaking tackles to go the last six yards. It was 14–0 and everyone breathed a small sigh of relief. No flags, no mistakes, just the good start they needed.

The defense took over for most of the third quarter, allowing the Green Wave just one first down. The offense couldn't repeat the opening drive, so it was left to the defense — and the special teams — to take control of the game. After the offense had gone three-and-out,

Schrum boomed a 46-yard punt to the Tulane 13. Keith Galloway blew down the field past all the Tulane blockers and nailed return man P. J. Franklin for a two-yard loss at the 11. That fired everyone on the bench up. Two plays later, halfback Horace Raymond fumbled and Robert Green jumped on the ball at the 15.

Getting into the end zone still wasn't easy — it took five plays — but McCoy finally scored on third-and-goal from the one, and with 2:17 left in the third they had command, 21–0. Another McCoy touchdown early in the fourth quarter ended any doubts about a miraculous Tulane rally.

In truth, no one was thinking that, because the defense continued to stuff the Green Wave on every possession. The rest of the afternoon was a joyride. On Tulane's next possession, Thompson intercepted a Shaun King long ball and returned it to the Navy 28. Two years earlier, Kevin Hickman, one of three ex-Mids playing in the NFL, had tossed a ball up into the brigade after a touchdown, and Thompson had never forgotten it. He had vowed to do it someday, but only if the game was safely in hand. Up by 28 in the fourth quarter, he figured it was safe. So, he hurled the ball into the stands.

Naturally, the officials flagged him for unsportsmanlike conduct, moving the ball back to the 13. Weatherbie, game face still firmly in place, was furious and told Thompson so, getting right up in his face. Thompson understood Weatherbie's anger, but he was still fighting a smile.

"I got yelled at," he said later, "but it was worth it."

And in spite of Weatherbie's fears that it might hurt the team, it didn't. In fact, it set up one of the most satisfying moments of the season. On first down, with Tulane figuring that Navy would try to run the ball out of the hole it was in, McCoy play-faked, dropped back, and threw the ball as far as he could. Scornavacchi, three steps behind everyone, ran under the ball at midfield and was long gone — for an 87-yard touchdown play, the longest in Navy history. No PIF, just a perfect throw and a perfect catch. It was too bad Mike Scornavacchi couldn't find the time to be there to see it.

Nonetheless, it provided a joyous capper to what turned out to be an almost perfect day. By game's end, no one on the Navy sideline was noticing the cold or the gray or anything except the scoreboard.

The only disappointment was not getting the shutout — which would have been the first against a I-A opponent since 1980. Tulane finally scored on a fluky, 58-yard pass against the second team defense. Even so, the 35–7 final was more than enough to cause a wild celebration.

As soon as they finished shaking hands with the Tulane players, Thompson led the other seniors into the stands so they could stand *with* the brigade during the playing of "Blue and Gold." All the bad feelings, or at least a lot of them, were a thing of the past. The brigade clearly enjoyed having a team it could really cheer for, one that was a part of the academy, rather than apart from the academy. And the players, sensing that support, enjoyed the bonding they could feel coming from their fellow students.

The locker room scene was a wild one, with the Supe and the 'Dant giving rah-rah speeches about what they were going to do to Army when they got to Philadelphia in two weeks. Bogle was particularly wound up. "We kicked Tulane's ass this week," he said, "and in two weeks we're going to kick Army's ass too!" he roared.

Seeing how excited Bogle was, Thompson approached him and asked if he would consider granting full liberty for the rest of the weekend to all football players — not just the varsity but scout team-ers, JVs, and plebes too. Bogle said absolutely, why not, everyone deserves it. When Thompson made the announcement, the room went wild. Liberty for the rest of the weekend, then on Wednesday they all got to go home for Thanksgiving.

No one was happier than Mark Hammond. He had played well in his last home game and now he could celebrate. Earlier in the week he had been put on restriction by his company officer for committing the dreaded book-bag-over-the-shoulder crime. Now, he was free — at least for this weekend.

About the only person in the room who wasn't thrilled by Bogle's decision was Kent Owens. As a company officer, Owens was very sensitive about anything that might be perceived in the brigade as special treatment for the football team. This was certainly that. None of the other varsity teams were given complete liberty after a victory. The rest of the brigade, which had been required to be at the game, wasn't getting liberty either.

Owens started to say something to Bogle, then thought better of it. Maybe, he thought, he was overreacting. He would just let it go and let everyone enjoy the victory. Later, he regretted the decision because there was grumbling within the brigade about Bogle's decision.

"What I should have done was suggest to him that the whole brigade be given liberty," he said. "That way, everyone would have been happy and the brigade would have felt as if the football team had done something for *them*."

Everyone else in the room was content to enjoy what had been accomplished. They had all come a long way since that first meeting with Weatherbie back in January. They were now 5–5. The winning season that had seemed at times to be little more than a hyperbolic fantasy was right there, close enough that they could almost reach out and touch it.

"All I've heard since I first got here is 'Army, Army, Army,' " Weatherbie told the players. "Well now, guys, it's time to take care of that piece of business. I can't wait to go up there and play the Black Knights of the Hudson.

"We got number five today, guys. Army is going to be number six."

As much as the seniors wanted win number six, that wasn't the number on their minds when they thought about Army. One was the number they thought about. They had one last chance to beat Army.

# 18

# THE LONG WAIT

ON that same afternoon, Army won its final home game too, but the victory didn't bring the same kind of happiness that they felt at Navy. It took almost three quarters to put away a spunky Bucknell team, and although the final score was 37–6, no one was jumping up and down when the final gun went off.

"We play like that against Navy," Joel Davis said, "and they'll kick our butts."

Actually, the lethargic performance was hardly surprising. Nothing the coaches were going to say, nothing the captains or anyone else was going to say or do was going to make the Air Force game easy to digest. The awful trip home left everyone tired and cranky. Sutton, who normally kept practices fairly simple and low-key during the season, had them out hitting hard in pads on both Monday and Tuesday to try and shake the cobwebs free.

In a sense, it was a tribute to how far the team had come that, even on a bad day, they would still handily beat a respectable I-AA team. Bucknell was 7–3 coming into Michie Stadium and the game was the last one for their seniors. The Bison played hard and were well coached. But even on a day when nothing felt quite right, the Cadets were never in serious danger of losing. They had, in the end, taken care of business. They would now go into the Navy game with a chance to salvage a .500 season and, they hoped, their coach's job.

There was a lot to do before they would finally get to play the game. Every year, Army and Navy play the week after Thanksgiving, meaning they have a Saturday off before the game. Occasionally, when the football calendar falls strangely, they have two Saturdays off, meaning they go three weeks between games. That makes everyone crazy.

This year would be more normal. The teams would practice Monday, Tuesday, and Wednesday before Thanksgiving. Army would have three full days off, returning Sunday for meetings and a light practice. Weatherbie had decided to bring his team back on Saturday. In order to give everyone extra time away from the Yard, the team practiced on Wednesday at 5:30 A.M. That meant everyone could leave right after their last class.

"Better, I guess, to go without sleep Wednesday morning and get out of here Wednesday afternoon," Andrew Thompson concluded.

Thompson, Garrett Smith, and Andy Person had a particularly hectic twenty-four hours before the break because they had to get up early Tuesday to drive to Philadelphia with Weatherbie and sports information director Tom Bates for the annual Army-Navy press conference. Sutton would also be there along with Cantelupe and Davis. They arrived in an Army helicopter. It would be the first time the players had met, even though they were all aware of one another, having played already and having watched one another on tape during game preparation.

The press conference is always held in the city where the game is being held — Philadelphia, most years, although the game had been moved to the New Jersey Meadowlands in 1989 and 1993 — to drum up media attention and sell some tickets. Army-Navy was not an automatic sellout the way it once had been. The crowds were always big — attendance had been 65,308 in 1994 — but every seat wasn't always sold. This year, however, with the two teams playing well and beating some solid opponents, there were already less than a thousand tickets left.

The players were curious to meet one another. Cantelupe and Thompson had become long-distance admirers of each other's play. Everyone at Navy knew how good Davis was, and Davis knew how good Person was. He also wanted to meet Smith, the one Navy lineman who would qualify for the Fat Men's Club.

Eddie Stover, who had spent Thanksgiving weekend at Davis's house, was skeptical when Davis speculated on the possibility that Smith might be a fellow Fat Man at heart.

"Impossible," Stover insisted. "He's from Navy."

Stover was even more surprised when Davis, the ultimate Army loyalist, returned to Philadelphia and told him, "Eddie, they're all good guys. They're just like us. Even the DB [Thompson] was a good guy."

"I don't believe it," Stover said.

"Believe it, Top," Davis said. "But we still have to kick their ass."

Cantelupe and Thompson hit it off right away. Thompson had heard about the Air Force trip and he commiserated with Cantelupe. "Bad enough losing to those SOBs," he said. "Then you have to take all night to get back."

"I don't mind them being good," Cantelupe said. "But you know what they are?"

"Punks," Thompson said.

"Yes!" Cantelupe said. "Exactly. They're punks."

A friendship was born.

For Weatherbie, this was all brand-new. Since his arrival at Navy, he had thought people on the Yard made too much of the rivalry with Army. Weatherbie remembered the importance of the Oklahoma–Oklahoma State rivalry from his college days, and he knew the games with the other service academies were a big deal when he was at Air Force. But he had never seen anything quite like the round-the-clock, twelve-months-a-year obsession with Army-Navy.

At the bottom of every piece of academy stationery were the words "Beat Army." Every time "Blue and Gold" was played it ended with everyone shouting, "Beat Army." The alumni and fans talked endlessly about beating Army and the horrific losses of the last three years.

"To tell you the truth," he said, "I think people want to make it a bigger thing than it is. I'm not saying it isn't a great rivalry or a big deal, but I don't see it as being any different than Oklahoma–Oklahoma State or Alabama-Auburn or Florida–Florida State. Those are all big rivalries. They all come at the end of the season, so that makes them seem bigger. Navy-Army" — Weatherbie insisted on calling it Navy-Army and made his assistants do the same — "is right up there with games like that. But I don't see it being something beyond that."

Sutton felt differently. He had coached in twelve Army-Navy games, eight as an assistant, four as a head coach. He had been involved in other rivalry games before arriving at Army, including Michigan–Ohio State and North Carolina State–North Carolina. In his mind, nothing came close to Army-Navy. If someone had told him he could coach only one more game in his life, it would be Army-Navy.

"It's not something you can understand until you've been through it," he said. "The feeling in the stadium is unlike any other football game. You want to win the game so much, and yet you can't help but be aware of the fact that the players on the other side of the field have worked just as hard and just as long to get to this point. The emotions are incredible. The seniors all know it's the last game they'll ever play, with maybe one exception every three or four years. They all want that last memory of football to be a good one, and they'll do anything to win."

Each year before the Navy game, Sutton told his players the same thing: "Think about how much you want to win this game. Think about the fact that you'd be willing to do absolutely anything to win. Then remember the fact that the team in the other locker room feels exactly the same way."

Sutton loved coaching in this game. He understood what it meant to the players on both teams and to the two schools. Weatherbie didn't. Not yet.

It was not surprising, then, that each man took an entirely different approach to the game. Weatherbie saw it as the final step, a chance to finish with a winning record for the first time in thirteen years. Sutton never mentioned to his team that a win would allow them to finish at .500. To him, the ten games past were just that — past. When he handed out schedules for the week, the words at the top said it all: "One Game Season."

No group of Army seniors had gone 4–0 against Navy since the class of '48 had won from 1944 through '47. That was what this game was about; that would be this senior class's legacy — four wins over

Navy. "There is nothing you can do that will make you feel prouder than beating Navy four straight times," Sutton told them. "This is something we should all be proud to be a part of."


EVEN though the Army coaches had been hearing all year about Navy's improved play, they were amazed when they began looking at tape. Navy didn't have that many new players, but they looked like a completely different team than that of a year before, especially on defense.

"They really go after the ball," Mike Sullivan said. "They played hard against us the last couple of years, but you expect that. Now they're playing hard against everyone."

Both teams were convinced that this would be the best played Army-Navy game in years. The teams had played well against good teams all year long. Army had played one bad game, one bad half really, all year — against Air Force. Navy had played poorly twice — against Wake Forest and against Air Force.

Navy had the edge over the Cadets in a couple of areas. It was deeper and quicker in the secondary, it had the more experienced defensive line, and in Brian Schrum it had one of the best punters in the country. Ian Hughes had come a long way since the Duke game, but he still wasn't in Schrum's class.

Army appeared to have a slight edge in a few areas. The Fat Men would have a considerable size advantage over the Navy defensive line. There was no doubt that Ronnie McAda was their quarterback, as opposed to the Fay/McCoy shuffle that Navy had been running in recent weeks. Perhaps most significant, Navy had no idea who would be its placekicker.

To say that Navy was haunted by the placekicking question was a vast understatement. While J. Parker had blossomed into a very dependable kicker for Army, Jason Covarrubias had gone backwards after starting the season so well against SMU and Rutgers. In the Tulane game it had been apparent that he had lost all his confidence and the coaches had no confidence in him. That was why Brian Graham had been kicking extra points on a bad ankle.

Graham's ankle was so sore it was unlikely he would be able to kick at all in the Army game. Covarrubias had become a risk.

Bucchianeri was ready and waiting in the wings, but the only way he was going to kick in the game would be if no one else on the Yard was capable of swinging their leg through a football.

"John Gainey [one of the offensive linemen] would get to kick before Booch would," Garrett Smith said one day. "Maybe they might try him if they were desperate in another game, but in the Army game — again — no way."

Deep down, Bucchianeri knew that was true even though he wished it weren't. Two weeks earlier, during a kicking drill when none of the kickers had been able to make anything, Weatherbie had sent receiver Astor Heaven in to kick rather than give Bucchianeri a shot.

"At least," Bucchianeri said later, "Astor made one."

That evening had convinced Bucchianeri once and for all that he would never be given a chance to kick in a game by this coaching staff. He had gone so far as to meet with Jack Lengyel about the situation and come out of the meeting even more frustrated. Lengyel had suggested that Bucchianeri's father should speak to Weatherbie. No, Bucchianeri had said, this is not my father's problem, it's mine. They had left it at that.

When the team assembled for practice after the Tulane game the kickers were told that they were all back to square one. There was no first-string kicker at the moment; no second-string kicker. After ten games, there would be, in effect, an open tryout for the kicking job. Whoever emerged as the best kicker over the next two weeks would be the kicker in the Army game.

The coaches were all hoping that Covarrubias would reassert himself, win the job back. They all cringed at the notion that Bucchianeri might kick so well that they would have to consider giving the job to him. But as the evenings wore on, in weather that was now very cold, a surprise was developing. Night after night, the best kicker on the field wasn't any of the veterans. It was the plebe, Tom Vanderhorst.

Vanderhorst was from Newnan, Georgia, and the idea of playing varsity football as a plebe had never really crossed his mind. He came out for the team as a walk-on in August and was so far down the depth chart that Kevin Bull didn't even issue him a helmet. But the coaches noticed he had a strong leg, although an erratic one. In JV games, he boomed kicks at times, but at others he missed extra points. Someone to look at in the future, they thought.

But with the kicking situation such a mess, they were forced to look at anyone and everyone. Night after night, Vanderhorst was the most consistent kicker. And at the end of practice, when the coaches would give one kicker a chance to make a field goal to keep the rest of the team from doing up-downs, Vanderhorst would coolly drill the kick, even with everyone standing around and yelling at him as a distraction to simulate game conditions.

By early in the second week, Todd Wright was convinced Vanderhorst should be the kicker in the game. So was Brian Schrum, who was the holder. Weatherbie watched and listened, waiting for his gut to tell him what to do. One evening, after watching Vanderhorst take the end-of-practice kick usually reserved for the first-string kicker, Lengyel pulled Weatherbie aside.

"Please tell me that you're not thinking of using a plebe kicker in the Army-Navy game," he said. "Please tell me you're joking."

"Navy-Army game," Weatherbie answered with a smile.

Lengyel just shook his head. "It'll take a lot of guts to do it," he said. "But I think he just might."

The other players watched the kicking soap opera unfold and shook their heads in disbelief. After all the work they had done, after they had come this far, the notion that this game might come down to another kick with another untested or unreliable kicker galled them.

"Here's the deal," Matt Scornavacchi said one evening as the kickers went to work. "If the game comes down to a kick for them or for us, I'm just leaving. I'm not even going to stay and watch. I'm going up the tunnel and someone can come and tell me what happened. They won't need to, though, because I'll know."

"It just can't come down to a kick," Thompson said. "We have to make sure it doesn't come down to a kick. We just can't take that chance."

"Men," Weatherbie said in their Monday meeting, "if it comes down to a kick, we're going to make that kick. I can feel it. I can see it. I believe it."

He did not say, however, exactly *who* would be making that kick.

NOTHING in the world is quite like Army-Navy week at the two academies. For all intents and purposes, all rules cease to exist. There is only one rule that really matters: you can do anything you want — as long as you don't get caught.

Statues are painted, first classmen are victimized by pranksters, very little attempt is made to sleep. Sometimes things get out of hand. It is not uncommon for cadets to try and run through the main area unclothed. That is usually written off as plebe foolishness. What could not be written off was a plebe who tried to set himself on fire running through the area in 1994. He ended up hospitalized and out of the academy.

It is a week filled with energy. Everyone has gotten a second wind, courtesy of Thanksgiving break. They are feeling well fed and rested for the first time since September. Exams loom, but while they are nerve-racking, they also mean the end of the semester and a chance to go home for a real break.

Everyone looks forward to the weekend because it means a trip to Philadelphia and a chance to be turned loose on the town — all the better to be turned loose after a victory. The plebes at both schools know that a win will make their life much better for the last few weeks of the semester. The upperclassmen will go easier on them. There won't be as many rating demands made during meals and they may even get away with not squaring every corner in the hallways.

Monday morning at West Point began with the first of many impromptu "rallies." Instead of wearily falling out at 6:15 in order to be in their spots for formation at 6:25, the plebes came bursting through the doors of their barracks screaming "RALLY!" at the top of their lungs. A group of them surrounded Washington Statue, which is right in front of the steps leading to the mess hall. Another group formed a circle in the main area on the other side of the barracks. The sun still wasn't even close to being up and it was a frigid November morning, but no one seemed to notice.

"It'll be like this all week," Joel Davis said, watching the screaming and yelling and hearing the "Beat Navy" cheers echoing off the buildings and statues.

One of the "spirit leaders" — Army-speak for cheerleaders — walked up to Davis and asked if he could make it back from his noon meeting on Wednesday to speak at a spirit lunch. Davis smiled.

"Tell you what. Buy me lunch at Grant Hall afterwards and I'll do it," he said. Grant Hall is the closest thing West Point has to a student union. Its small cafeteria was the unofficial headquarters of the FMC.

The spirit leader was baffled. "Don't you get lunch in the mess hall?" he asked.

"That's a snack," Davis answered.

The spirit leader smiled. "Deal," he said.

"I'll bring Top too," Davis said.

"To talk or to eat?"

"Both."

Davis smiled. "I like all this spirit stuff, I really do," he said. "But we have to watch our schedules this week. If we get too caught up in things, we won't be ready for the game." He shook his head. "Our last game together. I can't believe it."

Davis had learned over the weekend that Army-Navy would not be the last game of his football career. He had been invited to play in the East-West All-Star game in January, an honor in itself, but also an opportunity. A lot of pro scouts would be at the game. If Davis performed well, it would improve his chances of being drafted.

"I want it so bad," he said. "I can taste it."

This would be an emotional week for all the seniors, but in particular for Davis and the Fat Men. Although Davis would be given a brief reprieve because of the East-West game, the others would all have to begin to separate themselves not only from football but from fatness the following week. Both academies have strict rules on weight, on neck size, and on being able to run two miles in a certain time. If those qualifications weren't met, you couldn't graduate.

The weight loss was a very difficult thing to ask of the linemen. For four years they had been urged to bulk up, to lift weights to gain weight, to eat all they wanted in order to be bigger. Davis had gained 80 pounds during his four years, going from a 225-pound plebe to a 305-pound senior. ("Actually, 310 right after Thanksgiving," he said.)

Stover weighed just under 300; Bill Blair weighed 280; and Mike Wells — Slimsy — weighed 260. Wells, whose body fat was only slightly more than 10 percent, would have no trouble meeting the requirements for graduation. Davis, Stover, and Blair would have some work to do. Blair, who wasn't as tall as Davis or Stover, would really be hard-pressed to de-fat himself.

The weight requirements were radical enough that Bob Arciero, the team doctor, worried about the players. For several years he had been pushing the army to give football players an extra year to get their weight down. Even though they were monitored carefully, he felt asking anyone to lose that much weight that fast was potentially dangerous.

But losing the weight would be more than just a physical burden. It would represent a letting go of Fatness and all the feelings of camaraderie and brotherhood that came with it. Davis was in denial about it all. Since his slim-sentence had been pushed back until late January, he was talking about how both he and Top were going to end up in the pros, that it would all work out so they could stay Fat. At least in spirit.

"I like being big," he said, walking to a Monday morning class. "I like being strong and eating a lot and being bigger than other people. I'm not ready to give that up."

Stover was more realistic. Although some people thought he had just as much potential to play in the NFL as Davis, he saw the Navy game as an absolute ending. If by some chance that turned out not to be true, he would be delighted. But he didn't expect that to be the case.

"Joel," he said repeatedly that week, "how is it going to feel to not be football players anymore?"

"I don't know, Top," Davis replied, "because we're still going to be football players. Believe me on this. We're going to the pros together."

Stover would just nod, knowing there was no way to convince his buddy differently.

The one who was most ready for the end of football and of Fatness was Wells. It had taken him three years to become a full-time starter, and this season had been one big joyride for him. Unlike the three FMC Chiefs, Wells had to work at putting weight on. His natural weight was closer to 235 or 240, and it would be a lot easier for him to slide back in that direction than it had been to put on the weight.

Beyond that, Wells had made peace with the notion that football would soon be behind him. He was an engineering psychology major, one of the best students on the team, and had always seen football as something that was part of the here and now but not the future. He and Blair were the quiet Fat Men, often sitting and listening while Davis and Stover railed on about something.

They would hold their final Fat Fest on Thursday night. It would be an emotional evening for everyone. Over Thanksgiving weekend, Davis and Stover had gone out and had three silver spatulas engraved with the FMC crest. The three senior chiefs would pass their spatulas on to the three juniors who would replace them as FMC Chiefs the following year.

"I don't want the Fat Men's Club to be a one-year thing," Davis said. "I mean, it started as a fun thing, a way to bring the O-line together. But I also think having the younger guys aspire to be chiefs someday, and to be leaders of the club is something that will make them work harder and keep working to get better."

The final Fat Fest would be the least formal and most significant of the Army-Navy week events at West Point. There would also be an "impromptu" spirit rally on Tuesday night. The commandant had suggested that *if* the cadets felt like having a spontaneous rally at some point during the week, Tuesday night at ten o'clock might be a good time for it. The Comm's instructions were simple: "Have fun, do what you want. Just don't hurt yourselves jumping off buildings or setting yourselves on fire."

There would also be the spirit lunch on Wednesday that had earned Davis an extra meal, and a spirit dinner on Thursday night. That afternoon, the annual Goats vs. Engineers touch football game would be held, matching the top thirty students in the senior class against the bottom thirty students. Unfortunately for the goat team, Davis would not be available. After breakfast on Friday, the entire corps would form a cordon for the team leading to the buses. As soon as they boarded the buses, they would stop being West Point cadets and become Army football players one final time.

There was also the ongoing push-up contest with Navy. Each year, the two schools spent the week adding up push-ups done by the student body, totaling them and seeing who ended up with more. It was all based on honor, and, presumably, calculators. Before marching into lunch on Monday, the entire corps (minus the football team, which was already at its lunchtime meetings) was dropped for sixty. Everyone marched inside only to be informed by the first captain that the word from Navy was that the mids had gotten off to a very early start that morning in the contest and had already opened a huge lead. Everyone had to drop down in between the tables and do thirty more. Then they got to eat.

Up at Michie Stadium, Sutton was conducting business as usual as best he possibly could. He even held a recruiting meeting on Monday afternoon before practice since the coaches would be going on the road the following week — *if* they were still coaches.

All season long Sutton had dealt with the ongoing questions about his future with remarkable calm. But now, as the reality that this might be *his* last game began to set in, he was starting to feel the pressure.

"I almost wish they had called me in and said, 'Win or else,' " he said, standing on the practice field Monday afternoon while his players warmed up. "At least then, we know where we stand. At least that represents some kind of commitment. Right now, none of us knows where we stand. I know our minds should only be on the game, but when you're sitting there making plans for recruiting and you don't know . . ."

The rest of the sentence went unspoken. There was no need to finish. Sutton looked toward the far end of the stadium. The last of the leaves still hung from the trees behind the scoreboard and the sun was setting spectacularly in the distance.

"I love coaching these kids," he said.

He walked off to begin coaching them for at least one more week.


IF anything, Navy was wilder than Army during Army-Navy week.

Pranks weren't just a part of the tradition, they were a focal point of it. The fifth company stole the sixth company's wardroom furniture, then moved it into a first classman's room. Plebes broke into third classmen's rooms to wreak havoc. There was even a fistfight between a female plebe and a female third classman that landed the third classman in the hospital briefly. On Wednesday morning, Andrew Thompson's entire company was awakened at 5:21 A.M. — "Ninety-nine goddamn minutes before formation," as Thompson pointed out — by plebes running down the hallways screaming, "Beat Army, Beat Army, Beat Army!"

The upperclassmen were not amused — or inspired.

Garrett Smith's company had a West Point exchange student in it. Each semester, all three service academies had several exchange students from the other two join them. Needless to say, life could become difficult for those students during Army-Navy week. Early Monday morning, Smith's company officer called him in and asked him to speak to the company that morning about "not laying a hand" on the exchange student.

"If you ask on behalf of the football team, they might listen," the CO said. Smith was happy to give it a try.

Smith was to Navy what Davis was to Army: the offensive captain, the leader of the O-line, the closest thing Navy had to a Fat Man on its line. But he was completely different from Davis in every way. He knew his football career would end against Army, and that was fine. As much as he wanted to win the Army game, as tough as it would be to take the uniform off for the last time, he was also concerned about all the schoolwork he had gotten behind in during the season. Smith had a 2.64 GPA in systems engineering, but he had been Unsat (under 2.15) after the first six-weekers. That didn't make him happy. He took engineering seriously, carrying the black briefcase with engineering materials in it that the rest of the mids called "geekboxes" around the Yard with pride.

Smith was also one of the few football players at either school who was looking forward to his five-year service commitment. "I'm the football team nerd," he said. "I think being in the military is something to be proud of. It's actually something I want to do."

By midweek at Navy, nerves were starting to get a little bit frayed. Everyone woke up Wednesday morning to find it snowing, which was particularly galling to the members of the band, who had to be on the Astroturf field at 6 A.M. for practice, snow or no snow. Weatherbie had been scheduled to be "dunked" in a water tank in front of Tecumseh that morning — the Supe and the 'Dant would get their dunkings later — but he begged off, citing the cold weather and the cold that he had been fighting all season.

The word had floated down from Army that the cadets had rallied back to open up an impressive 100,000 push-up lead (some of the older mids and cadets suspected that the numbers were invented by the leadership at each school as an excuse to demand more push-ups), so the day began with everyone doing thirty-five push-ups — and a thirty-sixth to "Beat Army!"

If there were a contest every year to see whose students said "Beat ——" the most times, Navy would win in a romp. At Army, all announcements end with "Beat Navy," and the plebes are required to say "Beat Navy sir" whenever they end a conversation with an upperclassman or pass one anywhere on the post. At Navy, they take it a step farther. All phones must be answered "Beat Army" the week of the game, and the plebes are allowed to answer all rating questions by saying "Beat Army."

A typical upperclassman/plebe conversation during breakfast or lunch will sound something like this:

"Kline, what's the weather report for Saturday in Philadelphia?"

"Beat Army sir."

"Is it going to snow?"

"Beat Army sir."

"OK, fine. Kline, what's the latest on the budget?"

"Beat Army sir."

And so on. There are ways, of course, for the upperclassmen to get around those answers. If they ask a plebe what's for breakfast and he replies "Beat Army sir," the other upperclassmen may decide to concoct a potion called "Beat Army" that might include large quantities of, say, tabasco sauce and salad dressing or something similarly grotesque, and may demand that the plebe down the "Beat Army" drink in one swallow.

What's more, if a plebe slips and does answer a question ("Kline, is that salt or pepper in there?" "It's pepper sir"), then all "Beat Army" bets are off in that squad. The plebes must return to answering rating questions, either for the rest of the day or the rest of the week, depending on the mood and demeanor of the upperclassmen.

If you walked into King Hall during mealtime, you were bound to hear plebes screaming, "BeatArmysir, BeatArmysir, BeatArmysir" as a sort of nonstop mantra. On occasion, just for fun, the upperclassmen would demand that the plebes repeat the phrase as many times as possible for sixty seconds straight.

Most of these battles were staged between the plebes and third classmen, with some help from second classmen. For the most part, the first classmen stayed out of it. They were like world-weary travelers. They had been there, done that. Torturing plebes is the favorite sport of most third classmen because their memories of being tortured themselves are still so vivid. By the time they are in the second class, the memories are beginning to fade. As first classmen, about the only rating question they are likely to bother asking a plebe is "How many days until I graduate?" A plebe who does not know the answer runs the risk of encountering serious wrath.

"There are days," Andrew Thompson said, "where you really need to be reminded that the end is in sight."

First classmen often talk almost wistfully about Plebe Summer and their first year at the academy, shaking their heads and saying, "It really wasn't that bad." Inevitably, they also say, "These kids today have it so easy. . . ."

Actually, the plebes did have it a lot easier than the first class had it. Plebe hazing isn't anything close to what it was even a few years ago — the physical part of it has virtually been eliminated — and Larson had made a number of changes when he returned. For example: the plebes had to be allowed to eat. That hadn't been true when Thompson and Smith and other first classmen were plebes.

Then, they could be rated throughout a meal, and if they didn't get to eat, they didn't get to eat. Larson made it mandatory that the plebes be allowed to eat. He also asked that rating have a point behind it: "Ask them about the headlines in that morning's newspaper," he said. "Make it worthwhile. They don't have to know the score of every Army game."

Most of them did. It just wasn't worth the risk of being asked and not knowing. Meals were, without question, the most difficult part of the day for the plebes, relieved to some degree by the "BeatArmysir" cop-out. There was still considerable tension, though, because this was their week to "get" the upperclassmen, and to let that opportunity slip past was unthinkable.

One week a year — guess which one — plebes could do almost *anything* to an upperclassman during meals — throw food in their face, pour a drink down their pants, whack them on the side of the head with a book bag — as long as they then made it out of King Hall and back to their room without being caught. If a plebe was caught, the upperclassmen in question could do anything to *him* and also make him pay for it with extra duty later. But the challenge was there and the risks were considered part of the territory.

The football players, for the most part, weren't the least bit interested in any of this. About the only prank any of them had pulled had been the Ex-Lax cookies defensive lineman Cal Quinn had brought up to the hall in his company on Tuesday night. Quinn had hoped to nail some of the company nerds with the cookies. Instead, the trick backfired: the only ones to eat the cookies were Thompson and offensive lineman Greg Summa. They were both sick for twenty-four hours (Summa lost fourteen pounds because he couldn't eat) and vowed to kill Quinn as soon as the Army game had been played.

"All we want to do this week is get through class, get our rest, and be ready to play," Smith said at breakfast on Wednesday morning as all hell broke loose around him. "Next week is actually brutal because we have to start catching up on our schoolwork and we're all way behind. But next week we don't have to be rested, so if we pull all-nighters to finish papers and get ready for tests, it's OK. This week, you sleep whenever you can, day or night, because the halls are never quiet."

At Navy, sleeping in your room during free periods was allowed. At Army, it wasn't, but there was an unwritten rule at West Point that the football players were protected by the other members of their company when they slept during Navy week.

While Smith was eating, two plebes at the next table were downing a "Beat Army" drink. One of them sprinted from the room to get sick. The other sat down, smiled, and continued talking to a round of applause. Relatively speaking, breakfast was calm. Everyone was still waking up and getting ready to go to class. At lunch, with everyone wide awake and most classes over for the day, it would really get wild.

The one thing that didn't change during Army week was class. At Navy, where classes start at 7:55 — forty minutes later than at Army — each class runs for fifty minutes, or five minutes shorter than at Army. Of course, with formation at 7 A.M. as opposed to 6:25 at Army, the day also begins later at Navy. That the mids form inside when the weather gets cold proves that either mids are smarter or cadets are tougher, depending on your point of view. Everyone still had to go to class Army week, and the profs (at Army they are called P's) didn't let up. In fact, knowing that no one was going to be focused on Friday, they probably pushed just a little bit harder.

That didn't mean that football was ignored in the classroom. Garrett Smith's first period class on Wednesdays was robotics — the art of building robots. On the Wednesday of Army week, Professor Ken Knowles decided it would be a good idea for the class to build a "Beat Army-bot."

"What characteristics would we give it?" he asked.

"It depends sir," one of the mids answered. "What position would we want it to play?"

"How about a kicker," another mid piped up.

"Ouch!" Knowles said. "That's a sensitive issue."

Everyone, Smith included, giggled.

"Well," Knowles continued. "About the only thing a kicker needs is to see the ball and the uprights."

"Sir, last year Army's kicker couldn't see the ball and the uprights and he still made the winning kick." Army's Kurt Heiss was partially blind in one eye.

"Good point."

It would be like that all day and all week around the Yard. There would be a "Beat Army" bonfire (mandatory fun of course) on Thursday night that would include all the usual speeches. The first classmen had never seen the Yard so energized, even for Army week.

"I think it's because we have a pretty good team this year," Andy Person said. "It's not like other years where we were just trying to salvage some credibility by beating Army. This year we have credibility. Beating Army would just kind of top everything off."

While Weatherbie was delighted with all the enthusiasm, he was worried that all the adrenaline pumping through the brigade was being picked up by the players too soon. "They're ready to play the game right now," he said to the coaches on Tuesday after practice. "We have to slow them down."

They also had to get them some sleep. With all hell breaking loose on the halls every night, the players were getting even less sleep than normal. On Wednesday, Weatherbie went to Lengyel and asked him if he might be able to convince Bogle to let the team leave town on Thursday night right after the bonfire instead of the usual Friday morning departure. That would mean they could sleep in on Friday in the quiet of the hotel instead of waking up at 6:30 — if not earlier — for formation.

Lengyel thought it was a good idea. So did Bogle, who like the rest of the academy brass, wanted desperately to end the three-game Army losing streak. The players liked the idea of getting the extra sleep, but the seniors were a little disappointed because they had planned their own farewell dinner for Thursday after the bonfire. Now, that would have to be put off until after the season, when it wouldn't feel quite the same.


WHEN the players arrived for practice on Wednesday afternoon, they each found a note in their locker. It read as follows:

> This is just a short letter to each and every member of the 1995 Navy football team. The team captains would like to express their most sincere gratitude to each of the members of the respective classes of '96, '97, '98, and '99. It doesn't take a rocket scientist to figure out that this year's team is a special one. And, without the consistent efforts of each player, both on and off the field, we would not be in the position we are now. This is a TEAM that future teams will be measured by, and hopefully surpass. This group is made up of a bunch of blue-collar, hard-working, tough-mothers whose whole mission in life is to play for the guy next to them for the overall betterment of the team.

> All Navy football players know the task that is currently at hand. There is a lot to play for in the final game of the 1995 season. Seniors, it is the last game we will ever play as a member of this unit. It is the last shot we have to prove to the world who the best service academy football team is. All of the other guys, this also will be the last time that this team will be together. Your challenge is to take the lessons you have learned

from the older guys, and build upon them for the up and coming years. The biggest gift any of you younger guys could give your seniors would be just to continue the great effort that has been displayed all season and contribute to a great VICTORY on Dec. 2, 1995. Further, winning the Commander in Chief's trophy and winning a bowl game in the future will be the ultimate gift in and of itself. We know what is at stake and what needs to be accomplished. For many of us, this last 60 minutes of football will be a lifetime of memories. It's time to kick ASS!!

> Respectfully,
> The 1995 Team Captains

Since this was the team's last Wednesday practice of the season, it would also be their last post-practice, players-only meeting. Every Wednesday, the players would gather on the practice field after the coaches had left and talk about the upcoming game or what had happened the previous week or anything they felt the captains should talk to the coaches about.

Neither Thompson nor Smith was all that comfortable speaking in front of groups, whether it was the brigade at a pep rally or the team on Wednesdays. Both had grown with the job, though, gotten to the point where they felt more comfortable, especially in front of their teammates. But both were a bit uncertain how they would feel standing in front of the other guys on the practice field for the last time. To make sure that they said what they thought was important, they cowrote the letter to the team so everyone would know where they stood.

By now, everyone was in a countdown mode. Assistant coach Mike Vaught had started to count the number of practices the seniors had left in their careers, reminding them each day. Now, with the days dwindling rapidly, he had started to count down the periods (each football practice is broken into periods for each drill) that were left.

By the time they got to the last period of practice on Wednesday evening, the sun was down and the lights were on overlooking the Astroturf practice field. Normally, the team only practiced on the turf if bad weather made the grass fields too soft or muddy, but this week, since Veterans Stadium had an artificial playing surface, they stayed on the turf. This would be Navy's only game of the season on turf. At Army, where Michie Stadium had not had real grass since 1977, the opposite was true: the Cadets' only game on grass was the one at Air Force.

Practice ended with Vanderhorst being asked to kick a 28-yard field goal to "win the game," as Weatherbie put it. They all crowded around and screamed and yelled and waved their arms as Lester Fortney snapped the ball to Schrum, who placed it down and then watched Vanderhorst steer it through the uprights. A huge cheer went up from the players. The wanted to do everything in their power to encourage Vanderhorst even though Weatherbie still hadn't said who the kicker would be on Saturday.

Three were on the travel squad: Vanderhorst, Covarrubias, and Graham, but Graham wasn't even going to be in uniform because of his ankle injury. Bucchianeri would be in what was now a familiar place: the stands, with the rest of the brigade.

Todd Wright, who had been an all-American kicker at Arkansas, was convinced Vanderhorst was the best choice. Weatherbie knew the risks involved in using a plebe kicker against Army. But he had outkicked everybody for two weeks.

Once the coaches had left, the players all took a knee and gathered in a semicircle around Thompson and Smith. On occasion, Thompson had gotten himself a little too riled up at these meetings. Before the Air Force game, he had been so wound up, he had started hitting people, screaming in their faces that they had better be ready to play or else.

Now, he was calm, measured. He was recovering from Quinn's Ex-Lax cookies and could feel his adrenaline slowly building toward Saturday. "I just want to thank each guy here, everyone in every class, first of all for electing me captain of this team," he said. "It's the greatest honor I've ever received and I'm proud to have been with you guys this season.

"The reason we've gotten to this point is simple: we've worked our asses off. We all know this isn't the most talented group of guys in the world. That's part of the deal here. But no team has worked harder than we have and I'm proud of that. All you underclassmen, remember what it was like to work this hard, and come back next year and work harder. If you don't want to, well then, get the hell off the team. You don't belong if you don't want to work.

"One game, guys, and then it's over. Let's make sure we get the job done."

He moved aside for Smith, who had done a lot of thinking about what he was going to say.

"You know, in a lot of ways, it's been a long, tough four years for this senior class," he said. "We've been through a lot of tough times, on and off the field. But now, with one game left to play, when I think about how I feel about the whole experience, I can honestly say that the thing I feel most is thankful.

"Thankful to have known all you guys. Thankful to have been part of this team, especially *this* team, thankful you all thought enough of me to elect me a team captain.

"The other day I was going through some old clippings that my mom saved for me from my plebe year. There was this one story from my hometown paper, you know, the standard story we all have written about us, the hometown kid going to the academy. But in the story, they asked me what my goals were at Navy.

"The funny thing is, I can't remember what I said back then. At least I didn't remember it when I was reading the story. But my answer was 'I want to make a mark.'

"Now, I have no idea what I meant when I said that. I was probably thinking I was going to revolutionize Navy football or something, and if there's anything I've found out in four years it's that very few individuals make that kind of mark.

"But this *team* can make a mark. We have a chance to do something Saturday that no Navy team has done in twelve years. I know you guys don't need any rah-rah pep talks. You all know what this is about and I know every one of you is going to play your butt off on Saturday. But I just want to thank you for giving me a chance to make a mark, even a small one, on Navy football."

It was time to clear the practice field. The rest of the brigade was waiting so they could practice for the Saturday march-on. Most of the players headed for the cafeteria at Dahlgren Hall. This had become a Wednesday night ritual. Since Wednesday was the one night of the week no one — including the firsties — could leave the Yard, many of them went to Dahlgren together to eat, watch a ball game, and play video games.

Thompson was wearing an ice pack as he hobbled over to Dahlgren because his right knee had gotten twisted two weeks earlier. "The only thing I won't miss about playing football," he said, "is the pain. Everything else will be hard to let go of. Really hard."


THERE is probably no more emotional day in an Army football player's career than his last practice as a senior in Michie Stadium. During his years as coach, Jim Young had started a tradition of giving the firsties a private farewell after their last practice.

It was always conducted on the field, regardless of the weather, and it always ended with a lot of tears being shed.

On Thursday evening November 30, everyone dressed warmly for practice, knowing it wouldn't end until well after dark and that they would probably be on the field for a while once it was over. Practice itself was no different than any other Thursday. When it was over, everyone gathered at the 50 yard line. First, as had become tradition, the Supe addressed the team. He told them all how proud he was of the season they had produced and how confident he was that they could represent the academy well on Saturday, and, after that, how well the first classmen would go on to represent the army. It sounded as if he had pulled the speech from a folder marked, "Football team — last Thursday pep talk."

When the Supe left the field, it was Sutton's turn. He had spent a good part of the week at his desk making notes about each first classman. Those notes were now arranged alphabetically. He wouldn't start with the captains or the starters, he would start with the A's and end with the Z's. Sutton would call a name and the player would get up and stand next to him. Then Sutton would talk about him and what he had meant to the program.

In all, there were twenty-eight of them, including scout teamers and players who had been hurt and unable to play as seniors. Sutton had thoughts about, and memories of, every one of them.

He talked about Heath Bates and the long road he had traveled to get to West Point — not one year but two at prep schools — and his willingness to accept a backup role to Ron Leshinski at tight end. He remembered how much it had hurt Mike Bellack to miss his senior year because of repeated ankle injuries. Then there was Abdullah Muhammad, who had lost his starting job at cornerback midway through the season and, even though he didn't like it a bit, never let his disappointment drag the rest of the team down.

There were so many others: Joe Triano, who had played in the Notre Dame game with a cast on his broken wrist; Adrian Calame, who after foot surgery a month earlier had been told his career was over, but who had worked his way back to the point where he was going to try and play Saturday; Tom Burrell, who had struggled so hard to make himself eligible academically, then became a starter when Calame got hurt; Steve Carpenter, who had dealt with the disappointment of not becoming the starting quarterback as a junior and then became a starting halfback as a senior.

Special cases: Conroy, who could have quit a dozen times, but wouldn't; Jason Moura, who in his own way had become one of the team's leaders by working so hard on scout teams and special teams every single day; Derek Klein, who never cared about anything except making the Army football team better; Al Roberts, who played defensive tackle at 225 pounds for two years and proved every game that heart and guts were a lot more important than weight and strength; John Graves, who forced the coaches to notice him. Sutton made a prediction about Graves: "I have a feeling," he said, "that when we need a big play on Saturday, John Graves is going to be the guy to make that play."

He talked about each of the Fat Men and what the camaraderie they had brought to the team had meant, not only to the players but to the coaches. "The togetherness you guys felt for one another helped bring all of us together," he said.

Quietly, his voice filled with emotion, Sutton said he had never coached or met a better leader than Jim Cantelupe. "When it gets tough Saturday," he said, "I know I'll be looking to Jim and I know he won't let me down. He never has."

The loudest cheer was reserved for the one senior who wouldn't graduate with the class of '96: Leon Gantt, who would graduate in four weeks, six months later than he had planned. "We all know what

Leon went through to be part of this team again," Sutton said. "His heart is the epitome of what this football team has been all about."

Sutton finished with Abel Young, who had come a long way from the mean streets of Detroit to be a first classman at West Point and had performed well no matter how much or how little had been asked of him.

"Well," Sutton said, "I guess that's about it. I just want to say to each firstie . . ."

There was a commotion in the ranks. Sutton opened his eyes wide in mock surprise. "Did I forget somebody? Oh, I guess I did. Jim Zopolis!"

They all hooted loudly for Zopolis and for Sutton turning the tables on Zopolis, who was usually the prankster, not the prankee. Sutton spoke about how Zopolis had proven that being five eight and 185 pounds (at most) didn't mean you couldn't play Division I football. When he was finished, Zopolis had to get in the last word. Looking right at Doug Pavek, he repeated the Pavek mantra: "You know, I played in *no* bowls, none."

They all roared. Now, Sutton really was finished. It was time to say goodbye. While the seniors stood at midfield and waited, all the coaches, managers, staff members, and underclassmen formed a cordon leading from the field to the locker room. The coaches and staff came first, then the plebes, the third classmen, and finally, the second classmen, who would be the ones making this walk in a year.

One by one, the seniors moved slowly through the cordon. They shook hands with everyone, saying thanks, being thanked, saying goodbye. Close friends hugged one another. Tears came easily.

"You spend so much time on that practice field with those guys," Cantelupe said. "To realize you're never going to be out there again in uniform is a tough, tough thing. In a way, it's an achievement, a great feeling, because you remember how you felt about the first classmen who came before you and the fact that you hoped someday the team would look up to you the way you looked up to them.

"But when you walk through that cordon and it really is the last time, it hits you right in the gut."

As each player reached the end of the cordon, he walked one last time past the plaque that sits at the entrance to the field. On it is the quote from General George C. Marshall, the army chief of staff during World War II: "I want an officer for a secret and dangerous mission. I want a West Point football player."

Everyone on the field that night would tell you that the seniors had played a huge role in making them into a team that had overachieved in 1995. It was hard for everyone to see them go. Especially Sutton. He knew how hard they had worked to make this season memorable. When he had shaken the last hand, Sutton started to leave the field.

As he did, it occurred to him that this might be *his* last practice too. A chill swept over him. The seniors had to leave; that was part of football, part of college. He didn't want to leave. He wanted to be around to stand on the cordon again next year.

AT Navy, the last day of practice was far more routine. There were no speeches or cordons. Instead, after Vanderhorst had again been called on to kick the field goal to "win the game" (the first attempt was accidentally blocked; the second one just curved inside the upright), Weatherbie gathered the team to go through the itinerary for the trip to Philadelphia.

Since they were leaving that night, everyone had to be ready to leave on the buses right after the "Beat Army" bonfire that would be held at 7 o'clock.

When Weatherbie finished going over the travel schedule, Garrett Smith asked all the seniors to stand so that the rest of the team could recognize them. They did, everyone clapped, and then it was time to go eat. No tears. All business.

Unfortunately for the brigade, the change in schedule had put everyone a little bit behind in their preparation for leaving town. Everyone had gathered at Farragut Field for the bonfire shortly after the sun had gone down. It was a bitterly cold night and the hot cider was soon gone. So were the cookies. Everyone stood around in the dark while a band of mids played hard rock. No one had come to hear mids play hard rock. Actually, most people had come because they had to.

To entertain the restless troops while everyone waited for the team to show up, several of the cheerleaders tried to put on a couple of skits. At one point, one of the "panelists" on a mock TV show was asked what her major complaint was with life at the Naval Academy.

Before she could answer, someone in the crowd yelled out, "Mandatory pep rallies!"

That drew the biggest round of applause anyone had heard all evening.

It was 7:30 when the buses finally pulled up and the players spilled onto the podium. As it turned out, the highlight of the rally was the performance of the commandant, Randy Bogle.

When it was his turn to talk, Bogle grabbed the microphone and said to the brigade, "Is everybody cold?"

"YES!" came the answer.

"Well," Bogle said, "I don't think it's that cold." He then proceeded to take off his entire uniform, except for his undershirt and undershorts. Then he led several (brief?) cheers while the brigade went wild. The 'Dant in his underwear in twenty-five-degree weather. Now *that* was worth showing up for.

When it was Larson's turn, his first comment was "The only thing I guarantee you is that I'm *not* going to try and top *that*."

There were a few cries for the Supe to take it off too, but the Supe wasn't buying — or stripping. Bogle had promised that the team was going to go to Philadelphia and kick Army's ass. Larson was much too dignified to say anything like that. Instead, he talked about how great the brigade had been in supporting the football team and how happy he was that the team and the brigade were one again.

It was time to light the fire. As the flames climbed higher and higher and the surrounding area warmed, the players stood in small groups watching, while many of their schoolmates came up to wish them luck. In one sense, everyone wanted to get on the buses and get going. Bert Pangrazio was walking around yelling "Come on, everyone, let's go, let's get on the buses. Time to go to Philly!"

In another sense, especially for the seniors, this was another last in a series of them. Just when they had finally bonded with the brigade, their time was up. Getting on the buses meant leaving a party they wouldn't have minded hanging around for.

Before they left, as at any official Navy function, the band had to play "Blue and Gold." As everyone stood at attention, the now roaring fire framing them in orange flames against the black sky, they all began to sing:

*Now, college men from sea to sea*
*May sing of colors true;*
*But who has better right than we*
*To hoist a symbol hue?*
*For sailor men in battle fair*
*Since fighting days of old;*
*Have proved the sailor's right to wear*
*The Navy Blue and Gold . . .*

It is a hauntingly beautiful song, especially with four thousand voices raised against the night singing it. The players all took a deep breath, shook a few last hands, and boarded the buses. The last trip was under way.


RYAN Bucchianeri was standing a few feet away from the lead bus as his teammates boarded. He shook as many hands as he could, then stood and watched the buses pull away. He couldn't help but notice the Triton Light, which was directly across the street from where the buses were leaving. The bench where he had sat during the SMU game was right there, illuminated, just as it had been that night, by the light.

Bucchianeri hadn't expected to be on the travel squad. He knew that Vanderhorst and Covarrubias were going to be the kickers, although, like everyone else, he still wasn't certain which of them would kick in the game.

"If they go by performance the last two weeks," he said, "they have to go with Vanderhorst." He had made certain to shake hands with Vanderhorst as he boarded the bus and wish him luck. If anyone could understand what Vanderhorst was feeling that evening, it was Bucchianeri.

Not making the trip was devastating for Bucchianeri, but by now he was used to the feeling. The only good thing about Saturday, he decided, was that it was the last game of the season. There would be no more futilely trying to prove himself in practice, at least not for a while. He had vowed to meet with Weatherbie once exams were over and everyone had gotten a break and some rest. He was going to tell him straight out that he didn't think he had been treated fairly.

Under no circumstances, regardless of the outcome of the meeting, was Bucchianeri going to quit. "I'm going to be on the football team for my last home game next year," he said. "After all they've been through, my parents deserve to stand on the field and be acknowledged with the parents of the other seniors. I will make sure they aren't denied that moment."


NAVY'S trip to Philadelphia was routine. Almost everyone slept. They arrived at the Franklin-Wyndham Hotel a little before 11 o'clock. Everyone had a snack and went to bed. They would sleep late in the morning, then practice at Veterans Stadium at noon. Army would practice right after that.

For the Cadets, their trip from West Point the next morning wasn't nearly as routine. As scheduled, they stopped at a hotel near Giants Stadium for brunch. While everyone else went in to start devouring the food, Bill Doutt went to a telephone to phone home. This was the day that his fiancée, Theresa Coutts, was scheduled to give birth to their son.

Doutt had hoped that it might be possible to induce labor a week early when he had been home on Thanksgiving break. Salem, Oregon, is a long way from West Point, New York, and the only way Doutt was going to be able to see his son's birth was if he arrived during the break. No luck. The doctors didn't think inducing labor was a good idea, and Theresa wasn't quite ready. The projected date for Jonathan's arrival was still December 1 — the day before the Army-Navy game.

"It wasn't very good planning," Doutt said. "But that's because it wasn't planned."

Doutt had found out the previous spring that Theresa was pregnant. They had already been planning to get married as soon as he graduated from West Point — cadets and midshipmen are not allowed to be married, which is why so many weddings take place right after graduation — but they hadn't planned to start a family just yet. Now, they were starting one.

All fall, Doutt had been as nervous as you might figure an expectant father would be, especially when he is three thousand miles away from his future child's mother. Everyone on the team, especially the other seniors, had rallied around him, mostly by teasing him about his freedom coming to an end the minute he was commissioned as an army lieutenant — if not sooner.

Family was important to Doutt. He was twelve years younger than his sister, Monica, and his parents had split when he was in the sixth grade. John Doutt had been working in a gold mine in Honduras. He came home one day when Bill was getting his bicycle out to go to peewee football practice and told him he was very sorry but he and Bill's mother were splitting. There was another woman, someone he had met in Honduras.

"I was one of those kids who always thought, 'Other kids' parents may split, but never my parents,' " he said. "I was crushed. I remember crying all the way to practice on my bike."

His father moved back to Oregon after the divorce but was diagnosed with intestinal cancer — after an initial misdiagnosis — when Bill was in the eighth grade. He died a year later. Judy Doutt remarried when Bill was a high school senior, and his stepfather, Dale Duff, was an ex–Southern California football player. For the first time in his life, Bill had someone around the house he could talk football with. Even when Bill was a kid, his father hadn't been all that interested in football.

He chose West Point because he loved the campus and because he knew his mother couldn't afford to send him to an Ivy League school even though several of them were recruiting him. For two years, he was a scout team player, wondering if he would ever get a chance to play. As a junior, he was a backup linebacker. Only as a senior had he become a starter, and he had taken full advantage, becoming one of the defense's more dependable players.

Now, twenty-four hours before his last football game, he learned that he had become a father, Jonathan had arrived weighing six pounds, eleven ounces. Everyone was doing just fine. Doutt joined his teammates in the dining room and whispered the news to John

Conroy. He was too embarrassed to get up and make the announcement himself, so Conroy, who was never embarrassed, got up and
delivered the good news. A huge cheer went up.

"A first," Sutton said later. "Never had a baby born en route to
play Navy before."

While Navy stayed right in downtown Philadelphia the night before
the game, Army had always stayed on the outskirts, at the Eagle Lodge
Conference Center, a resort that gave everyone plenty of room to
spread out. Once they had gone through their workout at the stadium,
they all piled eagerly onto the buses to head for the lodge.

"It's always something everyone looks forward to because it isn't
like the other hotels we stay in," Cantelupe said. "There's just a lot
more to do, a lot more room to move around. It's almost like going
on a mini-vacation for a few hours."

The coaches liked that idea, the notion that everyone could relax
and briefly forget about the pressure of what was to come the next
day. With a noon kickoff, they would want everyone in bed early, but
there were still Friday night rituals to go through.

Those rituals are different the night before the Army-Navy game.
To begin with, each player finds a packet waiting for him when he
gets on the bus Friday morning. Inside the packet are letters, some of
them solicited by the coaches, some of them unsolicited. They come
from former players, from generals and privates, from civilians who
are football fans. They are all on the same topic: Army-Navy, what
the game means, why it is different than other football games.

Cantelupe had saved every letter from each of his four Army-Navy
games. It had become a Friday night tradition for him to read the
letters before he went to bed. "I remember my plebe year, wondering
exactly what the big deal was about Army-Navy," he said. "I mean
I was like everyone else, I knew it was important, but I didn't really
understand it because I hadn't played in one yet.

"Then, when the coaches gave us the letters and I looked through
them and realized what the game meant to so many different kinds
of people, I started to understand. It's the one game you play in that
people who might never see a football game in person will remember
and talk about for years. If you make a big play, or blow a big play,
it is going to be a part of you for the rest of your life."

Ryan Bucchianeri could certainly attest to that fact.

After dinner, the coaches showed the movie. This was not the usual Mike Sullivan/CEP production. This was the same movie they had watched before every Army-Navy game since Sutton had been the coach: "One Hundred Years of Army Football."

This was the fourth time some of the seniors had seen the film. They all remembered being fascinated by it the first time they had seen it, even being awed by some of the West Point history they hadn't been aware of.

"It's one of those things where you know Army has a great football tradition because they tell you about it all the time," Eddie Stover said. "But then when you see it right in front of you, you know, all the names: Blaik and Blanchard and Davis and Dawkins and Carpenter, all those guys, you go, 'Wow, this is something.'

"But then when you see it the second time and the third time, you kind of go, 'Yeah, yeah, I know all that.' But the last time, when you're sitting in that room and you are about to be part of Army *history* rather than Army *present,* it gives you chills. And it reminds you what you're playing for."

Which was exactly what Sutton wanted. He wanted his players to understand the unique nature of Army-Navy, that in spite of what Weatherbie thought at that moment, there was no rivalry quite like it. No rivalry had the kind of history that it had; no two teams shared the same kind of experiences these two teams shared — and might share in the future.

"In no other rivalry is it possible that the players will someday be fighting next to one another in war," Sutton said. "That isn't just a possibility, it's an historical fact. It's happened before and, unfortunately, there's a good chance it will happen again."

With American troops scheduled to leave for Bosnia before the end of the month, that notion was especially poignant before the playing of this game. The players had been talking all week about the signing of the Bosnian peace treaty and the commitment President Clinton had made to send troops to Bosnia. Most of them didn't like the idea, not because they were afraid to go — they had been trained to go if needed — but because they didn't think it was the right solution.

"Doesn't really matter what we think," Conroy said. "If we have

to go, we have to go. It isn't something that scares you; it's just something that sobers you.''

Or, as Andrew Thompson had put it earlier in the week: ''A lot
of people have invested a lot of time and a lot of money into making
sure we're ready to do this if we have to. We all know the deal. We're
all prepared to do whatever has to be done.''

This sort of conversation, these kinds of concerns, were slightly
different from those facing Nebraska or Florida or Penn State or
Southern California.

After the film was over, Sutton went through the schedule one more
time. Then, as he had done at Air Force, he and the coaches left the
players alone. Cantelupe had brought along some reading material that
he wanted to share with his teammates. Earlier that week, Keith Galloway, one of the Navy senior safeties, had sent an E-mail message to
a friend of his at West Point, Kevin Odfel. Galloway, Odfel, and Heath
Bates, Army's backup tight end, had all been friends at Wyoming
Seminary, a prep school in Pennsylvania.

Galloway's E-mail read as follows:

Kev:
Good to hear from you bud. I've been trying to get in touch
with you guys, but my messages keep getting returned. I just
saw Mike Neil. He said to say hello to you guys.
By the way, I don't want to talk trash, but you guys are going
to die. If you score a point, I will be embarrassed. Tell Heath,
he'd better not get on the field while I'm in because it could
mean his neck. On a lighter note, I'm looking forward to seeing
you guys. That's one cool thing about the Navy-Army game.
With Air Force, we hate those guys before and after the game,
but with you guys we only hate each other during the game.
Well, I've got to jet. Good luck to you guys, you'll need it.
                                                          Keith

Galloway was as gentle a soul as there was on either team, a
friendly, deeply religious young man who had roomed with Shaun
Stephenson for three years. His ''trash talk'' was clearly meant at least

half, if not wholly, in jest. That didn't prevent Odfel from passing it on to Bates, who immediately showed it to Cantelupe.

"If we score a point, he'll be embarrassed?!" Cantelupe grabbed the printout and stared at Galloway's boast. "Is this guy nuts? He's calling us out! Not score a point? What is he thinking about?"

Cantelupe wanted to make sure his teammates heard Galloway's prediction. He was a little concerned that evening that everyone had perhaps had a little bit *too* much fun relaxing around the resort. It was almost as if they showed up at dinner in a laid-back mood. This was not a night or a weekend for being laid back. He was fairly certain there was nothing laid back in Navy's approach to the game, and he didn't want his team to find itself quickly behind the next day because it came onto the field not quite ready to play.

Deep down, Cantelupe knew Galloway was probably just having fun with his old friends Odfel and Bates. That wasn't his problem. His problem was making sure everyone understood what this game meant to all of them and, as Sutton would say, that they understood that it meant just as much to the Navy players. If reading Galloway's E-mail would help bring everyone back into focus, he would not only read it, he would stand up in front of the team, wave the piece of paper, and say repeatedly, "The guy's calling us out! Are we going to let him do that?"

The response was just what he had hoped for. They were both surprised and angry. It wasn't like a Navy player to trash talk, that wasn't their style any more than it was Army's. But if they thought they could trash talk, they better come ready to back it up.

When the team meeting was over, the seniors again stayed behind the way they had at Air Force. This was a different kind of meeting than the one in Colorado Springs. There were no promises to kick anyone's butt; there was no talk about how important it was to win the game. It was more like a letting-go, a realization that there was no more football after this game, that something they had done most of their lives would be gone.

"We all said things to one another that we already knew," John Graves said. "But it still felt good to say them and to hear them. It was all about what football had meant to us and what we had meant to each other."

Naturally, John Conroy gave the lengthiest speech. ''I feel like something is being taken away from me,'' he said to his classmates. ''Most of the things I have in my life are because of football. I was always treated like a big shot as a kid because I could play football. I came to West Point because I could play football. It doesn't seem fair that this is it, but since it is, I just want to be able to go out as a winner. I want my last memory to be a good one.''

They all expressed that sentiment in different ways. Stover worried that he wouldn't be able to accept the end of his football career. Cantelupe said the important thing was that they meet their most important goal: getting Army football turned around in the right direction. To do that, they had to win this game. They had to finish at .500 and they had to save Coach Sutton's job.

It was Davis who pointed out that they had never given a game ball to Sutton during their four years. ''Let's give him the ball,'' he said. ''Let's win the damn game, then give Coach the ball. He deserves it.''

They made a pact to do that. Then they formed their huddle one more time. It was Leon Gantt who had the final say: ''I didn't come in with you guys,'' he said, ''but I can't think of a better group to go out with.''

# 19

# A CIVIL WAR

SATURDAY dawned clear and sunny, the temperature climbing toward the mid-forties. Army-Navy games are often played in frigid, close-to-unbearable conditions. That would not be the case for this game, and the 12:08 kickoff meant there would be none of the torturous waiting around the hotel, counting the minutes, watching the clock.

This would be the last Army-Navy game on ABC for at least six years. CBS had won the rights to the next five games, and ABC had responded by scheduling not one but two other games to follow Army-Navy that day: Texas–Texas A&M and the Southeast Conference championship game (or as the ABC flaks liked to say: "The Dr Pepper SEC Championship Game").

And, just to show Army and Navy how they felt about their game, they assigned not their number one broadcast team, not their number two broadcast team, but their number three braodcast team to the game. The shame of that decision was that the number two team, Brent Musberger and Dick Vermeil, loved doing the game.

Musberger was often criticized for his hyperbolic nature and Vermeil tended to talk in coach-speak a lot. But they were the right duo for this game. Musberger had opened the broadcast two years ago this way: "There is no bowl game at stake here. There is no coalition poll, no number one ranking. No Heisman Trophy is at stake either. This is bigger than all of that."

Exactly.

Vermeil had described the game in one sentence: "It's the only game you'll watch all year where eighteen guys will be on the ground on the opening kickoff."

Mark Jones would do the play-by-play and Todd Blackledge the color, with Dean Blevins on the sidelines. All were solid, professional announcers. All were working their first Army-Navy game. Each would come away wishing they could have the chance to do a second.

The teams' pregame routines were the same as they had been for ten weeks, except that Paul Johnson asked the seniors on the offensive unit to get up and speak to their teammates one last time during the offense's morning meeting.

Everyone talked about how much playing football at Navy had meant to them and how much they would miss being part of the team. Shaun Stephenson thanked everyone for making him feel part of the team even though his knee had limited him and he still hadn't caught a single pass. Brian Schrum thanked everyone for keeping him less busy. "Last year I punted seventy-two times," he said. "This year, I've only punted fifty-three. That shows how much you guys have improved."

The most impassioned speech came from John Moe, an offensive tackle who hadn't played a single down as a sophomore or a junior because of injuries and had come back to play a limited role as a senior. He would only play in this game if it turned into a rout.

"I am sick and tired of losing to these guys," he said. "I know I'm not really going to play a role today, so I'm asking all you guys to win the game so we'll all be able to walk away from all this as winners. I can't even stand the thought of losing to them again. Please, please go out and play like mother-------. It's the only way to win."

Moe was crying by the time he finished. He wasn't alone. Even Johnson, everyone's favorite curmudgeon, was a little bit misty-eyed. "I just want to find out about ringing this damn bell," he said, referring to the bell of the USS *Enterprise* — known on the Yard as the E-bell. Navy players get to ring the E-bell after a win over Army. No one in the room had ever had that pleasure. The room was quiet when Johnson finished. They all seemed to know that, unless they went to war someday, they would never again feel as close to a group of people as they all did that day.

The coaches spent a good portion of their pregame meeting talking about — what else? — the kicking game. Weatherbie asked everyone who they thought should kick. Wright went first, again saying he thought Vanderhorst could handle the pressure; that he had dealt with everything thrown at him during the week. He had gone to talk to Schrum again the previous evening to see how he felt since he was the one holding the ball for each of the kickers. Schrum said he liked Vanderhorst's mental approach, that it seemed as if none of this was a big deal each time he was asked to make a kick.

"It's going to be a lot bigger deal with 70,000 people watching than it was on that practice field," Weatherbie said.

A couple of the coaches pointed out that Covarrubias had kicked better near the end of the week. "Only after he thought he'd lost the job," Wright said. "The pressure was off."

Weatherbie nodded. "I agree with that."

It was the first time he had let his feelings show. All week he had been thinking that Vanderhorst should kick, but he didn't want to let anyone — even the coaches — know he felt that way because he didn't want their opinions swayed by knowing his.

They went through all the usual questions and answers. Johnson said he again planned to get McCoy into the game when the time was right but that Fay would play for at least the first few series because "I want to throw the ball around a little, loosen them up some." They had decided to go back to using Scornavacchi on punt returns. Mill might have more potential to break a long return, but being a plebe, he also had more potential for fumbling. "Can't give the ball up," Weatherbie said softly. "Not in this game."

Had he finally come around to the notion that this game was special? He shook his head and laughed. "It's special," he said. "But I still don't think it's as special as people want to make it out to be."

There was one other change that had to be dealt with. Scott Runyan, the receivers coach, hadn't been with the team all week because of the death of his father. Weatherbie had told him not to rush back for the game, to stay with his family as long as he was needed. That meant that Damon Dixon, who had been with the team all season as a graduate assistant coach, would be in charge of the receivers.

"Just stay with the regular rotation," Weatherbie told him. "I'll help you out whenever necessary."

Weatherbie was concerned about Stephenson. Even though the doctors had said it was OK for him to play, he was concerned about his ability to play on artificial turf, which has so much less give than real grass.

They broke up to go talk to their players one last time before boarding the buses. Todd Wright lingered in the doorway. "My gut really tells me it's Vanderhorst," he said one last time.

Weatherbie nodded. "So does mine," he said. Wright breathed a sigh of relief.

"I just hope," Weatherbie said as Wright left, "that both our guts are right."

The team buses arrived at the stadium at almost the same time that the march-ons were beginning. Navy, as the designated visiting team, went first, filling the playing field with blue and white. It was not yet 10 o'clock in the morning, but already the stands were beginning to fill up and a full-blown traffic jam was under way outside. Only at Army-Navy, because of the march-ons, is there more traffic two hours before kickoff than ten minutes before kickoff.

Many of the players on both teams walked down their respective tunnels — Veterans Stadium's locker rooms are set up so that the teams do not have to share a tunnel — to watch the march-ons. Some of them had participated in the past, some had not. It was an impressive sight, the entire student bodies — minus the football teams — marching onto the playing field in perfect precision, reaching their positions and then offering cheers: first one for the opposition, then one for themselves. The cheers for the opponent were just a little bit louder than a TV set sounds with the mute button on. The cheers for their own schools boomed through the stadium, off the empty seats, and back around again.

Weatherbie's pregame talk was similar to the other ten he had already given. He reminded them that this was their chance to do something special — produce a winning season — and told them that he had never seen a team more ready to play a football game than this one.

"All I want," he said, "is everything you got. Come back in here with nothing left."

Sutton's approach was a little different. He talked about desperation. "The most desperate team wins Army-Navy games," he said. "The effort will be there on both sides, we all know that. The question is, which team will be more desperate to win when it comes time to decide the game? I think this is the more desperate team."

Both teams were still in the locker room when the national anthem was played. Even though the sounds of the song were muted by the walls and the distance, they all stood and listened. In the Navy locker room, Mark Hammond felt himself choking up, knowing he wouldn't ever again listen to the anthem in a football uniform.

The Cadets came down the tunnel with Jimi Hendrix blaring in their eardrums, the music that last year's captains had chosen. Cantelupe and Davis had decided to stick with it. Conroy, who was more of a Sinatra fan when it came to music, loved hearing Hendrix on his way to the field. "There are times for Sinatra," he said. "And times for Hendrix. Football is Hendrix."

There was no music in the Navy tunnel. But as the players made their way to the field, they could hear their band at the far end of the stadium playing "Anchors Aweigh."

For some of the seniors, this was their last football game — but their first Army-Navy game in uniform. Stephenson and Ramon Vasquez had been on the lightweight team until this year. Moe had battled injuries. Billy Butler had played basketball for three years and Brad Snodgrass had played baseball before each came out for football as a senior. On the Army side, Conroy, Graves, and Tom Burrell — all of whom would start — had never played a down against Navy.

For Burrell, who had worked so hard to keep his head above water academically and as a football player, the whole scene when he got to the field — the packed house, the Corps of Cadets on one side, the Brigade of Midshipmen on the other — was overwhelming. "I had to get ahold of myself," he said. "It all hit me at once, that finally, after four years, I was living my dream to play in this game. I almost lost it before we even started playing."

Navy had one clear advantage right from the beginning: its sideline was bathed in sunshine; the Army sideline was already in shadows, and it was at least ten degrees colder as a result. Cantelupe and Davis walked to midfield to meet Thompson and Smith. The handshakes were warm, but there was no small talk. There would be time for that later. Smith, who always called the toss for Navy, called heads. It came up heads. It was the eleventh straight time Navy had won the coin toss in 1995. For the eleventh straight time, they elected to defer receiving the kickoff until the second half. Army would receive the kick and defend the west goal — the one at the locker room end of the field.

It was forty-one degrees in Philadelphia as Covarrubias teed the ball up to kick off. Veterans Stadium was completely full; not a ticket had gone unsold. On the message board, in the corner of the stadium where the brigade was located, the series history was neatly summed up:

The 96th Meeting
Army — 45 wins
Navy — 43 wins
Seven ties

The only thing it didn't mention was that through those 95 games, the total point differential was a grand total of 54 — Navy had the edge there. Fifty-four points apart after 95 games — a virtual deadlock.

Covarrubias's kick floated to Jeff Brizic at the five yard line. He got as far as the 16 before he was buried by a group of flying white shirts. Good start for Navy; poor field position for Army.

Army went into its grinding routine: Carpenter picked up three; Conroy went up the middle for four. That set up third-and-three at the 23. In the huddle, McAda called 54 option. He could give the ball to Conroy or pull it out and keep it himself. He took the snap and turned toward Conroy.

All the players had noticed during the practices the day before that the field was saturated after a week filled with rain. When they arrived on Saturday, the conditions were much better, but the field was still wet in spots — especially where the bases from the baseball field had been removed and covered over with new dirt that the turf was then placed over.

Coming out of his stance, Conroy slipped on one of those spots. As he fell forward, trying to catch himself, his helmet hit the ball, knocking it loose from McAda before he knew what had happened. In the blink of an eye, Andy Person, who had penetrated the backfield on the play, was on top of the ball.

The game was 71 seconds old and Navy had the first big break. It was first down on the Army 22. True to his word, Johnson came out "throwing the ball around." On first down, Fay looked deep for Cory Schemm in the end zone but just missed him. Undeterred, he ran a fake option on second down, dropped back, and found LeBron Butts wide open behind all the Army defenders in the end zone.

Touchdown. Vanderhorst trotted onto the field for the extra point. On the Army sideline, a lot of people wondered who number 78 was. They had never heard the name before. Vanderhorst easily kicked the point. No sign of jitters. Navy led, 7–0. The game was less than two minutes old.

"I thought, 'We're going to blow these guys out,' " Person said. "I really thought we were that much better than they were, that we were going to move the ball all day and the D would stuff them. It was probably a mistake thinking that. No one ever blows anybody out in the Army-Navy game."

Cantelupe was furious. This was exactly the kind of start he had worried about. They *had* gotten too laid back the day before and they had been sloppy, first on the fumble, then biting too easily on Fay's fake.

"That's it!" he screamed at his teammates. "That's all they get!"

The Army offense managed to pick up a first down on the next series but had to punt from the 39. Hughes calmly sailed a 41-yard punt to Scornavacchi on the 20. He tried to cut back to pick up yardage and was swarmed under by Al Roberts and Landis Maddox, two seniors willingly playing on special teams and playing as if their lives depended on it.

This time, the Army defense held and Schrum's punt was downed at the Army 48. With good field position, the Cadet offense finally got rolling. Abel Young picked up 19 yards on an option play to the 23. Then, on third-and-eight, McAda went back and looked, and looked. No one was open. Navy's coverage was perfect. Finally, just as he was about to be sacked by Hammond, he tossed a desperation knuckleball toward Young. Young reached for the ball, but it was over his head. He got a hand on it, deflecting it back to the middle of the field.

Graves had been running his route on the other side of the field. When he saw McAda in trouble, he broke his pattern and began looking for an open spot on the field. ''When I saw Ronnie throw the ball, I thought, 'Oh boy, that's an interception,' '' Graves said. ''I just started towards it, hoping I could break it up and get the ball on the ground.''

Instead, Graves saw the ball change direction and suddenly come right at him. He dove for it, just getting his hands underneath it as he fell, stretched across the six yard line.

The Navy bench couldn't believe it. They had played perfect defense and the result was a 15-yard Army pickup. On the Army side, Jack Hecker shook his head. ''Can you believe that kid?'' he said as Graves flipped the ball to the referee. ''He always finds a way.''

Not bad for the worst wide receiver in Army football history.

Three running plays later, Conroy pounded into the end zone from the one, and with 3:20 left in the first quarter, it was 7–7. The Navy defense came off the field angry, but not discouraged. ''They needed a lucky play,'' Thompson screamed at his teammates. ''Don't worry about it. It can't happen all day.''

Inside, his thoughts were churning. Why, he wondered, did it seem the lucky bounces always went Army's way? When would Navy's lucky bounce come?

Neither team did much bouncing one way or the other until late in the first half. The most action was in the stands, where the corps, reacting to the news that twenty-four mids had been charged as a result of the NCIS drug investigation done after the LSD arrests in October, began chanting ''Just Say No'' in the direction of the brigade. The spirit leaders eventually convinced them to return to the more standard cheers.

Slowly, Army seemed to be taking control of the line of scrimmage on both sides of the ball. The Fat Men were opening holes for the backs and the defense wasn't giving up very much. When Johnson brought McCoy in, hoping for a spark, he carried on three straight plays and netted four yards. Schrum's fourth punt of the half was caught by Cantelupe at the Army 34. He picked up two yards before Galloway brought him down. There were no conversations about E-mail messages.

On the second play of the Army drive, Conroy blasted up the middle for 10 yards before Sean Andrews stopped him. As he was going down, Conroy felt someone come in from behind to finish the tackle and heard the dull "thwack" of a helmet hitting bone. A sharp pain raced through him and he came up holding his rib cage.

He walked slowly back to the huddle. "You OK?" McAda asked.

"Fine," he said. "Just a little stiff."

Two plays later, Conroy carried again, this time for a yard. Once again as he was going down, he felt a sharp pain. This time he had been nailed in the ribs on the other side. It wasn't as bad as the first hit, but now he felt stiff on both sides. Still, he stayed in the game. "It wasn't like I couldn't breathe," he said.

The ball was now at midfield and it was third and nine. On the next play, McAda, finding no one open, somehow scrambled away from what looked like a sure sack and took off down the sideline for 23 yards. First down at the Navy 27.

"Wrap him up!" Weatherbie screamed. McAda had dodged four different potential tacklers.

They picked up another first down at the 17. The clock was under three minutes. Conroy, sore ribs and all, got seven more on second down to set up first-and-goal at the six. But now Navy dug in. Hammond and Person, Bruce and Harris. They could all hear Dick Bumpas's voice in their heads: "You do *not* let their ass run the ball into the end zone."

Conroy got two before Harris wrestled him down. They tried Carpenter as a change-up and Hammond stepped into the hole and knocked him down at the line of scrimmage. Person, Hammond, and Bruce were all over the field throughout the game. Bruce, who had played against McAda in high school, would end up with 16 tackles. Hammond was double-teamed constantly, but still made plays. He had even engaged in the first — and last — trash talking of his college career.

When the Army offense came on the field early in the second quarter with excellent field position at the 40-yard line, Joel Davis was screaming at his teammates: "Here we go, right now, we're rolling them!"

Three plays later as the Army punt team trotted on, Hammond couldn't resist yelling at Davis as he and the Fat Men left, "Guess you aren't going just yet!"

Hammond shook his head later at the memory. "I don't know what got into me," he said. "Usually, I don't say a word. But there was nothing usual about this game."

His tackle of Carpenter for no gain brought up third-and-goal from the four. With 1:29 left in the half, Sutton wanted to talk before calling the next play. He called time and McAda trotted over. The call was 59 Volvo, a play-action fake to Conroy with tight end Ron Leshinski as the primary receiver in the corner of the end zone.

As McAda turned to go back into the game, Sutton grabbed his arm. "Don't force anything," he said. "If it's not there, throw it away or take the sack and we'll get three."

McAda nodded. Bumpas was thinking Army would pass and no one on the defense bought the play-fake. Joe Speed was blitzing from the left side and came charging right at McAda, who could see that Sean Andrews had Leshinski well covered. There was no time to look for a secondary receiver.

*Throw it away or take the sack.* McAda could still hear Sutton's last words, but he wasn't listening. Instinct had taken over. "I have a tendency at times to force things," he said. "That's why Coach reminded me the way he did. I just think I can get the play done somehow and I throw it up there. Sometimes I get away with it."

This time he didn't. Andrews had been outjumped for a ball only once all season — by Derrick Mayes at Notre Dame. This time he was in perfect position, and he grabbed the ball without Leshinski ever getting a hand on it. Navy had the ball back. Army had no points. Sutton had a headache.

"What in the world were you thinking?" he demanded of McAda as he came to the sideline. McAda's sheepish look was the only available answer. There wasn't much more Sutton could say. The damage was done.

"I was thinking we could lead 14–7 and at worst we'd be up 10–7," Sutton said. "The second quarter had gone all our way. The next thing I know, I'm scared to death we're going to be *behind* at halftime."

They almost were behind. With 1:24 left, Fay came back in and, just as he had done at Notre Dame, pieced together an excellent last-minute drive. He hit Astor Heaven for 10. Then Tim Cannada took a screen, picked up 15 yards, *and* got out-of-bounds at the Navy 47. There were still 29 seconds left. Schemm got seven over the middle and they spent a time-out. Two incomplete passes and it was fourth-and-three with 15 seconds left. Johnson crossed Army up, calling an option on fourth down, and Cannada went up the middle for nine to the 37. First down. They used their last time-out.

Fay, under heavy pressure from new dad Bill Doutt, threw a pass over Scornavacchi's head. Six seconds left. Time for one last play. Scornavacchi went straight down the left side on a streak pattern with cornerback Garland Gay step for step with him. Fay threw the ball up and both players looked back for it. Ever so gently, Scornavacchi bumped Gay, getting him off balance just enough that he suddenly had enough room from the defender to reach out for the ball as it came down into his arms.

But the bump had also knocked Scornavacchi a little off balance. His hands were turned just a little bit sideways. Instead of being able to cradle the ball, he had to reach for it. With Gay desperately trying to knock him off balance, Scornavacchi felt the ball brush his hands and roll off. He made one last lunge for it, but it was too late. The ball hit the ground. The half was over.

Army 7, Navy 7.

"NO!" Scornavacchi screamed in frustration. He had done everything right. The official hadn't even seen his push — there was no flag on the play. A touchdown pass, one that would have given his team a huge boost while knocking Army for a loop, had literally been in his hands. And he had dropped it.

In the stands many members of the brigade shook their heads and said, "PIF."

It wasn't that simple. If Scornavacchi had made the play, it would have been both brilliant and controversial. Army would have screamed — justifiably — for pass interference. If the flag hadn't been thrown and Scornavacchi had held on, it would have gone down as one of the great plays in Army-Navy history.

Scornavacchi wasn't thinking about any of that, going up the tunnel. He was furious with himself. "Don't feel bad, Scorno," Tommy Raye said, putting an arm around him. "If you'da caught it, they'da flagged you."

Scornavacchi appreciated the encouragement. But he spent most of halftime pacing the locker room angrily while his teammates told him to forget it and get ready for the second half.

The feeling in each locker room was almost identical: *they're* lucky the score is tied. The Army players and coaches were convinced they had taken control of the game in the second quarter and that only McAda's misjudgment had prevented them from being in the lead. The Navy players and coaches were furious that they hadn't been more assertive, especially on the offensive line, and disappointed that they hadn't stolen a last-second touchdown.

Brian Dreschler, the sophomore center who rarely said anything during a game, screamed at his linemates as they left the field: "Saying you want to win is one thing, doing it is another. This is embarrassing!"

Johnson said roughly the same thing when he spoke to the offense. "In a way, we're lucky as hell to be tied because you can't possibly play any worse. I mean, fellas, why would you play scared in *this* game? Do you think they want it more than you? I can't believe that. You guys have let number 60 [Stephen King] run around in the backfield as if he was on our team."

He paused and looked around. At the other end of the locker room, Bumpas had paused in his talk to the defense, so everyone was listening. Weatherbie stood right in the middle of the room, hands on hips, listening with everyone else.

"Against a running team, you've got to make every possession count," Johnson continued. "*We're running out of NEXT TIMES,* guys. This is all that's left now — thirty minutes. They've given us two turnovers and we've got seven points. Not good enough. But you know what the good news is? If we win the game, 110 percent of the people won't care about or remember the first half."

Andrew Thompson's knee was killing him. He kept trying to stretch it out, hoping it would loosen up for him one last time. He hadn't slept a wink the night before but that didn't matter. He would worry about sleep later.

Down the hallway, the Army coaches were convinced they didn't need to make any major changes on either side of the ball, although they were frustrated by what had happened in the last 90 seconds.

They had dominated the statistics: 186 total yards to 102 for Navy — only 59 of them before the Mids' last drive against the prevent defense. They had 166 yards rushing, Navy 35. They had kept the ball almost 20 of the 30 minutes. But it was still 7–7. The two turnovers had hurt a lot. Sutton and Greg Gregory both reminded McAda to stay patient and not try to win the game on every play.

Conroy spent most of the break in the training room. Bob Arciero looked at his ribs and checked to make sure he wasn't having any trouble breathing. His breathing was fine, he was just having trouble moving around. Tim Kelly offered a pad that would cushion the ribs but might slow him down a little bit. Conroy said no. He was upset.

"My last game and I feel like I can't get the job done," he said. "I gave up the first touchdown" — causing the fumble by slipping — "and now I don't know what I'm going to feel like in the second half."

Sutton's message was the same as it had been before the game: stay desperate. "Thirty minutes, men," he said. "These games always come down to one or two plays. There's just no way to know what those plays will be. Let's go out and be the ones to make them happen."

Weatherbie still felt that the game was his team's to win or lose. "Hey, men, this game doesn't *have* to be close," he said. "Let's go out in this second half and show 'em what Navy football is all about. Turn it up a notch now and let's take care of business just like we did in the second half against Tulane. Thirty more minutes and then we'll really have some fun!"

And so they came back to the field: one team confident, the other team desperate. Navy's confidence seemed justified at the start of the third quarter. The Midshipmen took the kickoff and, as Weatherbie and Johnson had been convinced could happen, they went right down the field with it.

Not that it was easy. The Army defense gave ground — but grudgingly. Every time the Cadets seemed to have Navy stopped, the Mids came up with a big play. And the player who came up with the most big plays was Matt Scornavacchi.

First, he went over the middle on third-and-14 at the Army 47 and made a fingertip catch of a Fay pass just as cornerback Bobby Brown slammed into him. Scorno hung on. First down at the Army 33. Three plays after that, it was fourth-and-seven at the 30. Too far to try a field goal, so the Mids went for it. Again, Scornavacchi went over the middle. Fay found him, and this time it was Cantelupe trying to knock his head off. Scorno's head stayed on and the ball stayed in his hands. Another first down at the 21. Two plays later, it was Fay to Scorno again — over the middle one more time. Three passes, three tough catches. No PIF, just hard-nosed, clutch receiving.

Scornavacchi's third catch set up third-and-three at the 14. Fay tried the quarterback draw that had worked so well against both Villanova and Delaware. But this wasn't Villanova or Delaware. The Army coaches had seen the play on tape and were ready for it. Defensive tackle Scott Eichelberger nailed Fay for a three-yard loss. Fourth-and-six. Did they go for it again or bring in Vanderhorst to try a 34-yard field goal?

Everyone crowded around listening as the coaches decided. Finally, they sent the kicking team in. Lestor Fortney snapped the ball, Brian Schrum put it down, and Vanderhorst coolly sailed it through the uprights. There was just one problem. With all the hemming and hawing about what to do, the play clock had run out. The kick didn't count. Vanderhorst would have to move back five yards and try again. Everyone on the Navy sideline had the same thought: Here we go again.

This time, though, they were wrong. Calm as could be, Vanderhorst actually kicked the ball higher and farther from 39 yards than he had from 34. It was good. The Navy sideline was bedlam. The lead was just 10–7, but they had made a field goal!

"We made one!" Scornavacchi screamed as the ball sailed through the uprights. Like everyone else, he was amazed. What's more, they had eaten 7:31 off the clock, keeping the Army offense off the field.

In fact, the Army offense, sitting on the shaded south side of the stadium, had gotten cold during Navy's extended drive. Although McAda did pick up two first downs on option runs, the offense was stopped at the 40 and Hughes was forced to punt. They exchanged punts again, each defense controlling the other offense, and when Army punted the ball back to Navy with 1:20 left in the quarter, Johnson decided it was time to bring McCoy back in at quarterback.

He immediately picked up a first down, going from the 17 to the 28 on an option keeper that brought back memories of SMU as he ducked tackles. Then, with Army thinking run since McCoy was in the game, he rose up on second-and-seven and found Neal Plaskanos open on the sideline at the 48. Seventeen yards and another first down. As Plaskanos stepped out-of-bounds, the quarter ended. It was 10–7, Navy.

Fifteen minutes to play. As always, the Army-Navy game would be decided in the fourth quarter.

THROUGHOUT the game, the atmosphere in the stadium had been wild. The relatively warm weather meant that people didn't have to huddle to keep warm. The tight nature of the game made every possession and every play seem important. Both the brigade and the corps were convinced their school was going to win. The sense on the Navy side was that it was their turn. Army had escaped for three straight years. Now, with the new coaching staff, this was a different Navy team with a different attitude. They were gradually taking control. On the Army side, although the breaks had gone their way in Navy games, they certainly hadn't in other games during this season. Maybe this was the game that was going to make up for all those earlier disappointments.

Both sides thought they deserved to win. Both were probably right.

The fourth quarter started with another Navy explosion. McCoy, dashing and darting, picked his way for 42 yards, all the way to the Army 10 yard line. If it wasn't for Cantelupe, fighting off a blocker to get to him, McCoy would have scored.

By now, Cantelupe was exhausted. The defense had been on the field almost the entire third quarter and he had been all over the field all day. Just as Hammond, Harris, and Person were playing heroically for Navy's defense in their last game, Cantelupe, Burrell, King, Al Roberts, and nose guard Colin Kearns were coming up big for Army.

But Navy was rolling now. A touchdown could put them up 10 points, and even this early in the fourth quarter that could be a tough margin to overcome. Close to the goal line, though, McCoy's tendency to hang on to the ball and not pitch it made him less effective. Three times he ran the ball himself. Roberts got him the first time; Burrell and Cantelupe the second; King and Kearns the third when he had to scramble because of good pass coverage. The last run put the ball on the four — fourth down.

Vanderhorst had become the Mids man of the hour. He trotted on and made the 22-yard field goal. Nothing to this game when you're 18 and haven't missed a kick yet. There was 12:33 left to play and Navy now led, 13–7.

There was no panic on the Army sideline. Being behind in the fourth quarter against Navy was hardly unusual. The only game in the last three in which they had led throughout the fourth quarter was the Bucchianeri game — and that was the one they had come closest to losing.

The Navy players were convinced that was ancient history. Irrelevant ancient history. They were moving the ball. The defense was stuffing Army's offense. The vaunted Army running attack was doing very little damage. The Fat Men were no longer opening holes the way they had in the first half. With Sutton keeping the ball on the ground most of the time, Bumpas kept moving the defensive backs closer and closer to the line, calling more blitzes.

Covarrubias kicked off to Brizic, who for the first time all day got a good return, taking the ball to the 32. But Army was caught holding and the ball moved back ten yards to the 22.

It moved back another four yards on the first down. McAda pitched to Ron Thomas, who had been held in check all day. This play was no different. Keith Galloway, having talked the talk, was walking the walk. He brought Thomas down for a four-yard loss.

More important than the lost yardage was the lost player — McAda was hit hard as he pitched the ball and didn't get up. He had landed squarely on his tailbone and felt pain shoot through him. He had to be helped off the field. Army's sideline was starting to look like a MASH unit. Conroy was hurting and so was Al Roberts, who had a hip-pointer. Eichelberger had a sore knee. Now, most important of all, McAda. Arciero and Kelly began checking him immediately.

In the meantime, Adam Thompson, who had been a spectator for two and a half hours, had to rush into the game without the benefit of taking even one warm-up snap. By now, the entire field was in shadows, and the Army bench had been cold all day anyway. All year long, Thompson had been superb when forced to come in for McAda on the spur of the moment.

But this time, with cold hands — cold *small* hands — and in the cauldron of the fourth quarter of Army-Navy, he tried to get away from center just a little too quickly. Kyle Scott's snap never quite made it into his hands and the ball was lying on the turf. Fernando Harris, the quickest player Navy had, dove into the scrum for the ball, and when they picked all the players apart, he was clutching it.

The Navy bench was jubilant. They had the ball on the Army 17. Time to move into the end zone for the kill. As Garrett Smith grabbed his helmet and ran onto the field with the offense, he thought: "Score here and we can blow them out. We can get John Moe into this game."

For the first time on the Army sideline, the thought of losing began to creep into people's minds. When McCoy picked up 13 yards on two straight option plays to set up first-and-goal on the three, Sutton was screaming at the officials, convinced that his players were being held. He came all the way down to the 15 yard line, yelling, then realized he was risking a penalty and retreated.

The clock had ticked under 10 minutes. The only reason McCoy hadn't scored on the second option run was Cantelupe, who had come from the far side of the field to bring him down. Cantelupe talked often about Pat Work being the unsung hero of the Bucchianeri game because he had come from nowhere to trip Brad Stramanak up on the goal line just before the ill-fated kick. This play was reminiscent of Work's, Cantelupe refusing to give up on the play when it looked like McCoy was bound to score.

Now, though, it would take a miracle from the defense to keep Navy out of the end zone. Cannada got nothing on first down. On second down, McCoy ran left and Kearns and Cantelupe pulled him down for a loss of one. The Army bench was imploring the defense to dig in and force Navy to kick a field goal. By now, everyone in the stadium was standing, sensing that the game was about to reach a turning point.

Third down. Ball on the four. McCoy started backwards and to the right, then cut left. The Army defense had bought his first move to the right and had overrun the play. As McCoy started left, he appeared to have a clear path to the end zone. In complete desperation, Tom Burrell reached out and back with his right arm, hoping to get a hand on any part of McCoy's body.

Instead, he got his hand on his face mask. Since McCoy was going toward the goal line and Burrell was off balance, Burrell's grab didn't stop him, but it did slow him. As McCoy struggled to pull free, linebacker Ben Kotwica, who had initially been blocked, managed to pull himself loose just long enough to get his body between McCoy and the goal line. Still driving forward, McCoy was finally stopped no more than six inches away.

Lying on the ground, Burrell looked around for the flag that he knew had to come. He hadn't intentionally grabbed McCoy's face mask, but that didn't matter. Hc had grabbed it and that would mean the officials would move the ball half the distance to the goal line — in this case three inches — and, far more important, Navy would have an automatic first down. The Mids would have four cracks from three inches away to score.

But there was no flag. Later, looking at the play on tape, the Cadets — Burrell most of all — would be amazed to see one of the officials standing on the goal line, hands on his knees, looking right at the play. Or so it seemed. Somehow, he didn't pull his flag.

"To this day, I'll never know why he didn't throw the flag," Burrell said. "I just got lucky on the play, very lucky."

Navy's view of it was a little bit different. When he saw the tape, Weatherbie angrily sent it to the Big East office (the officials were from the Big East), but at that point it didn't matter.

What did matter was that, thanks to the non-whistle, Navy now had fourth down and inches. Weatherbie called time with 8:26 left in the game.

On the Army sideline, there wasn't any doubt in anybody's mind about what Navy was going to do. With Vanderhorst already two-for-two and the fourth quarter almost half over, putting Army in a nine-point hole would be huge. "At that point, nine was about as good as thirteen for them," Cantelupe said. "It was two scores. That wouldn't be impossible, but it would be tough."

By now McAda was on his feet. He was sore, but OK. Arciero had told him he could go back in the game. He was standing with John Graves, watching as the Navy coaches huddled on the sideline.

"They gotta kick it," McAda said to Graves.

"We need a good return on the kickoff," Graves said, already thinking ahead to what the offense would have to do with a nine-point deficit.

Weatherbie was on his handset, talking to Johnson in the press box. "We can score with A-pop," Johnson told him. "They'll have so many people on the line it'll be wide open."

Weatherbie's mind was racing. The field goal would be 18 yards. Somewhere, in the deep recesses of his brain, he remembered that Bucchianeri's miss had been 18 yards. That close, the angle could be a factor. They could take a delay-of-game penalty and move the ball back five yards, making it a little easier angle from 23 yards. Vanderhorst had been solid all day. But this was the fourth quarter; this was that moment with 70,000 people screaming that Weatherbie had wondered about in the pregame coaches meeting.

He looked at his offensive coaches, who were all nodding as Johnson explained how they could score. There was only one dissenting voice: defensive backs coach Gary Patterson. He knew it was none of his business telling the offense what to do, but Patterson thought going for anything but three was crazy. "It's all we need," he said. "They can't score twice, they just can't."

On the field, the offense waited. Smith and Bryce Minamyer, the two seniors on the offensive line, wanted to go for it; they wanted to explode off the ball one more time, push the Army defense back on its heels, and run the ball in for the score. "I'm thinking, 'Six inches. Come on, we can move the ball six inches,'" Smith said.

On the other side of the huddle, Matt Scornavacchi nudged Scott Zimmerman. "Zim," he said, "we gotta kick the field goal."

Zimmerman shook his head. "We're not. Look, Tom's not even standing up there near Coach."

A chill ran through Scornavacchi. He was reckless enough to appreciate the nature of the gamble, but a bit unnerved by what would now be at stake on this play.

Weatherbie put his arm around McCoy. "Three twenty-eight, A-pop," he said.

It was a quick pass play, a pop pass to the A-back, in this case Schemm. It was designed to take advantage of a defense lined up to stop the run at all costs. McCoy would take the snap, drop back a step, and throw the ball quickly to Schemm, who only had to take two or three steps to be open.

When the Army players saw McCoy trotting back onto the field, they were amazed. Cantelupe and Klein were both on the sidelines, since the "heavy," goal-line defense was in the game. "Has to be a fake," Cantelupe said. "They'll take the penalty, then kick."

As soon as he saw McCoy come back to the huddle, offensive line coach Ed Warriner began screaming for the O-line to get ready. "We're gonna stop 'em and get the ball back!"

No one was sitting on either sideline or in the stands. McCoy walked to the line and saw the entire Army defense pinching the middle to stop what they all thought would be a quarterback sneak or a fullback dive. "The play was wide open," he said. "No one was even on Cory."

Schemm was linked up on the right side, just behind the line. As soon as he stepped outside, toward the sideline, he would be all alone. On the other side, Scornavacchi noticed that no one was on Schemm and he took a deep breath. "It's right there," he thought.

McCoy got under Dreschler, and, to the surprise of the Army sideline, went on a quick count. No delay of game penalty coming here. He dropped quickly and saw Schemm all alone.

"I got too excited," he said later. "I rushed it and I didn't have to. I never quite got my arm back right or the ball off the way I wanted to."

The ball wobbled off McCoy's hand. Seeing that it was low, Schemm dove, got his hands on it, bobbled it a little as he hit the turf, and then watched helplessly as it just rolled off his fingertips. He lay there for a moment, pounding the ground in frustration.

For a split second it was as if no one was quite sure what had happened. Then everyone understood. The Army bench exploded as if it had just scored the winning touchdown. People were jumping into one another's arms.

The Navy defensive players sagged for a split second, then gathered themselves. "Come on!" Thompson screamed. "It's our game now! Let's go out there and stuff them like we have all day!"

Across the way, Cantelupe grabbed Klein by both shoulders. "Guess what!" he yelled. "We just won this goddamn game. You watch. We just won the goddamn game."

# 20

# THE DRIVE

AS Cantelupe spoke, the football was sitting 99 yards, two feet, and six inches from where it had to be for Army to win the game. And yet, there was no doubt that all the emotion in the stadium, all the adrenaline, all the momentum, was now on Army's side.

Before the offense took the field, McAda gathered everyone around him. Even though there was still 8:23 left in the game, there was a sense of urgency. They all knew that if they gave the football back now, they might not see it again. The defense was exhausted and it was entirely possible that, given another possession, Navy might run out the clock with two or three first downs.

"Listen up," McAda commanded. None of the Fat Men told him to shut up. They listened. "The D did its job, now we have to do ours. Right now!"

As they huddled up, deep in the end zone, waiting for the TV time-out to end, Davis turned to the other Fat Men. "This is our destiny," he said. "Ninety-nine yards to win. This is what the whole thing is all about."

The Navy defense was rested and ready. Everyone knew if they could hold Army without a first down and force a Hughes punt from the end zone, they would get great field position. "It was as if someone had decided that we were supposed to win the game," Person said. "There was part of me that liked that idea. I had no doubt we would get the job done."

Thompson, who had been frustrated all day because Army had consistently run the option away from him, didn't care anymore about where the plays went. All he wanted was a stop right now to get the damn game under control once and for all. He looked at Joe Speed, who just nodded his head as if reading Thompson's mind. "Now's the time," Speed said.

McAda knew what the first call was going to be even before Heath Bates trotted into the huddle carrying it: 60 short. It was a basic, straight-ahead fullback dive designed to create a little bit of room when the offense was backed up. They would never be more backed up than they were at that moment. McAda handed the ball to Conroy, the Fat Men pushed as hard as they could, and the Navy line pushed back. Conroy burrowed for almost two yards — putting the ball squarely on the two. His ribs were sore, but felt better than they had earlier.

Second down. Now McAda was at least standing on the playing field and not in the end zone as he called signals. The call was 204 option, meaning he would read the defense and decide whether to give to Conroy again or keep the ball himself. If he kept the ball and got trapped, a safety was possible. Turning to hand the ball to Conroy, McAda could see that Stover and Blair had blasted off the ball so hard that they had wedged a hole in the right side of the line. He stuck the ball in Conroy's gut and Conroy slid through the hole, broke a tackle at the five, and was finally brought down at the 14.

First down. A roar went up from the corps. At the very least they had now given Hughes some breathing room if he had to punt. Conroy was slow getting up. The ribs had gotten banged again. He was hobbling as he tried to go back to the huddle. "I couldn't take a step without pain," he said. "I knew I had to come out."

With a little more room to operate, McAda kept the ball on the first-down play and pitched it to Abel Young. He got six. Steve Carpenter got three more on a counter play, again running behind Stover. It was third-and-one at the 23. Now the noise was coming from the brigade, urging the defense to dig in and hold right now.

Conroy had taken his helmet off when he came to the sideline. The pain was almost unbearable. Kelly told him to take it easy and sit down. The message was: you're done, kid.

The third-down call was 46 stack reach. The fullback — now Demetrius Perry — was the decoy and the give would again be to Carpenter going over the right side. This time, though, Navy read the play and Clint Bruce had ahold of Carpenter two yards behind the line of scrimmage. Bruce was probably Navy's best tackler. But Carpenter somehow found some extra surge in his legs and pulled loose from Bruce just enough to dive past the line of scrimmage and land a foot beyond the first-down marker.

Bruce came up screaming in anger at himself. Carpenter, who always seemed to be the other guy during his four years at Army, had just become *the* guy. First down again. The ball was at the 24. The clock was now down to 6:25. Army's grind-it-out attack ate up the time quickly. More and more it looked like this drive would be now or never.

Sutton and Gregory knew they couldn't run the ball on every play. Navy was putting 10 men on the line to deny the option room. And so, on first down, Gregory suggested 29 Volvo, a three-man pass route with Leshinski as the primary pass receiver. McAda dropped and saw that Leshinski was covered.

Graves, coming from the right side, had gone about 15 yards when he saw Speed coming up to meet him. "If I ran the route just the way I was supposed to, the guy would have been right there," he said. "I looked up and figured I better flatten it out some and make sure I was open."

McAda saw him make his cut early and hit him on the numbers. Speed brought him down immediately on the 41. First down again. They went back to the option, but this time McAda dropped the ball as he turned away from the line. He picked it up before anyone from Navy could make a move at it, but Bruce was all over him. The gain was one. On second down, Perry, still in the game for Conroy, got two up the middle.

It was third-and-seven. The drive had now lasted seven plays and, more important, had eaten up almost four minutes. Sutton called for the fullback screen, a play Conroy had run very well all season. Only now he wasn't in the game. Bumpas, sensing a chance to make a big play, had both safeties, Thompson and Speed, blitzing. McAda dropped, and before he even had a chance to set up, Thompson and

Speed were on him. Somehow, using every bit of his six feet four inches, he managed to get his arm up and loft the ball just over the hands of the diving Thompson. Perry caught it, dodged a tackler, and crossed midfield. Michael Ogden got him down at the 47, but again, it was a yard late. Another first down.

Back behind the line of scrimmage, Thompson and Speed could not believe how close they had come to the sack. Thompson stood up and went to help Speed up. But Speed wasn't getting up. Diving for McAda he had felt a sharp pain in his legs. Both of them had cramped on him at the same time.

"I didn't adjust for the weather being warmer," he said. "I should have been drinking more fluids. The legs just went."

Speed had to come off. He didn't know it then, but his football career had just ended. Sophomore Kevin Lewis, who often came in on passing downs anyway, took his place.

Watching all this, Conroy still felt pain in his ribs. But it was duller now. He walked a few yards and felt all right. He looked at the clock and saw that he had less than five minutes to be a football player. "I've got the rest of my life to heal," he thought. "I have to get back in the game."

He went to get his helmet, but it was gone. "Hey!" he screamed. "Where's my helmet?" Everyone looked at him blankly. What was he raving about his helmet for? He didn't need it to watch the rest of the game. "Where's my helmet?" Conroy screamed again.

From behind the bench, someone was trying to get his attention. "Hey, Conroy," the man said. "It's under the bench, down at the end there."

Conroy had no idea who the man was. Maybe his guardian angel. He grabbed the helmet, stuck it on, and headed back to the field. He didn't bother to check with any doctors, trainers, or coaches. He just ran in and told Perry, "Hey D, Coach wants to see you."

Perry nodded and ran off. McAda grabbed his shoulder. "You sure you're OK?" The noise in the stadium was so loud now that everyone had to scream to be heard.

"I'm fine," Conroy yelled back. "Call the play."

McAda called Carpenter's number again and the little halfback picked up three to the Navy 44. Then, using Conroy as the decoy,

McAda faked the dive handoff, started right as if to run the option, then handed to Jeff Brizic on the counter. Davis and Wells opened a gaping hole and Brizic roared to the 26. Three and a half minutes left. There was now no doubt that this was it for both teams. The game would be decided on this possession.

Army went back to basics, McAda leaving the ball in Conroy's stomach on the option. He picked up six more to the 20. Then Brizic got five to the 15 for another first down. The Navy players were screaming at each other to dig in the way the Army players had done on the goal line a few minutes earlier.

Sutton called 54 option, the play that they had fumbled on way back in the first quarter. This time Conroy didn't slip, and McAda pulled the ball out of his stomach and started right. But Fernando Harris had read the play and he caught McAda from behind and pulled him down at the 17. The loss was two yards. The clock was at 2:03. Army took its second time-out.

Sutton and Gregory talked on the headsets while McAda waited. During the week they had worked on a play called 96 solid-suzy, a fake screen pass that ended up being a deep pass to one of the halfbacks. They had used the screen effectively all game, so a screen look might suck Navy in. They all agreed it was the right play. Coby Short, the best receiver among the halfbacks, went into the game.

McAda dropped, made his fake, and looked deep for Short. Kevin Lewis hadn't bought the fake even for a second. He was all over Short as they streaked to the left corner of the end zone together. A little voice was telling McAda to throw the ball away, but his gut was telling him there wasn't anymore time to waste plays. He tossed the ball in the direction of Short and Lewis and hoped for a miracle.

In a sense, he got it. Only one person had a chance to catch the ball: Lewis. He turned and saw it coming right at him. Short was reaching back to try and pull him away from the ball. Even so, Lewis had a clean shot at it. But he was a split second slow getting his hands up and the ball slid through them and hit him on the helmet. It bounced away harmlessly.

McAda's heart started beating again. "I thought for a second it was over," he said. "That I had lost the game. I got away with that one."

It was third-and-12. Sutton and Gregory were deep into their bag of tricks now. They called 28 willie-cross, a post pattern for Graves. Bumpas knew the Cadets had to pass and he called a full blitz. Again, Thompson came in clean. McAda saw him and spun to try and clear room. But Thompson was too close to him, and as he spun he tripped and fell, 12 yards behind the line of scrimmage.

Thompson jumped to his feet, screaming at the top of his lungs. The Navy players were in full celebration. It was fourth-and-24 at the 29. The clock was at 1:46. Army used its last time-out to try and regroup. All Navy had to do was stop this play and the game would be over. Army wouldn't be able to stop the clock again.

McAda trotted over to Sutton, who was talking again to Gregory. They were convinced that Navy would come with a full blitz package again, trying to make sure that McAda didn't have time to pick out a receiver down the field. They had little choice but to call a play that would commit McAda to throwing the ball to one receiver in one spot, do or die. There wouldn't be time for anything else. There was no doubt in Sutton's mind that Graves was the man to throw the ball to.

He looked at Graves, who was standing next to McAda. "Which do you want to run, post or corner," he said.

Graves thought for a split second. "Corner," he said, thinking he felt more comfortable running toward the sideline than over the middle. That was the answer Sutton wanted to hear. He thought Graves would have a better chance to get open running the corner route than the post if only because there was less chance for the defense to get help near the sideline.

"OK then," Sutton said. "Four-ninety-six, steve-key."

That meant there would only be two receivers in the pattern — Graves and Thomas — and Thomas was strictly a decoy. Everyone else would stay in to give McAda maximum protection against the blitz they all expected.

McAda and Graves returned to the huddle. Before McAda called the play, Joel Davis stepped in and pointed a finger around the circle of 11 players. "Who is going to step up?" he demanded. "Who steps up right now and makes the play?"

McAda's voice was much softer. "Just give me time," he said, looking into the eyes of the Fat Men. "Give me time, we'll make it work."

The look he got back told him all he needed to know: they would give him time, one way or the other. The rest would be up to him and to Graves.

IT took the Navy sideline a full minute to get a collective hold of itself after Thompson's sack. The offensive players and second-teamers were still hugging and screaming when Thompson and Bruce came to the sideline.

"Hey," Thompson yelled. "No celebrating yet. We still need one more play."

It was at that moment that Charlie Weatherbie came back into the football game. From the moment that the ball had rolled off Schemm's hands until the moment he heard Thompson's voice, he had mentally checked out. As soon as he saw McCoy's fourth-down pass fall incomplete, a wave of dread swept over him.

"*What have I done?*" he kept thinking over and over. "*What was I thinking? All we needed was a field goal.*"

"I was in an absolute state of shock," he said later. "I did the one thing I always tell the players not to do: I turned one mistake into two. Because I was standing there beating myself up and not thinking about the football game."

Bumpas was calling the defensive signals and Weatherbie heard them in his headset. But he wasn't listening. All he could see was Army moving down the field and the clock ticking down. He had a vague sense that there were moments when the defense had a chance to put him out of his misery by getting the ball back, but it didn't happen. Then he heard Thompson's voice and he snapped back to reality.

"I looked up and realized we were one play from winning," he said. "The kids were still battling, still trying to win the game after I had just put them in a position to lose it."

No one was thinking about the goal-line incompletion now, not even Weatherbie. They were thinking only about making one more play and getting almost everything they had wanted from the season. Bumpas was calling the play — full blitz with coverage in the defensive backfield backed off to give up a short pass. The key was to make McAda get rid of the ball (or sack him) before any of his receivers had the chance to get anywhere near the five yard line, which was where they had to get to pick up the first down.

Everyone was in agreement. Thompson looked at Speed, who was trying to stand up straight, the pain still biting at his legs. "Can't go?" he asked. Speed shook his head. There were tears in his eyes. Thompson reached out and grabbed Speed's mouthpiece out of his hand. He took his own mouthpiece, handed it to Speed, and stuck Speed's in his mouth. "You're out there with me, Joe," he said. "This is for you."

He ran back to the huddle. In the Army huddle, McAda calmly called "496 steve-key," and brought them up to the line. On the Navy side, Ben Fay and Lester Fortney kneeled, helmet-to-helmet, praying.

Sutton watched Graves trot out to the left side and saw that Kevin Lewis was alone out there with him. Sean Andrews was with Thomas on the other side. Everyone else was bunched in the middle of the field. Sutton's heart leapt. Graves was one-on-one with Lewis! If the protection would hold up long enough . . . "Greg," he said into his headset, "I think we've got a shot at this."

McAda took the snap and dropped and nine Navy players came at him. Hammond made a twist move coming up the middle and had a lane, but Carpenter stepped in his way. At the same time, Thompson was forced a step wider than he wanted to go and was still two steps from McAda when he saw the quarterback's arm come up.

Graves came off the line and ran straight at Lewis, who was back-pedaling to give him room, since anything caught short of the five yard line would be worthless to Army. Graves went down 15 yards and took a jab step toward the middle of the field. Lewis read post and took a tiny step in that direction.

As he did, Graves planted his right foot as hard as he could and spun to the outside. His heart was racing. He knew Lewis had bought the fake and he had a step on him. He looked back over his shoulder, hoping the ball would be dropping down toward him, because if it wasn't, that meant that McAda was in trouble.

McAda saw Carpenter pick up Hammond and saw Graves come open. His quarterback senses told him the ball had to be released right then because Thompson and Person and Bruce were bearing down on him. He stood up in the pocket as tall as he could and let the ball go.

For one horrifying millisecond he thought he had put too much on it and thrown it too close to the sideline. Then he saw Graves race under it and he knew everything was OK.

Graves wasn't worried about the sideline, but he wasn't absolutely certain what *yard* line he was on. As the ball dropped through the air into his waiting arms, he was tempted to look down for a yard marker. But his gut told him he was where he should be and he had to make sure he made the catch. He gathered the ball safely into his arms just as Lewis, lunging for him, pushed him out-of-bounds. Graves looked down as he went out and saw the flag — the end zone flag — almost on top of him.

"For a second, I thought I might be in," he said.

He wasn't, but he was close. The official spotted the ball on the one yard line. It was first-and-goal. The play had taken six seconds. That meant the Fat Men, with considerable help from Scott and Conroy and Carpenter and Leshinski, had held the blitzing Navy defense out for close to four seconds — an eternity.

Now it was the Army bench going crazy; the Navy bench in shock. Weatherbie called *his* last time-out to give his players a chance to regroup. A three-minute time-out wasn't going to be long enough to do that. They had gone from one play away from having the game won to one yard away from losing it.

"I just couldn't believe it," Hammond said later. "Fourth-and-twenty-four, you've got them. You have to have them. Only we didn't."

"How many times," Andy Person asked, "do you see someone pick up fourth-and-twenty-four?"

The defense wasn't going to give up. They had simulated this situation in practice 100 times. Dig way down, get underneath the offensive linemen, and, as Bumpas always put it, "move the line of scrimmage backward."

Sutton called 72 diamond, the play off right tackle that Conroy had scored the first touchdown on. Blair and Stover were screaming for the ball to come that way. The only person who wasn't sure was Conroy. "They'll be looking for that play," he said to Steve Carpenter in the huddle. "We should run forty-six and I can block for you."

Carpenter looked at Conroy. "John," he said, "just shut up and put the ball in the end zone."

Conroy thought he would do just that. Blair and Stover created space, but as he hit the hole, Thompson was waiting. Conroy hadn't been brought down by one tackler very often during the season. Thompson stood him up and Conroy heard him screaming, "NO, NO, NO!" He tried to drive forward, but Thompson was a wall. He brought him down on the one.

The clocked ticked toward a minute. "Actually," Jack Hecker said on the Army sideline, "it's probably better for us to take a couple of plays to get it in. Use up the clock."

Bob Arciero looked at him as if he were crazy. "Use up the clock!" he screamed. "Forget that! We've got to get the ball in the damn end zone!"

Cantelupe was already gathering the defense. "When we score, we've got to do our job one more time," he said. "Don't think the game is over when we score. Because it's not."

On second down, Sutton called 73 diamond: same play, only over the left side, behind Davis and Wells. This time, Conroy agreed with the call. "I figured *now* they would be looking for forty-six," he said.

As they broke the huddle, Davis looked back at him. "Just follow me, babe," he said.

McAda took the snap and handed the ball to Conroy for the 22d and last time of the afternoon. Conroy submarined to get his body as low as possible, and following orders, ran right behind Davis and Wells as they plowed open just enough space for him to squeeze through. Conroy heard the cannon go off and he knew he had scored. Lying on the ground, Davis pounded his fist on the turf joyfully. He was screaming to the heavens, "We did it, we did it, we did it!" Mike Wells was lying next to him, his eyes filling with tears.

"The last time my feet will ever touch a football field as a player," he thought, "and I was a part of *this*."

*This* was as epic a drive as anyone in the stadium had ever seen: 19 plays, seven minutes and 20 seconds, 100 yards, minus those fateful six inches. When Graves made his catch, they had driven the ball 99 yards — and still weren't in the end zone yet. It was a monumental drive because it came against a defense that stood in on every play and pushed and shoved and scrambled trying desperately to stop them.

But Army was just a little more desperate. The Fat Men refused to be denied their destiny. J. Parker came in and kicked the extra point —

putting it just a little closer to the right upright than anyone from Army cared for — and, after three hours, the Cadets led for the first time: Army 14, Navy 13.

But as Cantelupe had said, the game wasn't over. There were still 63 seconds left. Navy had one last chance.

THERE was nothing left to hold back on either side now. Neal Plaskanos took the kickoff at the eight and got as far as the 30 before Cantelupe and Maddox tackled him. It was Cantelupe's 13th tackle of the game.

Ben Fay came back at quarterback because Navy now had to throw the ball. The kickoff had taken six seconds. There were 57 seconds to play. On first down, Fay made an awful mistake. With no time-outs left, Johnson had called a pass play, but when he looked at the defense Fay thought he saw room in the middle. Going on instinct, rather than on the situation, he audibled to an option.

When Smith and Minamyer heard the check-off call they were shocked. But they couldn't turn around and call time to ask Fay what he was doing because there were no time-outs left. Having made a mistake by changing the play, Fay then made the wrong read on the option, handing the ball to Cannada on the fullback dive. He got nothing. Worse than that, the clock was running and Navy couldn't stop it. By the time Fay got them lined up so he could spike the ball to stop the clock there were only 36 seconds left.

They had wasted 21 critical seconds and faced third-and-ten. On third down, Fay dropped straight back and looked up to find Al Roberts in his face. Roberts would have taken him down 10 yards behind the line of scrimmage and Navy might not have gotten off another play if Fay hadn't smartly thrown the ball away just before Roberts piled into him.

It was fourth-and-ten and now *Army* was one play from winning. The Navy bench was almost silent. Fay took the snap and was again under heavy pressure. He rolled left, looking desperately for someone to throw to. "I knew I couldn't run with it because I probably wouldn't get the first down and if I didn't we were done," he said. "I was about out of room when I saw Astor."

Heaven had done the same thing Graves had done earlier, breaking his pattern when he saw his quarterback in trouble. Since Fay was running toward the sideline, Heaven ran in that direction, putting his hand up to get his attention. Fay spotted him and let go of the ball just as Roberts and Doutt were about to bury him.

For a moment it looked as if Jerrold Tyquiengco was in perfect position to intercept the ball or knock it down. But somehow the ball threaded its way past his arms and fell right into Heaven's hands. Heaven-sent, Heaven-*caught,* for Navy. Tyquiengco pushed him out-of-bounds on the Army 44, but it was a pickup of 26 yards.

Amazingly, with 26 seconds to go, the game still wasn't over. "I saw that and I thought, 'Oh my God, what's going on here?'" Graves said. "I thought maybe it was going to come down to another kick."

McAda's reaction was more direct: "Won't this damn game ever end?"

On the Navy sideline, the same thought went through everyone's mind: was the game going to come down to a kick? Again? Fortney, Schrum, and Vanderhorst went to the kicking area behind the bench to get ready, just in case . . .

The problem Navy had was that it was going into what had now become a strong wind. With no wind, getting the ball to the 35 yard line would have given Vanderhorst a fighting chance; anything closer than that would have been gravy. But because of the wind, they probably needed an extra 10 yards to have a chance.

Fay tried to pick up the 19 yards they probably needed on one play, looking again for Heaven, this time over the middle. The ball was on target, but as Heaven went down for it, Cantelupe dove in front of him and got both hands on it. Only Heaven wrestling with him and the impact of hitting the ground kept him from intercepting the ball.

Cantelupe picked himself up and looked at the clock. He didn't even pause to think about how close he had been to the interception. There was no time for that now. The clock was at 20 seconds.

Fay dropped once more and here came Al Roberts one more time. Navy simply couldn't keep him out of the backfield. The coverage downfield was perfect and Fay had no choice but to scramble. Desperately trying to get to the first-down marker since a first down would stop the clock, he was stopped three yards short by Ray Tomasits.

The clock was under 10 and running. Army was taking as much time as possible to unpile and line up. It looked as if the clock might run out, but Dreschler got the snap off with three ticks left and Fay spiked the ball to stop it with two seconds to go.

They had one play left. The ball was on the Army 37 yard line. If the wind had been the other way, their best chance probably would have been Vanderhorst. But 54 yards into a strong wind was an impossibility. They had no choice but to send everyone into the end zone, have Fay throw it up for grabs, and pray that this time the bounce would go their way.

Remarkably, they almost got lucky. In the bedlam that was the Army sideline, there was confusion about which defense they were supposed to be in. Some players thought the coaches wanted "prevent," others heard defensive coordinator Denny Doornbos screaming, "Victory, victory." The victory defense, used only on the last play of the game, consisted of nine defensive backs along with Roberts and Doutt.

Landis Maddox, who would have been one of the DBs, didn't hear Doornbos screaming "victory." As Navy lined up, Derek Klein thought they were a man short and started onto the field. But he was seized with panic: what if he had miscounted and he was the 12th man? He stopped and went back. Cantelupe *knew* they were a man short and started screaming for a time-out. But Army was out of time-outs so the officials ignored him.

Navy had an 11-on-10 advantage. Fay went back, and with Roberts again bearing down on him he lofted the ball as high and far as he could. Roberts crashed into him and the two of them went down together. Both of them listened to hear which direction the next roar would come from.

From the Army sideline, McAda thought briefly that Heaven had somehow gotten behind everyone. Then he saw a jumble of white and black uniforms converging on the spot where the ball was coming down. Everyone jumped, but no one from Navy made any kind of deflection. The ball somehow floated through everyone and into the hands of Donnie Augustus, in the game strictly for "victory." It was his only play of the game. Augustus clutched the ball safely in his chest as the corps screamed joyously.

Lying underneath Roberts, Fay heard the screams coming from his right and he knew no miracle had occurred. So did Roberts. He pulled Fay to his feet and offered him his hand.

The corps poured onto the field, everyone looking for their friends or company-mates. When Conroy looked up and saw half his company bearing down on him, he put his hands up and screamed, "Please, no hugging!" He was terrified at the thought of anyone crunching his ribs.

Sutton and Weatherbie found each other at midfield amid a crush of cameras. Both men were completely drained. "Your kids played a great game," Sutton said.

Weatherbie was still in a state of semi-shock. "I just hope," he said to Sutton, "that we at least helped your job situation."

He meant it. The only glimmer he could find in the whole thing was the thought that Sutton's job might have been saved by his mistake. Sutton thanked him. Then he went looking for Smith and Person and Thompson. He found Smith, who had tears rolling down his face, and hugged him. He did the same for Person. But he couldn't find Thompson.

Thompson and Speed were still on the sideline, locked in an embrace, their bodies racking with sobs. It just wasn't possible. How could this happen four years in a row? Four years, six points, impossible endings each time.

Cantelupe found Person and Smith just as Sutton had, but couldn't find Thompson in the crush of people on the field. Speed and Thompson didn't let go of one another until the teams were standing at attention in front of the Navy band for "Blue and Gold." Almost everyone in a Navy uniform — football or dress blue — was crying. A close-up shot of Mark Hammond on ABC said it all: Hammond stood at attention, hand on his heart, singing every word of "Blue and Gold," tears streaming down his face.

The Mids weren't alone. The Fat Men were all fighting tears, especially Eddie Stover. In the midst of the hugs and the cheers, it had occurred to him that this really was it, that he had played his last football game. As the players from both teams made their way to the Army side for the playing of "Alma Mater," Stover felt himself losing it. His knees started to quake. As the song ended, Stover began racing for the locker room. He didn't want to stay and celebrate. He couldn't think of a reason to celebrate. They had won, but so what? Football was over. How would he live without football? He couldn't imagine it.

THE last Navy player off the field was Thompson, who stood staring at the scoreboard, crying, somehow hoping that if he stood there long enough he could blink the numbers away. Speed and Gary Patterson finally took him by the arm and guided him up the tunnel to the locker room.

Once the doors closed, they all surrounded Weatherbie and kneeled to pray together one more time.

"Heavenly Father," Weatherbie began, "we come to you with pain, with sorrow, with hurt. Help us to learn a lesson from this to help us in life. Help us to learn a lesson, Lord, in dealing with disappointment."

He paused. "I just want to apologize to this team, Lord, for a stupid mistake."

"NO!" The shouts came from all over the room.

Weatherbie continued, his voice beginning to crack. "I just pray that you'll always be with these seniors, Lord." When he said the word "seniors," the crack became a sob. He paused, head still down, his arms stretched across the shoulders of the players kneeling next to him. For a few seconds it seemed he wouldn't be able to finish. The only sound in the room was his quiet sobbing. Then he forced himself to go on.

"Help them, Lord, as they go out to defend our country. Lord, I just thank you for their leadership and the guidance they gave us this year. I know you do have a plan for us, Lord. A plan to prosper us, not to harm us; a plan to give us a hope and a future. Thank you, Lord, for all these young men. Please put your healing hand on all those that are hurt. Help these young men hold their heads high and be proud to be part of the Naval Academy; the navy and the Marine Corps."

He paused once more as if trying to think of something else to say. He couldn't. "Thank you, Lord Jesus, for dying on the cross and for eternal life. In your name we pray; in your name we play. Amen."

Slowly, everyone stood. Weatherbie put his cap back on and stood in the middle of the room, the players fanning out on both sides of him.

"Guys, I tell you what, I made a stupid tactical error."

Again, the chorus: "No, no you didn't."

*"Yes I did, men!"* He shouted it back. "I did, gang. Now listen up. That's horsecrap on my part — horsecrap. You deserved to win that football game, gang. You *won* that football game. I was the one that screwed it up and *lost* it.

"Men, I'll tell you what, though. That ain't gonna happen again. It ain't never gonna happen again. You played your butts off, guys. You played your hearts out. I apologize."

He paused and looked at all of them, most of them still crying. "Underclassmen: juniors, sophomores, freshmen. Remember this feeling. Remember the pain. Remember how it hurts.

"Seniors. I appreciate your leadership. I appreciate what you've done for this football team. I'll never forget you." He was crying again. "I'm sorry."

He turned and fled into the coaches' locker room because now the tears were coming in a flood. Garrett Smith followed him into the coaches' room and found him sitting on a bench, curled up almost in the fetal position, his head down, his entire body racking with sobs. Gently, he stood him up.

"Coach," he said. "You always tell us, we win as a team, we lose as a team. This is no different."

He guided Weatherbie back into the locker room, where everyone stood waiting. Weatherbie and Smith moved into the middle of the huddle, and Thompson, his voice almost gone from shouting and crying, joined them.

"We're still a family no matter what!" he shrieked. "On three — *Family!*" They pushed and shoved to get as close as possible to each other and did one last team cheer. "One, two, three," Thompson called out.

*"Family!"* they all yelled back.

They broke the huddle. Now came the hard part. Taking off their uniforms and going on with the rest of their lives.

AT the other end of the hallway, the scene was as different as you might expect it to be. For several minutes, the players and coaches just circled the locker room, high-fiving and hugging and laughing and crying all at once.

The only person not joining in the celebration was Stover, who sat at his locker for a moment, then burst into the training room screaming at the top of his lungs, "I can't go on without football. How can I not play football anymore?"

It took considerable consoling and cajoling by the trainers and other players to get Stover to calm down and join the party. Davis and Cantelupe waited until all the big shots — General John M. Shalikashvili, the chairman of the Joint Chiefs of Staff; General Dennis Reimer, the army chief of staff; Joe Reeder, the Undersecretary of the Army; and Superintendent Graves all came into the room, followed by all their various functionaries.

"We wanted to be sure," Davis said later, "that all the stars" — generals — "were in the room before we did anything."

Once the "stars" were all in, Davis climbed on a chair, holding the game ball. "Coach, all the seniors got together last night and decided we wanted to win this game as a way to thank you for everything you've done for us for the last four years. You've helped make us better players and better people and we want to tell you how much we appreciate everything you've done for us.

"That's why we decided that this game ball is for you, from us."

The ball was for Sutton. The message was for the "stars."

They all cheered as Davis handed the ball to Sutton and then bear-hugged him. So did Cantelupe. Sutton was both surprised and touched. In all his years as a coach, he had never been given a game ball.

After that, the "stars" all gave their little speeches, telling the players how wonderful they were and how wonderful Army-Navy was and how this game proved again that both the academies were producing great future leaders. The players listened, or at least stayed quiet, until the speeches were done. There was still one thing left to do. As soon as Superintendent Graves was finished, Sutton jumped up on the chair.

"Everybody in here?" he asked.

They nodded.

"OK," he said. "On three . . ." And so, one more time, at the top of their lungs, they sang the Song:

*The Army team's the pride and dream of every heart in gray;*
*The Army line you'll ever find a terror in the fray;*
*And when the team is fighting for the Black and Gray and*
    *Gold;*
*We're always near the song and cheer and this is the tale*
    *we're told;*

*The Army team — Rah! Rah! Rah! Boom! . . .*
*On Brave Old Army Team!*
*On to the fraaay;*
*Fight on to victory;*
*For that's the fearless Army way;*
*Rah! Rah! Rah! . . .*

When the last notes of the second chorus died away, they fell into one last extended team huddle, filled with heartfelt handshakes, hugs, even a few kisses. In their final minutes of Fatness, the Fat Men never felt fatter.

In a corner of the room, Cantelupe and Klein gave one another a final victory hug, a mutual thank you for four years as teammates, four years of friendship. As they pulled apart, Cantelupe said, "I never found Andy Thompson on the field. I should go see him."

And so, as the party that would eventually move from the stadium to a downtown hotel and go on all night long continued, Cantelupe quietly slipped out of the locker room and walked down the hall to find and console his former foe, his future friend.

# EPILOGUE

IT was quiet in Bancroft Hall the next evening when Andrew Thompson sat down to make his last journal entry. At the top of the page, he wrote:

Army 14
Navy 13.

And then, it all tumbled out:

Six points in four games. What can I say? They proved who the best TEAM was. What a war. It's all I've been thinking about for the past two days, non-stop. It's like a bad dream. Those bastards knew I would destroy their option if they came to the wide side of the field. They never ran the option to me. The X's and O's of the game are soon to lose their significance. What won't ever lose meaning:

— Andy Person telling me that I was the best team captain he has ever had.

— Knowing, after the fellas told me, that I made a difference in their lives.

— Talking with Joe late in the game, saying, "We'll remember this feeling for the rest of our lives."

— Coach Weatherbie: ultimate example of accountability after the game.

— Leaving our program in better hands than we found it.

— Jim Cantelupe coming into the locker room one half hour after the game. We stepped into the hallway and spoke for a few moments at the end of successful service academy football careers. I respect the hell out of him.

This will probably be the last journal entry for awhile. One year and one season make for a great deal of learning and growing. '95 has been unreal.

At the bottom, Thompson signed off one last time: "AJT, #32."

WHILE the Navy players wrestled with their disappointment, Army's players still didn't know if their heroic effort had been enough to save their coach's job.

As he left the locker room on Saturday, Graves found Sutton. "We're still meeting Monday morning," he said. "We're going ahead just as planned. I'll let you know."

Sutton simply nodded and said, "I understand."

He had been told earlier in the week that Graves was planning a meeting for that Monday to discuss his job status. In a perfect world, Graves would have walked up to him in the locker room and said, "Bob, we don't even need to meet. I'll call you Monday to work out the details of your new contract."

Sutton didn't expect that, though; it wasn't Graves' style. If he had a plan, he stuck to it. Being told that the meeting was still on didn't make him feel any better or worse about his job standing.

One person who was convinced Sutton was going to be rehired was Al Vanderbush. He was standing a few feet from Graves and Sutton when they had their brief conversation. As Graves left, Vanderbush watched him go and said, "He'll do the right thing. The right thing is to rehire Bob. If we made a coaching change after *this* game, people would say we were rinky-dink." He paused, then added, "And they would be right."

Graves was going to be thorough in his research before making a decision. On Monday morning, Davis and Cantelupe both received phone calls asking them to be in the Supe's office at 11 A.M. They were a little surprised — having never been summoned there before — but Cantelupe guessed it had something to do with Sutton's status.

It did. Graves wanted to know how they *really* felt about the coach and about the program. They both said the same thing: Sutton had grown with the job. He was a better coach now than he had been when they were freshmen.

What about the staff, Graves asked. Do you like the staff? Is there anyone you would want him to change? They both said no. Both loved the coaches they had played for — Davis for Ed Warriner; Cantelupe for Johnny Burnett. They didn't argue when Graves said there were some people who thought the play-calling was sometimes too conservative. But they both said — again — that they thought both Sutton and Greg Gregory had improved in that area too. Just look, Cantelupe said, at what they came up with when the game was on the line Saturday.

Graves thanked them for their input. As they stood to go, he asked Davis if he still harbored hopes of playing pro football. Davis had been low-keying the idea in public all season. Now, though, with the season over, he told Graves that, yes, he would love to play pro football if the opportunity was there.

"Give the Army two years, Joel," Graves said. "I'll try to help you in any way I can if you do that. Anything less than that and I'm not on your side."

Davis said he understood and thanked him. He hadn't really expected him to say anything different.

That afternoon, sitting around the office waiting for the phone to ring, Sutton heard it ring. It was the Supe's office. But it wasn't the call he had been waiting for. They just wanted him to know that no decision had been made yet. What's more, the Supe wasn't sure when he would make a decision. It could be in forty-eight hours; it might not be until next week.

Sutton groaned. This was torture. His coaches were now on the road recruiting, not knowing if they were going to be employed for Christmas — or beyond. Everyone was on tenterhooks waiting for an answer, and Graves, it seemed, was taking his sweet time.

That wasn't really the case. Graves was simply being very methodical because he believed the decision to hire Sutton five years ago had been made too quickly — regardless of whether it was the right decision. Jim Young had simply walked into the Supe's office and said, "I'm retiring, Bob Sutton should replace me," and that had been it. The Army is all about chain of command and making sure everyone is briefed on everything. There were still hard feelings about that. If Sutton was going to come back, Graves wanted to be sure he was coming back with everyone even remotely involved having signed off on the decision.

So, he brought in just about everyone but the four mules — they were vacationing after the Navy game — and asked them what they thought. The answers were almost identical: outstanding person; ideal for West Point; understands the place and the players; has grown in the job. The last point, the one made by Cantelupe and Davis, was probably the most important. The Bob Sutton of 1991, still feeling his way as a head coach, probably would not have been rehired. The Bob Sutton of 1995 had virtually unanimous support. There were still a few holdouts among the old grads, but Graves knew they were waiting for Blanchard and Davis to resurface.

Sutton didn't know any of this. He just knew that every time he looked at his watch it was about one minute later than it had been the previous time he had looked. By Tuesday, he was beginning to crack. The strain was getting to him and he was also getting sick. By Wednesday morning when he came into the office he felt rotten.

"I'm not sure I can take this much longer," he said.

Shortly before noon Vanderbush came by to tell him that he would only have to take it for another few hours. Graves wanted to see him in his office at three o'clock. A decision had been made. Vanderbush had been in the meeting that morning when Graves had made his decision. But Graves had specifically asked him not to tell Sutton what it was because he felt he should be the one to do it.

Vanderbush tried to drop several positive hints without actually telling Sutton directly that the news was good. Sutton was so tired and drained, he didn't notice the hints. When Vanderbush left he still wasn't sure if he had a job or not.

"I didn't want Bob walking in there and not having any clue,"

Vanderbush said. "I didn't think he should have to wait any longer than he already had. But I also had an obligation to General Graves to honor his wish to be the one to tell Bob directly. I tried to tell him indirectly."

Sutton had no appetite. Even though he wasn't feeling well, he went for a long run. He kept trying not to think about the three o'clock meeting and what it might mean to his future, but he couldn't help himself. He looked around as he was running and thought about how much he had come to love West Point, how much his family enjoyed living here. He thought about his coaches and their families and what it would mean to them to be out of work. He thought about the 1996 schedule, how much he was looking forward to building on what had been accomplished in 1995, and how sad it would be if he wasn't part of that team.

He was drained and exhausted by the time he got in his car and made the short drive from Michie Stadium to the Supe's office in the central area of the post. He and Vanderbush walked in at exactly three o'clock. Graves was standing behind his desk.

"No sense making you wait any longer," Graves said. "I'm happy to tell you that everyone I spoke to was unanimous in thinking your contract should be renewed. We're prepared to offer you a two-year contract."

A wave of relief swept over Sutton. He had hoped for three years, but, as he said later, "a win is a win." This was a win. He was still the Army football coach. Christmas would be a time for celebration, not job-hunting. And he honestly believed that his team had the potential to do well enough in 1996 that a long-term extension would be very possible at the end of the season.

He thanked Graves, who told him he was truly sorry it had taken so long to tell him he was extended but that he had wanted to be completely thorough in his research because of the resentment that had existed the last time. Sutton told him he appreciated his concerns, his thoroughness, and the extension. They shook hands. The meeting lasted less than fifteen minutes.

But that was enough. Sutton raced back to his office to call Debbie and tell her and then to start calling the coaches on the road to tell them. It took so long to track everyone down that by the time he left the office there was only one restaurant he and Debbie had the energy to go to in order to celebrate: McDonald's.


CANTELUPE and Klein were at the Center for Enhanced Performance watching a tape of the game on the giant TV screen when Doug Pavek called to give them the news. Cantelupe immediately sat down and wrote out an E-mail message to send to the team:

> For those of you who have not heard, Coach Sutton received a two year extension this afternoon. He's going to take you to the next level!
>
> Thanks for sending the seniors out winners. The '96 team starts now, so start kicking butt and holding nothing back. The seniors enjoyed playing with you guys and we'll miss every one of you sons of bitches. My hat goes off to the scout team, the best by far that I've seen since being here. Make us proud of the 1996 team as you kick butt and make statements. Football only lasts so long, so "carpe diem" — seize the goddamn day.
>
> We will always be brothers.
>
> Your former captain checking out . . .
>
> — Lupe

Most of the other postseason news out of West Point was also good.

Joel Davis missed the football banquet because he was playing in the East-West Shrine game. The reports coming back from the West Coast were encouraging. In fact, he played well enough that he was invited to go to Hawaii the next week and play in another all-star game, the Hula Bowl. But the brass turned that down: too much missed class time. Davis was disappointed, but still hopeful that his performance in the East-West game would keep scouts interested in him. It did. Although he wasn't drafted, Davis signed a free-agent contract with the Cincinnati Bengals in April. He would use his summer leave time to try and make an impression. If he did, he would then have to decide how to deal with the army.

The rest of the Fat Men began dieting almost immediately. Naturally, Wells lost weight far more easily than the chiefs. Six weeks after the season had ended he was down to 238 pounds and looked like he could make a comeback as a linebacker. Stover and Blair battled themselves and their instincts toward Fatness, but they too began shedding the pounds. Only Davis, given the six-week reprieve, remained Fat into February.

It was no surprise that Davis was attracting interest from pro scouts. What was a surprise was an invitation Jim Cantelupe received when he returned from spring break: to attend a San Francisco 49ers minicamp in May. San Francisco owner Ed DeBartolo Jr, was from Ohio and knew about Cantelupe, so had arranged to have his team offer Cantelupe the chance to attend the camp.

Cantelupe was thrilled. "Just to have a shot like that is unbelievable," he said. "If I can go in there and get their attention, maybe a couple of years from now if I keep working, I might have a chance to make the team. I know it isn't very likely, but it's still exciting just to know someone in the NFL thinks I have some potential."

Unfortunately, Cantelupe didn't get that chance to prove to the 49ers that he had potential. Three days before he was scheduled to fly to California for the mini-camp he received word that Robert St. Onge, the Commandant of Cadets, had decided not to approve the four-day leave Cantelupe needed.

Cantelupe had received approval for the leave all the way up the chain of command and had planned his schedule so that he wouldn't get behind in any of his school work while he was away. Still, the word came back: no.

Stunned, Cantelupe went to see the Comm, an ex–football player who had always seemed sympathetic to football players. St. Onge said he worried about Cantelupe's "focus" a month before graduation. Cantelupe explained that this was no different than preparing to play for the team, as he had done for four years, except that it was *less* time-consuming. He also pointed out that since he had already been told he was going to be a graduate assistant coach at the prep school in the fall, exposure to the pro game could only help him be better prepared for that work.

St. Onge said he would think about it over the weekend. On Monday, he sent Cantelupe a note: the answer was still no. "I think right now you should just concentrate on being the best field artillery officer you can be,'' he said.

Cantelupe was convinced those were the words of Superintendent Graves more than they were those of St. Onge. But it was clearly nonnegotiable. He was supposed to leave for California on May 2 — the next day. Angry and embarrassed, he had to call the 49ers to tell them he couldn't come. If they still wanted to invite him to summer camp, he would definitely be able to attend, since by then he would be an officer entitled to summer leave.

He felt as if a door that had opened a tiny crack when he had never expected it to had been slammed in his face. The saddest thing about the whole affair was the shortsightedness of whoever — St. Onge or Graves — had made the decision. Sending someone like Cantelupe into the pro football world, regardless of how long he lasted, could only provide the army with positive publicity since his personality would make him a media magnet from day one. It appeared to be an opportunity lost for everyone — Cantelupe, the academy, and the army.

There was, however, a reprieve. The 49ers understood Cantelupe's unique circumstances and invited him to a second mini-camp in mid-June. By then he would be a West Point graduate, an army lieutenant. And most important, he would be on leave. No chain of command to go through, and no Supe to answer to.

There was one postseason engagement: Derek Klein, who had dated Christina Wills since high school, took her to New York for a weekend just before Christmas break and asked her to marry him. Apparently she had been drinking that night. She said yes.

When everyone got back to school in January, a number of the players were named to leadership positions within the corps for second semester: Cantelupe was named executive officer for the third regiment's third battalion. (At West Point there are four regiments, twelve battalions, thirty-six companies.) Heath Bates was named accountability officer for the first regiment's second battalion. Four other players — John Graves, Landis Maddox, Mike Wells, and Andy Krug — were named company commanders.

What did it all mean? That Sutton's feeling, that this senior class had more leaders in it than any group of seniors he had coached, was right.

At the end of January, they all received their branch assignments. Most of the team had put in for field artillery assignments, and that is what most of them got. Bill Doutt, who had asked for aviation, got it. So did Mike Bellack, although he received a scare on the night assignments came down.

Bellack had undergone surgery to remove a pin from his ankle because he had been told that as long as the pin was in, he would not receive an aviation assignment. With the pin out, he thought he was a lock to get an aviation assignment. On the night that all the first classmen went to Eisenhower Hall to pick up the envelopes with their branch assignments, Bellack opened his envelope and found "field artillery" written inside.

He was shocked. The following day he went to find out what had happened. The answer, as it turned out, was comforting: the paperwork on his surgery had somehow been misplaced. Once it was put through, his assignment was changed.

John Graves got the most oxymoronic assignment the army can offer: military intelligence.

Two players didn't go to Ike Hall that night for assignments. One was Abby Muhammad, who had been told the previous summer that he was uncommissionable because he had diabetes. "Happiest moment of my life," Muhammad said. He had never liked West Point or the prospect of five more years in the military. Only football — Army football honor — had kept him at the academy. To be able to graduate with his teammates and not have to go into the service made diabetes sound like good news to him.

"The only thing that got me through here was football," he said. "Every morning I put my feet on that cold floor in the barracks, I just tick off one more day until it's over."

The other player who did not receive an assignment was John Conroy. This was a shocker to everyone, including Conroy. He had known about his asthma for three years, but it had never affected him seriously. He was one of the fittest players on the team, the guy who always won the two-mile run. But during Christmas break he was hospitalized twice with attacks. When he came back, the doctors examined him and decided that the condition was now serious enough that he shouldn't be commissioned.

All of a sudden, four months prior to graduation, Conroy had to start putting together a résumé. Unlike Muhammad, he was *not* thrilled. He appealed and appealed the decision until the day before graduation. The answer never changed. Devastated, Conroy stood with his classmates to take the induction oath during graduation. But for once he had to be silent. He could only mouth the words.

When Joel Davis heard the news about Conroy, he told his teammates that he thought he needed to go see the doctors right away. "My breathing gets very labored when I climb steps," he said.

They all laughed. In four years no one had ever seen Davis walk up a flight of steps.

Conroy was still in charge of organizing the seniors' spring break trip to Cancún. The only player not going was Doutt. Fatherhood called. But he would see all his old teammates together on June 22. They were all planning to road-trip to Oregon after graduation for his wedding.

No doubt, they would sing the Song a record-breaking number of times before they reached Salem.


FOR all the players at both schools the weeks following the game were extremely hectic. Schoolwork that had been allowed to pile up had to be dealt with. There were less than two weeks to go prior to exams, and at both Army and Navy the rallying cry was now identical: "Beat the Dean!" as in the academic dean.

Social lives were also resumed. Most of the Navy seniors had made a pact to drink no alcohol until the end of the football season. They began making up for lost time the night of the game.

Without doubt, the most disappointed of the seniors was Shaun Stephenson. He had gotten into the game for exactly two plays: one in the first half, one in the second. At one point, when Damon Dixon tried to send him into the game, Weatherbie called him back, then yelled at Dixon for putting Stephenson in without first checking with him.

"He told me to follow the rotation," Dixon said. "That's what I was doing."

Stephenson was convinced things would have been different if

Scott Runyan had been at the game. Runyan had been his biggest supporter dating back to spring ball, and he had watched Stephenson carefully since his return after the arthroscopic surgery. He was convinced that even though Stephenson wasn't as fast as he had been, he could still be an asset to the team because he ran his routes so well and had such good hands.

And yet, they had never thrown a ball in his direction. In the Tulane game, Stephenson had broken wide open on one play and Fay had spotted him. But just as he drew his arm back to pass, he bobbled the ball and had to pull it down and run. When Stephenson got back to the huddle, Fay apologized.

"You were open," he said. "I blew it."

"Next time," Stephenson answered.

But there was no next time. Even on the last play of the game, when Navy could have used every sure-handed receiver available for the Hail Mary play, he was on the sideline, watching his college career tick down to zero, feeling helpless and miserable.

"If Coach Runyan had been at the game, he would have put me in and Coach Weatherbie wouldn't have questioned it," Stephenson said. "But he didn't have that kind of faith in Dix, which wasn't his fault or Damon's. It was just a very unfortunate circumstance."

As devastated as he was, Stephenson refused to feel sorry for himself. "If anyone knows that there are more important things in life, it's me," he said. "I feel bad that we lost the game because the other seniors deserved a better ending than that. I can't say I have no regrets, because I do. But I'll never forget this year."

And, proving that life does go on, Stephenson invited his girlfriend, Jennifer Ray, to visit his parents' house for the holidays. Then, on Christmas morning, he proposed. "I'm ready," he said. "I'm going to be twenty-five and I'm sure Jennifer is the right person for me."

Early in January, Stephenson underwent reconstructive knee surgery. The scar would always remind him of the 1995 season. No doubt, that memory would be a bittersweet one.

Andrew Thompson was not even close to being ready to get married. But he was ready to start dating again. He started dating another midshipman (all members of the brigade, male or female, are called midship*men*) shortly after the start of second semester, but insisted,

"It's nothing serious on either side. We just have a good time to-gether."

Like Stephenson, Thompson was still hoping to become a marine pilot. But they would have to take the flight test at least one more time. All four football players who had taken the makeup test the day after the Air Force game — Thompson, Stephenson, Joe Speed, and Brian Grana — had failed to make the grade. None of them would use the timing of the test as an excuse, but they were all glad to have another shot at it. Thompson finished first semester with one of his highest GPAs ever, 2.3, and was convinced that all four of them would pass the test on the next go-round.

"We have to pass," he said. "That's all there is to it. We have to pass."

THE entire brigade went through what would best be described as a mourning period after the game. As he made his way to class on Monday morning, Garrett Smith was stopped constantly by people who wanted to tell him how sorry they were, how much it had meant to them to see the team perform the way it had. "Some of them were crying," Smith said. "Actually crying. I thought, 'This is what we wanted, that kind of feeling from the brigade.' It was just a painful way to find out that we had it."

During classes, whenever a reference to the game came up — which it inevitably did — Smith felt as if all eyes in the room were on him. "It was almost like being the widow at a funeral," he said. "It was as if everyone wanted to see if I was all right."

They were all right, just disappointed, let down, unable not to think at times about what might have been. "You couldn't escape the feel-ing," Bryce Minamyer said, "that we almost had the perfect ending. Almost."

Joe Speed kept asking his teammates the same question: "How? How could it happen four years in a row?"

The only one of the seniors who even thought about playing more football was Brian Schrum, who had been told by the coaches that there might be some pro teams interested in looking at him in their free-agent camps. Schrum, low-key as ever, nodded when he heard this and said that would be very nice.

"The attitude I'm taking is that it won't happen," he said. "If someone does show an interest, well, then I can be surprised and happy about it then."

The rest of them knew they had played their last game, and when the team gathered in the meeting room at Ricketts Hall on the Monday after the game, they knew that it was time to clean out their lockers and make way for the younger players.

Postseason meetings are routine affairs. The coach thanks the team once more for its efforts and talks about how important it is to get to work on off-season conditioning. All the younger players knew that meant one thing: Satan. Weatherbie reminded them to make sure they got all their schoolwork done and made several administrative announcements about scheduling, the football banquet, and spring practice.

Then, finally, he turned one last time to the seniors. "What you've done in this last year," he said, "is build a foundation. Now, it's up to all of us to get the rest of the house built."

It was time for them to go; time for Weatherbie to talk in more detail about what had to be done to get ready for 1996. They would not be part of that.

"Thank you," Weatherbie said. "From the bottom of my heart, I thank you. We all thank you."

They stood to leave. In years past, when the seniors had left the postseason meeting, there had been some handshakes, maybe even a few hugs. But now, as they stood up — Thompson, Smith, Speed, Harris, Person, Hammond, Galloway, Schrum, Minamyer, Scornavacchi, Stephenson — to walk out the door for the last time, they found out exactly how their teammates felt about them.

In an instant, before they had even taken a step, the rest of the room was standing too. No cheers or hurrahs, just applause. Warm, heartfelt applause. In the back row, the coaches stood along with the players and applauded too. The seniors lingered for a moment, drinking it all in. One last moment with the brotherhood.

THE next day was December 5, the second anniversary of the accident that had killed Autumn Pevzner, Lisa Winslow, and Robin Pegram.

Mark Hammond walked over to Hospital Hill that afternoon, to the Naval Academy cemetery, to spend some time at Robin Pegram's grave. Every once in a while, when he was nearby, he would stop by, sit, and talk to her for a while. "More just to remember what it felt like than anything else," he said.

He spent some extra time on that afternoon, a bright cold day in Annapolis. As he got up to leave, one last thought occurred to him. "By the way," he said, forcing a smile, "they did it to us again."

WHILE the seniors were preparing to get on with Life After Football, Ryan Bucchianeri still had one more chance — or so he hoped.

He had ended his junior season by not suiting up for the last three games. He had gotten in for a total of two plays — kickoffs against Air Force and Villanova. He still felt he deserved another chance to prove to the coaches that he could be the team's kicker. He also knew the odds were stacked against him — especially after Vanderhorst's performance against Army, and even more so when he heard the coaches had recruited a highly rated kicker out of Texas.

"Once upon a time," he said, forcing a smile, "I was a highly rated kicker coming out of high school."

That seemed like several lifetimes ago as his junior year came to a close. Several weeks before spring practice, Bucchianeri requested a meeting with Weatherbie. Actually, he requested a meeting with Weatherbie, the kicking coaches — Todd Wright and Scott Runyan — and Jack Lengyel. He was told he had to meet with Weatherbie first.

On the afternoon of March 20, they met in Weatherbie's office. Nothing had really changed since they had met at the end of the spring a year earlier. Weatherbie told Bucchianeri that his status was based solely on his performance in practice; Bucchianeri insisted that if that were the case, he would have been the first-string kicker. Nothing was resolved.

The next day Bucchianeri met with Lengyel, who listened to him and took copious notes. At the end, Lengyel gave Bucchianeri a pep talk and told him to hang in and keep fighting. But the message was essentially the same: the final word would come — had to come — from the coaching staff.

Bucchianeri felt trapped. He knew that Weatherbie and the coaches were doing what they thought was best for the team as a whole. He knew they weren't responsible for the two infamous wide rights or the feelings within the team and the brigade that had made his life so difficult.

But he felt as if he had been sentenced to go through life with a scarlet "WR" on his forehead. Nothing he did could change that because he wasn't going to get the chance to change the "WR" to "good!" before December 7, 1996 — the date of his last Army-Navy game as a member of the brigade.

"I know in the grand scheme of things, in terms of what I'll become, football isn't important," he said, in a sad, choked voice one bright spring day. "But I worked so hard, for so long, it's painful to think that my identity in football will always be those two missed kicks."

He got one chance to attempt a field goal in the spring game. It was a 31-yarder and it had plenty of distance as it sailed toward the uprights. But it began drifting, first a little, then a little more. By the time it reached the uprights it was wide — wide right. The nightmare continued.

THROUGHOUT the spring semester, Cantelupe and Thompson kept in touch. In late February, Thompson and several of his friends drove to West Point for a weekend. It wasn't until May that Cantelupe got to make the return trip to Annapolis. When he did, though, he picked the right time: graduation weekend. He and Derek Klein were in the stands in Navy–Marine Corps Stadium to watch Thompson and the other twenty football seniors receive their degrees.

It was a hot, sunny day in Annapolis, and Thompson, who had battled hepatitis during the final weeks of the school year, felt weak and tired, but elated.

Perhaps no one was more elated than Shaun Stephenson, who had dreamed for years of graduating from the academy and becoming an officer in the marines. When it was his turn to receive his diploma, Stephenson walked proudly to the podium, shook hands with Joint Chiefs chairman John A. Shalikashvili (who was the graduation speaker), and then looked to the sky. He smiled and waved the diploma over his head as if to say, "I did it, Dion."

When the ceremony was over, the 115 graduates who had been sworn in as marines headed straight for the football team's locker room, where their new uniforms awaited them. Cantelupe and Klein, dressed in civilian clothes, made their way down to the field and headed straight for the locker room, knowing Thompson was there. At the door, a marine guard stopped them briefly.

"Are you members of the class of '96?" he asked.

Cantelupe grinned. "You bet we are," he said, telling the truth. Then just as he had done almost six months earlier, he walked inside a Navy football locker room looking for Andrew Thompson. This time was a little different than in Philadelphia. There were no tears when they hugged. But one thing hadn't changed: the bonds they felt. Football player to football player; team captain to team captain; cadet to midshipman. And finally, four long years after it began for both, lieutenant to lieutenant.

WHEN Charlie Weatherbie got back to his office in Annapolis on the Sunday after the game the first thing he wanted to do was get the field goal team together, run out to the practice field, and kick an 18-yard field goal. He knew that was lack of sleep invading his brain, so he put the idea aside and tried to concentrate on getting on with recruiting and beginning to prepare for 1996.

But 1995 was a long way from over. By the next afternoon, Weatherbie had been swamped by messages: E-mail from the brigade, telegrams, letters, phone calls. Every one of them said essentially, the same thing: we couldn't be prouder of the way you conducted yourself Saturday.

Thompson had talked in his journal about accountability. This is an era in sports when almost no one wants to be accountable. Losses are almost always someone else's fault. A lot of coaches in Weatherbie's position would have defended the decision to go for the touchdown in the fourth quarter. They would have pointed out that the play was wide open.

Many would have fallen back on that old coaching cliché: "It was a good call, we just didn't execute.'' Translated into English that means: "I coached good, but they sure played bad.''

Weatherbie did none of that. "*I lost the game.*" His players didn't really believe that, but he did, and he had no intention of changing that opinion no matter how many excuses people tried to hand him. He was the leader, he had a decision to make, and he made the wrong decision. Period. At a school where you are taught from day one that the three acceptable answers for a plebe are "Yes sir,'' "No sir,'' and "No excuse sir,'' Weatherbie had lived up to that kind of accountability. He had stood up in front of the world and said, "No excuse sir.''

When he walked into the Monday downtown quarterback club luncheon with Thompson and Smith, the entire room, filled with Navy fans and supporters, stood in unison to cheer for all three of them. One after another, people came to the microphone during the question-and-answer period to thank him for putting pride back into Navy football and for handling himself the way he had on Saturday. In his post-game press conference, Weatherbie had again taken responsibility for losing the game, although he had been far more composed than in the locker room.

When Thompson got up to talk at the Monday lunch, he turned to Weatherbie and said, "Coach, I just want you to know that I would follow you into a blazing inferno.''

Now Weatherbie knew what he couldn't have known before the game: Army-Navy *was* different. All season, he had wondered why everyone made such a big deal about Army-Navy as if it were somehow in a different category than other rivalry games. Now, having coached in one, having felt the emotion on the field and in the stadium for three hours, having gone through the aftermath, he understood.

He had lost the game and they still loved him because he had not only accepted responsibility for the loss but demanded it.

But there was more to it than that. The support and love he had felt in the locker room, the feeling he had now about what the game meant to the players and how much they put into winning it, made him realize that this *wasn't* Oklahoma–Oklahoma State.

It made him want to play the game again, right that instant. But he couldn't. He had to wait a year for another chance. "You can be sure," he told his coaches, "that I will understand what this game is all about on a completely different level next year than I did this year."

That afternoon, when he got back from the luncheon, Weatherbie found a message waiting for him from his old college coach, Jim Stanley. Once, Stanley had been an assistant at Navy. Weatherbie called him right back.

Stanley's first comment was right to the point. "Now," he said, "do you understand?"

For the first time since he had called 328 A-pop almost forty-eight hours earlier, Charlie Weatherbie heard himself laugh.

"Coach," he said, "*now*, I understand."

# ACKNOWLEDGMENTS

ONCE I knew I wanted to write this book, working out the details that would allow me to write about the rivalry and the schools and the players from the inside was not easy. The idea fell apart in 1991 when I first wanted to take on the project, and it wasn't until 1995 that I could put the pieces together to make the book happen. It took a lot of people working very hard to get me to this point.

First and foremost, I have to thank Navy athletic director Jack Lengyel and his football coach, Charlie Weatherbie. Lengyel was a supporter of this idea from the very beginning, even though there were some at Navy who worried about the notion of giving a reporter complete access to their team and school. After all, the Navy has taken a lot of publicity hits in recent years.

"Walking across the street is a gamble nowadays," Lengyel told people. "If we believe in our product, we should do this. I believe in our product."

With good reason, I might add.

Still, Lengyel would never force something like this on his coach, especially a rookie coach like Weatherbie. So, a month after he started a new job at a school that hadn't had a winning season in twelve years, Weatherbie found himself face-to-face with a complete stranger who was saying, "Let me into all your private meetings, your locker room . . ."

I know he had doubts — and why not? But he still said yes. And once he did, he never backed away from giving me complete access, even in some moments that were very difficult for him and his team. For that, I will be forever grateful.

Bob Sutton had doubts about this project from the very beginning. He worried — justifiably — that a reporter hanging around might be a distraction to his team or his assistant coaches. In 1995, facing a difficult year that would determine his future at Army, the *last* thing he needed was a stranger in the locker room. But, in large part I believe because he sensed that his players liked the idea, he came around to the project, cautiously at first, then enthusiastically as time went on.

I know 1995 was a tough fall for Sutton and for his athletic director, Al Vanderbush. Their willingness to listen to the players and to open their doors to me is something I will always remember.

At each school, there were many others whose help was invaluable to me.

Navy's erstwhile sports information director Tom Bates has been a friend for almost twenty years, which means he has put up with an awful lot. His staff — Scott Strasemeier, John Cornell, Tim Lanquist, and the fabulous duo of Beth Sherry and Amy Burgett — became my sounding boards and my friends.

No one worked harder to get this project off the ground at West Point than sports information director emeritus Bob Kinney. He deserves a medal of some kind, if only for listening to all my moaning and groaning on the phone. When Bob retired in June of 1995, his successor, Bob Beretta, was thrown right into the middle of what was, at the time, a difficult situation. He handled it like the pro he is. His staff — Mike (Mo) Albright, Mady (Coach) Salvani, John (JT) Terry, and Diane Baker — were invaluable to me throughout the season.

There are many others at both schools, too numerous to list, who deserve thanks, but I would be remiss if I didn't thank Superintendent Charles R. Larson at Navy and his commandant, Randy Bogle, and also Superintendent Howard D. Graves at Army. Thanks also to Gene Uchasz, Kip Nygren, Bob Arciero, Tim Kelly, Matt Oliver, Ben Russell, and the one and only Jack Hecker. I can't possibly thank equipment manager Dick Hall enough for, among other things, keeping me from drowning at Boston College; and Doug Pavek and Andy Smith, who were both responsible for making it appear that I was in two places at once during game week and on game day.

At Navy, I was aided immeasurably by Steve Orsini, Perry Martini, Gene Taylor, Beth Shumway, Phil Hoffmann, Phil (Satan) Emery, Bert Pangrazio, Kevin Bull, Rob Lawton, the one and only Red Romo, Dee Butler, Ed McDevitt, Mike Glynn, Tom Butler, Lael House, Scott Fuhrman, and Lois Gareis. Kent Owens helped keep me sane (or close to it) on the sidelines every week and, like Pavek and Smith, made me appear ubiquitous during that last week.

I know I tend to go on at length, but every one of these people deserves mention. So do all the assistant coaches at both schools, who no doubt were not always thrilled to have a reporter constantly in their midst, yet were nothing but helpful to me.

I also have to mention, as always, my agent, Esther Newberg, because if I don't she might fire me. She is only the best agent alive and a better friend. Thanks also to her assistant, Jack Horner. And at Little, Brown and Company: Charlie Hayward, as good a publisher as one could hope to work for; my long-suffering editor, Michael Pietsch (talk about listening to moaning and groaning); his ever-patient assistant, Nora Krug; and Holly Wilkinson and Lisa Singer, who deserve a special place in heaven for putting up with me.

My friends and family all know how much they mean to me: Mary and Danny, who make my life a joy; Dad, Margaret, Bobby, David (who actually taught me how to make a *fax* work!), and Jennifer. Not to mention Jim and Arlene, the best parents-in-law one could have, and Kacky, Stan, Annie, Gregg, Jim, and Brendan. And, of course, Norbert Doyle, who was once recruited by both Army and Navy.

Last, but certainly not least, the players. I hope this book has made apparent the tremendous respect and affection I have for them. As important as the help I received from all the above-mentioned people was, the players *are* this book. They allowed me to come into their lives and made me feel, at least for one season, a part of their football families.

When I walked out of Veterans Stadium on the afternoon of December 2, 1995, I was completely drained. I had never been through a game in which I wanted *both* teams to win so badly. I felt I knew what the game meant to all the seniors, and I didn't want any of them to walk off a football field for the last time feeling like losers.

Of course Navy did lose the game. But what I now know without a single shred of doubt is that no one in either locker room that day is anything but a winner. Army finished the season 5–5–1; Navy 5–6. I can honestly say I have never been around two groups of people who define the word "winner" more purely than the football players at Army and Navy.

From the bottom of my heart, I thank them for making this book so much fun from the first day until the last.

John Feinstein
*Bethesda, Maryland*

# INDEX

403